# An Expository And Contextual Commentary On Paul's Epistle To The Church At Rome
With additional notes.

*Daniel H. Coe, Sr.*, Ph.D.

Edited by: *Kathrine M. Rich and Gary Summers*

*An Expository and Contextual Commentary on Paul's Epistle to the Church at Rome* is copyright © 2021 by Daniel H. Coe, Sr. All rights reserved.

No portion of this book may be reproduced, stored in a retrieval system, or transmitted in any form or by any means—electronic, photocopy, recording, scanning, digital, audio, video, or any other method —without the prior written permission of the author.

All Scripture (unless otherwise noted) is from the King James Version.

Coe, Daniel H., Sr.
    ISBN: 978-1-947622-80-7

Religion/Christianity/Bible Study/Commentary/Romans

Printed in the United States of America
Cobb Publishing
Charleston, AR

# Commentary on Romans

| | |
|---|---|
| TABLE OF CONTENTS | ii |
| DEDICATION | iv |
| APPRECIATION | iv |
| FOREWORD | v |
| INTRODUCTION | vii |
| WORKS CITED | 443 |
| SCRIPTURE REFERENCES | 445 |

CHAPTER ONE
| | |
|---|---|
| VSS 1-7 | 1 |
| VSS 8-17 | 7 |
| VSS 18-32 | 16 |
| SUMMARY | 29 |

CHAPTER TWO
| | |
|---|---|
| VSS 1-11 | 32 |
| VSS 12-20 | 38 |
| VSS 21-29 | 46 |

CHAPTER THREE
| | |
|---|---|
| VSS 1-19 | 50 |
| VSS 20-31 | 57 |

CHAPTER FOUR
| | |
|---|---|
| VSS 1-8 | 63 |
| VSS 9-25 | 68 |

| | |
|---|---|
| CHAPTER FIVE (VSS 1-21) | 77 |

CHAPTER SIX
| | |
|---|---|
| VSS 1-2 | 96 |
| VSS 3-7 | 100 |
| VSS 8-10 | 105 |
| VSS 11-23 | 108 |

CHAPTER SEVEN
| | |
|---|---|
| VSS 1-7 | 117 |
| VSS 8-25 | 127 |
| SUMMARY OF VSS 14-25 | 141 |
| COMMENTS ON MARRIAGE DIVORCE, AND REMARRIAGE | 142 |

# Commentary on Romans

**CHAPTER EIGHT**
    VSS 1-8      144
    VSS 9-17      153
    VSS 18-28      167
    VSS 29-39      186
    WHEN DID INSPIRATION END?      194

**CHAPTER NINE**
    VSS 1-5      199
    VSS 6-17      204
    VSS 18-33      213

**CHAPTER TEN (VSS 1-21)**      226

**CHAPTER ELEVEN**
    VSS 1-6      238
    VSS 7-11      244
    VSS 12-24      250
    VSS 25-36      256

**CHAPTER TWELVE**
    VSS 1-8      267
    VSS 9-21      287

**CHAPTER THIRTEEN**
    VSS 1-10      315
    VSS 11-14      332
    CHAPTER END NOTES      345

**CHAPTER FOURTEEN**
    VSS 1-9      349
    VSS 10-18      356
    VSS 19-23      363

**CHAPTER FIFTEEN**
    VSS 1-7      368
    VSS 8-23      372
    VSS 24-33      390

**CHAPTER SIXTEEN (VSS 1-27)**      398

**WORKS CITED**      406
**SCRIPTURE INDEX**      407

# Commentary on Romans
## Dedication

This volume is dedicated to Katharine (Kathy) Rich. Over two years of reading, re-reading, editing, and correcting have been exhausted by Kathy in this effort. For her labors I am truly thankful. Writing is easy; editing and correcting manuscripts is the arduous work. This is true especially when the rules of grammar seem to change on a daily basis.

Kathy excels in her Christian character and conduct. She serves the Lord's church well as a grand example of what a godly woman should be. Kathy stands alongside of many great women of the Bible. She is not unlike women such as Sarah, Deborah, Mary, Martha, and Priscilla. Kathy has donned her robe of righteousness well and works diligently to maintain the cleanliness of her spiritual attire.

## Appreciations

Sister Ida Margit Habbershon (Marg) is deserving of much appreciation for her willingness to assist in the compiling of the Scripture references in this volume. Numerous were her days off work which she set aside to undertake this task. For her time, I am sincerely appreciative.

Appreciation is also expressed to Gary Summers for his editorial efforts. I have known brother Gary for over forty years and have known him to stand for the truth on every occasion. Gary excels as a preacher of the gospel and a grammarian. He has edited numerous brotherhood lectureship books and authored numerous articles for brotherhood publications. Gary is himself a prolific writer unequaled in his talent. He has served as an evangelist for the Lord's church for many decades.

# Commentary on Romans
## FOREWORD

The context of Scriptures is seldom considered by many who study the Word of God. Too often, passages of Scripture, are made to serve as *stand alone* verses. By such, we simply mean some find a verse or two in which a statement is made which seemingly lends credence to their beliefs or opinions. When context is set aside and opinion put in its place, one can teach whatever pleases him.

In this effort, I strongly and *repeatedly* emphasize the need to keep every verse of every chapter in context. Brother Foy E. Wallace often said that *a text taken out of context is a pretext.* Emphasis on context must always be front and center in the mind of the Bible student if he expects to ascertain truth. Context, context, context are the first three rules by which the Bible student must govern himself.

Much redundancy will be found in this effort, reminding the reader to whom the apostle is writing. When students lose sight of Paul's intended audience, the intent of his message is lost. There are seven laws of learning which must be continuously applied in Bible study. These seven laws are: repetition, repetition, repetition, repetition, repetition, repetition, and (lastly) repetition.

Who, what, when, where, why, to whom, and how are questions which must be posed in the study of every book, chapter, and verse of inspired Scripture. Such questions will be set forth in this volume and *repeatedly* emphasized.

There are times when chapter breaks are unfortunate in the Scriptures. The chapter break between fourteen and fifteen for example is unfortunate. The first seven verses of chapter fifteen are contextually tied to chapter fourteen. Not realizing such may cause the student to miss the intent of Paul as he addresses the eating of certain meats and the drinking of certain things.

The words *therefore* and *wherefore* are words which merit close attention in the study of the Scriptures. These words most often establish conclusions to things previously stated by authors. Further, the word *if* bears need of close attention to what authors have stated, the word establishes conditions. *If this, then that,* is

## Commentary on Romans

often the intent of an inspired author. Paul said of the gospel and salvation the following: *By which also ye are saved, if ye keep in memory what I preached unto you, unless ye have believed in vain* (I Cor. 15:2). The reward of which Paul wrote in this verse is salvation. The condition of salvation is based upon the word *if,* meaning the Corinthians would be saved *if* they did in fact *keep in memory* that which Paul preached.

It is the hope of this author this volume will be a profitable avenue by which diligent Bible students, who are willing to *launch out into the deep,* can come to a better and deeper knowledge of the truth, as God desires.

The matter of footnotes in this effort is an important one which we address here. Only authors will be referred to in the footnotes. Complete information regarding authors, publishers, printers, and the like can be found in the section of Works Cited. We feel it superfluous to have such information repeatedly supplied.

# Commentary on Romans
## Introduction to the Book of Romans

A thorough introduction to any book is an absolute essential if one expects to understand the book being studied. *A book well introduced is a book half taught.* An accurate knowledge of the author, date, purpose, theme, and the audience to whom a book is addressed are crucial in understanding the inspired text. Word studies are many times of a great benefit. Emphasis on numerous words shall be given to better expose the pictures set forth in this epistle. Many times a simple word study will make some passages much more clear. An example is found in Paul's first epistle to the church in Thessalonica.

*For this we say unto you by the word of the Lord, that we which are alive and remain unto the coming of the Lord shall not prevent them which are asleep* (I Thes. 4:15). The word *prevent* in this passage does not mean "to hinder or disallow." In this passage the word means "to go before or precede." Reading the passage with the definition makes the text clear. Notice: *For this we say unto you by the word of the Lord, that we which are alive and remain unto the coming of the Lord shall not go before or precede them which are asleep.* Those who remain living at the last advent of Christ shall not precede those who have died and gone to the realm of paradise when Christ brings them from the grave unto the resurrection.

Unger said, the book of Romans was Paul's greatest inspired work. Chrysostom said he read the book of Romans through twice every week. Samuel Coleridge said: *I think that the Epistle to the Romans is the most profound work in existence.*[1] Frederik Godet called the book of Romans, *The Cathedral of the Christian Faith.*[2]

Job 9:2 well summarizes the purpose of the book of Romans. *I know it is so of a truth: but how should man be just with God?* Romans answers Job's question and shows why God is righteous in His dealings with man.

The book of Romans is a thesis on the system of God's righteousness. Romans 1:15-16 are the thesis statement of the epistle. The gospel is the power of God unto salvation. Romans

---

[1] Samuel Taylor Coleridge.

[2] By F. Godet, D.D.

# Commentary on Romans

is the revelation of God's system of righteousness for man. The epistle shows how Divine justification is found. Spiritual justification is only found in the system of faith established by Christ. The *faith,* of which Paul writes in this epistle, is the system of faith established by the Godhead. The New Testament reveals the system by which man is to govern, guide, and guard his life. Further, the *faith* of which Paul writes in the book is most often not individual faith, but rather God's system of faith by which He declares man righteous. Paul shows in this Roman epistle man is to be faithful *to the system of faith* established by God. Man must comply with God's system in every detail. Man is neither justified nor forgiven until he complies with the ordinances God has mandated, after which God awards His forgiving grace (cf. Rom. 1:17; Heb. 5:8-9).

The theme of the book of Romans is the *righteousness of God*—that is, the system of faith by which God declares man righteous.

The Book of Romans is divided into different categories.

**We divide the book into the following categories:**
A. Paul's Introduction, Chapter 1:1-15
B. Justification by God's System of Faith, Chapters 1:16-11:36.
C. Rules for Christian Living, Chapters 12:1-16:27.

**Franklin Camp's divisions:**
A. The Problem of Sin, Chapters 1-8.
B. The Problems of the Jews, Chapters 9-11.
C. The Problems of Conduct, Chapters 12-16.

**Premillennialists divide the book as follows:**
A. Doctrinal Matters, Chapters 1-8.
B. The Dispensational Period, Chapters 9-11.
C. Practical Matters, Chapters 12-16.

Liberals have long assaulted the genuineness and the authenticity of this book. Numerous internal and external evidences prove Paul is the inspired author of the epistle.

**External witnesses:** Clement of Rome said Paul wrote the book, as did Ignatius. Romans is the most attested book of the New Testament regarding authenticity and authorship.

# Commentary on Romans

**Internal witnesses:** Paul claims authorship of the epistle. Peter also contends for Paul's authorship in II Peter 3:15-18.

Liberals object to Paul's authorship because the book of Acts does not mention the Roman epistle. However, Revelation never mentions the book of Hosea, but such does not negate Hosea's authorship of his inspired work. Such is to argue that because one purchases goods from a certain establishment, another does not sell the same goods.

Luke penned the book of Acts before Paul authored the book of Romans; therefore, the book of Acts can not contain any mention of the Roman epistle. Liberals have long tethered themselves to hitching posts of heresy to discredit the inspiration of every book of the Bible.

**Two major errors of liberals regarding the Book of Romans:**
1. Liberals teach "faith only" salvation from Romans 3:23.
2. Calvinists teach Premillennialism from chapters 9-11.

There are two key matters and two key words which must be contextually recognized in the study of Romans: 1) Paul addresses both Jewish and Gentile converts. He speaks to the Gentile converts in chapter 1 and the Jewish converts in chapter 2 and in chapters 4-11. The apostle addresses both in chapter 3 and in chapters 12-16. 2) The two key words of this epistle are *faith* and *spirit,* which are most often used metaphorically. These words must be properly ascertained for one to recognize the purpose and theme of the epistle.

### Overview of the epistle:

Chapter 1 – Righteousness revealed.
Chapters 2-3 – Righteousness required.
Chapter 4 – Righteousness recorded.
Chapters 5-8 – Righteousness realized.
Chapters 9-11 – Righteousness rejected.
Chapters 12-16 – Righteousness reproduced.

**The history of the church at Rome:** The church at Rome began with the conversion of some Jews which dwelt in Rome who were present on the day of Pentecost, as recorded in Acts 2:8-11. The Catholic Church teaches when Peter *went to another place* as recorded in Acts 12:17—that place was Rome. How-

## Commentary on Romans

ever, Acts 12:19 shows the other *place* to which Peter went was Caesarea. The Catholic Church also teaches the Lord established the church upon Peter, based upon Matthew 16:18.

**Reasons why Peter was not the founder of the church in Rome.** There is no record of Peter ever having been in Rome. Paul would not have failed to greet a fellow apostle (the alleged founder of the Roman congregation) if he were there. Further, why would Paul have purposed to visit the church at Rome if in fact Peter established the Roman congregation; especially in light of Paul having expressed his determination not to preach Christ where Christ was already preached? Paul had written:

> *For I will not dare to speak of any of those things which Christ hath not wrought by me, to make the Gentiles obedient, by word and deed, Through mighty signs and wonders, by the power of the Spirit of God; so that from Jerusalem, and round about unto Illyricum, I have fully preached the gospel of Christ. Yea, so have I strived to preach the gospel, not where Christ was named, lest I should build upon another man's foundation: But as it is written, To whom he was not spoken of, they shall see: and they that have not heard shall understand. For which cause also I have been much hindered from coming to you. But now having no more place in these parts, and having a great desire these many years to come unto you* (Rom. 15:18-23).

A close eye must be given to the above inspired text. Four reasons are here given. First, observe the above passage is found within the Roman epistle itself. Second, the passage is an inspired one. Third, Paul expressed his desire to preach the gospel to those of Rome and impart to them some needed spiritual gifts. Fourth, Paul declared, by inspiration, he was ready to and anxious to preach the gospel in Rome.

*"For I long to see you, that I may impart unto you some spiritual gift, to the end ye may be established; That is, that I may be comforted together with you by the mutual faith both of you and me."* Further, the apostle declared: *"So, as much as in me is, I am ready to preach the gospel to you that are at Rome also"* (Rom. 1:11-12, 15).

## Commentary on Romans

Paul declared, by inspiration, he would not preach Christ where Christ was already preached by others. Yet, by inspiration, Paul proclaimed he would indeed preach Christ in Rome. This solidifies the fact that neither Peter nor any other of the apostles were ever in Rome.

The sister epistle of the Roman letter is Paul's epistle to the church of Galatia. Paul's approach in the Galatian letter is the same as it is to Rome. Many of the same matters which troubled the church in Rome also troubled the church of Galatia.

When Paul reached the Appian Way, as recorded in Acts 28:15 the church was already established in Rome. Romans 16 mentions numerous individual saints, but Peter was not named among them. If Peter were in Rome, Paul would have recognized his presence and extended his salutation to his fellow apostle. Further, Paul wrote seven epistles from Rome none of which mention Peter.

The Catholic Church teaches between AD 51-54 Peter went to Rome to combat the heresy of Simon Magus. This argument is based on an error of Justin Martyr who saw a statue of the Sabine god of Semo Sancus and wrongly deduced it was a tribute to Simon Magus. Martyr assumed Simon Magus debated Peter and further assumed said debate took place in Rome. This is a Catholic tradition based upon Peter's correction of Simon Magus as recorded in Acts 8:21-22.

Suetonius said the Jews were banned from Rome by the Emperor Claudius because the Jews always caused much trouble there. Observe: *After these things Paul departed from Athens, and came to Corinth; And found a certain Jew named Aquila, born in Pontus, lately come from Italy, with his wife Priscilla; (because that Claudius had commanded all Jews to depart from Rome:) and came unto them* (Acts 18:1-2). These events occurred just before Nero's reign. Once Nero ascended to the throne, he married a third wife, who was a Jewess. Through her influence upon him, Nero permitted the Jews to return to Rome.

**The date of the epistle:** The epistle was written before Paul arrived in Rome, during his journey to the city as recorded in chapter 15:9-20. Paul also expressed his desire to journey to Rome (cf. Acts 19:21). The epistle was written about AD 57, most likely from Corinth.

# Commentary on Romans

In the epistle, Paul purposes to defend his apostleship before arriving in Rome. The character of the book is both doctrinal and practical. Paul uses much logic in the epistle. He does so especially in his dealings with Jewish converts. Paul puts his arguments into logical syllogisms, then refutes the Jewish oppositions with the gospel. Paul posed numerous questions he knew the Jews would ask, then answers the questions posed. Paul's approach is a threefold effort: 1. He uses the Old Testament. 2. He uses numerous illustrations. 3. He uses logic.

**The occasion of the letter:** Aquila and Priscilla were on their way to Rome, along with Phoebe. Paul sent the epistle to the church at Rome by the hand of Phoebe (Rom. 16:1-3). The form of the letter is strongly dogmatic because the church at Rome wanted to hear what Paul's views were on certain matters.

Keep in mind the date for which the Catholic Church contends for Peter being in Rome and supposedly having established the church there—AD 51-54. However, Acts 10 is dated about AD 41-43. According to Galatians 2:1 and 11, Paul confronted Peter in the city of Antioch 14 years after the events which are recorded in Acts 10. This shows Peter stayed in Jerusalem until about AD 54, and could not have established the church at Rome between the years of AD 51-54.

The Scriptures say: "*Then fourteen years after I went up again to Jerusalem with Barnabas, and took Titus with me also. But when Peter was come to Antioch, I withstood him to the face, because he was to be blamed*" (Gal. 2:1, 11).

Ambrosiaster and Hillary were historians and members of the first century church at Rome.[3] They insisted the Church of Rome was established without the aid of any of the apostles.[4] "*For I long to see you, that I may impart unto you some spiritual gift, to the end ye may be established*" (Rom. 1:11). If Peter were in Rome and established the church there, why did he not provide the church with the spiritual gifts Paul knew were lacking?

The names listed in Romans 16 are Latin, Greek, and Jewish, which shows that the tongues of Acts 2:1-4, in which the apos-

---

[3] Unpublished class notes on Romans.

[4] Ibid.

# Commentary on Romans

tles spoke included the Roman and Greek languages, which is confirmed by Acts 2:10.

**What kind of members made up the church at Rome?** The church consisted of all social ranks: the Aristocrat, the poor, and slaves. In Philippians 4:22, Paul said of the church in Rome: "*they of Caesar's household salute you.*" Because of the number of Greek names, the church consisted mostly of slaves.

**Some reasons why Peter could not have been the first pope.** 1) He was married (Matt. 8:14-15). 2) Peter was not infallible (Gal. 2:14). 3) He was a fellow elder (I Pet. 5:1-5). 4) He is not the head of the church (Eph. 1:22). 5) He is identified as an apostle in AD 66 more than 10 years after the Catholic Church declared him to be in Rome as the pope. 6) He was directed by the other apostles to go to Samaria, as recorded in Acts 8:14.

**Departures of the Catholic Church throughout history.** It is vital to understand the Catholic Church is not the apostate church, but it came about because of the apostasy of the Lord's church.

**1. The use of Holy Water was implemented in AD 120.** Holy Water is still used by the Catholic Church today. In the Catholic Church, *holy water* is water which has been blessed by a priest or bishop and used only in the Roman Catholic and Orthodox Christian traditions. Holy water figures in Roman Catholic rituals of exorcism. The use of specifically consecrated water is not required for a valid baptism under Roman Catholic religious law. A quantity of holy water is typically kept in a font, an item of church architecture, that typically appears in the baptistery. A smaller font, called a *stoup*, may be placed near the entrance of the church building, whereby Roman Catholics bless themselves when entering by dipping their fingers into the holy water and making the sign of the cross. Holy water is sometimes sprinkled upon the congregation during the Mass; this activity is called *aspersion*. In the theology of Roman Catholicism, holy water is sacramental.[5]

**Varieties of Holy Water:** Roman Catholic rituals distinguish four different kinds of holy water.

---

[5] Unpublished class notes on Romans.

## Commentary on Romans

- Holy water is water that has been blessed by a priest with a small amount of salt as a preservative; it is often found at stoups, and used in aspersions and blessings.
- Baptismal holy water contains a slight amount of anointing oil.
- Gregorian water, also called *water of consecration,* contains small amounts of wine, salt, and ashes added to it and is used by bishops for the consecration of a church building.
- Easter water is often distributed to the faithful on Easter Sunday for use at home.

The use of holy water is found only once in the Scripture which was used for the test of adultery.

> *Speak unto the children of Israel, and say unto them, If any man's wife go aside, and commit a trespass against him, And a man lie with her carnally, and it be hid from the eyes of her husband, and be kept close, and she be defiled, and there be no witness against her, neither she be taken with the manner; And the spirit of jealousy come upon him, and he be jealous of his wife, and she be defiled: or if the spirit of jealousy come upon him, and he be jealous of his wife, and she be not defiled: Then shall the man bring his wife unto the priest, and he shall bring her offering for her, the tenth part of an ephah of barley meal; he shall pour no oil upon it, nor put frankincense thereon; for it is an offering of jealousy, an offering of memorial, bringing iniquity to remembrance. And the priest shall bring her near, and set her before the Lord: And the priest shall take holy water in an earth-en vessel; and of the dust that is in the floor of the tabernacle the priest shall take, and put it into the water: And the priest shall set the woman before the Lord, and uncover the woman's head, and put the offering of memorial in her hands, which is the jealousy offering: and the priest shall have in his hand the bitter water that causeth the curse: And the priest shall charge her by an oath, and say unto the woman, If no man have lain with thee, and if thou hast not gone aside to uncleanness with another instead of thy husband, be thou free from this bitter water that causeth the curse: But if thou hast gone aside to another instead of thy husband, and if thou be defiled, and some man have lain with thee beside thine husband: Then the priest shall charge the woman with*

## Commentary on Romans

*an oath of cursing, and the priest shall say unto the woman, The Lord make thee a curse and an oath among thy people, when the Lord doth make thy thigh to rot, and thy belly to swell; And this water that causeth the curse shall go into thy bowels, to make thy belly to swell, and thy thigh to rot: And the woman shall say, Amen, amen. And the priest shall write these curses in a book, and he shall blot them out with the bitter water: And he shall cause the woman to drink the bitter water that causeth the curse: and the water that causeth the curse shall enter into her, and become bitter. Then the priest shall take the jealousy offering out of the woman's hand, and shall wave the offering before the Lord, and offer it upon the altar: And the priest shall take an handful of the offering, even the memorial thereof, and burn it upon the altar, and afterward shall cause the woman to drink the water. And when he hath made her to drink the water, then it shall come to pass, that, if she be defiled, and have done trespass against her husband, that the water that causeth the curse shall enter into her, and become bitter, and her belly shall swell, and her thigh shall rot: and the woman shall be a curse among her people. And if the woman be not defiled, but be clean; then she shall be free, and shall conceive seed. This is the law of jealousies, when a wife goeth aside to another instead of her husband, and is defiled* (Num. 5:12-29).

Other than this inspired record there is no mention or use of holy water recorded in the Scriptures. The source of the holy water used by the priests was most likely acquired from the laver, which was just before the door of the Holy Place. The priests were to wash themselves in the laver before entering the Holy Place.

The Lord detailed the location of everything regarding the Tabernacle. The Tabernacle and all of the furnishings thereof were adumbrative of the New Testament church. The Hebrew author wrote the following concerning things of the Old Testament: *"Who serve unto the example and shadow of heavenly things, as Moses was admonished of God when he was about to make the tabernacle: for, See, saith he, that thou make all things according to the pattern shewed to thee in the mount"* (Heb. 8:5). The location of the laver can be observed in the figure shown.

# Commentary on Romans

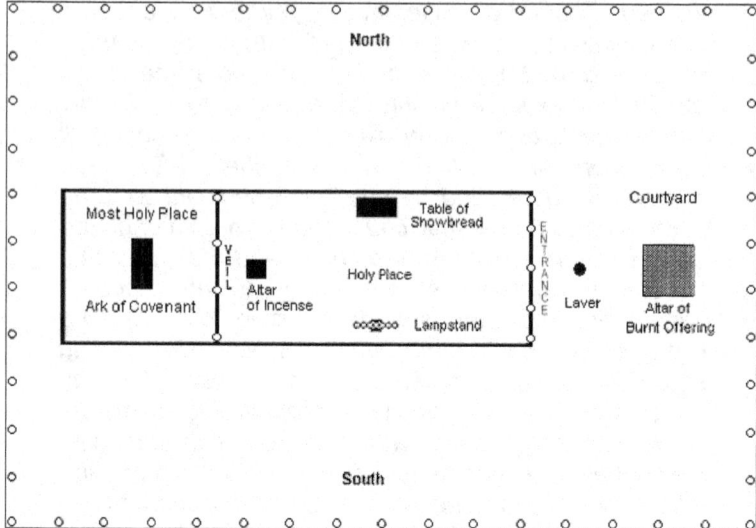

**2. Penance AD 157.** *Penance* is also called *reconciliation, forgiveness, confession* and *conversion*; it is also one of the two sacraments of healing. Catholics argue, Jesus Christ has willed that by this means the Church should continue in the power of the Holy Spirit—that is, by His work of healing and salvation. The priest, who is the minister of the sacrament, acts not in his own name, but on behalf of God; confession of sins is made to God, and absolution is received from God.[6]

**3. Mass AD 394.** Mass is an assembly of the Catholic members on December 25 which was declared by the pope to be the birthday of Christ. The term *Christmas* literally means "Christ-mass." The Bible, however, instructs the saints to remember the Lord's death. The doctrine of *Christmas* is a direct reversal of that which the Scriptures mandate.[7]

**4. The doctrine of Extreme Unction was adopted in AD 588.** This sacrament is administered to parishioners who, having reached the age of reason, begin to be in danger due to sickness or old age, except in the case of those who persevere obstinately in manifest grave sin. Proximate danger of death which occasions the administration of Viaticum is not required, but only at

---
[6] Unpublished class notes on Romans.
[7] Ibid.

# Commentary on Romans

the onset of a medical condition considered to be a possible prelude to death. The sacrament is also referred to as *Unction*, and in the past was referred to as *Extreme Unction*, which is one of the three sacraments that constitute *Last Rites*. It is used with the Sacrament of Penance and Viaticum. The sacrament is administered by a priest who uses olive oil or another pure plant oil to anoint the patient's forehead—and perhaps other parts of the body while reciting certain prayers. It is believed to give comfort, peace, courage, and (if the sick person is unable to make a confession) even forgiveness of sins. Several other churches and ecclesial communities have similar rituals.[8]

5. **The doctrine of Purgatory was introduced in AD 593.** It is a supposed intermediate state after physical death in which those destined for heaven *undergo purification,* so as to achieve the holiness **necessary** to enter the joy of heaven. Only those who die in the state of grace, but who have not reached a sufficient level of holiness can be in Purgatory. None in Purgatory will forever remain in that state or go to hell. This doctrine has ancient roots in early Christian literature; the poetic conception of Purgatory as a geographically existing place is the creation of medieval Christian piety and imagination.[9]

6. **The introduction of Mechanical music occurred in AD 666.** The word *acapella* is an Italian word which means "in a manner of the church," after the manner of the church, or in a manner of the chapel. History shows the early Church engaged in singing acapella and did not use mechanical instruments of music. Adam Clarke wrote the following in his commentary regarding II Chronicles 29:25.

> **With cymbals, with psalteries** – Moses had not appointed any musical instruments to be used in the divine worship; there was nothing of the kind under the first tabernacle. The trumpets or horns then used were neither for song nor for praise, but as we use bells, IE, to give notice to the congregation of what they were called to perform, etc. However, David did certainly introduce many instruments of music into God's worship for which we have already seen he was solemnly re-

---

[8] Unpublished class notes on Romans.
[9] Ibid.

## Commentary on Romans

proved by the prophet Amos, Amos 6:1-6. Here, however, the author of this book states he had the commandment of the prophet Nathan, and Gad the king's seer; and this is stated to have been the commandment of the Lord by his prophets: but the Syriac and Arabic give this a different turn – "Hezekiah appointed the Levites in the house of the Lord, with instruments of music, and the sound of harps, and with the Hymns of David, and the Hymns of Gad, the king's prophet, and of Nathan, the king's prophet: for David sang the praises of the Lord his God, as from the mouth of the prophets." It was by the hand or commandment of the Lord and his prophets that the Levites should praise the Lord; for so the Hebrew text may be understood: and it was by the order of David that so many instruments of music should be introduced into the Divine service. But were it even evident, which it is not, either from this or any other place in the sacred writings, that instruments of music were prescribed by Divine authority under the law, could this be adduced with any semblance of reason, that they ought to be used in Christian worship? No: the whole spirit, soul, and genius of the Christian religion are against this: and those who know the Church of God best, and what constitutes its genuine spiritual state, know that these things have been introduced as a substitute for the life and power of religion; and that where they prevail most, there is least of the power of Christianity. Away with such portentous baubles from the worship of that infinite Spirit who requires his followers to worship him in spirit and in truth, for to no such worship are those instruments friendly[10] [sic].

7. **The doctrine of the kissing of the pope's toe was introduced in AD 709.** Thus, the term *kiss my foot* was coined. A term used in order to belittle another by lofting one's self to a higher status, a term condescending to another. The practice of kissing the pope's toe was adopted at the election of Pope Leo IV (AD 847). It is observed liturgically in a solemn papal mass by the Latin and Greek sub-deacons and quasi-liturgically in the *"adoration"* of the pope by the cardinals after his election. It is also the normal salutation prescribed for papal etiquette. Fur-

---

[10] Adam Clarke.

## Commentary on Romans

ther, it is used for those who are presented to the Pope in a private audience. In his *De altaris mysterio* (VI:6), Pope Innocent III explains, this ceremony indicates "the very great reverence due to the Supreme Pontiff as the Vicar of Him whose feet" were kissed by the woman who was a sinner. The doctrine teaches the pope deserves the same reverence as Jesus, and refers to the woman who is believed to be Mary Magdalene who kissed and poured perfume on the feet of Jesus in preparation for his death and burial.[11]

8. **The doctrine of *Transubstantiation* was established in AD 1000.** *Transubstantiation* is a supposed change; whereby, according to the teaching of the Catholic Church, the bread and the wine used in the sacrament of the Eucharist become not merely a sign or a figure, but becomes the literal body and blood of Christ. The Catholic Church teaches the substance or reality of the bread is changed into the body of Christ, and the substance of the wine into his blood, while all that is accessible to the senses remains unchanged. What remains unaltered is also referred to as the *accidents* of the bread and wine, but this term is not used in the official definition of the doctrine by the Council of Trent.[12]

9. **The doctrine of Celibacy introduced in AD 1015.** Clerical celibacy is the discipline by which only unmarried men are ordained to the episcopate in the Catholic priesthood. Sometimes exceptions are made for individuals in some autonomous churches, and similarly for the deaconate. Though in this last case exceptions exist not only for single individuals, but for whole categories of people. In other autonomous churches the disipline applies only to ordination to the episcopate.[13]

10. **The doctrine of Indulgences came about in AD 1190.** This evil activity was practiced for nearly two centuries before it became Catholic doctrine. This difficult and complicated doctrine of indulgences is peculiar to the Roman Church, and was unknown to the Greek and Latin Fathers. It was developed by the medieval school-men and sanctioned by the Council of Trent (December 4, 1563); yet they did not clearly define it, and they

---

[11] Unpublished class notes on Romans.

[12] Ibid.

[13] Ibid.

## Commentary on Romans

expressly warned against abuses and evil gains. The Roman Catholic Church has yet to denounced this doctrine [14] [sic].

11. **The doctrine of Oracular Confession was introduced in AD 1215.** Roman Catholic Church bases its conclusions on Scripture, Divine revelation, and sacred tradition, as interpreted by the teaching authority of the Church. The belief is encapsulated in the Nicene Creed, the Apostle's Creed, and detailed in the Catechism of the Catholic Church, having been refined and clarified by major councils of the Church, convened by popes at important points throughout history.[15]

12. **The doctrine of Sprinkling adopted in AD 1311.** Introduced by Pope Cornelius I, who wrote that, as Novatian was about to die, *he received baptism in the bed where he lay by pouring* (Letter to Fabius of Antioch [AD 251]). This was cited by Eusebius in his works in which it is said: "Novation, at an adult age, grew sick. Nigh unto death he called for baptism which was administered by sprinkling. This later grew into the acceptance of either pouring or sprinkling in place of immersion, and became known as clinical baptism. The Catholic Church today now pours or sprinkles water upon the head of infants for baptism."[16]

13. **The doctrine of the infallibility of the pope was adopted in AD 1870.** Papal infallibility is a dogma of the Catholic Church which states, in virtue of the promise of Jesus to Peter, the pope is preserved from the possibility of error. When, in the exercise of his office as shepherd and teacher of all Christians, in virtue of his supreme apostolic authority, he defines doctrines concerning faith and morals to be held by the whole Church. In connection with papal infallibility, the Latin phrase **ex cathedra** means *from the chair.*

14. **Peter's bones were allegedly found in St. Peter's Basilica in AD 1953.** Supposedly, *Saint Peter's tomb* is a site under St. Peter's Basilica which includes several graves, and a structure said by Vatican authorities to have been built to memorialize the location of St. Peter's grave. Supposedly, Peter's tomb is near the west end of a complex of mausoleums that date between about AD 130 and AD 300. The complex was partially torn down

---

[14] Phillip Schaff.

[15] Unpublished class notes on Romans.

[16] Ibid.

## Commentary on Romans

and filled with earth to provide a foundation for the building of the first St. Peter's Basilica during the reign of Constantine I in about AD 330. Many bones were found at the site of the 2nd-century shrine as the result of two campaigns of archaeological excavation. Pope Pius XII stated in December of 1950, none could be confirmed to be Saint Peter's with absolute certainty. However, following the discovery of further bones and an inscription, on June 26, 1968, Pope Paul VI announced the relics of St. Peter had been identified.[17]

15. **Eating only fish on Friday was most likely instituted in AD 700.** Much research is needed to uncover the many myths and truth about this doctrine, which is seated in the assumption Jesus ate fish with the twelve apostles on Friday before His crucifixion. This doctrine was mandated by the Catholic Church to honor the Lord for His having abstained from meats other than fish on that occasion. While the date of when this doctrine began is in question, it is probable it occurred about AD 700. Additionally, it is argued fish is a food of fertility. The Catholic Church encourages large families—hence, the teaching. The doctrine was soon tied to the doctrine of Lent.[18]

16.) **The doctrine of Lent was adopted in AD 325.** The word *Lent* comes from the Anglo-Saxon word *Lencten,* meaning springtime. Forty days of Lent was part of the ecumenical Council of Nicaea in AD 325. Today Catholics are encouraged to choose from the areas of prayer, fasting, and alms-giving so they may unite themselves with Christ on all the 40 days of Lent in preparation for the celebration of the Resurrection on Easter Sunday.

17. **Contributions made by the Roman Empire to the spread of the early church are listed below.**

**Positive things:**

1. World peace.
2. Universalism.
3. The Greek culture.
4. The Greek language.
5. Travel—transportation.
6. Religious tolerance—a polytheistic society.

---

[17] Unpublished class notes on Romans

[18] Ibid

# Commentary on Romans

7. Universal law.
8. Synagogues.

**Negative things:**

1. There was no good common Roman religion.
2. Roman philosophy and religions were very subjective, and had no promise of eternal life.

**18. Main teachings of the Book of Romans:**

1. The failure of man.
2. Man has hope.
3. Doctrine of the Godhead.
4. Doctrine of Christ's system of salvation.
5. The cessation of the Old Law.
6. The possibility of apostasy of congregations.

**19. Contributions made by nations throughout history for the spread of the Gospel.**

1. Babylonian Empire—Synagogues.
2. Mede and Persian Empires—Law.
3. Grecian Empire—Language
4. Roman Empire—Transportation

**20. Important things to know about why Paul wrote the Roman Epistle in the style in which it was composed.**

1. First, Paul was directed by the Holy Spirit to do so.
2. God chose the most qualified human agent to compose the inspired book.
3. Paul was a Jew and understood the Jewish mindset. Jews made up the greater body of the church at Rome.
4. From the Jewish perspective, Paul could well relate to the difficulty the Jews had in giving up the Old Law.
5. Paul's education better qualified him to deal with Jewish attitudes.
6. Paul made arguments he knew the Jews would make to remain under the Old Law and then answers the arguments.

# Commentary on Romans

## Romans 1:1-7

*1 Paul, a servant of Jesus Christ, called to be an apostle, separated unto the gospel of God, 2 (Which he had promised afore by his prophets in the holy scriptures,) 3 Concerning his Son Jesus Christ our Lord, which was made of the seed of David according to the flesh; 4 And declared to be the Son of God with power, according to the spirit of holiness, by the resurrection from the dead: 5 By whom we have received grace and apostleship, for obedience to the faith among all nations, for his name: 6 Among whom are ye also the called of Jesus Christ: 7 To all that be in Rome, beloved of God, called to be saints: Grace to you and peace from God our Father, and the Lord Jesus Christ.*

These introductory verses reveal much for students willing to delve deeply into the inspired text. The deeper one dips his chalice of desire into the Word of God, the closer to the Lord one becomes—and the more astute in Scriptures. A good understanding of the Scriptures elevates the Bible student to a greater level in his ability *to give an answer to every man that asketh* him of the *reason of the hope that is in you with meekness and fear* (I Pet. 3:15).

Some have suggested Paul was his Roman name, Saul his Jewish name. Some suppose Paul adopted the use of his Roman name over his Jewish name to overcome the astigmatism of his blasphemous activity and persecution of the Lord's church. Paul declared of himself he was one *who was before a blasphemer, and a persecutor, and injurious* to the church. His past reminded him of his need to press on in the faith, and *labor more* than all others in order to work toward his salvation and the salvation of others (I Tim. 1:13; I Cor. 15:10).

**Verse 1.** *Paul, a servant of Jesus Christ, called to be an apostle, separated unto the gospel of God.* The word *servant* is defined as a slave, literally or figuratively, voluntarily or involuntarily. *Called* means invited or appointed, specifically referring to being called unto sainthood, especially unto an appointed office. Knowledgeable Bible students recall the Lord said to Ananias:

# Commentary on Romans

> *Arise, and go into the street which is called Straight, and inquire in the house of Judas for one called Saul, of Tarsus: for, behold, he prayeth, And hath seen in a vision a man named Ananias coming in, and putting his hand on him, that he might receive his sight. Then Ananias answered, Lord, I have heard by many of this man, how much evil he hath done to thy saints at Jerusalem: And here he hath authority from the chief priests to bind all that call on thy name. But the Lord said unto him, Go thy way: for he is a chosen vessel unto me, to bear my name before the Gentiles, and kings, and the children of Israel: For I will shew him how great things he must suffer for my name's sake* (Acts 9:11-16).

An apostle is a delegate, specifically an ambassador of the Gospel, officially a commissioner of Christ with miraculous powers.

The phrase, *separated unto the gospel of God*, is to be separated unto a specific purpose, and is akin to sanctification. Properly, *sanctification* means "to be set apart for the purpose of serving God." Jude, the servant of Jesus Christ, declared that saints *are sanctified by God the Father, and preserved in Jesus Christ, and called* (1). Saints are sanctified by God and by no other means. Paul declared only God justifies man (cf. Rom. 8:33).

**Verses 2-3.** *(Which he had promised afore by his prophets in the holy scriptures,) Concerning his Son Jesus Christ our Lord, which was made of the seed of David according to the flesh.* The Gospel was foreordained by the Godhead as the only avenue by which men may acquire salvation. Many fail to realize the Gospel and the church are as eternal as the Godhead.

> *Unto me, who am less than the least of all saints, is this grace given, that I should preach among the Gentiles the unsearchable riches of Christ; And to make all men see what is the fellowship of the mystery, which from the beginning of the world hath been hid in God, who created all things by Jesus Christ: To the intent that now unto the principalities and powers in heavenly places might be known by the church the manifold wis-*

dom of God, According to the eternal purpose which he purposed in Christ Jesus our Lord (Eph. 3:8-11).

This last sentence (quoted above) refers to the church – His kingdom. Just as the God is without beginning or ending, so the church has no beginning or ending. Though the Lord's church had an earthly beginning on the day of Pentecost it has forever been in the mind of God.

Premillennialism asserts the church was an alternative plan adopted by God, because Christ failed to establish His kingdom. To assert the Lord failed in His efforts to establish His Kingdom denies the all-powerful attributes and sovereignty of the Godhead. Jesus equated the church with the kingdom:

*And I say also unto thee, That thou art Peter, and upon this rock I will build my **church**; and the gates of hell shall not prevail against it. And I will give unto thee the keys of the **kingdom of heaven**: and whatsoever thou shalt bind on earth shall be bound in heaven: and whatsoever thou shalt loose on earth shall be loosed in heaven* (Matt. 16:18-19, emph. DHC).

What line of valid reasoning permits the conclusion the church and the kingdom are not one and the same? Why would the Lord declare He would build His church, and then give the apostles the *keys to the kingdom*—if they are in fact not both one and the same?

Consider some objections to such Premillennial thinking. First, such suggests the Lord realized before His three-and-one-half years of ministry were ended, He would be unable to establish His kingdom—thus making the Lord unable to complete the work the Father assigned Him. Second, such means Christ was totally ignorant and erred greatly when He said: *I have glorified thee on the earth: I have finished the work which thou gavest me to do* (Jno. 17:4). Third, if it is the case the church and the kingdom are not one and the same, then it is the case the apostles were not given the keys to either the church or the kingdom. Fourth, according to Premillennial thinking, the Lord promised the keys of the kingdom to the apostles; He did not promise the

# Commentary on Romans

apostles the keys to the church. Fifth, if therefore, the church was established as an afterthought, then it is the case there is no apostolic authority by which the Lord's church can be governed. Sixth, it must also be the case the apostles have no keys as of yet, and the giving of the keys to the kingdom is yet future. Seventh, consider the following passages with comments following.

*Who hath delivered us from the power of darkness, and hath translated us into the kingdom of his dear Son* (Col. 1:13). How could Paul have declared to the saints of the church of the Colossians they were *translated into* a kingdom which, according to Premillennial thinking, does not exist? The apostle John wrote of himself: *I John, who also am your brother, and companion in tribulation, and in the kingdom and patience of Jesus Christ, was in the isle that is called Patmos, for the word of God, and for the testimony of Jesus Christ* (Rev. 1:9). How could John have insisted he was in the kingdom of the Lord if it did not then exist?

Such foolishness is clear, the church and the kingdom are indeed both one and the same. Mark wrote: *And he said unto them, Verily I say unto you, That there be some of them that stand here, which shall not taste of death, till they have seen the kingdom of God come with power* (Mk. 9:1). Are any willing to assert there are still some of those to whom the Lord spoke on that occasion yet living, and will continue to live until such time the Lord succeeds in setting up His kingdom? What if the Lord fails to establish His kingdom the second time—or perhaps a third or fourth? Will He continue to allow some of those who heard the Lord say that *there be some of them that stand here, which shall not taste of death, till they have seen the kingdom of God come with power*—to live until the Lord gets it right?

**Verse 4.** *And declared to be the Son of God with power, according to the spirit of holiness, by the resurrection from the dead.* Christ is here described as the Son of God in a three-fold manner. First, Christ was declared to be the Son of God *with power.* Second, Christ is described as the Son of God according to the *spirit of holiness.* Third, He was declared to be the Son of God *by the resurrection from the dead.*

In human form, Christ demonstrated, by Divine power and mira-

# Commentary on Romans

cles, He was indeed the Son of God. The Pharisees knew, but refused to admit, the Son-ship of Christ. A few Pharisees did, however, ascend to that truth. For *there was a man of the Pharisees, named Nicodemus, a ruler of the Jews: The same came to Jesus by night, and said unto him, Rabbi, we know that thou art a teacher come from God: for no man can do these miracles that thou doest, except God be with him* (Jno. 3:1-2).

**Verses 5-6.** *By whom we have received grace and apostle-ship, for obedience to the faith among all nations, for his name: Among whom are ye also the called of Jesus Christ.* The grace under consideration here refers to the blessing of preaching the Gospel. Paul declared such to the church at Ephesus. *Unto me, who am less than the least of all saints, is this grace given, that I should preach among the Gentiles the unsearchable riches of Christ* (Eph. 3:8).

The phrase *for obedience to the faith* commands close attention. Paul opens this epistle with the edict, *the faith* must be obeyed; he closes this epistle with the same mandate, and he injects the same near the middle. Compare Romans 1:5, 6:17, and 16:26. The faith of which Paul writes is one which demands obedience. Truly, a faith that saves is a faith that obeys.

Isaiah wrote of the faith among the nations. *And it shall come to pass in the last days, that the mountain of the Lord's house shall be established in the top of the mountains, and shall be exalted above the hills; and all nations shall flow unto it* (Isa. 2:2).

Consider the words, *among whom*, in verse six; this phrase places the Gentiles among the nations of which Paul and the prophet Isaiah wrote. *All nations* is inclusive of both the Jew and the Gentile.

**Verse 7.** *To all that be in Rome, beloved of God, called to be saints: Grace to you and peace from God our Father, and the Lord Jesus Christ.* *To all* means Jew and the Gentile. All men are called to obey the gospel; *for the Lord is not willing that any should perish, but that all should come to repentance* (II Pet. 3:9).

# Commentary on Romans

How are men called? This has long been a controversy in the denominational world. There are, it seems, as many answers as there are denominations. However, the query is easily resolved by inspiration, and there need not be confusion; *for God is not the author of confusion, but of peace* (I Cor. 14:33). Paul declared, concerning the call issued by God that, *he called you by our gospel* (II Thes. 2:14). Man is called by the Gospel and by no other means. Many insist they were called by *some small still voice in the night.* However, the Lord declared: *I have not spoken in secret, in a dark place of the earth* (Isa. 45:19). Further, the Lord said: *I spake openly to the world; I ever taught in the synagogue, and in the temple, whither the Jews always resort; and in secret have I said nothing* (Jno. 18:20).

Those of the Lord's church are identified as the *beloved of God.* The word comes from the root word *agape,* which means "well-beloved—dearly beloved." Such love being awarded to those in the Lord's church should cause one to pause and deeply ponder the magnitude and depth of God's love for those in the church. The church is the only place where the scope, breadth, depth, and height of God's love can be found. Saints should well strain themselves in efforts to return their love to God as He has directed toward them. Jesus said: *A new commandment I give unto you, That ye love one another; as I have loved you, that ye also love one another* (Jno. 13:34). The phrase, *as I have loved you,* dictates the degree to which saints must go in loving their brethren. *For God so loved the world, that he gave his only begotten Son, that whosoever believeth in him should not perish, but have everlasting life* (Jno. 3:16). *But God commendeth his love toward us, in that, while we were yet sinners, Christ died for us* (Rom. 5:8).

*Grace be unto you and peace from God our Father and the Lord Jesus Christ* are the last words of Paul's salutation. Here there is a two-fold blessing from a two-fold source. First, Paul bids *grace* upon the church at Rome. Second, Paul beckons *peace* upon the church. Neither grace nor peace can be awarded without God's blessing. The grace and peace of which Paul wrote are spiritual blessings, the sources of grace and peace are *from God our Father and the Lord Jesus Christ.* Neither grace nor peace comes from denominational doctrine. *So then faith,* Paul

# Commentary on Romans

wrote; *cometh by hearing and hearing by the word of God.* Faith does not come from denominational doctrine (Rom. 10:17).

It is crucial to understand the word *so* in Romans 10:17 is an adverb of manner, which shows the process by which faith comes. Divinely approved faith comes by hearing that which God has mandated and by no other doctrine or means. The system of faith is found in and only in the Scriptures. The system of faith designed by God is the system in which men must abide and comply fully to secure eternal life. Unless one abides in Christ, His doctrine, and the system of faith established by Him, one cannot be a disciple of the Lord. Consider: *Abide in me, and I in you. As the branch cannot bear fruit of itself, except it abide in the vine; no more can ye, except ye abide in me* (Jno. 15:4). *Whosoever transgresseth, and abideth not in the doctrine of Christ, hath not God. He that abideth in the doctrine of Christ, he hath both the Father and the Son* (II Jno. 9).

Much more remains in the cornucopia of spiritual knowledge on which the student of God's Word may feast regarding this verse; therefore, it behooves all saints to delve deeply into the Word of God. Long sittings at the Lord's table are never out of style, but always in fashion. One moment deferred from in-depth Bible study for worldly things is a step taken far out of the way. Never has the pen of man equaled the magnitude of what inspiration has provided. Without deep, intense, and wearisome study of God's Word, men will stand before the throne of God empty-handed, empty-headed, and empty-hearted. Because God has revealed His truth to all men (Jno. 8:32), it behooves us to study in such a fashion as to gain the Lord's approval (cf. II Tim. 2:15).

## Romans 1:8-17

*8 First, I thank my God through Jesus Christ for you all, that your faith is spoken of throughout the whole world. 9 For God is my witness, whom I serve with my spirit in the gospel of his Son, that without ceasing I make mention of you always in my prayers; 10 Making request, if by any means now at length I might have a prosperous journey by the will of God to come unto you. 11 For I long to see you, that I may impart unto*

# Commentary on Romans

*you some spiritual gift, to the end ye may be established; 12 That is, that I may be comforted together with you by the mutual faith both of you and me. 13 Now I would not have you ignorant, brethren, that oftentimes I purposed to come unto you, (but was let hitherto,) that I might have some fruit among you also, even as among other Gentiles. 14 I am debtor both to the Greeks and to the Barbarians; both to the wise and to the unwise. 15 So, as much as in me is, I am ready to preach the gospel to you that are at Rome also. 16 For I am not ashamed of the gospel of Christ: for it is the power of God unto salvation to every one that believeth; to the Jew first and also to the Greek. 17 For therein is the righteousness of God revealed from faith to faith: as it is written, The just shall live by faith.*

**Verse 8.** *First, I thank my God through Jesus Christ*, wrote the inspired apostle. It is always a matter of importance to thank God for all His blessings awarded to us. Thanksgiving to the Father must always be *through Jesus Christ*—that is, through and by His authority. God graciously grants saints the blessing of approaching His throne in boldness. Observe: *Let us therefore come boldly unto the throne of grace, that we may obtain mercy and find grace to help in time of need. ... So that we may boldly say, The Lord is my helper and I will not fear what man shall do unto me* (Heb. 4:16; 13:6).

Paul's gratitude for the church at Rome enveloped a great commendation. *Your faith is spoken of throughout the whole world.* Every congregation should emulate the kind of faith adorned by the church at Rome. Such adorning does much good and multiplies God's blessings.

**Verse 9.** The apostle further declared, *God is my witness,* but to what does the apostle refer with the inspired comment? Before supplying due response, consider that God witnesses everything. The Father is witness to all things—things done openly and secretly, good or bad, through ignorance or intent. Nothing escapes His eye. Because the Father discerns every thought and intent of man's heart, it serves men well to do all they do,

# Commentary on Romans

whether *in word or deed in the name of the Lord Jesus* (cf. Rom. 14:12; Ecc. 12:14; Heb. 4:1; Col. 3:17).

The phrase, *Whom I serve with my spirit in the gospel of his Son,* contains a fourfold declarative. First, it was God whom Paul diligently served. Second, Paul's degree of service was couched in his heart and his service rose into action by an obedient spirit. Third, it was the Gospel to which Paul tethered his heart for service to God. Lastly, the matters declared heretofore find their place in Christ. All these things are found in the Gospel of God's Son.

*That without ceasing I make mention of you always in my prayers.* The purpose for Paul having said, *God is my witness,* lies within this phrase. God was the apostle's witness that he prayed without ceasing and offered continuous thanksgiving for the brethren in Rome. The apostle stated: *I make mention of you always in my prayers.* It is best for others that we often keep them in our prayers. Continuous prayers keep the avenue of communication with the Father always unblocked.

**Verse 10.** *Making request*—Paul wrote concerning his prayers on behalf of the saints at Rome. Though Paul was endowed with apostolic authority, he was not exempt from making his requests known to God. Such should cause saints to follow suit. Saints do well to realize they are not above the same need of making their requests known to the Father.

*If by any means now at length I might have a prosperous journey by the will of God to come unto you.* The phrase *at length* means "at last." Paul desired *a prosperous journey* as he pressed toward Rome. The prosperity for which the apostle hoped was not so much monetary, but rather spiritual. Paul desired to bring as many to Christ as possible, not only during his journey to Rome, but after his advent there.

It was *by the will of God* that Paul desired to enter Rome and be of good spiritual assistance to the saints. Our presence with the saints should always produce spiritual aid for them. It serves the church well when the brethren admonish one another.

# Commentary on Romans

**Verse 11.** *For I long to see you.* The word *long* means "to yearn, to dote upon—that is, intensely crave a possession lawfully or wrongfully, earnestly desire, greatly long after." All covetousness is not wrong. Paul instructed the Corinthians to *covet earnestly the best gifts* (I Cor. 12:31). The word *covet* means "to have warmth of feeling for, have desire, be jealous over, be zealously affected." Indeed, saints do well to covet company with the brethren.

Constant company with the saints should be desired and longed for by all those of *like precious faith* (II Pet.1:1). Saints often long for the company of worldly men and worldly things. The apostle John instructed the saints: L*ove not the world, neither the things that are in the world. If any man love the world, the love of the Father is not in him. For all that is in the world, the lust of the flesh and the lust of the eyes and the pride of life, is not of the Father, but is of the world. And the world passeth away and the lust thereof: but he that doeth the will of God abideth for ever* (I Jno. 2:15-17).

Men and the riches of the world perish and whither; earthly treasures are subject to moth and corruption, but spiritual men and blessings are not. Jesus instructed the godly to lay not *up for yourselves treasures...where...moth nor rust doth corrupt and where thieves...break through and steal, but rather lay up for themselves treasures in heaven* (Matt. 6:20). James wrote: F*or the sun is no sooner risen with a burning heat, but it withereth the grass, and the flower thereof falleth, and the grace of the fashion of it perisheth: so also shall the rich man fade away in his ways* (Jas. 1:11).

Paul had numerous reasons to covet company with the saints of Rome; among them was his desire to be among those whose *faith was spoken of throughout the whole world.* Further, the apostle wished to be with those for whom he continuously prayed. He also desired to be with them that he might impart to some of them some spiritual gift. The apostle wished to establish the Roman saints more strongly in the faith of Jesus Christ.

Paul wanted to impart unto some of the saints in Rome some *spiritual gift, to the end they would may be* [better] *established* in

# Commentary on Romans

their faith. It serves the church best when brethren seek to better establish themselves in the faith.

The phrase *to the end* means "for the purpose of." Paul's desire to be among the saints of the church at Rome was an honorable one. Often men of ill will work toward division and ruin within the Lord's church. Such men are after the pattern of Diotrephes of whom John wrote *unto the church: but Diotrephes, who loveth to have the preeminence among them, receiveth us not. Wherefore, if I come, I will remember his deeds which he doeth, prating against us with malicious words: and not content therewith, neither doth he himself receive the brethren and forbiddeth them that would and casteth them out of the church* (III Jno. 9-10).

**Verse 12.** The words, *that is*, reflects Paul's desire to impart to the saints of Rome some spiritual gift. Paul further declared such an impartation would be a comfort to both the church and himself. Saints must be bound together by mutual faith and the *common salvation* of Jesus Christ (Jd. 3). There should be *no divisions* among the saints, they should *be perfectly joined together in the same mind and in the same judgment* (I Cor. 1:10). Saints must be one in the Father and in the Son (cf. Jno. 17:21).

**Verse 13.** *Now I would not have you ignorant, brethren, that oftentimes I purposed to come unto you, (but was let hitherto,) that I might have some fruit among you also, even as among other Gentiles.* Paul was accused of numerous things by many Jews; some were deeply envious of Paul and his apostleship. Paul mentioned such strife and envy to the church of Philippi. Notice: *Some indeed preach Christ even of envy and strife* (Phil. 1:15).

Those clad with envy and strife toward Paul preached *Christ of contention, not sincerely, supposing to add affliction to my* (his) *bonds* (Phil. 1:16). They wished to have Paul kept in bonds to keep the apostle from the forefront of prominence among the saints. These were the kind of men who were much like unto *Diotrephes, who loveth to have the preeminence among* the saints (III Jno. 9). Those contentious and envious preachers preached for the purpose of compounding Paul's problem of incarceration. They hoped to have Paul suffer so greatly for the

# Commentary on Romans

church that the bonds with which Paul was fettered would not soon be loosed. The word *bond* is defined as "a band; that is, a shackle (of a prisoner) an impediment or disability—band, bond, or chain."

Contentious and envious preachers of Paul's day accused the apostle of intentionally refraining to go to Rome. Among such accusations was the charge that Paul was not an apostle and could in no way benefit the church at Rome. It was further declared by some that Paul had no apostolic powers and could not bestow spiritual gifts on anyone. Further, it was asserted Paul made many excuses to stay away from Rome lest he be found a liar should he present himself there. For these reasons the apostle wrote: *Now I would not have you ignorant, brethren, that oftentimes I purposed to come unto you.* With this inspired comment, Paul settled the matter and quelled the protest against him and his apostleship.

Paul assured the Roman church he *was let hitherto.* The word *let* in this verse is defined as having been hindered by means beyond the apostles' control. However, to reassure the Roman saints of Paul's true apostleship, he expressed his desire to be with them in order to *have some fruit among* the church at Rome as he also did *among other Gentiles.*

**Verse 14.** *I am debtor, both to the Greeks and to the Barbarians.* As a *debtor,* Paul meant he owed his fellowman the prize of the Gospel. Just as he had received grace from the Lord, so he desired all men to gain the same grace with which he had been blessed. Paul felt compelled to preach *for,* he said, *necessity is laid upon me; yea, woe is unto me, if I preach not the gospel* (I Cor. 9:16)!

*The Greeks* refers to those who spoke the Greek Language, *the Barbarians* refers to those who spoke some other. The word *barbarian,* as used today, means "savage, vicious, violent and uncivilized, or an untamed person." In Paul's time, such was not the case.

Paul considered himself a debtor *to the wise,* which referred to those of intellectual achievement. The word *unwise* describes

# Commentary on Romans

the sensual or foolish. Even these men deserve to have the Gospel preached unto them.

**Verse 15.** *So, as much as in me is, I am ready to preach the gospel.* The word *ready* means "being forward in spirit; that is, predisposed...always being ready and willing."

The word *so* is an adverb of manner, showing the manner in which Paul was *ready to preach.* The adverb *so* modifies the verb *preach.* The word *so* means in this way (referring to what precedes or follows), in this manner or fashion. The love of the Gospel and the preaching of it were well fettered in the heart of the apostle.

*As much as in me is* displayed the righteous obsession with which Paul was consumed. The prophet Jeremiah declared concerning God's Word: *his word was in mine heart as a burning fire shut up in my bones and I was weary with forbearing and I could not stay* [stay quiet about the Lord's message] (Jer. 20:9). Paul found himself in the same plight.

*To you that are at Rome also.* This phrase echoes the thoughts expressed in the comments of verse 13. Paul had no feelings of uncertainty or apprehensions about going to Rome, contrary to what his accusers declared.

**Verse 16.** *For I am not ashamed of the gospel of Christ: for it is the power of God unto salvation to every one that believeth; to the Jew first and also to the Greek.* The word *for* is "a primary particle; properly assigning a reason used in an argument, an explanation or intensification; often with other particles." Why was Paul *ready to preach the gospel* to those in Rome? Because *it is the power of God unto salvation.*

The preaching of any other gospel, warranted shame and cursing from God. Paul wrote to the Galatian church that, *though we, or an angel from heaven, preach another of a different kind of gospel unto you than that, which we have preached unto you, let him be accursed* (Gal. 1:8). The word *accursed* is defined as "a religious *ban* or an *excommunicated* thing or person, anathema."

# Commentary on Romans

The canvas of the mind is better adorned when one understands what the word *anathema* portrays. When the Jews brought animal sacrifices to the tabernacle for sacrifice, they were stalled until such a time the priest could tend to the sacrifices. Once the animal was stalled, it could not be redeemed. The animal was *anathema*—accursed, hopelessly fated unto death for sacrifice. The same is the case for those who preach a Gospel other than that which the Lord has both authored and authorized (cf. Gal. 1:6-9).

Paul wrote of the gospel; *it is the power of God unto salvation.* God's power to save man is found in the Gospel, and in the only Gospel; that is, the Gospel of Jesus Christ. By inspiration Luke penned: *Neither is there salvation in any other: for there is none other name under heaven given among men, whereby we must be saved* (Acts 4:12). James declared men are to *receive with meekness the engrafted word, which is able to save your souls* (Jas. 1:21). *The seed is the word of God*, as Luke 8:11 reveals, and only through it God saves men. Creeds of men are **of** men; they are not of God and cannot save.

*To every one that believeth.* Biblical *belief* is "to have faith in, or upon, with respect to a person or thing, to entrust one's spiritual well-being to Christ, as an obedient believer, with commitment to trust." To possess an active, busy, obedient belief is not mere mental assent, recognition, or acknowledgment of Christ's existence. *Thou believest that there is one God; thou doest well: the devils also believe and tremble* (Jas. 2:19).

Paul emphasized *everyone,* meaning both Jew and Gentile. Such is shown to be the case when one considers the phrase, *to the Jew first and also to the Greek.*

**Verse 17.** *For therein is the righteousness of God revealed from faith to faith: as it is written, The just shall live by faith.* The word *therein* has reference to the Gospel; that is, in the Gospel is God's saving power and righteousness revealed. The Gospel is here defined by Paul to be God's *righteousness. The righteousness of God* has reference to the system of faith by which God has made it possible to declare men righteous. This system is the system of the Gospel of Jesus Christ.

# Commentary on Romans

*The righteousness of God* is the New Testament system of faith established by Jesus Christ. The *righteousness of God* does not refer to qualities, characteristics, or attributes of God the Father. If such be the case, then none who lived before the time when *the righteousness of God* was revealed in the Gospel knew God was righteous. No one of the Old Testament period would have had any knowledge of God's attributes of righteousness. Can any logically conclude that of the men of faith, as recorded in Hebrews 11, or in the Old Testament, none knew God was righteous? Truly, those of the Old Testament period knew the Lord was righteous.

*Revealed from faith to faith* this is a portion of inspired text which has brought forth not a few controversies, uncertainties, and difficulties. The comments of countless commentators are too numerous to explore. However, the student is best served when he refers to the passage of inspired text from which Paul acquires the Old Testament quote. God's prophet of old wrote: *Behold, his soul which is lifted up is not upright in him: but the just shall live by his faith* (Hab. 2:4). The soul of the self-righteous man is not an upright one. However, those who live by an obedient faith do have an upright soul before the Lord. The justified one lives by the system of faith God designated. It is from an obedient heart by which God saves men. An obedient faith cannot be separated from the system of faith God has ordained if salvation is to be acquired. The two must be coupled to acquire salvation.

The word *faith* occurs twice in this passage, once in the verb form and once in the noun form. The former word *faith* is in the verb form, the latter in the noun form. The passage means for a man to be justified he must live by the system of faith ordained by God. Man must be obedient unto God's system of faith in all things. *From faith* (verb form—an obedient faith) *to faith* (noun form—to the system ordained by God). Saints must live faithfully, actively obedient to the system of faith God ordained.

It is well to observe the word *his* in the passage quoted by Paul (cf. Hab. 2:4). Such shows men who are obedient to the system of faith established by God are those under consideration by the apostle. That system is the one by which a person is to live.

# Commentary on Romans

The Gospel originated with God, it was authored by Christ, and it has been revealed by the Holy Ghost. Christ is *author of eternal salvation unto all them that obey him* (Heb. 5:9).

## Romans 1:18-32

*18 For the wrath of God is revealed from heaven against all ungodliness and unrighteousness of men, who hold the truth in unrighteousness; 19 Because that which may be known of God is manifest in them; for God hath shewed it unto them. 20 For the invisible things of him from the creation of the world are clearly seen, being understood by the things that are made, even his eternal power and Godhead; so that they are without excuse: 21 Because that, when they knew God, they glorified him not as God, neither were thankful; but became vain in their imaginations and their foolish heart was darkened. 22 Professing themselves to be wise, they became fools, 23 And changed the glory of the uncorruptible God into an image made like to corruptible man and to birds and fourfooted beasts and creeping things. 24 Wherefore God also gave them up to uncleanness through the lusts of their own hearts, to dishonour their own bodies between themselves: 25 Who changed the truth of God into a lie and worshipped and served the creature more than the Creator, who is blessed forever. Amen. 26 For this cause God gave them up unto vile affections: for even their women did change the natural use into that which is against nature: 27 And likewise also the men, leaving the natural use of the woman, burned in their lust one toward another; men with men working that which is unseemly and receiving in themselves that recompence of their error which was meet. 28 And even as they did not like to retain God in their knowledge, God gave them over to a reprobate mind, to do those things which are not convenient; 29 Being filled with all unrighteousness, fornication, wickedness, covetousness, maliciousness; full of envy, murder, debate, deceit, malignity; whisperers, 30 Backbiters, haters of God, despiteful, proud, boasters, inventors of evil things,*

# Commentary on Romans

*disobedient to parents, 31 Without understanding, covenantbreakers, without natural affection, implacable, unmerciful: 32 Who knowing the judgment of God, that they which commit such things are worthy of death, not only do the same, but have pleasure in them that do them.*

**Verse 18.** *For the wrath of God is revealed from heaven against all ungodliness and unrighteousness of men, who hold the truth in unrighteousness.* Quintuple observations should be considered regarding this passage. First, observe the words: *For the wrath of God.* God's wrath is real and concrete; it is strongly cast against all who oppose Him, His authority and His manates. The author of the Hebrew epistle wrote concerning God's wrath: *our God is a consuming fire* (Heb. 12:29). The word *consuming* is defined as "utterly to consume, or completely destroy." Further the Hebrew author wrote: *It is a fearful thing to fall into the hands of the living God* (Heb. 10:31). The word *fall* is in the verb form and means "to fall on; that is—literally—be entrapped by, or (figuratively) be overwhelmed with, or fall among, or into." When man willfully opposes God and His will, he subjects himself to the eternal trap of damnation with an overwhelming fire from which there is no escape. Indeed God is a consuming fire against the unrighteous and ungodly.

Second, it is observed, *the wrath of God is revealed.* As God has revealed His will and means by which He redeems man, He has also revealed the wrath He will impose against all ungodly men.

The word *hell* is used 22 times in the New Testament, of which Christ used the word 18 times. Man is therefore without excuse regarding God's wrath. Peter declared: *The Lord is not slack concerning his promise, as some men count slackness; but is longsuffering to us-ward, not willing that any should perish, but that all should come to repentance* (II Pet. 3:9).

Third, *the wrath of God is revealed from heaven.* God's wrath is not from men, but from the sovereign God of heaven and earth. Heaven is the home from which God has revealed His wrath. Not a few denominationalists reject the Bible doctrine of eternal

## Commentary on Romans

destruction in hell. However, the Bible teaching is both true and clear. The denial of eternal damnation has been adopted by those who wish for release from spiritual responsibility and accountability. The verity of the doctrine of eternal hell remains regardless of that which disobedient men avow. It is heaven to where God will take the obedient, but hell awaits those who disobey Him. Peter wrote: *The Lord knoweth how to deliver the godly out of temptations and to reserve the unjust unto the day of judgment to be punished* (II Pet. 2:9).

Fourth, *God's wrath is revealed from heaven against all ungodliness and unrighteousness of men.* Ungodliness and unrighteousness are rooted in willful disobedience. While Adam and Eve were yet in the Garden of Eden, that *old serpent, the Devil,* sowed the first seeds of sin in the soil of satanic trickery and deceit (Rev. 20:2). Wicked men have anxiously and aggressively harvested the fruits thereof since.

Of things holy and divine, not a few are willfully ignorant. Peter declared: *For this they willingly are ignorant of...* (II Pet. 3:5). Further, it is well to note that which Paul declared: *Be not deceived; God is not mocked: for whatsoever a man soweth, that shall he also reap. For he that soweth to his flesh shall of the flesh reap corruption* (Gal. 6:7-8).

Last, unrighteous men *hold the truth in unrighteousness.* Here the word *hold* means "to hold down in suppression." Unrighteous men cease not to hinder God's Word. They are ever working to change God's truth into a lie. Such men have always *changed the truth of God into a lie and worshipped and served the creature more than their Creator* (Rom. 1:25). When truth is altered, it becomes a lie. Though men seek to change God's truth into that which appeals to their fancies, the Lord declared, *My covenant will I not break, nor alter the thing that is gone out of my lips* (Psa. 89:34). The Scripture further states, *For ever, O Lord, thy word is settled in heaven* (Psa. 119:89).

**Verse 19.** *Because that which may be known of God is manifest in them; for God hath shewed it unto them.* God has never left man without knowledge of His ordinances. Paul, in this first chapter, begins to address the Gentile converts of the Roman

# Commentary on Romans

congregation. Paul set forth the argument that through the patriarchal dispensation God manifested His will. The apostle declared *that which may be known of God is manifest in them for God hath shewed it unto them.* God began revealing His will while Adam was yet in the garden. Moses wrote: *And the Lord God took the man and put him into the Garden of Eden to dress it and to keep it. And the Lord God commanded the man, saying, Of every tree of the garden thou mayest freely eat: But of the tree of the knowledge of good and evil, thou shalt not eat of it: for in the day that thou eatest thereof thou shalt surely die* (Gen. 2:15-17).

The death, which was to be suffered by Adam and Eve has long been contested. Many contend for physical death. Others insist spiritual death is the meaning of the passage. Both are submitted here for consideration. When Adam sinned, he died spiritually and lost his secure place with God. Adam also began to die physically. Their sin brought about both physical and spiritual death.

Bible students understand God revealed His will to the Patriarchal Fathers directly. Adam, Abel, Noah, Abraham, Isaac, and Jacob were among the patriarchs to whom God spoke directly. Never has man been without Divine Law. God has always subjected man to His Law regardless of which dispensation of time man has lived.

It has long been asserted it is an instinct of man to worship a higher being or power. Contrary to this assertion is the fact God instructed Adam of the need to worship. Adam in turn instructed his sons Cain and Abel. If it is the case man instinctively desires to worship, then we ask how was Abel able to offer *unto God a more excellent sacrifice than Cain, by which he obtained witness that he was righteous, God testifying of his gifts* (Heb. 11:4)?

Did Abel do so through *instinctive* knowledge, or did he do so based upon instructions received from Adam? If he did so through *instinctive* knowledge, then why did God not accept the offering of Cain. Would not have Cain had the same *"instinctive* knowledge?

# Commentary on Romans

**Verse 20.** *For the invisible things of him from the creation of the world are clearly seen, being understood by the things that are made, even his eternal power and Godhead so that they are without excuse.* Thus, man can never submit acceptable excuses for disobedience.

David wrote: *The heavens declare the glory of God; and the firmament sheweth his handywork. Day unto day uttereth speech and night unto night sheweth knowledge. There is no speech nor language, where their voice is not heard. Their line is gone out through all the earth and their words to the end of the world. In them hath he set a tabernacle for the sun* (Psa. 19:1-4). Both nature and Divine revelation declare God's Deity to man. Man is truly *without excuse.*

**Verse 21.** *Because that, when they knew God, they glorified him not as God, neither were thankful; but became vain in their imaginations and their foolish heart was darkened. Because that, when they knew God....* The word *knew* is a prolonged form of a primary verb meaning "to absolutely know." It also means "to be aware of, to feel, to have known, perceive, be resolved, to be sure and perfectly understand." The Gentiles of the patriarchal age absolutely *knew* God's will, but *they glorified him not as God, neither were thankful.* Disobedient patriarchs became men without gratitude toward God or his goodness. In so doing, they *became vain in their imaginations.*

The word *imaginations* refers to reasoning and thought. The word *vain* is defined as foolish, wicked, specifically idolatrous. Such immorality, wickedness, and idolatry resulted in having foolish and darkened hearts. The heart of man is his mind and thinking. The thoughts of the mind describe the activity of the heart. *For as he thinketh in his heart, so is he* (Pro. 23:7).

**Verse 22.** *Professing themselves to be wise, they became fools.* The Scripture here is not hard to understand. However, men today still navigate the same dangerous reefs of foolishness. The prophet of old was correct when he said: *O Lord, I know that the way of man is not in himself: it is not in man that walketh to direct his steps* (Jer. 10:23).

# Commentary on Romans

Solomon declared: *There is a way that seemeth right unto a man, but the end thereof are the ways of death"* (Pro. 16:25). Man shall never succeed in negating God's Word. Isaiah wrote: *So shall my word be that goeth forth out of my mouth: it shall not return unto me void, but it shall accomplish that which I please, and it shall prosper in the thing whereto I sent it* (Isa. 55:11).

**Verse 23.** *And changed the glory of the uncorruptible God into an image made like to corruptible man and to birds and fourfooted beasts and creeping things.* Idolatry was adopted by both Jews and Gentiles. It existed long before the Lord called the Israelites out of Egypt.

Jacob served Laban for a total of fourteen years for Rachel and Leah. Upon Jacob's departure from Laban, Rachel took with her the idols of her father. Of Jacob's father-in-Law, the Genesis record states that, upon Jacob's departure from Laban's house, *Laban went to shear his sheep: and Rachel had stolen the images that were her father's* (Gen. 31:19). On a later occasion, Jacob had his family get rid of any idols they yet retained.

> *God said unto Jacob, Arise, go up to Bethel and dwell there: and make there an altar unto God, that appeared unto thee when thou fleddest from the face of Esau thy brother. Then Jacob said unto his household and to all that were with him, Put away the strange gods that are among you and be clean and change your garments: And let us arise and go up to Bethel; and I will make there an altar unto God, who answered me in the day of my distress and was with me in the way which I went. And they gave unto Jacob all the strange gods which were in their hand and all their earrings which were in their ears; and Jacob hid them under the oak which was by Shechem* (Gen. 35:1-4).

The following purge occurred hundreds of years later when Moses was on Mount Sinai receiving the Law:

> *And when the people saw that Moses delayed to come down out of the mount, then the people gathered themselves together unto Aaron and said unto him,*

# Commentary on Romans

*Up, make us gods, which shall go before us; for as for this Moses, the man that brought us up out of the land of Egypt, we wot not what is become of him. And Aaron said unto them, Break off the golden earrings, which are in the ears of your wives, of your sons and of your daughters and bring them unto me. And all the people brake off the golden earrings, which were in their ears and brought them unto Aaron. And he received them at their hand and fashioned it with a graving tool, after he had made it a molten calf: and they said, These be thy gods, O Israel, which brought thee up out of the land of Egypt. And when Aaron saw it, he built an altar before it; and Aaron made proclamation and said, Tomorrow is a feast to the Lord. And they rose up early on the morrow and offered burnt offerings and brought peace offerings; and the people sat down to eat and to drink and rose up to play. And the Lord said unto Moses, Go, get thee down; for thy people, which thou broughtest out of the land of Egypt, have corrupted themselves* (Exo. 32:1-7).

From where did Aaron acquire the conception of constructing a *golden calf*? History records the worship of numerous things by the Egyptians. Many mummified animals have been unearthed by archaeologists for centuries in Egypt, among which have been birds, cats, frogs, and cattle. Numerous insects preserved by the Egyptians also have been uncovered. Of the ten plagues with which God afflicted the Egyptians was the murrain of cattle. Frogs, lice, and flies were worshiped by the Egyptians. The plague of the Nile River being turned into blood was an assault against Hapi, the Egyptian god of the Nile. Pharaoh's decree to cast the male children of the Israelites into the Nile was for the purpose of sacrificing the Hebrew children to the Egyptian god Hapi.

The Egyptians also worshiped the gods Moloch (Molech) and Chiun, as did other nations. Molech was fashioned like unto a half man and half bull creature, having the arms cradled for the placement of infants. The idol Chiun was a flat six-pointed star made of iron.

# Commentary on Romans

Molech was heated red-hot, and the infants were placed in the cradled arms of the idol and burned alive in the worship thereof. The idol Chiun was also heated and used to cook the human sacrifices for eating, especially the firstborn.

*And thou shalt not let any of thy seed pass through the fire to Molech, neither shalt thou profane the name of thy God: I am the Lord* (Lev. 18:21). *There shall not be found among you any one that maketh his son or his daughter to pass through the fire, or that useth divination, or an observer of times, or an enchanter, or a witch* (Deut. 18:10). *King Ahaz walked in the way of the kings of Israel, yea and made his son to pass through the fire, according to the abominations of the heathen, whom the Lord cast out from before the children of Israel* (II Ki. 16:3).

Among the many gods of the Egyptians, Molech and Chiun were well-favored. Many Israelites were strongly influenced by and were in involved in the worship of both Molech and Chiun. Many Israelites were so addicted to these gods they carried tabernacles of Molech and Chiun with them out of Egypt. *Have ye offered unto me sacrifices and offerings in the wilderness forty years, O house of Israel? But ye have borne the tabernacle of your Moloch and Chiun your images, the star of your god, which ye made to yourselves* (Amos 5:25-26).

Stephen refers to this passage in the book of Acts. *Then God turned and gave them up to worship the host of heaven; as it is written in the book of the prophets, O ye house of Israel, have ye offered to me slain beasts and sacrifices by the space of forty years in the wilderness? Yea, ye took up the tabernacle of Moloch and the star of your god Remphan, figures which ye made to worship them: and I will carry you away beyond Babylon* (Acts 7:42-43).

Chiun was the god of the planet Saturn. The worship of Chiun often involved the eating of one's first-born. Astrologers represented this planet as baleful in its influences, and hence the Phoenicians and other nations offered to Chiun human sacrifices, especially firstborn children. To the worship of Chiun, many of the Israelites were also strongly addicted (cf. Amos 5:25-26).

# Commentary on Romans

The Egyptians and Philistines, as well as other nations, worshiped numerous other gods, among which was Dagon, who was a god of fertility. The word *Dagon* means "fish-god." The worship of Dagon included gross promiscuity as well as incest.

*Then the Lords of the Philistines gathered them together for to offer a great sacrifice unto Dagon their god and to rejoice: for they said, Our god hath delivered Samson our enemy into our hand* (Jdg. 16:23). *When the Philistines took the ark of God, they brought it into the house of Dagon and set it by Dagon* (I Sam. 5:2).

Other examples of patriarchal idolatry can be provided, but these are sufficient to show the Gentiles worshiped numerous *idols made like to corruptible man and to birds and fourfooted beasts and creeping things.*

**Verse 24.** *Wherefore God also gave them up to uncleanness through the lusts of their own hearts, to dishonour their own bodies between themselves.* There are fifty-nine verses in Scripture which mention Balaam. In addition to infant sacrifice, promiscuity was often part of the worship of the god of the Moabites which is clearly seen in the Revelation letter: *But I have a few things against thee, because thou hast there them that hold the doctrine of Balaam, who taught Balak to cast a stumblingblock before the children of Israel, to eat things sacrificed unto idols and to commit fornication* (Rev. 2:14). Moses wrote: *And Israel abode in Shittim and the people began to commit whoredom with the daughters of Moab. And they called the people unto the sacrifices of their gods: and the people did eat and bowed down to their gods* (Num. 25:1-2).

The phrase, *Gave them up,* means "to surrender, to yield up, to entrust, to transmit, to betray, to bring forth, to cast, to commit, to deliver up, to give over, to hazard, or to be put in prison." Men who adhere themselves to wicked behavior will indeed be *given up* by God unto eternal destruction.

*To dishonor their own bodies* is "to render infamous, condemn, maltreat, despise, dishonor, suffer shame." Such amoral conduct *between themselves* was a dishonoring maltreatment of the

# Commentary on Romans

earthly body given by God. God will execute His righteous wrath upon all who shamefully despise their bodies. *Marriage is honorable in all and the bed undefiled: but whoremongers and adulterers God will judge* (Heb. 13:4).

**Verse 25.** *Who changed the truth of God into a lie and worshipped and served the creature more than the Creator, who is blessed forever. Amen.* The word *changed* here means "to change into or exchange for." Unrighteous men exchange the word of God for devilish doctrines. *Some shall depart from the faith,* Paul wrote, *giving heed to seducing spirits and doctrines of devils* (I Tim. 4:1). Departures from faith are as old as time. Adam and Eve departed from God's system of faith while yet in the garden, and they have been commonplace ever since.

The word *worshipped* means "to show and give adoration, to prostrate oneself, to bow down, to crouch, to fall down flat, to beseech humbly, to make obeisance, to do reverence, make to stoop down before."

The word *served* is closely fettered to the word *worshipped*. *Served* as used here is "to minister to; that is, render religious homage, serve, do the service, or to worship." Such conduct is a portrayal of humanism. Humanism is the belief in human-based authority in morality. It is a system of thought based on the values, characteristics, and behavior believed to be best for society. Humanism denies and rejects all Divine authority.

**Verse 26.** *For this cause God gave them up unto vile affections: for even their women did change the natural use into that which is against nature.* The *cause* here for which *God gave them up* is that of which Paul wrote in the previous verse. Two verses prior Paul stated, God gave wicked men up to *uncleanness through the lusts of their own hearts.* In this passage *God gave them up unto vile affections.* It should be observed, God *gave them over to a reprobate mind* as recorded in verse 28. Three times Paul informed the Gentiles God has never tolerated opposition to His mandates. God gives such men up and over to sin.

*Vile affections refer to* "indignity, disgraceful, dishonorable, reproachful, shameful, vile passions; but especially of concupis-

# Commentary on Romans

cence. Concupiscence is bestiality. Paul had earlier written of it: *Mortify therefore your members which are upon the earth; fornication, uncleanness, inordinate affection, evil concupiscence and covetousness, which is idolatry. Not in the lust of concupiscence, even as the Gentiles which know not God"* (Col. 3:5; I Thes. 4:5).

**Verse 27.** *And likewise also the men, leaving the natural use of the woman, burned in their lust one toward another; men with men working that which is unseemly and receiving in themselves that recompense of their error which was meet.* Moses had previously written: *Thou shalt not lie with mankind, as with womankind: it is abomination* (Lev. 18:22). *If a man also lie with mannd, as he lieth with a woman, both of them have committed an abomination: they shall surely be put to death; their blood shall be upon them* (Lev. 20:13).

It may seem superfluous to comment further about this matter, but in the culture of society today it is more needful to remind society that the Bible still mandates opposition to such amoral conduct. God does not and will not tolerate such behavior.

The word *unseemly* is, by definition, "indecency." The word also means "rude, uncouth, improper, indecorous, unsuitable, unbecoming, and tasteless."

**Verse 28.** *And even as they did not like to retain God in their knowledge, God gave them over to a reprobate mind, to do those things, which are not convenient.* The word *retain* is a primary verb meaning "to hold on to." The Gentiles of times past willingly refused to hold onto the knowledge of God and His mandates. Because of such conduct, *God gave them over to a reprobate mind.*

A *reprobate mind* is one of which God vehemently disapproves and rejects, it is greatly evil. *And with all deceivableness of unrighteousness, in them that perish; because they received not the love of the truth* (II Thes. 2:10). Reprobate minds are minds that are self-deceived. Everyone who deceives himself shall have the wrath of God visited upon him.

# Commentary on Romans

*To do those things which are not convenient. Convenient* means "fit or becoming." Involvement in the abominable conduct under consideration here makes one unfit for society. Such conduct is unbecoming of both man and society and must, therefore, be exposed and opposed.

**Verses 29-31.** *Being filled with all unrighteousness, fornication, wickedness, covetousness, maliciousness; full of envy, murder, debate, deceit, malignity; whisperers, Backbiters, haters of God, despiteful, proud, boasters, inventors of evil things, disobedient to parents, Without understanding, covenantbreakers, without natural affection, implacable, unmerciful.* To be *filled* with means "to be replete—literally crammed full, to furnish or imbue—to saturate." Men who stuff themselves full of unrighteousness are appropriately described above.

**Verse 30** is a summary of the evils of which Paul spoke in verses 24-28. The apostle John wrote saints must *love not the world, neither the things that are in the world. If any man love the world, the love of the Father is not in him. For all that is in the world, the lust of the flesh and the lust of the eyes and the pride of life, is not of the Father, but is of the world* (I Jno. 2:15-16). The activities mentioned in verses twenty four, twenty-six, and verse twenty-eight are rooted in the lust of the eyes, the lust of the flesh, and the pride of life.

**Verse 31.** *Without understanding, covenantbreakers, without natural affection, implacable, unmerciful. Without understanding* is "unintelligent; wicked foolish without any understanding by intent and will." Again, Peter declared: *For this they willingly are ignorant of* (II Pet. 3:5). Being without *natural affection* has reference to mothers who have no love for their children—only for themselves. Women who sacrifice the welfare of their children for their own pleasures are mothers *without natural affection.* Those who quickly and without reservation sacrifice the fruit of their wombs on altars of abortion are *without natural affection.*

Abortion has long been practiced by wicked mothers. Since they did not have the technology we do today, previous generations practiced infanticide. The child was born alive but allowed to die. Ezekiel spoke of this process as it pertained to Israel (figurative-

# Commentary on Romans

ly). *And as for thy nativity, in the day thou wast born thy navel was not cut, neither wast thou washed in water to supple thee; thou wast not salted at all, nor swaddled at all* (Eze. 16:4). During Ezekiel's time when a mother wanted her child to die, the navel was not cut from the placenta. Both were delivered and the child left to live only as long as the placenta could sustain life. Truly, such actions show such mothers to be *without natural affection.* Israel is pictured as left to die in this manner and was only saved by God's grace (Eze. 16:5-6).

Infanticide was also performed by filling the child's mouth with sand or soil causing suffocation. Being *without natural affection* for the fruit of the womb is a gross abomination for which God will strongly execute His Divine justice. Every child left to die (or aborted or both) is spiritually safe, having never sinned, but the mother *without natural affection* shall be punished unless she repents thereof and obtains God's pardon according to the mandates He has established.

Being *implacable* (also in verse 31) refers to a person incapable of being placated or satisfied. Such men love quarrels, strife, and division. Such men are infatuated by contention, divisiveness, and hostility. Many men are haters of good and lovers of evil; they have strong unquenchable thirsts for combative discourses and heated arguments. Such men influence others unto wickedness and urge contention. Such men always engage in vexatious behavior.

**Verse 32.** *Who knowing the judgment of God, that they which commit such things are worthy of death, not only do the same, but have pleasure in them that do them.* The word *who* has reference to those of whom the apostle described beginning with verse 18.

The Patriarchs knew of God's righteous judgments, but exchanged God's way for their own. God provided the Patriarchs with a system of faith by which they could obtain righteousness, yet they chose to invent unto themselves devilish doctrines by which they sought God's favor.

Such men are worthy of harsh physical death. The vile activities

## Commentary on Romans

recorded in these verses carried the punishment of a harsh death by stoning or burning under Old Testament Law. Not only is an unsympathetic physical death a fitting punishment for such behavior; but a flaming spiritual death is likewise a suitable penalty for such wicked conduct, such is reserved for those who engage therein.

Those who involve themselves in such ungodly behavior not only enjoy their own sinfulness, *but have pleasure in them that do them.* Men of such behavior are self-deceived; *God is not mocked: for whatsoever a man soweth, that shall he also reap. For he that soweth to his flesh shall of the flesh reap corruption* (Gal. 6:7-8).

The *corruption* of which the apostle wrote means utterly to perish in eternal destruction. The word *pleasure* here means "to think well of; that is, assent to, feelings of being self gratified, to allow, to be pleased with and have pleasure in evil conduct."

## Summary of Chapter One

Paul confirmed his apostleship and assured the saints of Rome that the Gospel was voluminously prophesied of in the Old Testament. He further established the Scriptures had much to say about the coming of the Son of God. Paul revealed, Jesus was declared to be the Son of God by the power of the resurrection. The apostle demonstrated the system of faith established by Jesus Christ must be obeyed by all men and that men are called unto holiness by the Gospel and all men must be obedient to it. Paul also declared, grace and peace come from both God the Father and His Son, Jesus Christ.

The apostle expressed his gratitude for the good faith of the Roman congregation. Paul assured the saints at Rome that he always had them in mind and ceased not to thank God for them. Paul longed to see the saints at Rome that he might better establish them in the faith of Jesus Christ.

Paul reminded the saints of Rome that they shared a common and mutual faith in Christ. He further told them he often wished to journey to Rome and share in their mutual faith. Paul also

## Commentary on Romans

spoke of his responsibility regarding the preaching of the Gospel and his indebtedness to it.

The apostle was always ready to preach the Gospel and was not ashamed of it. He showed the Gentile converts that the Gospel is where God's saving power is found. *The righteousness of God* was shown by the apostle to be the system of faith by which God saves men. God did not save the Gentiles by their system. Today, God's system by which He declares man righteousness is the system of the New Testament Gospel. Paul later wrote, *It is God that justifieth* (Rom. 8:33).

Paul displayed how the Gentiles made great efforts to develop their own system of faith by which to acquire salvation, but their system of amorality was deeply abominable and wicked. The wisdom the Gentile nations developed and to which they adhered was foolish, wicked, and a damnable choice. Paul revealed how Gentile nations took long strides to make their own gods and served them in lasciviousness.

The apostle further exposed the disobedient Gentiles had exchanged the God-ordained Patriarchal System of faith with their own system. Paul revealed the disobedient Gentiles worshiped and served man and creatures, rather than God.

Three times Paul expressed that God gave disobedient Gentiles up and over to ungodliness and works of abominations. The Gentiles distaste of retaining knowledge of God was also set forth by the apostle.

Finally, Paul exposed the wicked character of disobedient Gentiles, and he assured the Gentile converts God would indeed bring His judgments against all unrighteous men. We inject here the the reason why Paul addressed these matters of immorality. It was commonplace during the time Paul wrote. Many Roman elites, inclusive of Emperors, engaged in homosexuality and the abominations Paul identified. Orgies were common, as was infanticide, bestiality, adultery, and suicide.

# Commentary on Romans

God has revealed the system of faith by which He will redeem man, which consists of the New Testament. The Gospel system is the only one authorized by Jesus Christ. All men are amenable to it and must comply with it. Christ *is the author of eternal salvation unto all them that obey Him* (Heb. 5:8-9). When men set forth their own systems of salvation and engage in abominable works, they have exchanged truth of God for a lie. Every denominationalist has exchanged God's will for their own.

The Patriarchs strove to establish their own system of righteousness, but failed miserably. One step away from God's way is a long journey in the wrong direction.

God is the origin of eternal salvation, Christ is the author of it, and the Holy Spirit is the revealer thereof. Man cannot serve as God's advisor and better germinate the Lord's way and system of salvation. Christ is the only way authorized by Deity. Jesus affirmed: *I am the way, the truth and the life: no man cometh unto the Father, but by me* (Jno. 14:6). Man has been given *all things that pertain unto life and godliness* and cannot therefore alter God's word to suit his own fancies (cf. II Pet. 1:3).

Obedience to the system of faith which originated with God, authored by Christ, and revealed by the Holy Spirit, adds one to the only church authorized by Deity—that is, the church of our Lord and Savior Jesus Christ, in whom all spiritual blessings are found (cf. Eph. 1:3). Truly *the way of man is not in himself: it is not in man that walketh to direct his steps* (Jer. 10:23).

## Romans 2:1-11

*1 Therefore thou art inexcusable, O man, whosoever thou art that judgest: for wherein thou judgest another, thou condemnest thyself; for thou that judgest doest the same things. 2 But we are sure that the judgment of God is according to truth against them which commit such things. 3 And thinkest thou this, O man, that judgest them which do such things and doest the same, that thou shalt escape the judgment of God? 4 Or despisest thou the riches of his goodness and forbearance and longsuffering; not knowing that the goodness*

# Commentary on Romans

*of God leadeth thee to repentance? 5 But after thy hardness and impenitent heart treasurest up unto thyself wrath against the day of wrath and revelation of the righteous judgment of God; 6 Who will render to every man according to his deeds: 7 To them who by patient continuance in well doing seek for glory and honour and immortality, eternal life: 8 But unto them that are contentious and do not obey the truth, but obey unrighteousness, indignation and wrath, 9 Tribulation and anguish, upon every soul of man that doeth evil, of the Jew first and also of the Gentile; 10 But glory, honour and peace, to every man that worketh good, to the Jew first and also to the Gentile: 11 For there is no respect of persons with God.*

**Verses 1-2.** *Therefore thou art inexcusable, O man, whosoever thou art that judgest: for wherein thou judgest another, thou condemnest thyself; for thou that judgest doest the same things. But we are sure that the judgment of God is according to truth against them which commit such things.* Before delving into these verses, it is well to consider some of the twisted and distorted positions many have asserted from it.

Liberal, ignorant, and intentionally ill-willed men proclaimed this passage condemns the Divine mandate of judging others. Men who cower to such teachings are themselves men who seek not being judged for their own ungodly conduct. It is amazing just how judgmental such men become who contend for the non-judgment of anyone. *O consistency thou art a jewel.*

There are numerous passages of Scripture, which not only authorize judgments of others but command it. The church is to keep herself pure and engage in church purity through discipline. Every passage of Scripture which instructs the brethren to assist those weaker in faith or mark those who cause division and walk disorderly require judgments. How can such be accomplished without them?

The preaching of the Gospel to the lost is itself a judgment passed upon those outside of the church. Further, the Lord declared; *Judge not according to the appearance, but judge right-*

# Commentary on Romans

*eous judgment* (Jno. 7:24). These other passages all require making judgments: Matthew 18:15-18; II Thessalonians 3:6, 14; I Timothy 6:3-5; II John 9-11; Ephesians 5:11, and Romans 16:17-18.

Paul, having addressed the Gentile converts in chapter one, now directs his attention to Jewish converts. It is essential to keep in mind Paul understood the mindset of the Jews. Paul was himself a Jew, a Pharisee, and teacher of the Law. Paul charged the Gentile converts with numerous crimes against God, and exposed those who committed such things were worthy of death.

The Jews made the same charge against the Gentiles, while insisting they themselves were not worthy of the same because they were God's chosen people. However, the apostle effectively informed the Jews they were guilty of the same sins as the Gentiles. Thus, in judging the Gentiles, the Jews condemned themselves. Paul wrote to the Jewish converts, saying, *But we are sure that the judgment of God is according to truth against them which commit such things.* The Jews could in no way expect to escape the wrath of God while they themselves were as guilty as the Gentiles of the same sins. To the contrary, the Jews were subject to a more aggressive execution of God's wrath. God had given the Jews the Law of Moses, they knew more of God's will than the Gentiles. The Jews had the Law in written form. The Gentiles, on the other hand, were instructed orally by the Lord as He deemed it fitting. Therefore, the Jews should not have thought they would escape the wrath of God just because they were Jews.

All men treasure up for themselves God's wrath or His blessings. The more sin stored up the more wrath stored. The more righteousness stored, the greater the reward of God's goodness is stored. Men please God the most by not laying up for themselves *treasures upon earth, where moth and rust doth corrupt and where thieves break through and* steal, but rather lay up for *"themselves treasures in heaven* (Matt. 6:19-20).

The word *commit* is a primary verb meaning "to practice, perform repeatedly by habit, and by implication to execute, accomplish, to contagiously commit deeds, constantly do so, to exact and to

# Commentary on Romans

keep doing." The word differs from that which refers to a *single* act of sin when one is overtaken in a fault. *Brethren, if a man be overtaken in a fault, ye which are spiritual, restore such a one in the spirit of meekness; considering thyself, lest thou also be tempted* (Gal. 6:1). The word *overtaken* means "to be taken by surprise or off guard."

**Verses 3-5:** *And thinkest thou this, O man, that judgest them which do such things and doest the same, that thou shalt escape the judgment of God? Or despisest thou the riches of his goodness and forbearance and longsuffering; not knowing that the goodness of God leadeth thee to repentance? But after thy hardness and impenitent heart treasurest up unto thyself wrath against the day of wrath and revelation of the righteous judgment of God.* Paul had no difficulty getting the Jewish converts to concur the Gentiles were sinners. However, the task of making the Jews recognize and accept they themselves were sinners was a more arduous work. The Jews boasted of being God's chosen people, they boasted they were descendants of Abraham, they boasted they had the Law given to them, and they boasted in the fact they were the ones through whom the Messiah was to come.

Because of these facts they should have known better than to have been involved in the same sins as the Gentiles. Therefore, they were *without excuse.* Paul informed the Jews they had despised *the riches of his goodness and forbearance and longsuffering.* That God gave them the Law of Moses should have prompted them to repentance. They failed to see the goodness of God and His grace, because of their *hardness and impenitent hearts.* Because they were willfully ignorant of God's goodness; they treasured up to themselves God's *wrath and revelation of the righteous judgment of God* as equally the Gentiles.

**Verses 6-11.** *Who will render to every man according to his deeds: To them who by patient continuance in well doing seek for glory and honor and immortality, eternal life: But unto them that are contentious and do not obey the truth, but obey unrighteousness, indignation and wrath, Tribulation and anguish, upon every soul of man that doeth evil, of the Jew first and also of the Gentile; But glory, honor and peace, to every man that worketh*

## Commentary on Romans

*good, to the Jew first and also to the Gentile: For there is no respect of persons with God.*

God will render His rewards unto every man according to the works in which man involves himself. *So then every one of us shall give account of himself to God* (Rom. 14:12). *For God shall bring every work into judgment, with every secret thing, whether it be good, or whether it be* evil (Ecc. 12:14). *For we must all appear before the judgment seat of Christ; that every one may receive the things done in his body, according to that he hath done, whether it be good or bad. Knowing therefore the terror of the Lord, we persuade men; but we are made manifest unto God; and I trust also are made manifest in your consciences* (2 Cor. 5:10-11). God reserves eternal life for the obedient, but eternal destruction for the disobedient.

*Indignation* refers to God's fierceness. *Our God is a consuming fire* (Heb. 12:29). Countless saints insist the *God of the Old Testament* is immensely different from *the God of the New Testament.* Such is as far from the truth as the east is from the west. God caused Ananias and Sapphira, to fall dead before the apostles for their disobedience, having lied to God and the church.

> *But a certain man named Ananias, with Sapphira his wife, sold a possession and kept back part of the price, his wife also being privy to it and brought a certain part and laid it at the apostles' feet. But Peter said, Ananias, why hath Satan filled thine heart to lie to the Holy Ghost and to keep back part of the price of the land? Whiles it remained, was it not thine own? and after it was sold, was it not in thine own power? why hast thou conceived this thing in thine heart? thou hast not lied unto men [only], but unto God [also]. And Ananias hearing these words fell down and gave up the ghost: and great fear came on all them that heard these things. And the young men arose, wound him up and carried him out and buried him. And it was about the space of three hours after, when his wife, not knowing what was done, came in. And Peter answered unto her, Tell me whether ye sold the land for so much? And she said, Yea, for so much. Then Peter said unto her,*

# Commentary on Romans

> *How is it that ye have agreed together to tempt the Spirit of the Lord? behold, the feet of them which have buried thy husband are at the door and shall carry thee out. Then fell she down straightway at his feet and yielded up the ghost: and the young men came in and found her dead and, carrying her forth, buried her by her husband* (Acts 5:1-10).

Another instance likewise demonstrates God's wrath:

> *And when they had gone through the isle unto Paphos, they found a certain sorcerer, a false prophet, a Jew, whose name was Barjesus: Which was with the deputy of the country, Sergius Paulus, a prudent man; who called for Barnabas and Saul and desired to hear the word of God. But Elymas the sorcerer (for so is his name by interpretation) withstood them, seeking to turn away the deputy from the faith. Then Saul, (who also is called Paul,) filled with the Holy Ghost, set his eyes on him and said, O full of all subtlety and all mischief, thou child of the devil, thou enemy of all righteousness, wilt thou not cease to pervert the right ways of the Lord? And now, behold, the hand of the Lord is upon thee and thou shalt be blind, not seeing the sun for a season. And immediately there fell on him a mist and a darkness; and he went about seeking some to lead him by the hand. Then the deputy, when he saw what was done, believed, being astonished at the doctrine of the Lord* (Acts 13:6-12).

A third example makes the same point: *And upon a set day Herod, arrayed in royal apparel, sat upon his throne and made an oration unto them. And the people gave a shout, saying, It is the voice of a god and not of a man. And immediately the angel of the Lord smote him, because he gave not God the glory: and he was eaten of worms and gave up the ghost* (Acts 12:21-23).

If *the God of the New Testament* is not *the God of the Old Testament*, then we worship and serve a god unknown to the prophets of old. We worship and serve a god other than the Great and

# Commentary on Romans

Sovereign Jehovah, the El-Shaddai and Elohim, the Almighty—if the God of old is not the God of today.

There is no respect of persons with God so far as gender, race, education, pedigree, genealogy, or heritage are concerned. Paul declared unto the church at Galatia: *There is neither Jew nor Greek, there is neither bond nor free, there is neither male nor female: for ye are all one in Christ Jesus. And if ye be Christ's, then are ye Abraham's seed and heirs according to the promise* (Gal. 3:28-29).

However, there is an element of respect of persons with God so far as spiritual blessings and eternal inheritance are concerned. Only those who are the children of God have the spiritual blessing of the Godhead. For God *hath blessed us with all spiritual blessings in heavenly places in Christ* (Eph. 1:3). Faithful saints in the church are His children. *The Spirit itself beareth witness with our spirit, that we are the children of God: And if children, then heirs; heirs of God, and joint-heirs with Christ; if so be that we suffer with him, that we may be also glorified together* (Rom. 8:16-17). *And if ye be Christ's, then are ye Abraham's seed and heirs according to the promise* (Gal. 3:29).

God has respect for those who obey His will. Moses said, regarding Abel, that *he also brought of the firstlings of his flock and of the fat thereof. And the Lord had respect unto Abel and to his offering* (Gen. 4:4). On the contrary, *unto Cain and to his offering He had not respect* (Gen. 4:5). Observe, it was by *faith Abel offered unto God a more excellent sacrifice than Cain* (Heb. 11:4).

The Jews, as well as the Gentiles, had lost God's respect when they discarded His way. Both lost the respect of God, and both were lost. We are respected by God when we cheerfully do His work. When men fail to comply with God's mandates, He reserves for them eternal punishment.

In the Roman epistle, when Paul informed the Jewish converts they were not saved by works, he was speaking of the works of the Old Law. He was not speaking of the works of the New Law. *Knowing that a man is not justified by the works of the law but by*

# Commentary on Romans

*the faith of Jesus Christ* (Gal. 2:16). When James declared man is saved by works he was speaking of the works of the New Law. *Ye see then how that by works a man is justified* (Jas. 2:24).

Martin Luther could not harmonize the book of Romans and the epistle of James because Luther failed to understand Paul spoke of the works of the Old Testament; while James spoke of the works of the New Testament. Luther, thus, declared the epistle of James was *a right strawy epistle.* Luther believed James' epistle was lacking in authenticity and credibility.

The phrase *no respect* in verse eleven means absolutely no favoritism with God towards man's pedigree, status, or gender. When one becomes a child of God, he becomes an equal heir to the blessings of God. Paul wrote: *And if children, then heirs; heirs of God and joint-heirs with Christ* (Rom. 8:17). The phrase *joint-heirs* means to be an equal heir with Christ.

The apostle made powerful arguments regarding the Jews, and how they had become disrespected by God because of the works in which they had become involved. Both men of disobedience *and* their works must be counted disrespectful by those in the church today. Saints must *have no fellowship with the unfruitful works of darkness, but rather reprove them* (Eph. 5:11).

## Romans 2:12-20

> 12 *For as many as have sinned without Law shall also perish without Law: and as many as have sinned in the Law shall be judged by the Law;* 13 *(For not the hearers of the Law are just before God, but the doers of the Law shall be justified.* 14 *For when the Gentiles, which have not the Law, do by nature the things contained in the Law, these, having not the Law, are a Law unto themselves:* 15 *Which shew the work of the Law written in their hearts, their conscience also bearing witness and their thoughts the mean while accusing or else excusing one another;)* 16 *In the day when God shall judge the secrets of men by Jesus Christ according to my gospel.* 17 *Behold, thou art called a Jew and restest in the Law and makest thy boast of God,* 18

# Commentary on Romans

*And knowest his will and approvest the things that are more excellent, being instructed out of the Law; 19 And art confident that thou thyself art a guide of the blind, a light of them which are in darkness, 20 An instructor of the foolish, a teacher of babes, which hast the form of knowledge and of the truth in the Law.*

**Verse 12.** *For as many as have sinned without Law shall also perish without Law: and as many as have sinned in the Law shall be judged by the Law.* This verse has suffered no little wresting and perversion. The phrase *for as many* has reference to the Gentiles who lived under the Patriarchal System. Paul pointed out, the Gentiles who did not have the Law of Moses revealed to them, *sinned without the Law.* Here two observations warrant attention. First, Paul informed the Jewish converts that the Gentiles who did not have the Law of Moses revealed to them were indeed guilty of sin. However, their sins were in violation to the Law under which they lived and to which they were subject, not the Law of Moses. The phrase *without the Law* means not having the Law Moses. Second, Paul wrote the Gentiles would *be judged* by the Patriarchal Law. For God to hold the Gentiles subject to the Law of Moses would make God unrighteous in His judgments. God has never held man accountable to a Law which He did not reveal.

*And the times of this ignorance God winked at; but now commandeth all men every where to repent.* It is essential to understand that at which God *winked.* God *winked* at **the times** of *ignorance.* **God did not wink at ignorance.** God knew the Gentiles were ignorant of His more fully revealed truth given to the Jews; he therefore could not hold the Gentiles accountable to the Law of Moses.

That Paul declared the Gentiles were to *be judged by the Law,* is to be understood God would judge the Gentiles according to the Law He revealed to them, not the law revealed to the Jews.

Here we feel strongly compelled to give commentary on Deuteronomy 29:29. The passage does not teach what most affirm. Most contend there are things men cannot and do know because God has kept certain secrets from them. While such is true, it is

## Commentary on Romans

not the case the Deuteronomy passage teaches this doctrine. Many times men reach right things from wrong passages; this is a classical example.

Moses wrote: *The secret things belong unto the Lord our God: but those things which are revealed belong unto us and to our children for ever, that we may do all the words of this law* (Deut. 29:29). The passage is speaking of that which God revealed to the Jews through the Law of Moses. Observe the phrase *those things which are revealed belong unto us.* The *things revealed* to the Jews was the Old Law. *The secret things belong unto the Lord our God* refers to that which God had yet to reveal regarding the gospel. Once God, through inspired men, revealed His complete will, the secret things were no longer a mystery. Consider the following passages.

*Having made known unto us the mystery of his will, according to his good pleasure which he hath purposed in himself* (Eph. 1:9).

*How that by revelation he made known unto me the mystery; (as I wrote afore in few words, Whereby, when ye read, ye may understand my knowledge in the mystery of Christ)* (Eph. 3:3-4).

*And for me, that utterance may be given unto me, that I may open my mouth boldly, to make known the mystery of the gospel* (Eph. 6:19).

*Even the mystery which hath been hid from ages and from generations, but now is made manifest to his saints: To whom God would make known what is the riches of the glory of this mystery among the Gentiles; which is Christ in you, the hope of glory* (Col. 1:26-27).

Until God revealed His mystery, the things pertaining to the New Testament remained *secret things.*

The number of commentaries is endless wherein it is contended God will judge the Gentiles by the Law of Moses. If such were the case, how could inspiration have declared Cornelius, who was a Gentile, to be a righteous man, as recorded in Acts 10? Why would God command the Gentiles to comply with the Patri-

# Commentary on Romans

archal System and all the mandates thereof, and yet judge them according to the Law of Moses? Such is far from the righteous character of God. *Cornelius was a Gentile and was not a proselyte to the Jewish faith as many maintain.* We shall address this matter further into this work, with several proofs.

**Verses 13-15.** *(For not the hearers of the Law are just before God, but the doers of the Law shall be justified. For when the Gentiles, which have not the Law, do by nature the things contained in the Law, these, having not the Law, are a Law unto themselves: Which shew the work of the Law written in their hearts, their conscience also bearing witness and their thoughts the mean while accusing or else excusing one another).* These verses are Paul's commentary on verse 12. Paul declared in verse 13 *the doers of the Law shall be justified.* The doers of the Law under which they lived were the justified ones. The obedient Gentiles were justified or condemned under the Patriarchal Law, and the Jews were justified or condemned by the Law of Moses.

**Verse 14.** Paul plainly declared the Gentiles had *not the Law,* meaning they had not Law of Moses, but the Gentiles did by nature the things contained in the Law of the Gentiles. It was by *nature,* meaning it was natural for the obedient Gentiles to comply with the System of Law which God revealed to them.

God set forth the same *principles* in both the Law of Moses and the Patriarchal Law. *God's principles have never changed, but his Law did.* God changed the Law for the Jews at Mount Sinai, but the Law for the Gentiles remained the same. *The principles of both the Patriarchs and the Jews did not change.* God has always demanded worship, service, sacrifice and obedience.

**Verse 15.** The Gentiles had a *Law unto themselves* just as the Jews had a Law unto themselves. Paul reminded the Jews while they had a written Law on tables of stone; God caused the Patriarchal Law to be *law written in their hearts.* The Gentiles had no written or recorded law as the Jews had; thus, the obedient Gentiles did by *nature* the things of their law.

# Commentary on Romans

The witness of the law for the Gentiles was etched on their conscience and was not in written form. However, the law of the Jews was etched on tables of stone. The stones were written on both front and back.

*And Moses turned, and went down from the mount, and the two tables of the testimony were in his hand:* **the tables were written on both their sides**; *on the one side and on the other were they written* (Exo. 32:15, emph. DHC). *On both their sides* does not mean left and right; it means front and back. When one writes on both sides of two sheets of paper it is clearly understood there is writing on both sheets, front and back of each sheet. Notice the passage plainly says o*n both their sides.*

Further, the details of the tabernacle were a part of the Mosaical Law. God showed Moses the pattern of the tabernacle while Moses was on the mount. *Moses was admonished of God when he was about to make the tabernacle: for, See, saith he, that thou make all things according to the pattern shewed to thee in the mount* (Heb. 8:5). The pattern shown to Moses was also provided in written form.

The details of the things of the tabernacle are recorded for us in the book of Exodus. Additionaly, David declared he was given the details of the things of the tabernacle written by God. *And look that thou make them after their pattern, which was shewed thee in the mount* (Exo. 25:40). *And thou shalt rear up the tabernacle according to the fashion thereof which was shewed thee in the mount* (Exo. 26:30). *Hollow with boards shalt thou make it: as it was shewed thee in the mount, so shall they make it* (Exo. 27:8). *And this work of the candlestick was of beaten gold, unto the shaft thereof, unto the flowers thereof, was beaten work: according unto the pattern which the Lord had shewed Moses, so he made the candlestick* (Num. 8:4). *All this, said David, the Lord made me understand in writing by his hand upon me, even all the works of this pattern* (I Chr. 28:19).

The Law of the Gentiles was that by which they were commended or condemned, *accused or excused* before and by God. Such was true for the Jews as well; it was their Law by which

## Commentary on Romans

they were either commended or condemned, *accused or excused* before God.

**Verses 16-20.** *In the day when God shall judge the secrets of men by Jesus Christ according to my gospel. Behold, thou art called a Jew and restest in the Law and makest thy boast of God, And knowest his will and approvest the things that are more excellent, being instructed out of the Law; And art confident that thou thyself art a guide of the blind, a light of them which are in darkness, An instructor of the foolish, a teacher of babes, which hast the form of knowledge and of the truth in the Law.* It is needful to keep in mind the apostle is addressing the Jewish converts here. Doing so aids in a better understanding of the of the apostle's purpose in these verses.

**Verse 16.** *In the day when God shall judge the secrets of men by Jesus Christ according to my gospel.* Here the apostle set forth the edict the day had come where God shall judge the deeds of men, Jew or Gentile, neither by the Law of Moses nor by the Patriarchal Law; rather God will judge the world *according to the gospel of Jesus Christ.*

**Verse 17.** *Behold, thou art called a Jew and restest in the Law and makest thy boast of God.* The Jews boasted much because they were the people through whom God would send the Messiah. They believed they were the standard by which the world should go. John the baptizer made great efforts to dismiss that dogma during his preaching.

John told the Jews: *And think not to say within yourselves, We have Abraham to our father: for I say unto you, that God is able of these stones to raise up children unto Abraham* (Matt. 3:9). The Jews felt God had to save them because they were Jews, but in truth they were Jews because God saved them. They were saved them from Egyptian captivity for the purpose of preserving the seed line through whom the Messiah would come. God further saved them for the purpose of setting forth shadows, figures, ante-types and anti-types, all of which were fulfilled in Christ.

**Verse 18.** *And knowest his will and approvest the things that are*

## Commentary on Romans

*more excellent, being instructed out of the Law.* The Jews knew more of God's revealed will than the Gentiles and *approved* the things of it. The word *approved* means "to have, discern, and to examine." The Jews could have discerned and examined more of God's revealed will than the Gentiles, for God more fully instructed them things regarding the coming Messiah. Even though God had revealed the coming of the Messiah to the Patriarchs of old, He revealed it more so to the Jews.

*The Lord thy God will raise up unto thee a Prophet from the midst of thee, of thy brethren, like unto me; unto him ye shall hearken; According to all that thou desiredst of the Lord thy God in Horeb in the day of the assembly, saying, Let me not hear again the voice of the Lord my God, neither let me see this great fire any more, that I die not. And the Lord said unto me, They have well spoken that which they have spoken. I will raise them up a Prophet from among their brethren, like unto thee and will put my words in his mouth; and he shall speak unto them all that I shall command him. And it shall come to pass, that whosoever will not hearken unto my words which he shall speak in my name, I will require it of him* (Deut. 18:15-19).

The Jews had revealed unto them those things which were more excellent than the things God revealed unto the Gentiles. The word *excellent* in verse 18 means to surpass in value; to be better, to be more excellent and to be of a far greater value. Indeed, that which God revealed to the Jews was of far greater value than that which was revealed to the Gentiles. However, the things of the Law of Moses, though greater in value than which was revealed to the Gentiles, were still in promise and painted a prophetic picture of the Messiah's Law which was yet future.

*Who serve unto the example and shadow of heavenly things, as Moses was admonished of God when he was about to make the tabernacle: for, See, saith he, that thou make all things according to the pattern shewed to thee in the mount.... For the Law having a shadow of good things to come, and not the very image of the things, can never with those sacrifices which they offered year by year continually make the comers thereunto perfect* (Heb. 8:5; 10:1).

# Commentary on Romans

The Jews, during the Mosaical dispensation were *instructed out of the Law.* The Old Testament contains well over three hundred prophecies of Christ, all of which have come to fruition. It was from *out of the Law* the Jews had made known unto them the way of Christ which was yet to come.

**Verse 19.** *And art confident that thou thyself art a guide of the blind, a light of them which are in darkness.* The Jews, with their false trust and hope in the fact they were Jews, were no different from the Gentiles whose *foolish hearts were darkened* because of their unbelief. The Jews insisted they were the only hope for the world.

Paul informed the Jewish converts they were spiritually blind. What was worse, the Jews believed themselves to be the guide to the Gentiles, even though they themselves were in spiritual darkness. The Jews were like countless men today, who believe the Jews will once again serve as God's His chosen people and have the throne of David once again occupied by the Lord in Jerusalem.

**Verse 20.** *An instructor of the foolish, a teacher of babes, which hast the form of knowledge and of the truth in the Law.* The apostle's remarks here are sarcastic, and are not to be considered as matter of fact. Premillennialists insist the Jewish Nation will be physically restored, and Christ will reign over an earthly Kingdom, even though Jesus said, *my kingdom is not of this world* (Jno. 18:36).

The apostle's remark is one of condemnation and rebuff for the Jews, not of commendation contrary to what many affirm. It is interesting to observe that nowhere in the Old Testament did God ever command the Jews to *convert* Gentiles to the Law of Moses. The Jews could make proselytes of the Gentiles if they chose to do so, but were not commanded to do so. There are those insist the Jews were required by the Law of Moses to make proselytes of all the Gentiles. This shall receive commentary later.

## Romans 2:21-29

21*Thou therefore which teachest another, teachest*

# Commentary on Romans

*thou not thyself? thou that preachest a man should not steal, dost thou steal? 22 Thou that sayest a man should not commit adultery, dost thou commit adultery? thou that abhorrest idols, dost thou commit sacrilege? 23 Thou that makest thy boast of the law, through breaking the law dishonourest thou God? 24 For the name of God is blasphemed among the Gentiles through you, as it is written. 25 For circumcision verily profiteth, if thou keep the law: but if thou be a breaker of the law, thy circumcision is made uncircumcision. 26 Therefore if the uncircumcision keep the righteousness of the law, shall not his uncircumcision be counted for circumcision? 27 And shall not uncircumcision which is by nature, if it fulfill the law, judge thee, who by the letter and circumcision dost transgress the law? 28 For he is not a Jew, which is one outwardly; neither is that circumcision, which is outward in the flesh: 29 But he is a Jew, which is one inwardly; and circumcision is that of the heart, in the spirit and not in the letter; whose praise is not of men, but of God.*

**Verses 21-23.** *Thou therefore which teachest another, teachest thou not thyself? thou that preachest a man should not steal, dost thou steal? Thou that sayest a man should not commit adultery, dost thou commit adultery? thou that abhorrest idols, dost thou commit sacrilege? Thou that makest thy boast of the law, through breaking the law dishonourest thou God?* The prophets Ezekiel and Zephaniah well summarized the conduct of the teaching Jews. *Her priests have violated my law and have profaned mine holy things: they have put no difference between the holy and profane, neither have they shewed difference between the unclean and the clean and have hid their eyes from my sabbaths and I am profaned among them.... Her prophets are light and treacherous persons: her priests have polluted the sanctuary, they have done violence to the law* (Eze. 22:26; Zeph. 3:4).

Not only had the Levitical priesthood involved themselves in such conduct, the Jews as a people did likewise. In these verses the apostle reminded the Jews they had no cause to castigate

# Commentary on Romans

the Gentiles for their illicit behavior and insubordination to God while they were guilty of far more offensive transgressions against God and the temple.

**Verse 24.** *For the name of God is blasphemed among the Gentiles through you, as it is written.* The word *blasphemed* means "to vilify; specifically to speak impiously, defame, rail on, revile, or to speak evilly of and or against." The Jews had become a *hissing* and a *byword* among the Gentiles because of their apostasy, which was well observed by numerous Gentile nations.

The prophet Isaiah declared:

> *Now therefore, what have I here, saith the Lord, that my people is taken away for nought? they that rule over them make them to howl, saith the Lord; and my name continually every day is blasphemed* (Isa. 52:5).

God informed the Jews they would become a by-word among the nations round about for their departure from God's ways.

> *All that pass by clap their hands at thee; they hiss and wag their head at the daughter of Jerusalem, saying, Is this the city that men call the perfection of beauty, The joy of the whole earth* (Lam. 2:15)?

> *And thou shalt become an astonishment, a proverb and a byword, among all nations whither the Lord shall lead thee* (Deut. 28:37).

> *Then will I cut off Israel out of the land which I have given them; and this house, which I have hallowed for my name, will I cast out of my sight; and Israel shall be a proverb and a byword among all* people (I Ki. 9:7).

> *Then will I pluck them up by the roots out of my land which I have given them; and this house, which I have sanctified for my name, will I cast out of my sight and will make it to be a proverb and a byword among all nations* (II Chro. 7:20).

# Commentary on Romans

*Thou makest us a byword among the heathen, a shaking of the head among the people* (Psa. 44:14).

**Verse 25.** *For circumcision verily profiteth, if thou keep the law: but if thou be a breaker of the law, thy circumcision is made uncircumcision.* Some Jews deduced circumcision alone was the standard by which God chose to save the Jews. The Jews believed just because they were of the covenant of circumcision they were entitled to the benefits of God. They failed to realize circumcision was a **token** of God's agreement with Abraham and Abraham's agreement with God. *This is my covenant, which ye shall keep, between me and you and thy seed after thee; Every man child among you shall be circumcised. And ye shall circumcise the flesh of your foreskin; and it shall be a token of the covenant betwixt me and you* (Gen. 17:10-11).

The Jews failed to realize that keeping the mandates of the covenant was the avenue by which they gained God's approval—not just circumcision, They needed to obey the edicts of the covenant. The Jews boasted of the covenant, but broke it daily, which left them *without excuse* (cf. Rom. 2:1).

The word *excuse* is a negative particle and a derivative of *indefensible*—meaning "inexcusable." It is the word for apology, which means to give a defense for one's self. The disobedience of the Jews made them unable to give an acceptable defense for their apostasy.

**Verse 26.** *Therefore if the uncircumcision keep the righteousness of the law, shall not his uncircumcision be counted for circumcision?* The word *uncircumcision* is used two ways in this verse. First, the word applies to the Gentiles. The Patriarchs who obeyed the Laws of the Patriarchal System had also kept the principles of the Law of the Jews.

The second use of the word *uncircumcision* has reference to the fact the Gentiles were not circumcised according to the covenant God made with Abraham. An obedient Gentile was considered by God as one who complied with the covenant given to them by God; therefore, the obedient Gentile was considered as one who had been circumcised.

# Commentary on Romans

**Verse 27.** *And shall not uncircumcision which is by nature, if it fulfill the law, judge thee, who by the letter and circumcision dost transgress the law?* Once again the *uncircumcised* here refers to the Gentiles. The obedience of the Gentiles was the judge of the disobedient Jews.

The word *judge* means "to distinguish, decide judicially, to try, condemn, punish, avenge, conclude, condemn, damn, decree, determine, esteem, judge at the law and or ordain." The obedience of the Gentile was the avenue by which disobedient Jews were being judged.

Paul used the same argument regarding obedient saints of the church and the disobedient men of the world. *Do ye not know that the saints shall judge the world? and if the world shall be judged by you, are ye unworthy to judge the smallest matters? Know ye not that we shall judge angels? how much more things that pertain to this life* (I Cor. 6:2-3)? The same argument is used by the author of Hebrews: *By faith Noah, being warned of God of things not seen as yet, moved with fear, prepared an ark to the saving of his house; by the which he condemned the world and became heir of the righteousness which is by faith (11:7).*

The *letter* of the verse has reference to the Law of Moses; the word *circumcision* has reference to the covenant. Thus, it was Paul's purpose to show the Jews they were guilty of both violating the Law of Moses and the covenant.

**Verses 28-29.** *For he is not a Jew, which is one outwardly; neither is that circumcision, which is outward in the flesh: But he is a Jew, which is one inwardly; and circumcision is that of the heart, in the spirit and not in the letter; whose praise is not of men, but of God.* A Jew was a Jew regardless of how he lived before man, but he was not God's Jew unless he lived according to the covenant of circumcision and the Law of Moses.

All men bear outward evidences of things done, but unless the heart is the seat from which obedience, love, service, and devotion arise, outward signs are little value. Just as *Some men's sins are open beforehand, going before to judgment; and some*

# Commentary on Romans

*men they follow after,* some men's sins are secret (I Tim. 5:24). Some men's righteousness is self-righteousness which is not put into action from a good heart. Self-righteousness is motivated by *the lust of the flesh, the lust of the eyes, and the pride of life* (I Jno. 2:16).

Men too often look on the outward man, but God looks upon the heart. It is best to seek the favor of God than the praises of men. *The Lord seeth not as man seeth; for man looketh on the outward appearance, but the Lord looketh on the heart* (I Sam. 16:7b). Men can only see and judge action and fruits, but God sees both the fruit and the heart from which actions are made known.

## Romans 3:1-19

*1 What advantage then hath the Jew? or what profit is there of circumcision? 2 Much every way: chiefly, because that unto them were committed the oracles of God. 3 For what if some did not believe? shall their unbelief make the faith of God without effect? 4 God forbid: yea, let God be true, but every man a liar; as it is written, That thou mightest be justified in thy sayings and mightest overcome when thou art judged. 5 But if our unrighteousness commend the righteousness of God, what shall we say? Is God unrighteous who taketh vengeance? (I speak as a man) 6 God forbid: for then how shall God judge the world? 7 For if the truth of God hath more abounded through my lie unto his glory; why yet am I also judged as a sinner? 8 And not rather, (as we be slanderously reported and as some affirm that we say,) Let us do evil, that good may come? Whose damnation is just. 9 What then? are we better than they? No, in no wise: for we have before proved both Jews and Gentiles, that they are all under sin; 10 As it is written, There is none righteous, no, not one: 11 There is none that understandeth, there is none that seeketh after God. 12 They are all gone out of the way, they are together become unprofitable; there is none that doeth good, no, not one. 13 Their throat is an open sepulchre; with their tongues they have used deceit; the poison of asps is under their lips:*

# Commentary on Romans

*14 Whose mouth is full of cursing and bitterness: 15 Their feet are swift to shed blood: 16 Destruction and misery are in their ways: 17 And the way of peace have they not known: 18 There is no fear of God before their eyes. 19 Now we know that what things soever the Law saith, it saith to them who are under the Law: that every mouth may be stopped and all the world may become guilty before God.*

**Verse 1.** *What advantage then hath the Jew? or what profit is there of circumcision?* It is well to recall the apostle's purpose in chapter two was to show the Jewish converts they had taken the Law of Moses and the covenant of circumcision for granted. They had falsely assured themselves, because they were Jews by heritage, they were Jews in heart. We recall the apostle's words of 2:28: *For he is not a Jew, which is one outwardly; neither is that circumcision, which is outward in the flesh.*

Such being the case, the apostle understood the mental attitude of the Jew. Paul poses their inquisitions and supplies his inspired response. The Jews, in their thinking, had several major questions the apostle needed to address. Their first question: *What advantage then hath the Jew?* The second question: *What profit is there of circumcision?* Both questions were valid so far as the Jews were concerned and warranted a goodly reply.

**Verse 2.** The Jews were *greatly advantaged because that unto them were committed the oracles of God* (vs.2b).

**Verse 3.** *For what if some did not believe? shall their unbelief make the faith of God without effect?* What if some of the Jews *did not believe* is the elliptical thought here. An ellipsis is a figure of speech from which there is an omission of one or more words when what is omitted is clearly understood by the context.

The second question; *shall their unbelief make the faith of God without effect?* The *faith of God* here means the system of faith God established in Christ—the Gospel system!

We are reminded of the words of the prophet Isaiah who wrote:

# Commentary on Romans

*For my thoughts are not your thoughts, neither are your ways my ways, saith the Lord. For as the heavens are higher than the earth, so are my ways higher than your ways and my thoughts than your thoughts. For as the rain cometh down and the snow from heaven and returneth not thither, but watereth the earth and maketh it bring forth and bud, that it may give seed to the sower and bread to the eater: So shall my word be that goeth forth out of my mouth: it shall not return unto me void, but it shall accomplish that which I please and it shall prosper in the thing whereto I sent it* (Isa. 55:8-11).

**Verse 4.** The apostle's response to the query was; *God forbid: yea, let God be true, but every man a liar; as it is written, That thou mightest be justified in thy sayings and mightest overcome when thou art judged.* When an inspired author refers to that which was written in the Old Testament, it is essential to know where such things were written. But just where is this passage found? Suggestions are seemingly without number, among which are: Psalm 35:5, 11; 55:13-14; I Samuel 18:5, 7; 23:12, 19-20; II Samuel 15:6, 31; Matthew 21:9, and John 19:15. Psalm 51:4 has also been suggested.

While it is the case no one single Old Testament passage houses the words of verse four as Paul cites them; it is the case the principle of the passage is set forth in an accumulation of numerous Old Testament passages. Matthew used this same approach when he wrote concerning Christ: *And he came and dwelt in a city called Nazareth: that it might be fulfilled which was spoken by the prophets, He shall be called a Nazarene* (Matt. 2:23). The word *Nazarene* means "branch, root, shoot, stalk, or stem." Consider Isaiah 11:1 and Zechariah 6:12. There is no specific Old Testament passage wherein it is said of Christ, *He shall be called a Nazarene.*

**Verses 5-6.** *But if our unrighteousness commend the righteousness of God, what shall we say? Is God unrighteous who taketh vengeance? (I speak as a man). God forbid: for then how shall God judge the world?* Here we have another objection from the Jews. They assumed God was unrighteous for condemning

# Commentary on Romans

them, according to Paul's arguments. Paul, therefore, demonstrated the more rebellious and disobedient the Jews became, the more righteous God was in exercising His wrath against them.

Was God unjust in His dealings with the Jews? Not at all. Better yet, as Paul noted, *God forbid.* If God be unjust, how then can He execute final judgment upon men or any judgment whatsoever against the world? Note again verse 6, *God forbid: for then how shall God judge the world?*

**Verses 7-8.** *For if the truth of God hath more abounded through my lie unto his glory; why yet am I also judged as a sinner? And not rather, (as we be slanderously reported and as some affirm that we say,) Let us do evil, that good may come? whose damnation is just.* The Jews contended the system of Christ was a blasphemous lie. Paul's work was indeed an arduous one as he addressed his fellow Jews.

The fact Paul was a preacher of the gospel of *Jesus Christ and him crucified* made Paul a liar, so far as the Jews were concerned. *For I determined not to know any thing among you, save Jesus Christ and him crucified* (I Cor. 2:2). Paul had earlier stated he was *not ashamed of the gospel of Christ: for it is the power of God unto salvation to every one that believeth; to the Jew first and also to the Greek* (Rom. 1:16). This too was considered blasphemous from the Jews' perspective.

It is once again expressed—there is a strong need to keep in mind the apostle is addressing the Jewish converts in this portion of Scripture. Paul is dealing with the Jews from their perspective. The Jews theorized their sins brought about a greater display of God's righteousness. "On that theory, the Jew regarded Christianity as a lie, Since Paul preached the message, it became **his** lie. Since he forsook Judaism for Christianity, he committed about the greatest sin that a Jew could commit. Paul is here adopting the objector's method of reasoning. If you justify your sins on the grounds that your sins brought out and displayed God's righteousness, why condemn me for what you consider my great sin? On that theory, "Why not (as we are slanderously reported and as some affirm that we say), let us do

## Commentary on Romans

evil, that good may come?" If the theory stated in the objection were correct, then the more we sin, the better it would be for us. But Paul adds that the condemnation of such slanderers is just"[19] [sic].

**Verse 9.** *What then? are we better than they? No, in no wise: for we have before proved both Jews and Gentiles, that they are all under sin.* The Jews were not in any better spiritual condition than the Gentiles, nay, *in no wise.*

The Jews had a great advantage over the Gentiles; they had a more detailed and clear revelation of God's Law. However, they failed to take proper advantage of it. The Jews failed to live up to the covenant God gave them and were, therefore, no better than the Gentiles who had also failed in living up to the Law God gave them. Both had failed and both were lost. Thus, we have the apostle's commentary wherein he said; *for we have before proved both Jews and Gentiles, that they are all under sin.*

**Verses 10-11.** *As it is written, There is none righteous, no, not one: There is none that understandeth, there is none that seeketh after God.* Many Jews were great students of the Law, but failed to understand it. The Jews failed to realize the Law was a temporary Law, a temporary system; a system which was to provide numerous types, shadows, figures and adumbrations of the Gospel system which found fruition in the Gospel of Christ.

The Law of Moses was a Law which *was to be done away* (II Cor. 3:7-11). The Jews believed the Mosaical Law to be permanent. They failed to realize that of which Paul wrote to the church of Galatia. *Wherefore the Law was our schoolmaster to bring us unto Christ, that we might be justified by* (the system of the New Testament) *faith. But after that* (system of the New Testament) *faith is come, we are no longer under a schoolmaster* (Gal. 3:24-25). The apostle further demonstrated to the Jews *there is none* (Jew or Gentile) *that understandeth, there is none that seeketh after God,* according to God's mandates. The Jews failed to seek God on God's terms, just as the Gentiles failed in so doing.

---

[19] Robertson L. Whiteside.

## Commentary on Romans

The Jews studied the Law to win the favor of their fellow Jews, and reap the reward of the praises of men. However, they should have studied to find the favor of God and win His approval. It is for this very reason Jesus *said unto them, Ye are they which justify yourselves before men; but God knoweth your hearts: for that which is highly esteemed among men is abomination in the sight of God* (Lk. 16:15).

When men search the Scriptures for reasons other than to know God's will and submit to it, it does them no good. Men must *follow on to know the Lord,* rather than to merely obtain knowledge, favor, and praises of men (Hos. 6:3). Note also the words of Christ; *Ye search the scriptures; for in them ye think ye have eternal life: and they are they which testify of me* (Jno. 5:39). The searching of Scriptures is good, but obedience and understanding must be applied. The ellipsis of this passage contains the understood *you.* The ellipsis would read: *You Jewish dignitaries search the scriptures; for in them ye think ye have eternal life: and they are they are the very Scriptures which testify of me* (Jno. 5:39). The Scripture-searching Jews thought that because they did so, they had eternal life. They failed to realize the Scriptures were those things which testified of Christ Himself. Truly, searching of the Scriptures must be fettered to the submission of them.

**Verse 12.** *They are all gone out of the way, they are together become unprofitable; there is none that doeth good, no, not one.* When men go out of God's way, they are of no value to Him. The Jews had gone away from the Lord just as Cain *who went out from the presence of the Lord* (Gen. 4:16). They failed to realize the purpose for which God had intended for them. They were to exist as a nation only until Christ, the seed, came. Once Christ came, both the Jewish Nation and the Old Law became defunct.

**Verses 13-14.** *Their throat is an open sepulchre; with their tongues they have used deceit; the poison of asps is under their lips: Whose mouth is full of cursing and bitterness.* This is a statement which is very strong in its intended message. An open grave reeks: from the depths of a decaying cadaver comes foul stenches. Paul equates the speech of the Jews to the same

# Commentary on Romans

odious stench of an open sepulcher. From the depths of the throat of the disobedient Jews came filthiness of speech. The ill will and filth the Jews promoted and vaunted toward God was equal to the *poison of asps.* Indeed their *mouths were full of cursing and bitterness* against God.

**Verse 15.** *Their feet are swift to shed blood.* This verse equates to which Peter stated as recorded in Acts on the day of Pentecost. Observe: *ye* (the Jews) *have taken and by wicked hands have crucified and slain* (Acts 2:23).

The thirst for blood by the Jews is seen in the numerous occasions wherein saints suffered martyrdom for the cause of Christ. We recall Stephen (Acts 7), James (Acts 12), and Paul who was stoned and left for dead (Acts 14). Paul wrote: it was the Jews *Who both killed the Lord Jesus, and their own prophets, and have persecuted us; and they please not God, and are contrary to all men* (I Thes. 2:15).

**Verses 16-18.** *Destruction and misery are in their ways: And the way of peace have they not known: There is no fear of God before their eyes.* The Jews had become a rebellious people; they had neither tolerance nor mercy for the Gentiles, Samaritans, or other peoples. They knew not how to live peaceably with men.

The inspired record requires us to *live peaceably with all men* (Rom. 12:18). This the Jews refused to do. They could not live in peace with either man or God—not with men because of their distaste for the Gentiles—not with God for there *was no fear of God before their eyes.*

**Verse 19.** *Now we know that what things soever the Law saith, it saith to them who are under the Law: that every mouth may be stopped; and all the world may become guilty before God.* Every mouth was *stopped; n*either Jew or Gentile had an acceptable reply to God for their disobedience. None could be found with God's favor. Indeed they were *without excuse* (Rom. 2:1). All men are subject to God's judgment and must comply with His commands. All must be endowed with mercy, compassion, and contrition.

# Commentary on Romans

The Jews could in no way deny that of which their own prophets had spoken. They were quick to subject the Gentiles to harsh judgments of while exempting themselves from the same, even though they were guilty of the same crimes against God. However, Paul had demonstrated the Jews were likewise subject to the same judgment of God as were the Gentiles.

## Romans 3:20-31

*20 Therefore by the deeds of the Law there shall no flesh be justified in his sight: for by the Law is the knowledge of sin. 21 But now the righteousness of God without the Law is manifested, being witnessed by the Law and the prophets; 22 Even the righteousness of God which is by faith of Jesus Christ unto all and upon all them that believe: for there is no difference: 23 For all have sinned and come short of the glory of God; 24 Being justified freely by his grace through the redemption that is in Christ Jesus: 25 Whom God hath set forth to be a propitiation through faith in his blood, to declare his righteousness for the remission of sins that are past, through the forbearance of God; 26 To declare, I say, at this time his righteousness: that he might be just and the justifier of him which believeth in Jesus. 27 Where is boasting then? It is excluded. By what Law? of works? Nay: but by the Law of faith. 28 Therefore we conclude that a man is justified by faith without the deeds of the Law. 29 Is he the God of the Jews only? is he not also of the Gentiles? Yes, of the Gentiles also: 30 Seeing it is one God, which shall justify the circumcision by faith and uncircumcision through faith. 31 Do we then make void the Law through faith? God forbid: yea, we establish the Law.*

**Verse 20.** *Therefore by the deeds of the Law there shall no flesh be justified in his sight: for by the Law is the knowledge of sin.* Here lies a passage which has caused no little confusion among Bible students; it has been abused by countless commentators and misused for centuries.

This passage has become the seat from which the erroneous

# Commentary on Romans

conclusion, that none who lived under the Law of Moses could keep it. We ask, where is the passage that remotely suggests that none could keep the Law of Moses? *It does not exist!*

The Jews needed the New Law ushered in; wherein, grace was both fulfilled and made available. It has long been wrongly asserted there was no grace found under the Old Law. Such is far from being true. What is true, however, regarding this passage, is Paul was addressing the Jewish converts and showed them, had they as a nation, kept the Law as a nation, then justification would have been awarded to them by the Lord. Paul had proven even their own inspired prophets declared they as a nation had not kept the Law. The very Law by which they could have obtained grace and righteousness was the very Law which condemned the Jews as a nation.

The Law of Moses revealed sin to be sin. The apostle would later write: *I had not known sin, but by the Law* (Rom. 7:7). As a nation, the Jews were condemned as the people of God and no longer His chosen people. God had chosen a New Israel, a new nation, a new people, and a New Jerusalem no longer physical in nature, but spiritual.

Those who have, and still insist none could be declared righteous under the Old Law, err, not knowing the Scripture. Such students fail to realize the apostle is discussing the Jewish Nation as a whole and not Jews as individuals. As a nation, they failed to keep the Law. However, there were individuals who were indeed justified—in fact, found grace and righteousness under the Law of Moses.

Countless Jews of the Old Testament kept the commands of God and were, in fact, rewarded with grace and righteousness for their obedience. The Lord spoke to Elisha, saying, *Yet I have left me seven thousand in Israel, all the knees which have not bowed unto Baal, and every mouth which hath not kissed him* (I Ki. 19:18).

We have some Old Testament examples recorded in the New Testament of Jews who were found righteous and blameless before God. Of the parents of John the baptizer, Luke wrote;

# Commentary on Romans

*There was in the days of Herod, the king of Judaea, a certain priest named Zacharias, of the course of Abia: and his wife was of the daughters of Aaron and her name was Elisabeth. And they were both righteous before God, walking in all the commandments and ordinances of the Lord blameless* (Lk. 1:5-6). Further, Paul declared of himself that he was *circumcised the eighth day, of the stock of Israel, of the tribe of Benjamin, an Hebrew of the Hebrews; as touching the Law, a Pharisee; Concerning zeal, persecuting the church; touching the righteousness which is in the Law, blameless* (Phil. 3:5-6). Zacharias, Elisabeth, and Paul all kept the Law blamelessly. What of those Jews mentioned in Hebrews 11? Why have they been given place in the hall of fame of faith if they did not keep the Law blamelessly? It is not at all the case the Old Law could not be kept. The Law could indeed be kept and was kept by not a few.

If it be the case the Law of Moses could not be kept, then it is the case God gave the Jews a law up to which they could not live, a standard which they could not keep. However, it was in fact, kept by every Jew who found grace and righteousness under it. The righteousness which was found under the Old Law needed to be fulfilled, however. Paul spoke of that fulfillment when he wrote: *That the righteousness of the Law might be fulfilled in us, who walk not after the flesh, but after the Spirit* (Rom. 8:4).

The apostle had well solidified his case to his Jewish audience. Just as the Gentile Nations had lost God's favor because of their disobedience to their Law, the Jews lost their grace, favor, and righteousness for the same reasons. Thus, there were *none righteous, no not one,* Jew or Gentile (Rom. 3:10).

**Verse 21.** *But now the righteousness of God without the Law is manifested, being witnessed by the Law and the prophets.* The word *now* is emphatic, present. *Now* meaning under the system of faith that *now* exists is under Jesus Christ. The New Testament System of Jesus Christ was *witnessed by the Law and the prophets.* It is *the righteousness of God*—His system of faith by which He now declares obedient men righteous.

The New Testament System of Jesus Christ was not a new in the sense the Jews had never heard of it. They should not have

# Commentary on Romans

been ignorant of it. The New Covenant of Jesus Christ was prophesied of by the prophets, as in: *Behold, the days come, saith the Lord, that I will make a new covenant with the house of Israel and with the house of Judah: Not according to the covenant that I made with their fathers in the day that I took them by the hand to bring them out of the land of Egypt; which my covenant they brake, although I was an husband unto them, saith the Lord: But this shall be the covenant that I will make with the house of Israel; After those days, saith the Lord, I will put my Law in their inward parts and write it in their hearts; and will be their God and they shall be my people. And they shall teach no more every man his neighbor and every man his brother, saying, Know the Lord: for they shall all know me, from the least of them unto the greatest of them, saith the Lord: for I will forgive their iniquity and I will remember their sin no more* (Jer. 31:31-34).

**Verses 22.** *Even the righteousness of God which is by faith of Jesus Christ unto all and upon all them that believe: for there is no difference: For all have sinned and come short of the glory of God; Being justified freely by his grace through the redemption that is in Christ Jesus.* Again we emphasize the phrase, *the righteousness of God* has reference to the system of righteousness by which God will declare men righteous. Though the Gospel was for the Jews first, it was not for the Jew only, for God gave it *unto all and upon all them that believe.*

*For all have sinned and come short of the glory of God,* so wrote the apostle. The meaning is both the Jews and the Gentiles sinned and fell well short as nations and peoples. They both fell short of the glory of God. The Jews would then inquire as to how God would justify anyone, Jew or Gentile, if such was not to be accomplished through the Law of Moses? The answer was clearly provided by the apostle. Man will *now* be *justified freely by his grace through the redemption that is in Christ Jesus,* not the Patriarchal or Mosaical Laws.

**Verses 25-26.** *Whom God hath set forth to be a propitiation through faith in his blood, to declare his righteousness for the remission of sins that are past, through the forbearance of God; To declare, I say, at this time his righteousness: that he might be just and the justifier of him which believeth in Jesus.* The apostle

# Commentary on Romans

John said of Christ: *And he is the propitiation for our sins: and not for ours only, but also for the sins of the whole world. Herein is love, not that we loved God, but that he loved us and sent his Son to be the propitiation for our sins* (I Jno. 2:2; 4:10).

The word *whom* of verse 25 has reference to Jesus Christ, *Whom God hath set forth to be a propitiation through faith in his blood.* The righteousness of the New Testament of Jesus Christ was to provide remission of sins not fulfilled under the Old Law. Brethren have long taught that the sins of those who lived under the Old Testament *had their sins rolled forward.* There is no such passage in all of the Scripture which teaches such. To the contrary, the blood of Christ flowed backward to cover the sins of the people of old. Consider, *the remission of sins that are past, through the forbearance of God.*

Those of the Old Testament period, whether Jew or Gentile, who found grace in the eyes of the Lord (such as Noah and others), believed in the coming of the Messiah. Job said: *For I know that my redeemer liveth and that he shall stand at the latter day upon the earth* (Job 19:25). Many are the number of prophecies in the Old Testament which refer to the coming of Christ. All who lived obediently under their respective systems believed in the coming of the Messiah and longed to see that day. Jesus said to the Pharisees regarding Abraham: *Your father Abraham rejoiced to see my day: and he saw it and was glad* (Jno. 8:56). Further, Jesus said regarding the Scriptures that *they are they which testify of me* (Jno. 5:39). Christ is *the justifier of him which believeth in Jesus,* both of the Old Testament and the New Testament.

**Verse 27.** *Where is boasting then? It is excluded. By what Law? of works? Nay: but by the Law of faith.* The Jews boasted both in and of the Law of Moses. Paul however, removed that source of pride from them. Boasting in the Law was now *"excluded"* under Christ.

Boasting was now in Jesus Christ and His Law. *The Law of faith* was now the Law not only for the Jews, but also for the Gentiles. *The Law of faith* was established by Jesus Christ—that is, the New Testament System of faith.

# Commentary on Romans

**Verse 28.** *Therefore we conclude that a man is justified by faith without the deeds of the Law.* Complete justification and righteousness were not found under the Old Law. Paul argued it was not the Law that justified the Jew but rather God. The Jew would then pose the question about the system God *elected* to employ for the Jew.

*Who shall lay any thing to the charge of God's elect? It is God that justifieth* (Rom. 8:33). The *elect*, as used in Romans 8:33, refers to the system by which God *elected* to save all men, whether Jew or Gentile. Jude informs us it is God who sanctifies (cf. Jd. 1). *God's elect* does not refer to men elected by God according to the Calvinistic doctrine of predestination.

**Verses 29-30.** *Is he the God of the Jews only? is he not also of the Gentiles? Yes, of the Gentiles also: Seeing it is one God, which shall justify the circumcision by faith and uncircumcision through faith.* Here the apostle continues to solidify his argument with the asking of the rhetorical questions posed in verse 29.

The apostle answers with an emphatic, *Yes!* Indeed, God is the God of all men, both Jew and Gentile. Verse 30 is Paul's inspired answer. God justifies both the circumcision (the Jew) and the uncircumcision (the Gentile) through the New Testament System of faith, not the Law of Moses.

**Verse 31.** *Do we then make void the Law through faith? God forbid: yea, we establish the Law.* Paul again posed the question he knew the Jews would ask and supplies his inspired response. Paul's reply is clear, and the Jews well understood the apostle. The establishment of the New Law of Christ brought to fruition the prophecies of the Old Law. The Law of Moses served to bring the Jews to Christ (cf. Gal. 3:21-26).

## Romans 4:1-8

*1 What shall we say then that Abraham our father, as pertaining to the flesh, hath found? 2 For if Abraham were justified by works, he hath whereof to glory; but not before God. 3 For what saith the scripture? Abraham believed God and it was counted unto him for righteousness. 4 Now to him that worketh is the reward*

# Commentary on Romans

> *not reckoned of grace, but of debt. 5 But to him that worketh not, but believeth on him that justifieth the ungodly, his faith is counted for righteousness. 6 Even as David also describeth the blessedness of the man, unto whom God imputeth righteousness without works, 7 Saying, Blessed are they whose iniquities are forgiven and whose sins are covered. 8 Blessed is the man to whom the Lord will not impute sin.*

**Verse 1.** *What shall we say then that Abraham our father, as pertaining to the flesh, hath found?* The Jews were strongly fettered with great pride to their Abrahamic heritage and equally important to the Jews was their pride in the Law of Moses.

Many Jews, who had obeyed the Gospel, began asserting the Law of Moses was to be kept in conjunction with the Law of Christ. They also insisted the covenant of circumcision must be kept. *And certain men which came down from Judaea taught the brethren and said, Except ye be circumcised after the manner of Moses, ye cannot be saved* (Acts 15:1). As a result of this infraction, *the apostles and elders came together for to consider of this matter* (Acts 15:6). After much discussion;,

> *it pleased the apostles and elders, with the whole church, to send chosen men of their own company to Antioch with Paul and Barnabas; namely, Judas surnamed Barsabas and Silas, chief men among the brethren: And they wrote letters by them after this manner; The apostles and elders and brethren send greeting unto the brethren which are of the Gentiles in Antioch and Syria and Cilicia: Forasmuch as we have heard, that certain which went out from us have troubled you with words, subverting your souls, saying, Ye must be circumcised and keep the Law: to whom we gave no such commandment* (Acts 15:22-24).

The phrase *hath found* indicates Abraham had *found* something, but what was it he *found?* Verse 2 reveals it to us.

**Verse 2.** *For if Abraham were justified by works, he hath whereof to glory; but not before God.* Abraham found justification,

# Commentary on Romans

however, the *justification* he found was not through his obedience to the Law of Moses. Abraham was not justified by the works of the Old Law; rather, he was justified by God long before the Law of Moses was given.

**Verse 3.** *For what saith the scripture? Abraham believed God and it was counted unto him for righteousness.* The phrase, *what saith the scripture,* is known in hermeneutics as *personification*, which is the giving of human attributes or characteristics to the inanimate, be they concrete or abstract in nature. Here the attribute of human speaking is awarded to the Scripture. While the Scripture itself can not speak, Paul uses personification to give the Scripture the characteristic of doing so.

The Scripture quoted in this passage comes from Genesis 15:6. *And he believed in the Lord; and he counted it to him for righteousness.* James gives his inspired commentary on this Genesis passage which solidifies the argument made by Paul. *But wilt thou know, O vain man, that faith without works is dead? Was not Abraham our father justified by works, when he had offered Isaac his son upon the altar? Seest thou how faith wrought with his works and by works was faith made perfect? And the scripture was fulfilled which saith, Abraham believed God and it was imputed unto him for righteousness: and he was called the Friend of God. Ye see then how that by works a man is justified and not by faith only* (Jas. 2:20-24).

Two matters warrant attention here. First, James informs his reader that Genesis 15:6 was a prophecy concerning Abraham which was not fulfilled until after Abraham had offered up Isaac for a sacrifice.

> *And it came to pass after these things, that God did tempt Abraham and said unto him, Abraham: and he said, Behold, here I am. And he said, Take now thy son, thine only son Isaac, whom thou lovest and get thee into the land of Moriah; and offer him there for a burnt offering upon one of the mountains which I will tell thee of. And Abraham rose up early in the morning and saddled his ass and took two of his young men with him and Isaac his son and clave the wood for the*

## Commentary on Romans

*burnt offering and rose up and went unto the place of which God had told him. Then on the third day Abraham lifted up his eyes and saw the place afar off. And Abraham said unto his young men, Abide ye here with the ass; and I and the lad will go yonder and worship and come again to you. And Abraham took the wood of the burnt offering and laid it upon Isaac his son; and he took the fire in his hand and a knife; and they went both of them together. And Isaac spake unto Abraham his father and said, My father: and he said, Here am I, my son. And he said, Behold the fire and the wood: but where is the lamb for a burnt offering? And Abraham said, My son, God will provide himself a lamb for a burnt offering: so they went both of them together. And they came to the place which God had told him of; and Abraham built an altar there and laid the wood in order and bound Isaac his son and laid him on the altar upon the wood. And Abraham stretched forth his hand and took the knife to slay his son. And the angel of the Lord called unto him out of heaven and said, Abraham, Abraham: and he said, Here am I. And he said, Lay not thine hand upon the lad, neither do thou any thing unto him: for now I know that thou fearest God, seeing thou hast not withheld thy son, thine only son from me* (Gen. 22:1-12).

Second, James clearly showed a man's faith must be married to works. Without works, faith is nothing, and without works, faith cannot be displayed. Indeed, *faith without works is dead* (cf. Jas. 2:20).

A faith that saves is a faith that obeys. Further, James and Paul agreed Abraham was not justified under the Law of Moses; rather, Abraham was justified by being obedient to the system of faith under which he lived. For Abraham it was the Patriarchal Law. Regardless of the Law under which men may have lived or now live, God has always required works of obedience.

**Verses 4-5.** *Now to him that worketh is the reward not reckoned of grace, but of debt. But to him that worketh not, but believeth on him that justifieth the ungodly, his faith is counted for right-*

## Commentary on Romans

*eousness.* These verses have long served as a sweetener for the caustic cocktail of Calvinists. Calvinism teaches man can do no works whatsoever that would in any way merit God's reward.

No Law provided forgiveness. The Law under which Abraham lived, the Law under which the Jews lived, nor the Law of Christ could or did provide forgiveness. Laws provide avenues unto grace, forgiveness, and salvation only through obedience. No Law awards forgiveness, grace, or salvation. Forgiveness is only awarded by God's grace. God's grace is awarded to man based upon obedience to His Law. Men *are sanctified by God the Father and preserved in Jesus Christ,* and *it is God who justifies* (Jd. 1: Rom. 8:33).

The rewarding of God's grace and salvation has always been conditional. It is without question God's grace is awarded based upon the condition of obedience. The number of passages which contain *if this, then that* statements regarding rewards is many. *Now therefore, if ye will obey my voice indeed and keep my covenant, then ye shall be a peculiar treasure unto me above all people: for all the earth is mine* (Exo. 19:5). *If ye love me, keep my commandments* (Jno. 14:15). *Ye are my friends, if ye do whatsoever I command you* (Jno. 15:14). *And being made perfect, he became the author of eternal salvation unto all them that obey him* (Heb. 5:9).

**Verses 6-8.** *Even as David also describeth the blessedness of the man, unto whom God imputeth righteousness without works, Saying, Blessed are they whose iniquities are forgiven and whose sins are covered. Blessed is the man to whom the Lord will not impute sin.* Paul demonstrated Abraham was not justified by the Law of Moses, or by the Patriarchal Law in verses 2-7. He now shows none were saved or awarded God's grace and forgiveness under the Law of Moses. Paul does so by quoting David. Under the Law of Moses, David clearly showed God's grace was not awarded by the Law of Moses, but God's grace and salvation were awarded by God to those who obeyed the Law of Moses. There is a vast difference between keeping a Law and receiving grace. Grace is the reward for keeping God's Law. No Law can award either grace of forgiveness (cf. Jd. 3; Rom. 8:33). God's Laws revealed grace can be acquired, but

# Commentary on Romans

the acquisition of God's grace and salvation is granted based upon obedience.

Obedience to the New Law of Christ results in the reward of grace and forgiveness. But no Law contains grace or forgiveness. The Jews believed that, just because they were the offspring of Abraham and because they had the Law of Moses, they were entitled to God's grace and forgiveness. Calvinists insist just because one believes in Jesus Christ as the Son of God, he is entitled to God's grace and forgiveness. They also assert that, because they *accept Jesus Christ,* He saves them, and works are not required by the Lord. Salvation is not a matter of man *accepting the Lord as Savior,* but rather it is a matter of the Lord accepting man. The Lord does so based on one's obedience to God's will.

No amount of works can save anyone, given the Calvinistic doctrine. Yet Paul declared, men are to *work out their salvation with fear and trembling* (Phil. 2:12). Calvinism further insists *faith only* saves man. However, it is well to note there is only one passage of inspired Scripture in which the words *faith* and *only* appear together. It is interesting to note in that same passage the words *faith only* are preceded by the words *not by. Ye see then how that by works a man is justified and not by faith only* (Jas. 2:24).

Why so many proclaim man cannot work his way toward salvation is amazing! In response to the multitude which asked the Lord; *What shall we do, that we might work the works of God? Jesus answered and said unto them, This is the work of God, that ye believe on him whom he hath sent* (Jno. 6:28-29). The church has become so fearful of teaching the commands given in the Scriptures to *work* toward salvation because they have no concept how to refute Calvinism.

Just as there are works of God, there are works of the devil. Jesus said: *He that committeth sin is of the devil; for the devil sinneth from the beginning. For this purpose the Son of God was manifested, that he might destroy the works of the devil* (I Jno. 3:8). There are 48 passages of Scripture which contain *work of God,* and there are 31 passages which contain *works of God.*

# Commentary on Romans

**79** total passages of Scripture couple *work* and *works* together with the phrase *of God*. How is it saints have become so cowardly and faint of heart that they fail to realize the urgent need to *work out their salvation* and *work the works of God* and be about their *Father's business* (Lk. 2: 49)?

## Romans 4:9-25

*9 Cometh this blessedness then upon the circumcision only, or upon the uncircumcision also? for we say that faith was reckoned to Abraham for righteousness. 10 How was it then reckoned? when he was in circumcision, or in uncircumcision? Not in circumcision, but in uncircumcision. 11 And he received the sign of circumcision, a seal of the righteousness of the faith which he had yet being uncircumcised: that he might be the father of all them that believe, though they be not circumcised; that righteousness might be imputed unto them also: 12 And the father of circumcision to them who are not of the circumcision only, but who also walk in the steps of that faith of our father Abraham, which he had being yet uncircumcised. 13 For the promise, that he should be the heir of the world, was not to Abra-ham, or to his seed, through the Law, but through the righteousness of faith. 14 For if they which are of the Law be heirs, faith is made void and the promise made of none effect: 15 Because the Law worketh wrath: for where no Law is, there is no transgression. 16 Therefore it is of faith, that it might be by grace; to the end the promise might be sure to all the seed; not to that only which is of the Law, but to that also which is of the faith of Abraham; who is the father of us all, 17 (As it is written, I have made thee a father of many nations,) before him whom he believed, even God, who quickeneth the dead and calleth those things which be not as though they were. 18 Who against hope believed in hope, that he might become the father of many nations, according to that which was spoken, So shall thy seed be. 19 And being not weak in faith, he considered not his own body now dead, when he was about an hundred years old, neither yet the deadness of Sara's*

# Commentary on Romans

*womb. 20 He staggered not at the promise of God through unbelief; but was strong in faith, giving glory to God; 21 And being fully persuaded that, what he had promised, he was able also to perform. 22 And therefore it was imputed to him for righteousness. 23 Now it was not written for his sake alone, that it was imputed to him; 24 But for us also, to whom it shall be imputed, if we believe on him that raised up Jesus our Lord from the dead; 25 Who was delivered for our offenses and was raised again for our justification.*

**Verse 9.** *Cometh this blessedness then upon the circumcision only, or upon the uncircumcision also? For we say that faith was reckoned to Abraham for righteousness.* The *blessedness* under consideration has reference to the blessing of forgiveness as mentioned in verses 6-8. Circumcision refers to the Jews, uncircumcision refers to the Gentiles.

The phrase, *for we say,* is to be understood as *we all, both Jew and Gentile, say.* There was one thing upon which both the Jew and Gentile agreed—Abraham's obedient faith was that which was reckoned to him for righteousness. Paul had clearly shown Abraham was justified before the Law of Moses was given.

A careful reading of Genesis 12-21 will show Abraham was already spiritually safe with God long before he was called out of Ur. In Genesis 16, when Abraham was eighty-six years old, he begat Ishmael through Hagar the Egyptian, Sara's handmaid. God had not given the covenant of circumcision to Abraham until Ishmael was thirteen years old. Abraham was ninety-nine years old when the covenant of circumcision was given. Abraham was one hundred years of age when Isaac was born. Ishmael and Isaac were fourteen years apart; thus, Paul had shown the Jews that Abraham had the blessing of forgiveness and had obtained righteousness from the Lord—not only 430 years before the Jews left Egypt and before the Law of Moses was given—but God had declared him forgiven at least fourteen years before the covenant of circumcision. The argument constructed by Paul established Abraham was the father of both the Jews and the Gentiles (cf. Gen. 15:13: Exo. 12:41).

# Commentary on Romans

**Verses 10-12.** *How was it then reckoned? when he was in circumcision, or in uncircumcision? Not in circumcision, but in uncircumcision. And he received the sign of circumcision, a seal of the righteousness of the faith which he had yet being uncircumcised: that he might be the father of all them that believe, though they be not circumcised; that righteousness might be imputed unto them also: And the father of circumcision to them who are not of the circumcision only, but who also walk in the steps of that faith of our father Abraham, which he had being yet uncircumcised.* How was it then reckoned? The *it* of this passage refers to the *blessedness* of forgiveness and righteousness Abraham received as recorded in verses 6-9.

Though these verses are not hard to be understood, the passage was indeed difficult to accept for the Jews, who were strongly married to the Law of Moses and the covenant of circumcision. Most refused to accept the truth of the Gospel Paul proclaimed.

**Verse 13.** *For the promise, that he should be the heir of the world, was not to Abraham, or to his seed, through the Law, but through the righteousness of faith.* This *promise* was the one given to Abraham: *Now the Lord had said unto Abram, Get thee out of thy country and from thy kindred and from thy father's house, unto a land that I will shew thee: And I will make of thee a great nation and I will bless thee and make thy name great; and thou shalt be a blessing: And I will bless them that bless thee and curse him that curseth thee: and in thee shall all families of the earth be blessed* (Gen. 12:1-3).

**Verse 14.** *For if they which are of the Law be heirs, faith is made void and the promise made of none effect.* The passage contains an understood ellipsis. We are to understand the passage as follows; *For if they which are of the Law be the only heirs, then the faith of Abraham is made void, and the promise God made to Abraham is of none effect.*

**Verse 15.** *Because the Law worketh wrath: for where no Law is, there is no transgression.* The Jews questioned Paul's reasoning and, therefore, posed additional questions. If it is the case, so the Jew reasoned, salvation, justification, and righteousness came about because of obedient faith, for what then was the

# Commentary on Romans

Law of Moses good? The Law, Paul noted, was that which made the wrath of God known to the Jews. The Law of Moses revealed sin to be sin, and revealed the measure of God's wrath upon those who failed to work the works of faith through obedience.

**Verse 16.** *Therefore it is of faith, that it might be by grace; to the end the promise might be sure to all the seed; not to that only which is of the Law, but to that also which is of the faith of Abraham; who is the father of us all.* The *it* of which Paul writes in this passage is once again salvation, justification, and righteousness.

For Abraham and the Jews, salvation came by an obedient faith which was not acquired through the Law of Moses. Keep in mind the apostle is addressing Jewish converts. In so doing, it eliminates the needless confusions of Calvinism. When one fails to understand this salient point, one cannot but come to the wrong conclusion; he cannot perceive the intent of the apostle.

The phrase *to the end* means "for the purpose of." The purpose of the promise God gave to Abraham was to assure him it was through his seed that all the families of the earth would be blessed (Gen. 12:3). Thus, salvation was unto all men and *not to that only which is of the Law, but to that also which is of the faith of Abraham; who is the father of us all* (Jew and Gentile).

**Verse 17.** *(As it is written, I have made thee a father of many nations,) before him whom he believed, even God, who quickeneth the dead and calleth those things which be not as though they were.* The passage from which the apostle quotes is Genesis 17:4-5, but it is also helpful to consider Genesis 17:16 and 20, 25:1-34, and 28:3.

To rightly grasp the magnitude Paul intended by his reference to Genesis 17:4-5, it is essential to recall the events of Genesis 17: 1-14. The Lord appeared to the prophet Abraham when he was 99 years of age and told him: *I am God Almighty; walk before me and be thou perfect. And I will make a covenant between me and thee* (Gen. 17:1-2). The passage reveals a covenant was about to be made between God and Abraham, showing it was the land covenant with circumcision as the sign of it. Later, the Lord gave

# Commentary on Romans

the sacrifice of the covenant, which is addressed in verse 19. It is essential to remember God promised Abraham through his seed, all the families of the earth should be blessed. Peter quoted this promise and declared it to indeed be a covenant as recorded in Acts 3:25.

"That was not the covenant that God proposed to make with Abraham in Gen. 17:2. When this covenant was proposed, "Abraham fell on his face: and God talked with him, saying, As for me, behold, my covenant is with thee and thou shalt be the father of a multitude of nations." "My covenant is with thee"— that is, he had already covenanted with him to make him a father of a multitude of nations. Hence, he says in the next verse that "the father of a multitude of nations have I made thee." He had already constituted him a father of many nations. This shows that the covenant to make him the father of a multitude of nations, which was made in Ur of the Chaldees, was distinct from the land and circumcision covenant"[20] [sic].

This distinction should cause one to better grasp the meaning of the rest of the verse: *and calleth those things which be not as though they were.* It is well to realize the use of the prolepsis here. A *prolepsis* is a hermeneutical figure of speech in which there is a representation or assumption of a future act or development as if it presently existed or was already accomplished.

**Verse 18.** *Who against hope believed in hope, that he might become the father of many nations, according to that which was spoken, So shall thy seed be.* The promise God gave to Abraham, *so shall thy seed be,* was given to Abraham before the birth of Ishmael.

Sarah was barren; hence, could not bear Abraham a son. However, Abraham in hope believed in the hope God gave him; he also trusted he would beget a son with Sara in spite of her barrenness.

**Verse 19.** *And being not weak in faith, he considered not his own body now dead, when he was about an hundred years old, neither yet the deadness of Sara's womb.* Abraham's faith and

---
[20] Robertson L. Whiteside.

# Commentary on Romans

trust in God were strong. His faith was so strong that he gave no consideration whatsoever to the facts he and Sara were both past the age of procreation. Neither did Abraham give consideration to the deadness of Sara's womb.

Abraham's faith was a confident faith—one which well established his trust in the Lord. However, Abraham desired to know if God would secure the promise of the land.

*After these things the word of the Lord came unto Abram in a vision, saying, Fear not, Abram: I am thy shield and thy exceeding great reward. And Abram said, Lord God, what wilt thou give me, seeing I go childless and the steward of my house is this Eliezer of Damascus? And Abram said, Behold, to me thou hast given no seed: and, lo, one born in my house is mine heir. And, behold, the word of the Lord came unto him, saying, This shall not be thine heir; but he that shall come forth out of thine own bowels shall be thine heir. And he brought him forth abroad and said, Look now toward heaven and tell the stars, if thou be able to number them: and he said unto him, So shall thy seed be. And he believed in the Lord; and he counted it to him for righteousness. And he said unto him, I am the Lord that brought thee out of Ur of the Chaldees, to give thee this land to inherit it.* **And he said, Lord God, whereby shall I know that I shall inherit it?** *And he said unto him, Take me an heifer of three years old and a she goat of three years old and a ram of three years old and a turtledove and a young pigeon. And he took unto him all these and divided them in the midst and laid each piece one against another: but the birds divided he not. And when the fowls came down upon the carcasses, Abram drove them away. And when the sun was going down, a deep sleep fell upon Abram; and, lo, an horror of great darkness fell upon him. And he said unto Abram, Know of a surety that thy seed shall be a stranger in a land that is not theirs and shall serve them; and they shall afflict them four hundred years; And also that nation, whom they shall serve, will I judge: and afterward shall they come out*

## Commentary on Romans

> with great substance. And thou shalt go to thy fathers in peace; thou shalt be buried in a good old age. But in the fourth generation they shall come hither again: for the iniquity of the Amorites is not yet full. And it came to pass, that, when the sun went down and it was dark, behold a smoking furnace and a burning lamp that passed between those pieces. In the same day the Lord made a covenant with Abram, saying, Unto thy seed have I given this land, from the river of Egypt unto the great river, the river Euphrates (Gen. 15:1-18).

The passing between the sacrificed animals was a covenant ceremony of the time, sealing the promises of a covenant. If one of the parties of a covenant broke the covenant, the one who breached the covenant would be as the divided animals—that is, dead. Here God Himself walked between the divided sacrifice, as verse 17 shows. This custom is explained by the prophet Jeremiah.

> Therefore the word of the Lord came to Jeremiah from the Lord, saying, Thus saith the Lord, the God of Israel; I made a covenant with your fathers in the day that I brought them forth out of the land of Egypt, out of the house of bondmen, saying, hath been sold unto thee; and when he hath served thee six years, thou shalt let him go free from thee: but your fathers hearkened not unto me, neither inclined their ear. And ye were now turned and had done right in my sight, in proclaiming liberty every man to his neighbor; and ye had made a covenant before me in the house which is called by my name: But ye turned and polluted my name and caused every man his servant and every man his handmaid, whom ye had set at liberty at their pleasure, to return and brought them into subjection, to be unto you for servants and for handmaids. Therefore thus saith the Lord; Ye have not hearkened unto me, in proclaiming liberty, every one to his brother and every man to his neighbor: behold, I proclaim a liberty for you, saith the Lord, to the sword, to the pestilence and to the famine; and I will make you to be removed into all the kingdoms of the earth. And I will give the men

# Commentary on Romans

*that have transgressed my covenant, which have not performed the words of the covenant which they had made before me, when they cut the calf in twain and passed between the parts thereof, The princes of Judah and the princes of Jerusalem, the eunuchs and the priests and all the people of the land, which passed between the parts of the calf; I will even give them into the hand of their enemies and into the hand of them that seek their life: and their dead bodies shall be for meat unto the fowls of the heaven and to the beasts of the earth. And Zedekiah king of Judah and his princes will I give into the hand of their enemies and into the hand of them that seek their life and into the hand of the king of Babylon's army, which are gone up from you. Behold, I will command, saith the Lord and cause them to return to this city; and they shall fight against it and take it and burn it with fire: and I will make the cities of Judah a desolation without an inhabitant* (Jer. 34:12-22).

*And when the fowls came down upon the carcasses, Abram drove them away.* Genesis 15:11 has reference to the seriousness of the punishment God would put upon the man who broke a covenant between God and man. The one who broke the covenant would be as food for the fowls of the air. The apostle John makes use of this principle in the Revelation.

*And I saw an angel standing in the sun; and he cried with a loud voice, saying to all the fowls that fly in the midst of heaven, Come and gather yourselves together unto the supper of the great God; That ye may eat the flesh of kings and the flesh of captains and the flesh of mighty men and the flesh of horses and of them that sit on them and the flesh of all men, both free and bond, both small and great* (Rev. 19:17-18).

Abraham's chasing away of the fowls was the Patriarch's assurance to God that he was unwilling to break the covenant between them.

The Lord's presence is seen by Him passing between the two

# Commentary on Romans

parts of the sacrifice *when the sun went down and it was dark,* and when *a smoking furnace and a burning lamp passed...between those pieces* (Gen. 15:17).

God gave Abraham the sealing of the promise and covenant made between them when the sacrifice was offered. Circumcision was the *sign of the covenant* between the Lord and Abraham, but the event of Genesis 15:1-18 was the *sacrifice of the covenant* between the Lord and Abraham.

**Verses 20-22.** *He staggered not at the promise of God through unbelief; but was strong in faith, giving glory to God; And being fully persuaded that, what he had promised, he was able also to perform. And therefore it was imputed to him for righteousness.* That God declared Abraham righteous by his obedient faith is affirmed in no less than four separate occasions, covering a period of perhaps fifty years.

Paul was not writing to show the Jews how alien sinners were justified, but rather he was showing the Jewish converts their insistence the Gentiles had to keep the Law of Moses in conjunction with the gospel system was not at all the case. It is vital to keep in mind Paul was meeting the demands of the Judaizers.

Justification of the alien sinner *was not* Paul's topic. The issue Paul was addressing was whether a Christian was required to keep the Law of Moses in conjunction with the Law of Christ to be justified by God. Paul negated that Jewish dogma, showing throughout Abraham's whole life and service to God he was righteous because he had an obedient faith, not because he was a Jew or kept the Law of Moses.

**Verses 23-25.** *Now it was not written for his sake alone, that it was imputed to him; But for us also, to whom it shall be imputed, if we believe on him that raised up Jesus our Lord from the dead; Who was delivered for our offenses and was raised again for our justification.* Abraham's faith was reckoned and accounted unto him as righteousness, and was written for the sake of the Jewish converts. Just as it was the case with Abraham under the Patriarchal Law, and for the Jews under the Law of Moses, so it is with those under the Law of Christ. The faith of the

# Commentary on Romans

obedient believer will be reckoned unto him for righteousness. Men must believe in the resurrection of Christ as well as His death, for without His resurrection his death would have availed nothing. There must be a union of faith and works. Paul shows works without faith cannot save, and James shows faith without works is dead and is, therefore, worthless. *Ye see then how that by works a man is justified, and not by faith only. For as the body without the spirit is dead, so faith without works is dead also* (Jas. 2:24, 26).

## Romans 5:1-21

*1 Therefore being justified by faith, we have peace with God through our Lord Jesus Christ. 2 By whom also we have access by faith into this grace wherein we stand and rejoice in hope of the glory of God. 3 And not only so, but we glory in tribulations also: knowing that tribulation worketh patience; 4 And patience, experience; and experience, hope:5 And hope maketh not ashamed; because the love of God is shed abroad in our hearts by the Holy Ghost which is given unto us. 6 For when we were yet without strength, in due time Christ died for the ungodly. 7 For scarcely for a righteous man will one die: yet peradventure for a good man some would even dare to die. 8 But God commendeth his love toward us, in that, while we were yet sinners, Christ died for us. 9 Much more then, being now justified by his blood, we shall be saved from wrath through him. 10 For if, when we were enemies, we were reconciled to God by the death of his Son, much more, being reconciled, we shall be saved by his life. 11 And not only so, but we also joy in God through our Lord Jesus Christ, by whom we have now received the atonement. 12 Wherefore, as by one man sin entered into the world and death by sin; and so death passed upon all men, for that all have sinned: 13 (For until the Law sin was in the world: but sin is not imputed when there is no Law. 14 Nevertheless death reigned from Adam to Moses, even over them that had not sinned after the similitude of Adam's transgression, who is the figure of him that was to come. 15 But not*

# Commentary on Romans

*as the offence, so also is the free gift. For if through the offence of one many be dead, much more the grace of God and the gift by grace, which is by one man, Jesus Christ, hath abounded unto many. 16 And not as it was by one that sinned, so is the gift: for the judgment was by one to condemnation, but the free gift is of many offenses unto justification. 17 For if by one man's offence death reigned by one; much more they which receive abundance of grace and of the gift of righteousness shall reign in life by one, Jesus Christ.) 18 Therefore as by the offence of one judgment came upon all men to condemnation; even so by the righteousness of one the free gift came upon all men unto justification of life. 19 For as by one man's disobedience many were made sinners, so by the obedience of one shall many be made righteous. 20 Moreover the Law entered, that the offence might abound. But where sin abounded, grace did much more abound: 21 That as sin hath reigned unto death, even so might grace reign through righteousness unto eternal life by Jesus Christ our Lord.*

**Verse 1.** *Being therefore justified by faith, we have peace with God through our Lord Jesus Christ.* Literally, the passage means, *Having been justified by faith, we have peace with God.* The Greek language was exact in the use of participles. In English one would say, *Mounting a horse, he rode away,* but the Greeks would say, *Having mounted a horse, he rode away.* The mounting preceded the riding. It is imperative to attune ourselves to this structure. Paul shows in this language justification precedes peace with God.

To justify a person is to pronounce him free from guilt or blame. When one, through faith, puts sin out of his heart and life by submission to the will of God, he is forgiven. He is then declared by God to be righteous. Guilt and blame are no longer attached to him—he is justified.

It is evident in the structure of Paul's language; righteousness and justification are one and the same. Paul argues that one is made righteous only through obedient faith. He then added to

## Commentary on Romans

his argument, saying: *Having therefore been justified by faith, we have peace with God.* Paul insists that men are made righteous by an obedient faith in Christ instead of by the works of the Law of Moses. In other words, one becomes righteous by obedience to the Gospel of Christ rather than by obedience to the Old Law.

The apostle had demonstrated faith in Christ means fully accepting and being obedient to the will of God and Christ. Those who seek to establish the false doctrine man is justified by *faith only* err grossly. The phrase *justified by faith* does not mean one is justified by a verbal confession of faith, or faith only. A *faith only* religion eliminates everything which is not faith. *Faith only* eliminates prayer, it excludes obedience, it refuses hope, it removes hearing the Word of God, it severs one from receiving any knowledge of the Word of God. A meal of potatoes only eliminates everything other than potatoes. Just as *potatoes only* means only potatoes, so *faith only* means only faith.

A proper exegesis of every passage requires the student to understand the use and meaning intended by the inspired author. Then and only then can one deduce the intent of the subject passage. It is not difficult to understand why Paul makes use of of the phrase in question. Paul uses the phrase *by faith* more than all other writers of the New Testament. Observe the following examples in Hebrews 11.

**1.** *By faith Abel offered unto God a more excellent sacrifice than Cain* (v. 4). Every step Abel took and every lick that he struck in preparing the altar, the wood and the sacrifice were included in the phrase *by faith.*

**2.** *By faith Noah, being warned of God concerning as yet, moved with godly fear, prepared an ark to the saving of his house* (v. 7). The task of building the ark required 120 years to complete; it was all done *by faith.* All the labor and toil expended in building that ark are included in the phrase *by faith.* It was a working faith by which Noah built that ark. Unless one is willing to affirm the ark stood completed the moment Noah believed, one should not contend a person is justified the moment he believes.

**3.** *By faith the walls of Jericho fell down* (v. 30). Here the phrase

# Commentary on Romans

*by faith* includes thirteen trips around the walls of the City of Jericho. The walls did not fall by *faith only*.

**4.** Through faith also Sara herself received strength to conceive seed and was delivered of a child when she was past age, because she judged him faithful who had promised. Therefore sprang there even of one and him as good as dead, so many as the stars of the sky in multitude and as the sand which is by the sea shore innumerable (Heb. 11:11-12). Isaac was not conceived by *faith only*.

**5.** *But the angel said unto him, Fear not, Zacharias: for thy prayer is heard; and thy wife Elisabeth shall bear thee a son and thou shalt call his name John* (Lk. 1:13). John was not conceived by *faith only*.

So also is our deliverance from sin. The phrase *by faith* includes our baptism, which is preceded by belief, repentance, and confession of Christ.

Paul made the same argument in Galatians, saying, *For ye are all sons of God, through faith, in Jesus Christ. For as many of you as were baptized into Christ did put on Christ* (Gal. 3:26-27). They were children of God by faith in Christ because their faith led them to be baptized into Christ.

These illustrations confirm faith is taking God at His Word and doing all things God commands. Taking God at His Word and doing what he said, Noah built an ark. Taking God at His Word means one must do what He tells one to do. Doing so results in one's justification.

James was correct when he wrote, *faith without works is dead being alone* (Jas. 2:17). Those who refuse to do what God commands will not acquire justification from Him. There is more rebellion enveloped in the heart of the one who refuses to comply with all of God's will than faith.

Peter established that proper faith demands obedience. *Unto you therefore which believe he is precious: but unto them which be disobedient, the stone which the builders disallowed, the*

# Commentary on Romans

*same is made the head of the corner* (I Pet. 2:7). It is of profound interest Peter contrasts belief to disobedience. A faith that is a valid faith is an obedient faith. Valid faith compels one to be in compliance to all of the Lord's commands.

Men may feel compelled to comply with many things God commanded—not because God commanded them, but because certain things are agreeable to them. Obedience must be in compliance to God's will and executed from the heart. Paul would later write: *But God be thanked, that ye were the servants of sin, but ye have obeyed from the heart that form of doctrine which was delivered you* (Rom. 6:17).

When someone feels compelled to refrain from lies because he agrees they are bad or because he believes telling them is morally wrong does not mean said individual is in compliance to God's will. The one who refrains from lies because it is God's will is the one who is obedient to God. A compulsion to do right things based upon one's own volition is one who complies with his own will and not the Lord's. The one who feels compelled to do right because God said so is doing God's will—because God said so. Phillip declared obedience must come from a heart which conforms to and complies with God's will (Acts 8:37).

**Verse 2.** *By whom also we have access by faith into this grace wherein we stand and rejoice in hope of the glory of God.* The words *by whom* have reference to Jesus Christ. Having access into grace through Christ was not an attractive message to the Jews. The Jews hardly desired to surrender the Law of Moses and the covenant of circumcision.

Paul, in the Second Corinthian Epistle, was faced with the same matter when he addressed Jewish converts there. Consider the apostles' address to the church at Corinth wherein he wrote: *But if the ministration of death, written and engraven in stones, was glorious, so that the children of Israel could not steadfastly behold the face of Moses for the glory of his countenance; which glory was to be done away: How shall not the ministration of the spirit be rather glorious? For if the ministration of condemnation be glory, much more doth the ministration of righteousness exceed in glory. For even that which was made glorious had no*

# Commentary on Romans

*glory in this respect, by reason of the glory that excelleth. For if that which is done away was glorious, much more that which remaineth is glorious* (II Cor. 3:7-11).

Unto the church at Galatia Paul wrote:

> *Wherefore then serveth the Law? It was added because of transgressions, till the seed should come to whom the promise was made; and it was ordained by angels in the hand of a mediator. Now a mediator is not a mediator of one, but God is one. Is the Law then against the promises of God? God forbid: for if there had been a Law given which could have given life, verily righteousness should have been by the Law. But the scripture hath concluded all under sin, that the promise by faith of Jesus Christ might be given to them that believe. But before faith came, we were kept under the Law, shut up unto the faith which should afterwards be revealed. Wherefore the Law was our schoolmaster to bring us unto Christ, that we might be justified by faith. But after that faith is come, we are no longer under a schoolmaster. For ye are all the children of God by faith in Christ Jesus. For as many of you as have been baptized into Christ have put on Christ. There is neither Jew nor Greek, there is neither bond nor free, there is neither male nor female: for ye are all one in Christ Jesus. And if ye be Christ's, then are ye Abraham's seed and heirs according to the promise* (Gal. 3:19-29).

Other examples can be cited, but these clearly show the Jews were deeply steeped in the keeping of the Law of Moses and the covenant of circumcision. The apostle spent no little time refuting their craving.

Paul continued preaching the cessation of the Law of Moses and the covenant of circumcision. He was the best human agent God could have chosen to do so. As a Pharisee, a staunch defender, teacher, and master of the Law of Moses—who better was there to serve as God's agent for the Jewish converts? Who was better equipped to relate to the emotions of the Jews?

# Commentary on Romans

As the apostle went about negating Judaizing teachers, he was doing as he was instructed by the council of the apostles and elders at Jerusalem, as recorded in Acts 15. Remember, it was the inspired decision of those apostles and elders to write a letter and send it by the hands of Paul and Barnabas. In the close of that apostolic letter, they wrote: *Forasmuch as we have heard, that certain which went out from us have troubled you with words, subverting your souls, saying, Ye must be circumcised and keep the Law: to whom we gave no such commandment: It seemed good unto us, being assembled with one accord, to send chosen men unto you with our beloved Barnabas and Paul, Men that have hazarded their lives for the name of our Lord Jesus Christ* (Acts 15:24-26).

The phrase, *wherein we stand*, was not a little difficulty for the Jewish converts. No longer were the Jews able to stand in the strength of the Law of Moses nor in the covenant of circumcision. The Law was fulfilled in Christ, and it was only in Him where the Jews could *rejoice in hope of the glory of God.*

**Verse 3.** *And not only so, but we glory in tribulations also: knowing that tribulation worketh patience.* Not only was it the case the Jews had access to God only through the grace of Christ once the church was established and should have gloried therein, they were to glory in their tribulations as well.
The *tribulations* of which the apostle speaks are the *tribulations* which came upon Jews obedient to the Gospel of Christ from unbelieving Jews. Here the word *patience* means "cheerful or hopeful endurance, constancy: an enduring patience; that is, a patient continuance."

**Verses 4-5.** *And patience, experience; and experience, hope: And hope maketh not ashamed; because the love of God is shed abroad in our hearts by the Holy Ghost which is given unto us.* The tribulation through which Jewish converts were then going worked patience for them. The word *worketh* is defined as "to work fully; that is, accomplish; by implication to finish, fashion: cause, do (deed), perform, or to work out." As tribulation works unto patience, so patience works unto experience. Experience in turn works toward hope. Hope removed the shame embellished on the obedient Jews by disobedient ones.

# Commentary on Romans

The reason why such shame was removed from the obedient Jews was *because the love of God is shed abroad in their hearts.* But just how was the love of God shed abroad? The apostle answers the query with the following phrase. It was *by the Holy Ghost which is given unto them.*

The Holy Ghost given unto them was not a *personal non-miraculous indwelling* as many contend. The phrase *non-miraculous personal indwelling of the Holy Ghost* occurs no where in the Scripture! The Holy Ghost that was given was a miraculous gift of the Holy Ghost for the confirmation of the Word of the Gospel.

It is imperative to keep in mind the time frame in which this letter to the church at Rome was authored. It was written during the time of inspiration and miracles in the New Testament church. If one realizes, the four works of the Holy Ghost were: 1) to glorify Christ [Jno. 16:14]; 2) to reveal truth [Jno. 16:13]; 3) to reprove men of sin [Jno. 16:8]; and, 4) to confirm the revealed Word [Dan. 9:26-27], then it is not at all difficult to understand the use of the phrase, *by the Holy Ghost which is given unto them.* By *the Holy Ghost* simply means through a miraculously endowed spiritual gift. *The Holy Spirit has never non-miraculously dwelt in anyone!* We shall address this subject later.

**Verse 6:** *For while we were yet weak, in due season Christ died for the ungodly.* Perhaps it is more clearly stated this way: when we were weak, Christ died for us. The language used by the apostle here refers to man's helplessness and hopelessness without Christ's death. Before the death of Christ, all men were condemned sinners; none had a means of escape from sin and the penalty thereof. However, the death of Christ provided the way of escape and removed man's hopelessness. Christ had to die to facilitate man's salvation.

Christ died in *due time*—that is, when the scheme of redemption developed and unfolded as it was revealed by the prophets. Paul made this matter clear to the church of Galatia when he wrote: *But when the fullness of the time was come, God sent forth his Son, made of a woman, made under the Law, To redeem them that were under the Law, that we might receive the adoption of sons* (Gal. 4:4-5).

# Commentary on Romans

**Verses 7-8.** *For scarcely for a righteous man will one die: yet peradventure for a good man some would even dare to die. But God commendeth his love toward us, in that, while we were yet sinners, Christ died for us.* The surrendering of one's life for another is indeed rare and uncommon. While such has been performed by a few, it remains far from the norm. It is not hard to understand that which is intended by the apostle. In the cases of both a good and righteous man, as Paul narrated, it is understood the quality of those described are men of good value.

However, the apostle sets forth the antithesis of such exceptional behavior in this passage. While man was not only lacking righteousness and goodness so far as Deity is concerned, Christ died for the ungodly, for the unrighteous, yea, even for those not at all good. The reason for Christ's willingness to die for ungodly men was seated in the Father's love for mankind. *For God so loved the world, that he gave his only begotten Son, that whosoever believeth in him should not perish, but have everlasting life. For God sent not his Son into the world to condemn the world; but that the world through him might be saved* (Jno. 3:16-17). It was God who *commendeth his love toward us, in that, while we were yet sinners,* which prompted Christ to die *for the ungodly.*

To die for a good man is great love, but Jesus died for sinners to save those, who in all things, *obey Him* (Heb. 5:8-9). Christ died for those who were His enemies while they were His enemies. To die for those who hate and abuse us is love supreme. He died for those who mocked Him, for those who scourged Him, for those who crucified Him, and for those shed His blood.

**Verse 9.** *Much more then, being now justified by his blood, we shall be saved from wrath through him.* Christ died for us while we were enemies. Only the death of the Son of God can bring about man's justification. It is only through the blood of Christ and man's obedience to the Father's will by which man can acquire Divine justification. Once justified by the Father, through the blood of the Son, man becomes a friend of the Father and the Son.

**Verse 10.** *For if, when we were enemies, we were reconciled to*

# Commentary on Romans

*God by the death of his Son, much more, being reconciled, we shall be saved by his life.* Verses 8 and 9 receive emphasis in this verse. Before the death of Christ occurred, men were enemies of God, but through His death men may be reconciled to God. The death of Christ provided the only way through which men can be reconciled to the Father.

**Verse 11.** *And not only so, but we also joy in God through our Lord Jesus Christ, by whom we have now received the atonement.* We rejoice in God, and we rejoice in the glory of His being—the perfection of His attributes. We should also rejoice in what He is to us and what He has done for us. These great benefits and blessings come to us through obedience to our Lord Jesus Christ through *whom we have now received the atonement.* It is only through obedience to the Lord Jesus Christ that men can be reconciled to God.

The remaining portion of this chapter is considered truly difficult by most. Again, we must remember Paul was still setting forth the blessings of the Gospel, and that God now justifies men through the Gospel. The apostle is still addressing Jewish converts who needed to understand God now justifies man through the Gospel of Christ, and not through the Law of Moses.

Persistence in reminding us that Paul is addressing the Jewish converts in chapters 4 through 11 is always needed. When the student keeps the context of the inspired text within the framework in which the author places his arguments, it is far less difficult to ascertain the principles and intent of the inspired author.

**Verse 12.** *Wherefore, as by one man sin entered into the world and death by sin; and so death passed upon all men, for that all have sinned.* Calvinism teaches all men have inherited Adam's sin and are born sinners; however, this passage teaches the exact reverse. Calvinists believe Adam's sin is passed upon all men. However, the apostle plainly reveals: that which has been passed upon all men from Adam is not the *guilt* of Adam's sin, but rather the *consequence* of Adam's sin. While Adam suffered spiritual death because of his sin, Adam also suffered the consequence of physical death. It is not spiritual death which has been passed upon all men because of Adam's transgression, but

# Commentary on Romans

rather the consequence of physical death.

Ezekiel wrote: *The soul that sinneth, it shall die. The son shall not bear the iniquity of the father, neither shall the father bear the iniquity of the son: the righteousness of the righteous shall be upon him, and the wickedness of the wicked shall be upon him* (Eze. 18:20).

Adam had not yet eaten of the tree of life before he partook of the tree of the knowledge of good and evil. God prevented him from doing so because it would have allowed Adam to be a perpetual being.

> *And the Lord God said, Behold, the man is become as one of us, to know good and evil: and now, lest he put forth his hand, and take also of the tree of life, and eat, and live for ever: Therefore the Lord God sent him forth from the garden of Eden, to till the ground from whence he was taken. So he drove out the man; and he placed at the east of the garden of Eden Cherubims, and a flaming sword which turned every way, to keep the way of the tree of life* (Gen. 3:22-24).

Because God denied Adam and Eve access to the tree of life, physical death, from that point *was passed upon all men.* It was *not* spiritual death, but physical.

Calvinists teach the doctrine of inherited sin from their gross ignorance of Genesis 3:22-24 and Psalm 51:5. *Behold, I was shapen in iniquity; and in sin did my mother conceive me.* Psalm 51 was authored by David after his sin of adultery with Bathsheba. David was of a contrite heart and sought God's blessing and forgiveness. He strongly desired to go to the tabernacle and offer a sacrifice for his sin of adultery with the wife of Uriah. However, he knew the Law of Moses prohibited him from doing so. Calvinists would do well to understand the background of Psalm 51. Doing so allows for the proper exegesis of the text.

David knew that Moses had written: *A bastard shall not enter into the congregation of the Lord; even to his tenth generation shall*

# Commentary on Romans

he not enter into the congregation of the Lord (Deut. 23:2). David knew that his lineage which went back to Pharez (one of a pair of twins born of Judah and Tamar (who were not married), which prohibited him from entering the congregation of the Lord. David's lineage is recorded for us in Genesis 38:12-30:

> And in process of time the daughter of Shuah Judah's wife died; and Judah was comforted, and went up unto his sheepshearers to Timnath, he and his friend Hirah the Adullamite. And it was told Tamar, saying, Behold thy father in law goeth up to Timnath to shear his sheep. And she put her widow's garments off from her, and covered her with a vail, and wrapped herself, and sat in an open place, which is by the way to Timnath; for she saw that Shelah was grown, and she was not given unto him to wife. When Judah saw her, he thought her to be an harlot; because she had covered her face. And he turned unto her by the way, and said, Go to, I pray thee, let me come in unto thee; (for he knew not that she was his daughter in law.) And she said, What wilt thou give me, that thou mayest come in unto me? And he said, I will send thee a kid from the flock. And she said, Wilt thou give me a pledge, till thou send it? And he said, What pledge shall I give thee? And she said, Thy signet, and thy bracelets, and thy staff that is in thine hand. And he gave it her, and came in unto her, and she conceived by him. And she arose, and went away, and laid by her vail from her, and put on the garments of her widowhood. And Judah sent the kid by the hand of his friend the Adullamite, to receive his pledge from the woman's hand: but he found her not. Then he asked the men of that place, saying, Where is the harlot, that was openly by the way side? And they said, There was no harlot in this place. And he returned to Judah, and said, I cannot find her; and also the men of the place said, that there was no harlot in this place. And Judah said, Let her take it to her, lest we be shamed: behold, I sent this kid, and thou hast not found her. And it came to pass about three months after, that it was told Judah, saying, Tamar thy daughter in law hath played the harlot;

# Commentary on Romans

*and also, behold, she is with child by whoredom. And Judah said, Bring her forth, and let her be burnt. When she was brought forth, she sent to her father in law, saying, By the man, whose these are, am I with child: and she said, Discern, I pray thee, whose are these, the signet, and bracelets, and staff. And Judah acknowledged them, and said, She hath been more righteous than I; because that I gave her not to Shelah my son. And he knew her again no more. And it came to pass in the time of her travail, that, behold, twins were in her womb. And it came to pass, when she travailed, that the one put out his hand: and the midwife took and bound upon his hand a scarlet thread, saying, This came out first. And it came to pass, as he drew back his hand, that, behold, his brother came out: and she said, How hast thou broken forth? this breach be upon thee: therefore his name was called Pharez. And afterward came out his brother, that had the scarlet thread upon his hand: and his name was called Zerah.*

In Ruth 4:18-22, the genealogy states: *Now these are the generations of Pharez: Pharez begat Hezron, And Hezron begat Ram, and Ram begat Amminadab, And Amminadab begat Nahshon, and Nahshon begat Salmon, And Salmon begat Boaz, and Boaz begat Obed, And Obed begat Jesse, and Jesse begat David.* In this record ten generations are listed. David was of that tenth generation, and because of such he was prohibited from going to tabernacle of the congregation in order to offer a sacrifice unto the Lord. The Law of Deuteronomy 23:2 prohibited him from doing so.

Of those recorded in the inspired record of Genesis 5, it is stated of each of them they all died, with the exception of Enoch whom God took. *For it is appointed unto men once to die* after which comes the judgment (cf. Heb. 9:27). All men will die a physical death, except for those of who remain living at the second coming of Christ. *For this we say unto you by the word of the Lord, that we which are alive and remain unto the coming of the Lord shall not prevent* [go before, DHC] *them which are asleep. Then we which are alive and remain shall be caught up together with them in the clouds, to meet the Lord in the air: and so shall we*

# Commentary on Romans

*ever be with the Lord* (I Thes. 4:15, 17).

Therefore, it is the case *death passed upon all men.* It is the consequence of physical death which has been passed upon all men not Adam's sin. This is a passage from which Calvinism, in part, acquires its false doctrine of inherited sin; when it reality, it is one of the very passages which refutes the false doctrine.

Of Adam and his sin Paul speaks of it merely to draw a contrast between the effects and consequences of what Adam's sin did and the effects of what Christ did. Paul was demonstrating for Jewish converts how the Gospel of Christ more than overcomes the consequences of Adam's sin.

**Verse 13.** *For until the Law sin was in the world: but sin is not imputed when there is no Law.* The question which must be asked here is, "What *Law* does the apostle intend?" There are but three plausible considerations: the Patriarchal Law, the Mosaical Law, the Law of Christ.

If one adheres to the argument Paul was speaking of the Patriarchal Law, then the passage should read: *For until the Patriarchal Law came sin was in the world.* Such a position suggests before God gave the Patriarchal Law, sin existed. Further, it must be concluded once the Patriarchal Law was given to Adam, then sin had the penalty of death removed. Such is not the case.

If the apostle was speaking of the Mosaical Law, then it must be the case once the Law of Moses was given then the penalty of death was removed at that set time. However, when one considers the Law of which Paul spoke to be the Law of Christ, then we properly conclude the penalty of death was removed through the Law of Christ.

**Verse 14.** *Nevertheless death reigned from Adam to Moses, even over them that had not sinned after the similitude of Adam's transgression, who is the figure of him that was to come.* It needs to be asked, "What is the *death* which *reigned from Adam to Moses?"*

We yet again emphasize Paul has been speaking of physical

# Commentary on Romans

and not spiritual death, which reigned from the time of Adam unto the end of the Law of Moses. It is also essential to keep in mind whom the apostle was addressing—the Jewish converts. He continued to do so through chapter 11.

The passage should be understood this way: *For until the Law of Christ came sin was in the world: but sin against Christ's Law was not imputed to anyone until the Law of Christ was given; Nevertheless physical death reigned from Adam, the father of the patriarchs, to the completion and fulfillment of the Law of Moses, even over them that had not sinned after the similitude of Adam's transgression, who is the figure of him that was to come.* The sin *after the similitude of Adam's transgression* was his having eaten of the forbidden fruit. None have been guilty of that sin except than Adam and Eve. The phrase, *who is the figure of him that was to come,* is inspiration's declaration that Adam serves as an anti-type of Christ as well as an ante-type. Proof is seen in verses 17 and 18 (see comments below).

**Verse 15.** *But not as the offense, so also is the free gift. For if through the offense of one many be dead, much more the grace of God and the gift by grace, which is by one man, Jesus Christ, hath abounded unto many.* Spiritual life came through Christ as well as the release of spiritual condemnation. It did not come through the Law of Moses as the Jews contended. Again, it is essential to recall the apostle is addressing the Jewish converts who insisted it was only through the Law of Moses man could acquire righteousness with God. We have continued to press this point and shall continue doing so.

Without obedience to, and keeping the Law of Christ the Jews were spiritually dead. Paul further affirmed such when he said; *For the Law of the Spirit of life in Christ Jesus hath made me free from the Law of sin and death* (Rom. 8:2). The Law of sin and death as used in this passage is the Mosaical Law. For the Jew to continue in the Mosaical Law was sinful and led to spiritual death.

**Verse 16.** *And not as it was by one that sinned, so is the gift: for the judgment was by one to condemnation, but the free gift is of many offenses unto justification.* Consider Paul's argument in

# Commentary on Romans

his epistle to the church at Galatia. *Is the Law then against the promises of God? God forbid: for if there had been a Law given which could have given life, verily righteousness should have been by the Law. But the scripture hath concluded all under sin, that the promise by faith of Jesus Christ might be given to them that believe. But before faith came, we were kept under the Law, shut up unto the faith which should afterwards be revealed. Wherefore the Law was our schoolmaster to bring us unto Christ, that we might be justified by faith. But after that faith is come, we are no longer under a schoolmaster* (Gal. 3:21-25).

**Verse 17.** *For as by one man's disobedience many were made sinners, so by the obedience of one shall many be made righteous.* Calvinists cling closely to this passage, insisting Adam's sin and the guilt thereof has been passed to all men. However, the passage in no way affirms *all* were made sinners. First of all, the passage plainly states *many were made sinners.* If it is the case *all were made sinners*, having inherited Adam's sin and the guilt thereof, then it must follow *all have been made righteous* by Jesus Christ.

There must be an equal utilization to both phrases of the passage. Because the Calvinist defines *many* as *all,* in applying Adam's sin and guilt to *all men*, then the application must be likewise applied to the righteousness being applied to all men. The Calvinist, however, denies the righteousness of Christ is passed unto all men. They exchange *many* for *all* when dealing with Adam's sin, yet refrain from changing the word *many* to *all* so far as the righteousness of Christ is concerned.

Calvinism teaches Adam's sin has been passed unto all men, but then insists the righteousness of Christ is only passed unto some. Calvinists teach those unto whom the righteousness of Christ is passed is only upon those identified as *the elect.* A gross misunderstanding of what the Scriptures mean regarding the *elect* exists among most in the religious world. The Scriptures speak of *God's elect* in only two New Testament passages, which shall be later addressed.

**Verse 18.** *Therefore as by the offense of one judgment came upon all men to condemnation; even so by the righteousness of*

## Commentary on Romans

*one the free gift came upon all men unto justification of life.* Paul asked the church at Rome: *Who shall lay any thing to the charge of God's elect? It is God that justifieth* (Rom. 8:33). The words *God's elect* do not refer to men. Rather the phrase refers to the system of faith by which God has elected to save man.

Second, the apostle wrote: *Paul, a servant of God and an apostle of Jesus Christ, according to the faith of God's elect and the acknowledging of the truth which is after godliness* (Titus 1:1). Just as it is the case that *God's elect* refers to the system of faith by which God elected to save man in the Romans' passage, so it is the case here. There is a vast difference between the election of a man and the election of a plan. *God elected a plan* by which to save men, *He did not elect some men* for salvation. God chose to save those who choose to obey the plan He *elected.*

Peter wrote: *The Lord is not slack concerning his promise, as some men count slackness; but is longsuffering to us-ward, not willing that any should perish, but that all should come to repentance* (II Pet. 3:9). Luke wrote; *And the times of this ignorance God winked at; but now commandeth all men every where to repent* (Acts 17:30). Luke does not in any way suggest God winked at ignorance. What Luke wrote is God winked *at the times* of ignorance. God has never winked at sin nor ignorance of it. The Jews were to offer sacrifices for sins committed unwittingly (cf. Lev. 4:2, 13, 27; Num. 15:24, 25, and 27). God has never winked at sin nor ignorance of it and never will.

**Verse 19.** *For as by one man's disobedience many were made sinners, so by the obedience of one shall many be made righteous.* God would be both unjust and unmerciful to insist all men to come to repentance with no intention of issuing to them a pardon from sin except unto those He had already *elected.*

Additionally, the Lord's mercilessness and unjustness would be further compounded for His having *commanded all men everywhere to repent.* Why issue the command for all men to repent if all penitent and obedient men are not going to receive the promise of pardon?

**Verse 20.** *Moreover the Law entered, that the offense might*

# Commentary on Romans

*abound. But where sin abounded, grace did much more abound.* This passage need not be difficult. Regardless of which Law is under consideration in this passage, it needs to be understood God's Law *entered* into man's life; that entering Law revealed sin to be sin and offensive toward God.

As mentioned in verse 13, there are only three possible Laws which can be considered here: the Patriarchal, the Mosaical, or the Law of Christ. One must keep the context of the apostle in mind. Paul is still addressing Jewish converts. The Jews needed constant reminders that the Law of Christ *entered* the world at the time God appointed. Paul declared; *when the fullness of the time was come, God sent forth his Son* (Gal. 4:4).

God's full grace entered the world through Jesus Christ, not by the Law of Moses. John, declared of Christ: *He came unto his own and his own received him not. But as many as received him, to them gave he power to become the sons of God, even to them that believe on his name: Which were born, not of blood, nor of the will of the flesh, nor of the will of man, but of God. And the Word was made flesh and dwelt among us, (and we beheld his glory, the glory as of the only begotten of the Father,) full of grace and truth. John bare witness of him and cried, saying, This was he of whom I spake, He that cometh after me is preferred before me: for he was before me. And of his fullness have all we received and grace for grace. For the Law was given by Moses, but grace and truth came by Jesus Christ* (Jno. 1:11-17).

Luke recorded; *the Law and the prophets were until John: since that time the kingdom of God is preached and every man presseth into it* (Lk. 16:16). Jesus, in His conversation with the Pharisees, clearly revealed the Law of Moses was to be done away with once the Kingdom of God was established. The grace of God brought salvation through Jesus Christ and not through the Law of Moses. That God's grace was extended to all men through Jesus Christ, and not through Moses, was a difficult and thorny challenge for the Jews, hard to be received.

Paul later wrote that *the grace of God that bringeth salvation hath appeared to all men* (Titus 2:11). It is through Jesus Christ grace is acquired not through the Mosaical Law. Yet again, em-

## Commentary on Romans

phasis is made, the audience to whom the apostle wrote included Jewish converts. Keeping such in mind alleviates the difficulties of the passage.

**Verse 21.** *That as sin hath reigned unto death, even so might grace reign through righteousness unto eternal life by Jesus Christ our Lord.* How did sin reign? Sin reigned with the power of death; that is, *unto death.* Paul wrote to the church at Corinth: *the sting of death is sin; and the strength of sin is the Law. But thanks be to God, which giveth us the victory through our Lord Jesus Christ* (I Cor. 15:56-57). Through Jesus Christ comes the victory over spiritual death. Further, only through the power of Christ (that is, through His reign) is there victory over physical death. Neither was accomplished through the Law of Moses.

*Even so, might grace rein through righteousness unto eternal life by Jesus Christ our Lord.* The righteousness unto eternal life is ruled by the system of grace established by Jesus Christ. Paul had much work in convincing the Jews it was through Jesus Christ eternal life was gained, rather than through the Mosaical Law or through the covenant of circumcision.

How does grace reign? It does so through *righteousness.* What is the *righteousness* through which it reigns? The *righteousness* through which grace reigns is the now present system of faith by which God declares man righteous. That system is the Gospel system of Jesus Christ, not the Mosaical system as the Jews contended.

The apostle now begins to more aggressively address the Jewish converts. When one keeps in the forefront of his thinking the Jewish converts were Paul's targeted audience, the flow of his arguments is better navigated. The greatest difficulty students have in the study of any book of the Scriptures is to keep the context of every given subject within the framework and purpose for which it was written. Once such becomes one's second nature to do so, difficult passages become less challenging.

### Romans 6:1-2

*1 What shall we say then? Shall we continue in sin,*

# Commentary on Romans

*that grace may abound? 2 God forbid. How shall we, that are dead to sin, live any longer therein?*

**Verse 1.** *What shall we say then? Shall we continue in sin, that grace may abound?* It is important to inquire as to what the *sin* is under consideration here. Most conclude the *sin* under consideration is sin in general. Again, we remind the reader, Paul is *still* addressing Jewish converts, showing the New Testament system of Christ—the Gospel system, had replaced the Law of Moses. To remain under the Mosaical Law was sin. Thus, the *sin* under consideration here is the *sin* of remaining under or returning to the Old Law. Paul had been addressing the fact the Jews were not to intertwine the Old Law of Moses, and the New Law of Christ, as many Judaizing teachers insisted.

Twice inspiration set forth the same argument in the Hebrew epistle. First, the record states; *For if we sin willfully after that we have received the knowledge of the truth, there remaineth no more sacrifice for sins* (Heb. 10:26). The willful sin of this passage is the willful sin of returning to the Old Law. Second, the Hebrew author declared: *For it is impossible for those who were once enlightened and have tasted of the heavenly gift and were made partakers of the Holy Ghost and have tasted the good word of God and the powers of the world to come, If they shall fall away, to renew them again unto repentance; seeing they crucify to themselves the Son of God afresh and put him to an open shame* (Heb. 6:4-6).

The Jews who were converted to the Gospel of Christ, but succumbed to Judaizing teachers by returning to the Old Law of Moses, no longer had an acceptable sacrifice for sin. The meaning of verse 6 is; *If they (converted Jews) shall fall away,* from the Law of Christ, it would be impossible under the Old Law, *to renew them again unto repentance,* under the Old Law.

**Verse 2.** The phrase, *shall we continue in sin*, of verse 1 means shall we, the Jewish converts, continue under the Old Law that the grace of the New Law of Christ may abound? The apostle's answer is absolute, pointed and brief. *God forbid.*

Though the reply was brief, it carried much weight. The apostle

## Commentary on Romans

intended the Jews to understand it is God, not him, who forbade the Jews to remain under the Old Law. The Mosaical Law was no longer binding; God had authorized a new system. Again we note the epistles of Romans and Galatians are parallel epistles. Paul addressed this issues in both letters. Twice the apostle informed the Jewish converts of Galatia the Old Law was no longer endorsed of God, yet the Jews continued to champion it as though it was still authorized. Paul wrote for the benefit of the Jewish converts in Galatia: *For ye have heard of my conversation in time past in the Jews' religion, how that beyond measure I persecuted the church of God and wasted it: And profited in the Jews' religion above many my equals in mine own nation, being more exceedingly zealous of the traditions of my fathers* (Gal. 1: 13-14).

Knowing the context of these passages, it becomes clear what Paul intended the Jewish converts to understand when he wrote:

> *Wherefore then serveth the Law? It was added because of transgressions, till the seed should come to whom the promise was made; and it was ordained by angels in the hand of a mediator. Now a mediator is not a mediator of one, but God is one. Is the Law then against the promises of God? God forbid: for if there had been a Law given which could have given life, verily righteousness should have been by the Law. But the scripture hath concluded all under sin, that the promise by faith of Jesus Christ might be given to them that believe. But before faith came, we were kept under the Law, shut up unto the faith which should afterwards be revealed. Wherefore the Law was our schoolmaster to bring us unto Christ, that we might be justified by faith. But after that faith is come, we are no longer under a schoolmaster. For ye are all the children of God by faith in Christ Jesus. For as many of you as have been baptized into Christ have put on Christ. There is neither Jew nor Greek, there is neither bond nor free, there is neither male nor female: for ye are all one in Christ Jesus. And if ye be Christ's, then are ye Abraham's seed and heirs according to the promise* (Gal. 3:19-29).

# Commentary on Romans

The Law of Moses did indeed bring the Jews to Christ and His Law, though most did not accept it. Paul had earlier asked in the Roman letter, *For what if some* (of the Jews,) *did not believe* (the gospel of Christ)*? shall their unbelief make the* (system of) *faith of God* (in Christ) *without effect* (Rom. 3:3)? Paul's reply was: *God forbid* (Rom. 3:4).

The second question posed in this passage is; *How shall we, that are dead to sin, live any longer therein?* The *we* of the verses pertains to Jewish converts. The Law of Moses was now a dead Law, no longer in force or endorsed by God.

The phrase, *that are dead to sin*, is not without weighty importance. Paul was establishing his forthcoming argument, which he presents in 7:1-6. Paul will have much to say about the subject of death in that text. However, to properly understand the latter passage, it must be preceded by a proper understanding of the former. The deadness of the Law of Moses is the apostle's intent here. Paul will heavily expound on this *deadness* as he develops his inspired argument.

The Jews could no longer live under the Law of Moses without being in sin, for the Law of Moses had become *dead* and was nailed to the cross as Paul affirmed in the Colossian epistle. *Blotting out the handwriting of ordinances that was against us, which was contrary to us and took it out of the way, nailing it to his cross* (Col. 2:14). The Law of Moses had become sin—that is, it missed the mark of reconciliation. *For if, when we* (the Jews) *were enemies, we were reconciled to God by the death of his Son, much more, being reconciled, we shall be saved by his life. And all things are of God, who hath reconciled us to himself by Jesus Christ* (not by the Law of Moses) *and hath given to us the ministry of reconciliation* (Rom. 5:10; II Cor. 5:18).

The Law of Moses was nailed to the cross; thus, it was crucified and died thereat. The Law of Moses was blotted out. God erased it out of existence—no longer to be obeyed and no longer alive. From whom was The Law of Moses taken out of the way? The Law of Moses was no longer the way by which the Jews were to be governed. The new way by which the Jews were to be guided is described as a *new and living way* in contrast to the

# Commentary on Romans

old dead way. *Having therefore, brethren, boldness to enter into the holiest by the blood of Jesus, By a new and living way, which he hath consecrated for us, through the veil, that is to say, his flesh* (Heb. 10:19-20). Jesus expounded the same to Thomas when he said, *I am the way, the truth and the life: no man cometh unto the Father, but by me* (Jno. 14:6).

When Christ said He was *the way,* He meant it would no longer be the way of Moses. When Christ declared He was *the truth,* He meant He was the one through whom completed truth was given. When He said he was *the life,* He meant He was the one through whom spiritual life was to be obtained and not Moses.

The Jews spent no little time listening to the preaching of Christ. Some readily accepted Him as the Messiah; most did not. The Jewish converts understood the arguments the apostle was making. However, most students fail to place the arguments made by the New Testament authors and speakers within the context, framework, and settings to which they belong. This failure is miserable and results in a gross misunderstanding the Scriptures. Contexts must be properly recognized by those who wish to ascertain truth.

## Romans 6:3-7

*3 Know ye not, that so many of us as were baptized into Jesus Christ were baptized into his death? 4 Therefore we are buried with him by baptism into death: that like as Christ was raised up from the dead by the glory of the Father, even so we also should walk in newness of life. 5 For if we have been planted together in the likeness of his death, we shall be also in the likeness of his resurrection: 6 Knowing this, that our old man is crucified with him, that the body of sin might be destroyed, that henceforth we should not serve sin. 7 For he that is dead is freed from sin.*

**Verse 3.** *Know ye not, that so many of us as were baptized into Jesus Christ were baptized into his death?* The question posed by Paul is one of rhetoric. The Jews who had obeyed the gospel had indeed been well taught what baptism represented, and all

# Commentary on Romans

the things associated with it. They, as the Gentile converts, understood baptism was symbolic of the death, burial, and resurrection of Jesus Christ. However, there is another connotation directed to the Jewish converts involved in Paul's directive.

Be it remembered, many Jews insisted the Law of Moses was to be kept in conjunction with the gospel. The apostle made numerous arguments against the validity of the defunct Law of Moses. The Old Law was dead and no longer in force. Paul used a logical process by which to assist the mindset of the Jewish converts. Paul uses the words *death and dead* in a two-fold fashion. His first purpose was to remind the Jews baptism was symbolic of the death, burial, and resurrection of Christ. It was equally important for the apostle to persuade the Jewish converts the Old Law was both dead and buried. Paul strongly broaches this matter as his argument proceeds in chapter 7.

**Verse 4.** *Therefore we are buried with him by baptism into death: that like as Christ was raised up from the dead by the glory of the Father, even so we also should walk in newness of life.* The word *therefore* establishes the conclusion of the apostle's query of verse 3. Because the Jews were baptized into Jesus Christ and His death, they had become *dead* to the Old Law. As Christ was raised from the grave in a new form, so were the Jews raised from the grave of baptism unto a new form of life under the Law of Christ. For the Jews, their baptism was the grave of the Old Law as well as the grave of the old man of sin. Their resurrection from the watery grave of baptism should have brought forth a new creature. The *newness of life* in which the converted Jews were to walk was not after the Law of Moses, but after the Law of Christ. Twice Paul declared to the Jewish converts they had become *dead to sin*. Both dead to the sin of living under the Old Law and dead unto sin in general.

Just as *Christ was raised up from the dead by the glory of the Father,* so the converted Jews were raised up from the grave of baptism *by the glory of the Father.* Consider the apostle's words of exhortation to the Jewish converts recorded in Colossians epistle: *Buried with him in baptism, wherein also ye are risen with him through the faith of the operation of God, who hath raised him from the dead* (2:12). In the Romans' passage, Paul

# Commentary on Romans

declared there was a raising from the dead *by the glory of the Father.* In the Colossians' passage, Paul described being raised from the dead as an *operation of God.*

**Verse 5.** *For if we have been planted together in the likeness of his death, we shall be also in the likeness of his resurrection.* Whiteside commented:

> In being buried in baptism there is a likeness of his death; so also there is a likeness of his resurrection in our being raised from baptism to a new life. Hence, in being baptized we are united with him in the likeness of his death and resurrection. We are, therefore, partakers with him in death and also in being raised to a new life. Jesus was buried and arose to a new life; we are buried in baptism and arise to a new life. These verses show the act of baptism and also its spiritual value[21] [sic].

Just as Christ was raised unto a new life, so the Jews were raised unto a new life in Christ; in so doing they had become *dead to the Old Law.* The obedience of the Jewish convert involved a departure from both Law and from sin. Today, those who obey the Gospel surrender their former denominational ties, becoming dead thereunto as well as dying to sin.

**Verse 6.** *Knowing this, that our old man was Crucified with him, that the body of sin might be done away, that so we should no longer be in bondage to sin.* The apostle continues his comparison between the death of Christ and of man's death to sin. Just as Christ was crucified because of our sins, so *our old man was crucified.* Just who is the old man that was crucified? Some contend it was man's corrupt nature. Others insist it was man's desire to sin. However, it is vital to realize that *Paul does not view man's nature as corrupt.* The Bible nowhere teaches such a doctrine!

If it is the case the nature of man is corrupt, then by necessity it would have to be the case Satan's wiles of temptation are futile. Why would Satan trouble to tempt man if he were corrupted by

---

[21] Robertson L. Whiteside.

## Commentary on Romans

nature? Their would be no purpose for Satan to walk *about, seeking whom he may devour* (I Pet. 5:8). Satan tempts not only the righteous, but he tempts the wicked as well. He tempts the righteous to corrupt them, and he tempts the wicked to keep them wicked.

The tally of scholars and Bible students is without number who teach man is corrupt in his nature. Sadly, this is also true among many in the Lord's church. *The doctrine is false.* Man is no more corrupt in his nature than God. Man has never been corrupt by nature. God made man in His image, as recorded in Genesis 1:26-27. The image in which God made man was in sinless perfection. While it is true all men have sinned, it is not true that man **must** sin. If it is the case all must sin, then it is the case God created man in such a way as to predestine him to sin. God neither predestined men to sin, nor did He predestine men to be obedient to His will. To insist men are destined or predisposed to sin is to assert the Calvinistic doctrine of predestination to be true.

Nothing can be further from the truth. Man is in no way predisposed *to* or *unto* sin. The Lord's brother, James, forever settles this matter. *But every man is tempted, when he is drawn away of his own lust and enticed* (Jas. 1:14). Man has full charge over all his faculties and will; man is not compelled to sin. He chooses to sin or not sin; such is the free moral agency of man so given by the Lord. It is often echoed, *Nobody's perfect.* Indeed, such is true; however, such does not at all mean one cannot be without sin. Christ lived a sinless life as a man. *Christ did not live a sinless life with or by the aid of the Holy Spirit!*

We are aware of the sinlessness of Christ, yet it is held by many Christ was sinless because he was Deity. The sinlessness of Christ was not achieved because He was God, but because He chose to be without sin. *Christ did not overcome temptation by the intervention of the Holy Spirit as many insist.* He did not overcome sin because He was Christ. He overcame sin by His own human will. If it were the case Christ overcame sin by the intervention of the Holy Spirit, then it is the case Christ can in no way serve as a mediator between men and God. Christ serves as the mediator for saints *as a man. For there is one God and*

# Commentary on Romans

*one mediator between God and men,* **the man** *Christ Jesus* (I Tim. 2:5). Christ intercedes because He is both *man* and Deity. If he were not a man, overcoming sin as a man, He could not fully understand our position. It is for this cause he *was in all points tempted like as we are, yet without sin* (Heb. 4:15).

Further, Satan spent no little time tempting Christ. Satan knew, as a man, Christ could indeed sin. If the Lord overcame sin with the aid of the Holy Spirit, then Satan was tempting not Christ but the Holy Spirit as well.

Both Matthew and Luke record an account of some of the temptations of Christ. Luke informs us that after the temptations recorded in those passages, *when the devil had ended all the temptation, he departed from him for a season* (Lk. 4:13). The word *season* is defined as for a while—for a more convenient time. The Devil is indeed wise; he always knows the best of times to cast fiery darts our direction. Why it is that countless folks assume Satan tempted Christ only once is baffling. Nonetheless, it remains true: just as Satan leaves saints alone *for a season,* he left Christ alone *for a season.* Satan always returns to tempt us, just as he returned to tempt the Lord when it was more convenient for him to do so. Because there is no inspired record of Satan tempting Christ on other occasions does not negate the fact that he did so.

Paul continues the analogy between Christ's death and our death to sin. Christ was crucified—"our old man was crucified." What is the old man that was crucified? Some say: "Our corrupt nature." But Paul does not view our nature as corrupt. Besides, our nature is not put to death in the process of conversion to Christ. Read the verse again and observe the *"our old man"* and *"the body of sin"* are the same thing, for certainly *"our old man"* is not crucified in order that something else might be put to death. If one will keep in mind what Paul had been saying, one will see that to crucify the old man is the same thing as to die to sin. Of himself Paul said: "I have been crucified with Christ" (Gal. 2:20)[22] [sic].

---
[22] Robertson L. Whiteside

# Commentary on Romans

**Verse 7.** *For he that is dead is freed from sin.* The word *he* has reference to the converted Jew. The word *for* establishes the cause set forth in verse 6. In other words: Because he (the converted Jew) was dead to sin, he was freed from the penalty of sin; so long as he, the converted Jew, remained faithful to the New Law of Christ, and did not return to the Old Law. Consider the words of the Hebrews' author: *For it is impossible for those* [Jewish converts] *who were once enlightened, and have tasted of the heavenly gift and were made partakers of the Holy Ghost and have tasted the good word of God and the powers of the world to come, If they shall fall away* [by returning to the Old Law], *to renew them again unto repentance* [under the New Law of Christ]; *seeing they crucify to themselves the Son of God afresh and put him to an open shame* (Heb. 6:4-6).

Further, Paul had shown the Jews they were to die to the Old Law. Many of the Jews had been teaching that men were to keep both the Old Law and the New Law; it should become evident the apostle had shown the Jews they had been released from the Law of Moses—*widowed* from it. Being now *widowed* from the Law of Moses, the Jews were to be *married* to Christ. To the Jewish converts Paul wrote: *Wherefore, my brethren, ye also are become dead to the Law by the body of Christ; that ye should be married to another, even to him who is raised from the dead, that we should bring forth fruit unto God* (Rom. 7:4).

The apostle addressed the same issue with the Jewish converts at Galatia. The record states: *I marvel that ye are so soon removed from him that called you into the grace of Christ unto another gospel: Which is not another; but there be some that trouble you and would pervert the gospel of Christ* (Gal. 1:6-7). The *another gospel* of which the apostle spoke was the insistence of many Jews that the Old Law had to be kept in conjunction with the New Law of Christ.

Luke informed us of these things when he wrote:

> *And certain men which came down from Judea taught the brethren and said, Except ye be circumcised after the manner of Moses, ye cannot be saved. When therefore Paul and Barnabas had no small dissension*

# Commentary on Romans

*and disputation with them, they determined that Paul and Barnabas and certain other of them, should go up to Jerusalem unto the apostles and elders about this question. And being brought on their way by the church, they passed through Phenice and Samaria, declaring the conversion of the Gentiles: and they caused great joy unto all the brethren. And when they were come to Jerusalem, they were received of the church and of the apostles and elders and they declared all things that God had done with them. But there rose up certain of the sect of the Pharisees which believed, saying, That it was needful to circumcise them and to command them to keep the Law of Moses* (Acts 15:1-5).

## Romans 6:8-10

*8. Now if we be dead with Christ, we believe that we shall also live with him: 9 Knowing that Christ being raised from the dead dieth no more; death hath ho more dominion over him. 10. For in that he died, he died unto sin once: but in that he liveth, he liveth unto God.*

**Verse 8.** The word *now* establishes a crucial conclusion to which the apostle expected the Jewish converts to come as a result of his efforts beginning in verse 1. It does the student well to fix the eye closely to the number of times Paul uses the words *dead* and *death* in chapters 6 and 7.

Paul had been much involved in the work of showing the Jewish converts the Law of Moses had become *dead*. It was a law under which the Jews were no longer to live. It had been replaced by the Law of Christ. The Law of Moses had been nailed to the cross. Concerning the first covenant, Paul wrote there was a *blotting out the handwriting of ordinances that was against us, which was contrary to us and took it out of the way, nailing it to his cross* (Col. 2:14).
The Jews had been *married* to the Law of Moses for more than one-and-a-half millennia, but the advent of the cross of Christ brought about the death of their first spiritual spouse. The apostle will greatly detail this in chapter 7. Being *dead with Christ*

# Commentary on Romans

means the Old Law was *dead*. The Jews were *widowed* from it and must, therefore, be *married* to a new spiritual husband. Their new spiritual husband was indeed Christ.

The apostle further wrote that *we believe that we shall also live with him.* No longer were the Jews to live with Moses under the Old Law; rather, they were to live with Christ under His Law. For *the Law was our schoolmaster to bring us unto Christ* (Gal. 3: 24). Being brought to Christ was to be brought to a new husband, as well as a new law.

**Verse 9.** *Knowing that Christ being raised from the dead dieth no more; death hath ho more dominion over him.* This verse provides a stark contrast between Moses and Christ. While both Christ and Moses died, Moses was not resurrected. Christ, however, was resurrected unto life again. There were many witnesses to that fact.

> For I delivered unto you first of all that which I also received, how that Christ died for our sins according to the scriptures; And that he was buried and that he rose again the third day according to the scriptures: And that he was seen of Cephas, then of the twelve: After that, he was seen of above five hundred brethren at once; of whom the greater part remain unto this present, but some are fallen asleep. After that, he was seen of James, then of all the apostles. And last of all he was seen of me also, as of one born out of due time (I Cor. 15:3-8).

Both Moses and the Old Law *died* once and forevermore. Moses will be resurrected at the last day—the last and final return of Christ. The Old Law of Moses was forever nailed to the cross and will never be resurrected. The nailing of the Old Law of Moses to the cross served as the death certificate provided by the great physician regarding the Old Law.

From the time the Roman army destroyed Jerusalem in AD 70, no Jew has been able to keep the Old Law. The genealogical records were destroyed. Since that time the Jews have not been able to keep the Law of sacrifices, temple worship, nor any other

# Commentary on Romans

mandates of the Law. Further, the Jews have not made the mandatory journeys to Jerusalem three times each year, as the Old Law required. The Old Law was forever ended. It is also true the Jews have not been civilly governed as mandated by the Old Law since the Roman army destroyed the city of Jerusalem in AD 70. The *religious system* of the Old Law was then nailed to the cross when the Jews crucified the Lord. *The civil Law of the Jews was forever abolished in AD 70* to be kept no more. Christ, in contrast to Moses, was resurrected unto life; He remained on the earth for 40 days, ascended to heaven, and forever established His abiding Law of the New Testament.

Lastly, Paul declared in verse 8 that *death hath no more dominion over him.* The *him* under consideration does not refer to man, nor does it refer to Moses. The word refers to Christ. Moses is still in the paradise of Abraham, still bound by the chains of death, and will remain there until the resurrection of all men from the dead. Christ, however, was not bound by the Hadean realm; rather, Christ was resurrected and ascended to heaven: *This Jesus hath God raised up, whereof we all are witnesses. Therefore being by the right hand of God exalted and having received of the Father the promise of the Holy Ghost, he hath shed forth this, which ye now see and hear* (Acts 2:32-33). Christ is not, nor was not, dominated by the fetters of death in the Hadean Realm. Christ forever conquered death!

**Verse 10.** *For in that he died, he died unto sin once: but in that he liveth, he liveth unto God.* The meaning here is Christ died once and for all, never to die again. Christ died and was resurrected and now *liveth unto God,* we must do likewise. The Jews were no longer to live unto Moses or the Old Law but unto God under the New Law of Christ. There remained no more sacrifice for sin under the Old Law. Christ became the ultimate sacrifice which was once and for all delivered. Hebrews 10:18-26 says:

> *Now where remission of these is, there is no more offering for sin. Having therefore, brethren, boldness to enter into the holiest by the blood of Jesus, By a new and living way, which he hath consecrated for us, through the veil, that is to say, his flesh; And having an high priest over the house of God; Let us draw near*

# Commentary on Romans

with a true heart in full assurance of faith, having our hearts sprinkled from an evil conscience and our bodies washed with pure water. Let us hold fast the profession of our faith without wavering; (for he is faithful that promised). And let us consider one another to provoke unto love and to good works: Not forsaking the assembling of ourselves together, as the manner of some is; but exhorting one another: and so much the more, as ye see the day approaching. For if we sin willfully after that we have received the knowledge of the truth, there remaineth no more sacrifice for sins (Heb. 10:18-26).

## Romans 6:11-23

11 Likewise reckon ye also yourselves to be dead indeed unto sin, but alive unto God through Jesus Christ our Lord. 12 Let not sin therefore reign in your mortal body, that ye should obey it in the lusts thereof. 13 Neither yield ye your members as instruments of unrighteousness unto sin: but yield yourselves unto God, as those that are alive from the dead and your members as instruments of righteousness unto God. 14 For sin shall not have dominion over you: for ye are not under the Law, but under grace. 15 What then? shall we sin, because we are not under the Law, but under grace? God forbid. 16 Know ye not, that to whom ye yield yourselves servants to obey, his servants ye are to whom ye obey; whether of sin unto death, or of obedience unto righteousness? 17 But God be thanked, that ye were the servants of sin, but ye have obeyed from the heart that form of doctrine which was delivered you. 18 Being then made free from sin, ye became the servants of righteousness. 19 I speak after the manner of men because of the infirmity of your flesh: for as ye have yielded your members servants to uncleanness and to iniquity unto iniquity; even so now yield your members servants to righteousness unto holiness. 20 For when ye were the servants of sin, ye were free from righteousness. 21 What fruit had ye then in those things whereof ye are now ashamed? for

# Commentary on Romans

*the end of those things is death. 22 But now being made free from sin and become servants to God, ye have your fruit unto holiness and the end everlasting life. 23 For the wages of sin is death; but the gift of God is eternal life through Jesus Christ our Lord.*

**Verse 11.** *Likewise reckon ye also yourselves to be dead indeed unto sin, but alive unto God through Jesus Christ our Lord.* The word *likewise* is here provided for the purpose of comparison and parallelism. Just as that which Paul asserted in the previous verses (1-10) was the case for the Jews, so it is with that which follows.

Paul argued the Jews were to be *dead* unto (*widowed from*) the Old Law and Moses. They should now be *married* to the New Law and to Christ. Their first spiritual husband was *dead*. Neither the Old Law nor Moses had been resurrected. However, Christ had been resurrected; He also ushered in the New Covenant which superseded the Old Law (Col. 2:14). The New Covenant Christ ushered in was prophesied by Jeremiah the prophet.

*Behold, the days come, saith the Lord, that I will make a new covenant with the house of Israel and with the house of Judah: Not according to the covenant that I made with their fathers in the day that I took them by the hand to bring them out of the land of Egypt; which my covenant they brake, although I was an husband unto them, saith the Lord: But this shall be the covenant that I will make with the house of Israel; After those days, saith the Lord, I will put my Law in their inward parts and write it in their hearts; and will be their God and they shall be my people. And they shall teach no more every man his neighbour and every man his brother, saying, Know the Lord: for they shall all know me, from the least of them unto the greatest of them, saith the Lord: for I will forgive their iniquity and I will remember their sin no more* (Jer. 31:31-34).

Inspiration declared through Jeremiah, a *new covenant* was to be ushered in under Christ. The Jews were espoused to the Old

# Commentary on Romans

Law only for the time dictated. Paul wrote: *Wherefore then serveth the Law? It was added because of transgressions, till the seed should come* (Gal. 3:19). That seed did come, and that seed was Christ. Thus, the days would come when the Jews would be *married* to a new husband and a New Law. Not a few passages in the Hebrew epistle refer to the prophecy of Jeremiah. Two of those follow.

> *But now hath he obtained a more excellent ministry, by how much also he is the mediator of a better covenant, which was established upon better promises. For if that first covenant had been faultless, then should no place have been sought for the second. For finding fault with them, he saith, Behold, the days come, saith the Lord, when I will make a new covenant with the house of Israel and with the house of Judah: Not according to the covenant that I made with their fathers in the day when I took them by the hand to lead them out of the land of Egypt; because they continued not in my covenant and I regarded them not, saith the Lord. For this is the covenant that I will make with the house of Israel after those days, saith the Lord; I will put my Laws into their mind and write them in their hearts: and I will be to them a God and they shall be to me a people: And they shall not teach every man his neighbour and every man his brother, saying, Know the Lord: for all shall know me, from the least to the greatest. For I will be merciful to their unrighteousness and their sins and their iniquities will I remember no more. In that he saith, A new covenant, he hath made the first old. Now that which decayeth and waxeth old is ready to vanish away* (Heb.8:6-13).

> *And for this cause he is the mediator of the new testament, that by means of death, for the redemption of the transgressions that were under the first testament, they which are called might receive the promise of eternal inheritance. For where a testament is, there must also of necessity be the death of the testator. For a testament is of force after men are dead: otherwise it is of no strength at all while the testator liveth. Where-*

# Commentary on Romans

*upon neither the first testament was dedicated without blood* (Heb. 9:15-18).

Of Jeremiah 31 consider the phrase, *I was an husband unto them, saith the Lord*, in verse 32. These words emphatically and undeniably set forth the proof the Jews were indeed *married* to the Old Law and to Moses. The prophet's declaration, *Behold, the days come, saith the Lord, that I will make a new covenant*, should have forever settled the problem the Jews had concerning the escorting in of the *new covenant* under Christ.

Further, Moses had himself informed the Jews there would come a time when they would no longer be subject to either the Old Law or to Moses. Moses also declared it was Christ whom they should later hear, obey, and to whom they were to later *marry*. Moses also declared it was that new prophet to whom the Father would give authority to speak on His behalf. Moses warned those who refused to listen and comply with the new Prophet and His New Law would be held accountable to both the Father and His new prophet for failing to do so.

> *The Lord thy God will raise up unto thee a Prophet from the midst of thee, of thy brethren, like unto me; unto him ye shall hearken; According to all that thou desiredst of the Lord thy God in Horeb in the day of the assembly, saying, Let me not hear again the voice of the Lord my God, neither let me see this great fire any more, that I die not. And the Lord said unto me, They have well spoken that which they have spoken. I will raise them up a Prophet from among their brethren, like unto thee and will put my words in his mouth; and he shall speak unto them all that I shall command him. And it shall come to pass, that whosoever will not hearken unto my words which he shall speak in my name, I will require it of him* (Deut. 18:15-19).

**Verse 12.** *Let not sin therefore reign in your mortal body, that ye should obey it in the lusts thereof.* The *sin* which was not to *reign in the mortal bodies* was remaining under the Old Law. The Jews were no longer to be governed by the Old Law. Paul argued the same in the Galatians' epistle when he wrote: *Stand*

# Commentary on Romans

*fast therefore in the liberty wherewith Christ hath made us free and be not entangled again with the yoke of bondage. Behold, I Paul say unto you, that if ye be circumcised, Christ shall profit you nothing. For I testify again to every man that is circumcised, that he is a debtor to do the whole Law. Christ is become of no effect unto you, whosoever of you are justified by the Law; ye are fallen from grace* (Gal. 5:1-4).

The *lusts* of which Paul wrote in Romans. 6:12 were the lusts the Jews had for the Old Law. The Jews put great stock in the fact they were Jews, being God's chosen people. In such, they contended because they were God's chosen, they were without condemnation. However, John the baptizer declared to the Jews they should *think not to say within yourselves, We have Abraham to our father: for I say unto you, that God is able of these stones to raise up children unto Abraham* (Matt. 3:9).

**Verse 13.** *Neither yield ye your members as instruments of unrighteousness unto sin: but yield yourselves unto God, as those that are alive from the dead and your members as instruments of righteousness unto God.* When one secures a good grasp upon that which Paul has been affirming, this passage is not hard to be understood.

The *instruments of unrighteousness unto sin* here is two-fold. The Jews would serve as the instruments of the Old Law. *Sin* refers to the Old Law. Rather than serving as instruments in and of the Old Law, the Jews were to *yield* themselves unto God under the New Law of Christ.

In contrast to serving as instruments to the Old Law, Paul instructed the Jews to serve *as instruments of righteousness unto God. Righteousness* has reference to the New Law of Christ. The Jews were to be *as those that are alive from the* deadness of the Old Law, resurrected unto the newness of the Law of Christ.

**Verse 14.** *For sin shall not have dominion over you: for ye are not under the Law, but under grace.* It was the Old Law which no longer had *dominion* over the Jews. They were now under the dominion of the New Law of Christ. The passage could, in other

# Commentary on Romans

words, read: *For the Old Law shall not have dominion over you: for ye are no longer under the Old Law of Moses, but under grace.* The *grace* under which the Jews were to be was the Law of Christ—the Gospel. The consequences of sin remained upon the Jews so long as they remained subject to the Old Law.

**Verse 15.** *What then? shall we sin, because we are not under the Law, but under grace? God forbid.* Here again the Law is the Old Law of Moses. The *grace* under which the Jews were now under was the New Law.

The phrase, *What then? shall we sin*, is better understood as follows: *What then, are we—the Jews—in sin because we are no longer under the Old Law of Moses, but under the New Law of Christ? God forbid.*

**Verse 16.** *Know ye not, that to whom ye yield yourselves servants to obey, his servants ye are to whom ye obey; whether of sin unto death, or of obedience unto righteousness?* As has been the apostle's custom, he continues to pose questions of rhetoric.

We are to understand the passage thus: *Of course you Jews realize, that to whom ye yield yourselves servants to obey, whether it be Moses or Christ, his servants ye are to whom ye obey; whether of sin unto death, which is the Old Law, or of obedience unto righteousness, which is the New Law?*

**Verse 17.** *But God be thanked, that ye were the servants of sin, but ye have obeyed from the heart that form of doctrine which was delivered you.* *Ye*, the apostle stated, *were the servants* of the Old Law which was now a law unto spiritual death.

In contrast, Paul showed that the Jews, which had obeyed the New Law of Christ, did so from an obedient heart. The *doctrine* they had obeyed was indeed the New Law of Christ. Again, it is essential to recall there were many Jews who insisted both the Old Law and New Law were both to be kept simultaneously, which Acts 15:5 demonstrates: *There rose up certain of the sect of the Pharisees which believed, saying, That it was needful to circumcise them and to command them to keep the Law of Mo-*

# Commentary on Romans

*ses* (Acts 15:5).

**Verse 18.** *Being then made free from sin, ye became the servants of righteousness.* The sin from which the Jews had been made free was remaining under the Old Law of Moses. The Jews had become liberated from the Old Law by the Law of Christ. Consider the following passages with comments added in brackets.

*Now the Lord is that Spirit: and where the Spirit of the Lord is, there is liberty* [from the Old Law] (II Cor. 3:17*).*

*And that because of false brethren unawares brought in, who came in privily to spy out our liberty* [from the Old Law] *which we have in Christ Jesus, that they might bring us into bondage* [again under the Old Law] (Gal. 2:4).

*Stand fast therefore in the liberty* [of the New Law] *wherewith Christ hath made us free,* [from the Old Law] *and be not entangled again with the yoke of bondage* [of the Old Law] (Gal. 5:1).

**Verse 19.** *I Speak after the manner of men because of the infirmity of your flesh: for as ye have yielded your members servants to uncleanness and to iniquity unto iniquity; even so now yield your members servants to righteousness unto holiness.* Paul realized he was in need of addressing the Jewish converts on their level. He understood the mindset of the Jews; therefore, he identifies the Jewish mindset as their *infirmity;* that is, their weakness.

Remaining under the Old Law resulted in spiritual uncleanness and spiritual death. The Old Law was now one of *iniquity* so far as the Lord was concerned. The apostle revealed obedience to the New Law of Christ was the avenue by which they were to obtain *holiness.* Being a *servant to righteousness* was to be a servant of Christ and His New Law.

**Verse 20.** *For when ye were the servants of sin, ye were free from righteousness.* The *sin* to which the Jews had been servants was the Old Law. The apostle stated they *were* at one time *servants* of the Old Law which shows they were no longer

# Commentary on Romans

such. Rather, the obedient Jews had become servants unto Christ under the New Law.

The phrase *ye were free from righteousness* means so long as the Jews remained under the Old Law they were not liberated from it. They were not at all freed from obeying the New Law of Christ as they asserted.

**Verse 21.** *What fruit had ye then in those things whereof ye are now ashamed? for the end of those things is death.* Questions of rhetoric continue from the apostle. The answer to the query here posed was that there was no fruit produced from the things of which they were then ashamed. Of what were the Jews ashamed?

The Jews were ashamed (guilty) of listening to mischievous Jews perverting the gospel (cf. Gal. 1:6) who taught there must be a keeping of both the Law of Moses and the Law of Christ (cf. Acts 15:5). The keeping of both the Old Law and the New Law resulted in spiritual death. Therefore, Paul declared, *the end of those things is death;* that is, spiritual death.

**Verse 22.** *But now being made free from sin and become servants to God, ye have your fruit unto holiness and the end everlasting life.* Having been made free from the Old Law, the obedient Jews had become servants, not unto Moses, but rather unto Christ. It was in their new service to Christ under the New Law they acquired the eternal life they thought they had under the Old Law.

The concluding words of verse 21 are: *for the end of those things is death.* The concluding words of verse 22 are; *and the end everlasting life.* The phrases are antithetical. Just as it was the case the result of trying to keep both the Old Law and New Law at the same time was spiritual death, so it is the case keeping only the New Law was *everlasting life.*

**Verse 23.** *For the wages of sin is death; but the gift of God is eternal life through Jesus Christ our Lord.* The *sin* under consideration here is the Old Law. The wages of remaining under the Old Law resulted in spiritual death.

# Commentary on Romans

Again, the need to strongly emphasize context is here repeated. The context is Paul's comparisons and contrasts between the Old Law of Moses and the New Law of Christ. Further, there are other contrasts provided in this passage. One contrast is beween death and everlasting life. The second contrast is between wages and a gift. It is essential to keep in mind it is through Christ the gift of eternal life is awarded. The word *but* shows the contrast intended by the apostle.

Much effort was made by Paul to show the Jewish converts God had declared through Moses that another Lawgiver was to be given. It was unto Him, Moses declared; the Jews were to come, listen and obey (Deut. 18:15-19).

Through the prophet Jeremiah, the Jews were informed a *New Covenant* was to come through the Messiah. The new covenant would be that which replaced the Law of Moses (Jer. 31:31-34).

The Old Law was *dead and buried* having been *nailed to the cross* (cf. Col. 2:14). The Old Law served as the first husband to whom the Jews were spiritually married, but from whom they were now widowed. Again we note the Old Law being nailed to the cross was the death certificate of the Law of Moses issued and certified by God (Col. 2:14).

Because both the Old Law and Moses were dead, the Jews were to be *married* to the Prophet of whom Moses spoke as recorded in Deuteronomy 18:15-19. To remain *married* to the Old Law of Moses was to remain married to the corps of the Old Law. Remaining married to the old corps of the Old Law was a spiritual sin which led to their spiritual demise.

## Romans 7:1-7

*1 Know ye not, brethren, (for I speak to them that know the Law,) how that the Law hath dominion over a man as long as he liveth? 2 For the woman which hath an husband is bound by the Law to her husband so long as he liveth; but if the husband be dead, she is loosed from the Law of her husband. 3 So then if, while her*

# Commentary on Romans

*husband liveth, she be married to another man, she shall be called an adulteress: but if her husband be dead, she is free from that Law; so that she is no adulteress, though she be married to another man. 4 Wherefore, my brethren, ye also are become dead to the Law by the body of Christ; that ye should be married to another, even to him who is raised from the dead, that we should bring forth fruit unto God. 5 For when we were in the flesh, the motions of sins, which were by the Law, did work in our members to bring forth fruit unto death. 6 But now we are delivered from the Law, that being dead wherein we were held; that we should serve in newness of spirit and not in the oldness of the letter. 7 What shall we say then? Is the Law sin? God forbid. Nay, I had not known sin, but by the Law: for I had not known lust, except the Law had said, Thou shalt not covet.*

Whiteside wrote on Romans 7:1-7 and cited the American Standard Translation often in his Scripture references. (We have italicized the entirety of Whiteside's comments.)

*Some of the efforts to explain Romans 7:1-6 have not been very helpful. The meaning is sometimes obscured by injection into the passage things that the Holy Spirit did not put into it. Paul was not teaching a lesson on the relation of husband and wife, but was using that well known relationship as an illustration to show the brethren their relation to the Law and to Christ. There is always one main point of comparison in an illustration and to seek to extend the illustration to points not intended by the user is confusing. What is the purpose of Paul's marriage illustration? He still has in mind freedom from the Law... (Rom. 6:14, 15). His illustration not only shows that we are free from the Law, but that Christians are bound to Christ. He now is our master.*

**Verse 1.** *Know ye not, brethren, (for I speak to them that know the Law,) how that the Law hath dominion over a man as long as he liveth?*

# Commentary on Romans

> Paul credits them (the Jews, DHC) with knowing that the Law has dominion over man so long as he lives and no longer. The Law is the Law of Moses, though what is here affirmed of the Law of Moses is true of any Law under which a man lives. When a man dies, the Law governs him no longer—he is dead to the Law and the Law is dead to him.

**Verse 2.** *For the woman which hath an husband is bound by the Law to her husband so long as he liveth; but if the husband be dead, she is loosed from the Law of her husband.*

> This is the general Law of marriage. Whatever exceptions there might be are not here taken into consideration, for they had no part in the truth that Paul was illustrating. It was intended that both parties to a marriage should be faithful to their marriage vows and that only death should separate them. If they remained true to each other, only death could separate them. As Paul was using this illustration to show that the brethren were released from the Law so as to be married to Christ, it is easy to see why he speaks of the wife's obligations instead of the husband's (emph. DHC). The death of the husband releases the wife from the Law of her husband—that is, it releases her from the Law that bound her to that husband.

**Verse 3.** *So then if, while her husband liveth, she be married to another man, she shall be called an adulteress: but if her husband be dead, she is free from that Law; so that she is no adulteress, though she be married to another man.*

> Here again is a fixed Law concerning the marriage relation. When one pledges one's self to another in marriage, it is a base thing to break the marriage vows by immoral practices. But let us not forget that Paul is using this marriage relation to illustrate a principle that is involved in our relations to the Law and to the Christ. Our close union with the Lord Jesus Christ, Paul, by a figure of speech, speaks of as marriage to him. The

# Commentary on Romans

*relation of the people of Israel to Jehovah under the Old Testament was frequently spoken of under the same figure of speech. When the people then turned from Jehovah to worship idols and to mix in the religions of other people, Jehovah accused them of being guilty of whoredom and adultery. "She committed adultery with stones and with stocks" (Jer. 3:9). "With their idols have they committed adultery" (Ezek. 23: 37). So long as the Law was of force, they could not be married to another.*

**Verse 4.** *Wherefore, my brethren, ye also are become dead to the Law by the body of Christ; that ye should be married to another, even to him who is raised from the dead, that we should bring forth fruit unto God.*

*This is the application of the principle set forth in the marriage illustration. They became dead to the Law that they might be joined, or married, to Christ. They became dead to the Law through the body of Christ— that is, through the death of the body of Christ. It would be difficult to understand how they became dead to the Law through the body of Christ were it not for light gained from other passages. People became dead to the Law when it ended, or was abolished. "For he is our peace, who made both one and brake down the middle wall of partition, having abolished in his flesh the enmity, even the Law of commandments contained in ordinances; that he might create in himself of the two one new man, so making peace; and might reconcile them both in one body unto God through the cross, having slain the enmity thereby" (Eph. 2:14-16). The Law of Moses is here called the enmity between Jew and Gentile, because it acted as a barrier between them. Paul here affirms that this enmity was slain by the cross, or by the death of Christ on the cross. "Having blotted out the bond written in ordinances that was against us, which was contrary to us: and he hath taken it out of the way, nailing it to the cross" (Col. 2:14). The Law had dominion over those under it so long as it lived, but it was abolished at the cross. They then be-*

# Commentary on Romans

came dead to it, for it no longer had dominion over them. It is well to notice that this passage definitely settles two things: (1) They were not married to Christ before his death—the Law was taken out of the way at the cross that they might be joined to the risen Christ. (2) When Paul wrote this letter, these Roman brethren had been joined to Christ. That is made clear by the fact stated: that they were joined to Christ that they might bring forth fruit unto God. It is certain that Christians are expected to bear fruit in this life. But the marriage, or joining, to Christ precedes the fruit bearing. Verse 6 shows that the bearing of fruit is done in serving God in newness of the spirit. Besides, if the closeness of the relationship that existed between Jehovah and the Jews was spoken of as a marriage, certainly the closer union between Christ and his followers would also be spoken of as a marriage. In another place Paul uses the marriage relationship to illustrate the close union between Christ and the church (See Eph. 5:22-33). Notice specially verse 23: "For the husband is the head of the wife, as Christ also is the head of the Church, being himself the Savior of the body." Here is a comparison: The husband is head of the wife, as Christ is head of the church—in the same manner as Christ is head of the church. How could that be if, as some say, the church is now only espoused to Christ? That Paul in this entire passage is using the marriage relation to illustrate the relationship existing between Christ and the church is evident to any unbiased reader. Verse 32 shows conclusively that such is his purpose: "This mystery is great: but I speak in regard of Christ and of the church." So, then, in speaking of husband and wife, he was by way of illustration speaking of Christ and the church

**Verses 5-6.** *For when we were in the flesh, the motions of sins, which were by the Law, did work in our members to bring forth fruit unto death. But now we are delivered from the Law, that being dead wherein we were held; that we should serve in newness of spirit and not in the oldness of the letter.*

"Flesh" here does not mean the human body, for their

# Commentary on Romans

being "in the flesh" was a thing of the past. Paul's marriage illustration to show their relation to the Law and to Christ shows that he had in mind the Jewish brethren. No others were delivered from the Law that they might be joined to Christ. "In the flesh" refers to the time they were under the Law of Moses, for Paul immediately adds by way of contrast: "But now we have been discharged from the Law." They had been "in the flesh" but had been "discharged from the Law." It is not strange that Paul spoke of them as "in the flesh" during the time they were under the Law. The old covenant was a flesh covenant. They were members of the covenant by virtue of their flesh connection with Abraham and circumcision in the flesh was a sign of membership in that covenant. "Sinful passions," or passions of sin. Our passions are not essentially sinful and they certainly did not come to us through the Law of Moses—the Law of Moses did not create passions. They are sinful only when they lead us to do things contrary to God's will. In this way they became sinful through the Law—that is, through the violation of the Law. These sinful passions work through our bodies to bring forth fruit unto death. The statement that they had been discharged from the Law is a positive declaration that they were no longer under the Law. They had died to that wherein they were held and had no longer any connection with it. "Newness of the spirit" is the new life of the spirit into which they were raised at their baptism (6:4). The "oldness of the letter" was the Old Law. They were not then serving God in the Law of Moses.

**Verse 7.** *What shall we say then? Is the Law sin? God forbid. Nay, I had not known sin, but by the Law: for I had not known lust, except the Law had said, Thou shalt not covet.*

Hence, the Law Paul had in mind included the command, "Thou shalt not covet," which itself was one of the Ten Commandments. The Ten Commandments were a part of that Law from which these brethren had been delivered. Because people violated the Law and

# Commentary on Romans

*thereby became sinful, did not prove the Law to be sinful. The Law defined and condemned sin. Paul had not known coveting—that is, he had not known the real nature of coveting—had not the Law said, "Thou shalt not covet." Then he knew coveting—knew the nature of it, knew it to be sin. At the time Paul learned coveting to be sinful he was under the Law of Moses and it was his only source from which to learn the nature of coveting. Any one can now learn from the gospel of Christ the sinfulness of coveting. In fact, the gospel of Christ condemns coveting as idolatry and thus condemns coveting more severely than does the Law*[23] [sic].

Whiteside's comments are astute and perceptive. The Old Law of Moses was now dead—no longer in force and no longer binding on the Jews. Their first spiritual husband was now dead. The Jews, then being without spiritual guidance, needed a new spouse to whom to be married. The husband, being the head of the wife, makes it needful for the wife to subject herself to her husband. The new spiritual husband was Christ and the New Testament System of faith rather than the old, dead, and buried first husband—the Old Law of Moses.

The apostle continues to pose questions he knew the Jews would ask. The word *sin* means to miss the mark. Thus, it was the case the Jews concluded, Paul had been arguing the Law of Moses had fallen short of which God intended for it to do—that it missed the mark God intended.

Paul refuted the charge, reminding the Jews, if it were not for the Law of Moses, the Jews would have no idea just what sin was. He refers to Exodus 20:17, which addressed the Law of covetousness. "Thou shalt not covet," was one of the Ten Commandments, which were a part of that Law from which these brethren had been delivered. Because people violated the Law, and thereby became sinful, did not prove the Law to be sinful. The Law defined and condemned sin. Paul had not known coveting —that is, he had not known the real nature of coveting—had not the Law said, Thou shalt not covet. Then he knew coveting—

---
[23] Robertson L. Whiteside.

# Commentary on Romans

knew the nature of it, knew it to be sin. At the time Paul learned it to be sinful, he was under the Law of Moses, and it was the only source from which to learn the nature of coveting. Anyone can now learn from the Gospel of Christ the sinfulness of coveting. In fact, the Gospel of Christ condemns coveting as idolatry and thus condemns coveting more severely than does the Law.[24]

**Verse 4.** This verse solidifies that the Jews were to *married* to Christ. *Wherefore, my brethren, ye also are become dead to the Law by the body of Christ; that ye should be married to another, even to him who is raised from the dead, that we should bring forth fruit unto God.*

**Verse 5.** Whiteside commented earlier on this verse.

**Verse 6.** This verses solidifies the same facts addressed above. *But now we are delivered from the Law, that being dead wherein we were held; that we should serve in newness of spirit and not in the oldness of the letter.* This verse is profoundly important and needs to be well understood. Paul plainly declared the Old Law was in fact *dead*. The apostle then declared why the Old Law was *dead—that we should serve in newness of spirit and not in the oldness of the letter.* The *newness of the spirit* is the newness of the New Law of Christ; the *oldness of the letter* was the old dead letter of the Old Law.

When we realize what Paul has been working to achieve, it is far less difficult to properly ascertain the intent of the apostle. Coming to this understanding is vital, and it well prepares the Bible student to better grasp the future intents and meanings the apostle will set forth. Proper exegesis of the text under consideration eliminates the sad delusions and wrong conclusion held by most. Only through valid hermeneutics can one ascertain the conclusion intended through the inspired hand of the apostle.

No wonder that Peter wrote: *And account that the longsuffering of our Lord is salvation; even as our beloved brother Paul also according to the wisdom given unto him hath written unto you; As also in all his epistles, speaking in them of these things; in which are some things hard to be understood, which they that*

---
[24] Robertson L. Whiteside.

# Commentary on Romans

are unlearned and unstable wrest, as they do also the other scriptures, unto their own destruction (II Pet. 3:15-16).

Paul spent much time addressing the Jewish converts in his efforts to make known to the Jews the Old Law of Moses was now *dead* and buried, having been nailed to the cross (Col. 2:14). Paul's arduous efforts however, were enveloped in great empathy. In that he himself was a Jew, he well related to the desire to remain under the Law of Moses. However, his empathy was furrowed far more deeply than may be realized. Paul was a Pharisee, a great teacher of the Law; he was well endowed with a great zeal for the Law of Moses. Paul said of himself:

> *I am verily a man which am a Jew, born in Tarsus, a city in Cilicia, yet brought up in this city at the feet of Gamaliel and taught according to the perfect manner of the Law of the fathers and was zealous toward God, as ye all are this day* (Acts 22:3).

> *Though I might also have confidence in the flesh. If any other man thinketh that he hath whereof he might trust in the flesh, I more: Circumcised the eighth day, of the stock of Israel, of the tribe of Benjamin, an Hebrew of the Hebrews; as touching the Law, a Pharisee; Concerning zeal, persecuting the church; touching the righteousness which is in the Law, blameless* (Phi. 3:4-6).

> *I say then, Hath God cast away his people? God forbid. For I also am an Israelite, of the seed of Abraham, of the tribe of Benjamin* (Rom. 11:1).

The apostle understood the painfulness the Jews had in giving up the Old Law. The very thing he did not want to do is the very thing he had to do. He had to accept the Old Law was no longer the one which God approved. He had to accept Jesus Christ had ushered in the New Covenant of which Jeremiah wrote in Jeremiah 31:31-34. He had to accept Jesus was that prophet of whom Moses spoke as recorded in Deuteronomy 18:15.

Paul had become a *wretched man* because the Old Law was

## Commentary on Romans

now nailed to the cross. The Old Law was no longer in force, God abolished the Law of Moses and now required all men, both Jew and Gentile, to come to Christ. Paul will address his *wretched* condition further into chapter 7, and will explain how he and the Jews were to be delivered from such a *wretched* state. It was indeed difficult for the Jews to admit the Old Law of Moses was now defunct; it was a far greater difficulty for one who was a Pharisee.

Given these observations it becomes less difficult to understand the balance of chapter 7. That many efforts to emphasize the need to keep the context of this study within the spiritual framework in which inspiration intended is true, the student will well understand why such has been the case.

Brother Foy E. Wallace once stated: *a text taken out of context becomes a pretext.* Indeed brother Wallace was correct. Just as men today dislike that which they have either said or penned to be taken out of context, the Lord dislikes it more so.

It is also the case chapter 8 will be far less burdensome to understand. Once one is able to grasp the basics of any given matter, one's ability to address the matter becomes far less difficult. The flow of the book of Romans will become far less torrential, which will eliminate the delusions of many.

**Verse 7.** *What shall we say then? Is the law sin? God forbid. Nay, I had not known sin, but by the law: for I had not known lust, except the law had said, Thou shalt not covet.* "The objection which is here urged is one that would very naturally rise, and which we may suppose would be urged with no slight indignation. The Jew would ask, "Are we then to suppose that the holy Law of God is not only insufficient to sanctify us, but that it is the mere occasion of increased sin? Is its tendency to produce sinful passions, and to make people worse than they were before?" To this objection the apostle replies with great wisdom; he shows that the evil was not in the Law, but in man—that though these effects often followed, yet that the Law itself was good and pure"[25] [sic].

---
[25] Adam Clarke.

# Commentary on Romans

*Is the law sin?* Much has been written promoting countless controversies about this phrase. The word *sin* must be defined to ascertain the truth of this phrase. Sin can be either a noun, adjective, or a verb, depending on the context in which it is found. Paul uses the word here as a noun. The word *sin* is defined as missing the mark; however, this etymological meaning of the word is widely lost. The intention of the apostle was to ask the question he knew the Jews would pose regarding the Law of Moses. The Jewish converts deduced the Law of Moses to have fallen far short of what God intended. Paul's reply to the question was, *God forbid.*

Through the phrase, *for I had not known lust, except the law had said, Thou shalt not covet,* Paul reminded the Jewish converts he *had not known sin, but by the law.* If not for the Law, there would have been no knowledge of the sin of covetousness. Without the Law there would be no knowledge of the sin of lust. The Law did what God intended for it to do. The Law of Moses revealed sin to be sin. Contrary to the arguments made by the Jews, the Law had not missed the mark to which God assigned it. From these verses is also another false doctrine regarding marriage, divorce and remarriage. See comments at the end of the chapter.

## Romans 7:8-25

*8 But sin, taking occasion by the commandment, wrought in me all manner of concupiscence. For without the Law sin was dead. 9 For I was alive without the Law once: but when the commandment came, sin revived and I died. 10 And the commandment, which was ordained to life, I found to be unto death. 11 For sin, taking occasion by the commandment, deceived me and by it slew me. 12 Wherefore the Law is holy and the commandment holy and just and good. 13 Was then that which is good made death unto me? God forbid. But sin, that it might appear sin, working death in me by that which is good; that sin by the commandment might become exceeding sinful. 14 For we know that the Law is spiritual: but I am carnal, sold*

# Commentary on Romans

*under sin. 15 For that which I do I allow not: for what I would, that do I not; but what I hate, that do I. 16 If then I do that which I would not, I consent unto the Law that it is good. 17 Now then it is no more I that do it, but sin that dwelleth in me. 18 For I know that in me (that is, in my flesh,) dwelleth no good thing: for to will is present with me; but how to perform that which is good I find not. 19 For the good that I would I do not: but the evil which I would not, that I do. 20 Now if I do that I would not, it is no more I that do it, but sin that dwelleth in me. 21 I find then a Law, that, when I would do good, evil is present with me. 22 For I delight in the Law of God after the inward man: 23 But I see another Law in my members, warring against the Law of my mind and bringing me into captivity to the Law of sin which is in my members. 24 O wretched man that I am! who shall deliver me from the body of this death? 25 I thank God through Jesus Christ our Lord. So then with the mind I myself serve the Law of God; but with the flesh the Law of sin.*

**Verse 8.** *But sin, taking occasion by the commandment, wrought in me all manner of concupiscence. For without the Law sin was dead.* The first word of this verse shows the contrast which Paul had argued in verses 1-7. Whiteside quotes James Macknight on the epistles.

> James Macknight translates this verse: "But I say that sin taking opportunity under the commandment, wrought effectually in me all strong desire. For without Law sin is dead." The Authorized Version reads: "But sin, taking occasion by the commandment, wrought in me all manner of concupiscence. For without the Law sin was dead." Many others render the verse substantially the same as do Macknight and the Authorized Version. It is a fact that the phrase, "by the commandment," or "through the commandment," in the Greek text, comes before wrought and seems to connect directly with "taking occasion." This makes the commandment only the occasion for sin to assert itself. The commandment was only the occasion for sin to over-

# Commentary on Romans

ride the authority of God. It is certain that God's command was not the source of the evil desires. Let it be remembered that sin is here personified and represented as an enemy that is trying to get us into trouble. There is no occasion for any one to think that a command of God creates or stirs up evil desires. The desire was there, even if God had issued no command, but became an evil desire when it sought to override the command. Hence, without the Law sin was dead. As sin is Lawlessness, sin would not be operative where there is no Law. Neither does Law apply to a person who is not responsible for his deeds. To such a person there is really no Law and, therefore, no sin"[26] [sic].

**Verse 9.** *For I was alive without the Law once: but when the commandment came, sin revived and I died.* Some have encountered much difficulty with this passage. The intent of the apostle is to show, before one becomes accountable to God for sin, there is no spiritual death. The word *revived* here means to be brought to life. When one becomes accountable for his sinful conduct, he is no longer spiritually alive. The point at which this occurs is when an individual develops the ability to reason properly. The consequence of sin is spiritual condemnation. When sin comes to life, spiritual death is the result. It would do the student well to realize the argument of the apostle here refutes the Calvinistic doctrine of inherited sin. Paul had clearly shown that, until man reaches the age of accountability, he does not subject himself the consequences of sin. Once one becomes accountable for his sins, he becomes accountable to God and must, therefore, become obedient to God to secure pardon.

Again, it is impressed upon the student, Paul's audience is the Jewish converts. We shall continue to drive this point. It would be well to understand this passage as follows: *I was spiritually alive without the Law of Christ before the Law of Christ came. But when the Law of Christ came the sin of remaining under the Old Law of Moses became alive. At that point the Jews, who remained compliant to the Old Law of Moses died.* Why was Paul once *spiritually alive without the Law?* Paul declared of himself:

---
[26] Robertson L. Whiteside.

# Commentary on Romans

*Concerning zeal, persecuting the church; touching the righteousness which is in the law, blameless* (Phil. 3:6).

**Verse 10.** *And the commandment, which was ordained to life, I found to be unto death.* The commandment, which was ordained to life is the New Testament System of Christ. The Old Law, Paul found to be *unto death.*

Paul understood the New Law of Christ brought about the *death* of the Old Law of Moses. The Old Law had become a Law *unto death.* Paul will address this subject in greater detail in chapter eight.

**Verse 11.** *For sin, taking occasion by the commandment, deceived me and by it slew me.* Bible skeptics make much of this passage, insisting the commandment of God is the avenue by which men are deceived. However, men are deceived by sin and not the commandments of God. James provided good commentary on this passage when he wrote: *Let no man say when he is tempted, I am tempted of God: for God cannot be tempted with evil, neither tempteth he any man: But every man is tempted, when he is drawn away of his own lust and enticed. Then when lust hath conceived, it bringeth forth sin: and sin, when it is finished, bringeth forth death* (Jas. 1:13-15).

**Verses 12-13.** *Wherefore the Law is holy and the commandment holy and just and good. Was then that which is good made death unto me? God forbid. But sin, that it might appear sin, working death in me by that which is good; that sin by the commandment might become exceeding sinful.* The Jews argued, if they had to be delivered from the Old Law before they could be made free from sin, such meant the Law of Moss was sin; that is, it missed the mark of what God intended.

The commandment was just and intended for good; it did not work death. Sin brought death—not the commandments of God. Sin brings death through disobedience.

**Verse 14.** *For we know that the Law is spiritual: but I am carnal, sold under sin.* The word *we* has reference to the converted Jews of the church at Rome. This is an essential factor on which

# Commentary on Romans

to strongly hold if one wishes to ascertain the passage properly. *We* (the converted Jews) *know that the Law* (of Christ) is a *Spiritual* (Law). It is well to recall there were some *of the sect of the Pharisees which believed, saying, that it was needful to circumcise them and to command them to keep the Law of Moses* (Acts 15:5).

The word *believe* as used in Acts 15:5 is defined as "to have faith in, or upon, or put in trust with." Those who are described as *believers* in Acts 15:5 have reference to the Pharisees who had believed and obeyed the gospel, but had later adopted the doctrine of keeping both the Old Law of Moses in conjunction with the New Law of Christ.

Paul said much about himself when he said, *I am carnal, sold under sin.* To be *carnal* is to be fleshly. He had earlier written: *For when we were in the flesh, the motions of sins, which were by the Law, did work in our members to bring forth fruit unto death. But now we are delivered from the Law, that being dead wherein we were held; that we should serve in newness of spirit and not in the oldness of the letter* (Rom. 7:5-6).

When Paul made use of the word *carnal* he meant he was *fleshly-minded—Old-Lawly-minded.* To be *fleshly-minded* was to be *carnally-minded.* In other words, Paul was showing his fellow Jews that, just as they were Old Lawly-minded, he was at one time Old Lawly-minded. The apostle is not at all addressing physical, natural, fleshly, or carnal matters as they relate to our natural lives. The words *flesh* and *carnal,* as used by the apostle are synonyms and metaphors for the Old Law of Moses. The use of these synonyms and metaphors is one of the most misunderstood matters in the study of the Scriptures.

To remain Old Lawly-, carnally-, and fleshly-minded was to remain desirous for the Old Law. To be Old Lawly-minded, carnally-minded, or fleshly-minded was to be Old Testamently-minded. To remain in such a state would be sin.

Paul well related to his fellow Jews; he also had no desire to give up the Law of Moses and obey the Law of Christ. As a Jew, he wished to remain under the Old Law, as did his fellow Jews.

# Commentary on Romans

Just as the Jews believed and felt it to be sinful to give up the Old Law, so Paul felt it sinful in so doing; that is, before his conversion. However, Paul required and received instruction from the Lord about the matter. *But I certify you, brethren, that the gospel which was preached of me is not after man. For I neither received it of man, neither was I taught it, but by the revelation of Jesus Christ* (Gal. 1:11-12).

**Verse 15.** *For that which I do I allow not.* The exact opposite of what Calvinism teaches is what Paul intends here. *For that which I do I allow not* has reference to the very thing Paul was in fact doing. But what was it the apostle was doing? What was it for which he *allowed not?* Paul was complying with the New Law of Christ and giving up the Old Law. One of the definitions of the word *allow* in this verse is "understand." Paul, like his fellow Jews, found it hard to *understand* how God would require the Jews to give up the Old Law of Moses.

Paul had earlier stated he was speaking *after the manner of men because of the infirmity* of their flesh (Rom. 6:19). In other words, the apostle was speaking from the mindset of the Jews. Paul was showing the Jews that, just as they had such a great difficulty in giving up the Old Law, he had the same difficulty.

Once Paul became instructed by the Lord in the matter (Gal. 1:11-12) and became inspired, he was able to understand why God required the Jews to give up the Old Law. Having become an inspired preacher of the New Law of Christ made it possible and qualified him to instruct his fellow Jews as they needed.

Understanding these things makes the remainder of the verse far less difficult. The passage further reads; *for what I would, that do I not; but what I hate, that do I.* That which Paul *would* do, he did not do. What is it Paul *would* have preferred to do? As a Jew, Paul *would* have preferred to remain under the Old Law. As a Jew, Paul had no desire to surrender to the New Law of Christ. As a Jew, he preferred to remain under the Old Law.

Doing what he wanted to do was the very thing he realized he could not do. Having to give up the Old Law of Moses and obey the New Law of Christ is the very thing he, as a Jew, *hated.* He

## Commentary on Romans

understood the hatred the Jews had in having to give up the Old Law of Moses, and how they hated to obey the New Law of Christ. This caused Paul to be a *wretched* mess. He will explain how he was released from his *wretched* state further into the chapter.

Paul declared the Jews were to no longer be *married* to the Old Law of Moses, but were now to be *married* to the New Law of Christ. The Old Law was now dead, *nailed to the cross,* and buried. The Jews were to be *married* to the body of Christ rather than to Moses. *Wherefore, my brethren, ye also are become dead to the Law by the body of Christ; that ye should be married to another, even to him who is raised from the dead, that we should bring forth fruit unto God* (Rom. 7:4). Paul's argument here was crystal clear to his Jewish audience.

**Verse 16.** *If then I do that which I would not, I consent unto the Law that it is good.* Doing what he *would not* was inclusive of both having to give up the Old Law of Moses and obey the New Law of Christ. In so doing, the apostle *consented* to the fact the Old Law was good.

What does the apostle mean by his statement, the *Law was good?* If it were *good,* why then did God not allow the Jews to remain subject to it? Paul explains why the Law *was good*: *Wherefore the law was our schoolmaster to bring us unto Christ, that we might be justified by faith. But after that faith is come, we are no longer under a schoolmaster* (Gal. 3:24-25).

**Verse 17.** *Now then it is no more I that do it, but sin that dwelleth in me.* Some of the comments of the most revered and respected brethren regarding this passage are amazing to say the least. Whiteside, while having made many astute and scholarly remarks on other passages, misses the mark widely here:

> This verse furnishes conclusive evidence that Paul is not, in these verses, representing the condition of the Christian, for it certainly cannot be said that sin dwells in the Christian. The Holy Spirit dwells in the Christian and it is not possible that the Holy Spirit and sin inhabit the same dwelling place. True, sin slips in at times

# Commentary on Romans

when the Christian is off guard, as a thief might slip into your dwelling place. He who dwells in a house has charge of the house. To say that sin dwells in a person is to say that sin has the control of him. When sin enters into a Christian, it enters as an intruder and not as a dweller.

Paul's language does not free the sinner from responsibility for his conduct. His language is a figure of speech, often found in the Bible, in which one member of a sentence is negative in order to emphasize the other member. Here is an illustration: "He that believeth on me, believeth not on me, but on him that sent me" (John 12:44). We would say: 'He that believeth on me, believeth not on me alone, but also on him that sent me.' And so with Paul: 'So now it is not I alone that do evil, but rather it is sin that dwells in me.' His urge to follow the flesh was greater than his desire to do what his moral judgment dictated"[27] [sic].

Whiteside's comments are not at all in harmony with the context of the passage. He too made the same error as have so many others. What then did the apostle mean when he said, *Now then it is no more I that do it?* Question: *Did what?* The word *it* has reference to something but to what? Understanding what *it* is resolves the difficulty of the passage. What ever *it* was, the apostle was not involved in the doing of *it*. The *it* to which the apostle refers is the keeping of the Old Law.

*But sin that dwelleth in me.* The *sin* which dwelt in Paul was the Old Law. The apostle was in the same quandary as his fellow Jews. He desired to remain under the Old Law as a Jew. Doing so however, was sin. Paul well understood the dilemma his fellow Jews suffered.

**Verse 18.** *For I know that in me (that is, in my flesh,) dwelleth no good thing: for to will is present with me; but how to perform that which is good I find not.* The parenthetical phrase *(that is, in my flesh)* shows Paul was once again relating to his Jewish

---
[27] Robertson L. Whiteside.

## Commentary on Romans

brethren. The apostle made arduous efforts to assure his fellow Jews he understood their dilemma. He was showing his fellow Jews, just as they found it hard to understand why they were commanded by God to give up the Old Law of Moses, so he was in the same plight.

*For I know that in me (that is, in my flesh,) dwelleth no good thing.* The *no good thing* which dwelt in the apostle was his desire to remain under the Old Law. The phrase, *for to will is present with me* means as a Jew, Paul's wish was to remain under the Old Law.

*But how to perform that which is good I find not.* The apostle found it just as difficult to perform the good thing God demanded in giving up the Old Law, and obeying the New Law as did his fellow Jews. He could not, as a diligent Jew, find in himself the answers. He needed a resolution to his dilemma. The Lord did in fact provide the resolution.

**Verse 19.** *For the good that I would I do not: but the evil which I would not, that I do.* The *good* Paul needed to do was to give up the Old Law of Moses, but as a Jew had no desire to do so.

We are compelled to comment on the errors of the New International Version (NIV). Sadly, countless brethren warmly embrace the NIV with deep devotion. The New International Version is a detestable and gross commentary on the doctrine Calvinism regarding Romans 7:14-23. The NIV comes nowhere close to representing that which inspiration intended in said verses. The NIV reads as follows in Romans 7:14-23.

*14 We know that the Law is spiritual; but I am unspiritual, sold as a slave to sin. 15 I do not understand what I do. For what I want to do I do not do, but what I hate I do. 16 And if I do what I do not want to do, I agree that the Law is good. 17 As it is, it is no longer I myself who do it, but it is sin living in me. 18 For I know that good itself does not dwell in me, that is, in my sinful nature. For I have the desire to do what is good, but I cannot carry it out. 19 For I do not do the good I want to do, but the evil I do not want to do—this I keep on doing. 20 Now if I do what I do not want to do, it is no*

# Commentary on Romans

*longer I who do it, but it is sin living in me that does it. 21 So I find this Law at work: Although I want to do good, evil is right there with me. 22 For in my inner being I delight in God's Law; 23 but I see another Law at work in me, waging war against the Law of my mind and making me a prisoner of the Law of sin at work within me.*[28]

The NIV was designed to be Calvinistic. It was created for the purpose of teaching "trans-denominational"[29] doctrines. Below are excerpts from the introduction of the NIV. The bold texts are for emphasis and are matters which need strong consideration. They show the intent and dishonesty of the NIV *translators.*

The New International Version is a completely new translation of the Holy Bible made by over a hundred scholars working directly from the best available Hebrew, Aramaic and Greek texts. **It had its beginning in 1965 when, after several years of exploratory study by committees from the Christian Reformed Church and the National Associations of Evangelicals, a group of scholars met at Palos Heights, Illinois and concurred in the need for a new translation of the Bible in contemporary English. This group, though not made up of official church representatives, was trans-denominational.** Its conclusion was endorsed by a large number of leaders from many denominations who met in Chicago in 1966.

Responsibility for the new version was delegated by the Palos Heights group to a self-governing body of fifteen, the Committee on Bible Translation, composed for the most part of biblical scholars from colleges, universities and seminaries. In 1967 the New York Bible Society (now the International Bible Society) generously undertook the financial sponsorship for the project—sponsorship that made it possible to enlist the help of many distinguished scholars. **The fact that participants from the United States, Great Britain, Cana-**

---

[28] The Holy Bible, New International Version.
[29] Ibid.

## Commentary on Romans

da, Australia and New Zealand worked together gave the project its international scope. That they were from many denominations including Anglican, Assemblies of God, Baptist, Brethren, Christian Reformed, Church of Christ, Evangelical Free, Lutheran, Mennonite, Methodist, Nazarene, Presbyterian, Wesleyan and other churches—helped to safeguard the translation from sectarian bias.

It was further contended the first concern of the translators has been the accuracy of the translation and its fidelity to the thought of the biblical writers. They have weighed the significance of the lexical and grammatical details of the Hebrew, Aramaic and Greek texts. At the same time, **they have striven for more than a word-for-word translation.** Because thought patterns and syntax differ from language to language, faithful communication of the meaning of the writers of the Bible demands frequent modifications in sentence structures and constant regard for the contextual meaning of words.[30]

We now return to the passage under consideration: *For the good that I would I do not: but the evil which I would not, that I do* (Rom. 7:19). The meaning of this verse can be expressed as follows: *The good that I, Paul, should do in giving up the Old Law and accepting the New Law is that which I do not want to do.* Both Paul and his fellow Jews thought the New Law of Christ to be an *evil* thing.

Paul thought the New Law of Christ and Christianity were deadly *evils.* Paul felt it so much so he persecuted the church beyond measure, and did so without compassion. We recall during the early days of the church: *Saul, yet breathing out threatenings and slaughter against the disciples of the Lord, went unto the high priest and desired of him letters to Damascus to the synagogues, that if he found any of this way, whether they were men or women, he might bring them bound unto Jerusalem* (Acts 9:1-2).

---

[30] The Holy Bible, New International Version.

# Commentary on Romans

Paul further described the persecutions in which he involved himself against the Lord's church in his address to the Jewish converts of Galatia. The apostle wrote: *For ye have heard of my conversation in time past in the Jews' religion, how that beyond measure I persecuted the church of God and wasted it* (Gal. 1: 13).

**Verse 20.** *Now if I do that I would not, it is no more I that do it, but sin that dwelleth in me.* This verse is a re-statement of verses 16 and 17. *I am doing,* Paul would say, *The very thing I do not want to do, but it is the very thing I have to do; that is, I have to give up the Old Law and obey the New Law. It is not my Jewish will to give up the Old Law, but I have to do so. However, as Jew, I feel as if I am in sin in so doing.*

Understanding Paul was making strong efforts to empathize with his fellow Jews makes these verses easier to understand. Paul was as troubled as were his fellow Jews. Giving up the Old Law was contrary to his Jewish nature. He and his fellow Jews were to do so, nonetheless.

**Verses 21-22.** *I find then a Law, that, when I would do good, evil is present with me. For I delight in the Law of God after the inward man.* As a Jew, Paul's conscience bothered him much for having to set aside the Old Law of Moses and accept the New Law of Christ. The apostle felt as if were indeed a sinful thing to give up the Old Law and obey the New Law. Doing so made the apostle feel *evil.*

Paul was making his deep feelings known to his fellow Jew. His misery was genuine and his emotions ran deep. His love of the Law of Moses was unmatched. Paul made much of his pedigree and his study of the Law of Moses. He was proud of his education and zeal for the Law. Consider the following passages.

> *I am verily a man which am a Jew, born in Tarsus, a city in Cilicia, yet brought up in this city at the feet of Gamaliel and taught according to the perfect manner of the Law of the fathers and was zealous toward God, as ye all are this day* (Acts 22:3).

# Commentary on Romans

*Though I might also have confidence in the flesh. If any other man thinketh that he hath whereof he might trust in the flesh, I more: Circumcised the eighth day, of the stock of Israel, of the tribe of Benjamin, an Hebrew of the Hebrews; as touching the Law, a Pharisee; Concerning zeal, persecuting the church; touching the righteousness which is in the Law, blameless* (Phil. 3: 4-6).

The apostle was indeed deeply empathetic with his fellow Jews. As a Pharisee, he more than other Jews, felt the sense of sin in having to give up the Old Law.

**Verse 23.** *But I see another Law in my members, warring against* the *Law of my mind and bringing me into captivity to the Law of sin which is in my members.* Thus far, there have been two Laws under consideration. One was the Law of Moses; the other Law is the Law of Christ. In this verse, Paul introduces yet *another Law.* What is this third Law introduced by the apostle? It pertains to Paul's *members.* The third Law introduced here is the *Law* of Paul's conscience. Paul is at war with his conscience not wanting to give up the Old Law which he knew he had do.

On one hand, Paul wars within himself wanting to remain under the Old Law; however, he realized should he do so, he placed himself in captivity of the Old Law. The *Law of sin* is the Old Law. On the other hand, he understood he must overcome the difficulty and serve the Lord under the New Law.

*The Law of sin which is in my members* refers to the fact that, as a Jew, Paul still possessed the desire to remain under the Old Law. This desire was in his *members*—that is, in his mind and conscience. This condition made Paul a *wretched man.* He needed deliverance from his quandary, as did his fellow Jews. Paul needed to be delivered from the old corpse of the Law of Moses.

Paul spent much time informing the Jews the Old Law of Moses was now *dead.* The death of the Old Law occurred three days before Christ was crucified (cf. Matt. 23:38). When the Old Law died, the corpse of the Law of Moses remained and needed

# Commentary on Romans

burying. It is important to recall the number of times Paul used the words *dead* and *death* in this chapter. The *death* of the Old Law received much attention from the apostle. The Law of Moses was *dead* and needed to be *buried*. The Jews became *widowed* from the Old Law and needed a new husband. The Old Law was nailed to the cross and was forever dead (cf. Col. 2:14). When Pilate had the accusation written and set up over the Lord's head, saying, *This is Jesus the King of the Jews*, it served as the death certificate of the Old Law (Matt. 27:37).

*Wherefore, my brethren, ye also are become dead to the Law by the body of Christ; that ye should be married to another, even to him who is raised from the dead, that we should bring forth fruit unto God* (Rom. 7:4). The Jews were spiritually *widowed* once the Old Law died. They were to be *married* to a new husband. Their *new husband* was to be Christ.

Being *widowed* from the Old Law of Moses put Paul and his fellow Jews in a state of despair. That despair needed a resolution. How could Paul be delivered from such a *wretched* state? The *wretched* state of the apostle could only be resolved one way. That way was Christ (Jno. 14:6). The Old Law was now a dead corpse onto which the Jews continued to hold.
Under the Law of Moses, *Whosoever toucheth the dead body of any man that is dead, and purifieth not himself, defileth the tabernacle of the Lord; and that soul shall be cut off from Israel: because the water of separation was not sprinkled upon him, he shall be unclean; his uncleanness is yet upon him* (Num. 19:13). The Jews, however, were determined to cleave to the dead body of the Old Law of Moses which made them unclean under the New Law of Christ. Perhaps one can better grasp what Paul meant when he wrote: *Blotting out the handwriting of ordinances that was against us, which was contrary to us, and took it out of the way, nailing it to his cross* (Col. 2:14).

The Jews, as well as Paul, needed deliverance from that *body of death*. But how or who could deliver Paul from such a *wretched* state? Who could cleanse and deliver him and the Jews from that *dead body* of the Old Law? The apostle answers the question in the following verse.

# Commentary on Romans

**Verse 24.** *O wretched man that I am! who shall deliver me from the body of this death?* The *body of death* of which the apostle speaks is the *dead body of the Law of Moses*. It was a body of death in a two-fold manner. First, it was a *body of death* because it represented the Old Law which was indeed dead. Second, it was a *body of death* because remaining under it resulted in spiritual death.

Paul wrote elsewhere: *Who also hath made us able ministers of the New Testament; not of the letter, but of the spirit: for the letter killeth, but the spirit giveth life. But if the ministration of death, written and engraven in stones, was glorious, so that the children of Israel could not stedfastly behold the face of Moses for the glory of his countenance; which glory was to be done away* (II Cor. 3:6-7).

The question of *who shall deliver me from the body of this death?* needed an answer. Paul provided that answer in the following verse.

**Verse 25.** *I thank God through Jesus Christ our Lord. So then with the mind I myself serve the Law of God; but with the flesh the Law of sin.* Here the apostle first gave thanks to God that He provided an avenue by which this needed deliverance could be acquired.

The question Paul asked was not *what* could deliver him from his quandary; rather the question was through *whom* his needed deliverance could come. The answer was *through Jesus Christ our Lord.* Christ was the one through whom Paul's deliverance was to come—not the Law of Moses. The apostle was now able to serve God through the New Law of God with a clear conscience.

## Summary of verses 14-25

Paul informed his fellow Jews the very thing he wanted to do was to remain under the Old Law of Moses which was the very thing he could not do. The thing he had to do was to surrender to the New Law of Christ which he also did not want to do. In his Jewish heart, Paul wanted to remain under the Old Law.

# Commentary on Romans

The context of these verses has nothing to do with the works of the physical flesh. Countless members of the Lord's church are also deeply duped by the devilish doctrine of Calvinism as set forth in the NIV. It is sad indeed to see so many members of the Lord's church cling so tightly to their NIV "Bibles." The NIV *translates* this section of Scripture with caustic Calvinistic doctrine. Calvinism teaches it is the nature of man to sin and that nature to do so overrides man's ability to be the spiritual creature he ought to be.

The New International Version reads as follows, with emphasis added.

> *18 For I know that good itself does not dwell in me, that is, in my **sinful nature**. For I have the desire to do what is good, but I cannot carry it out. 19 For I do not do the good I want to do, but the evil I do not want to do—this I keep on doing.* [31]

*It is not man's nature to sin!* Man is tempted and taught to sin. The serpent tempted Adam and Eve to sin as recorded in Genesis 3. *Until the serpent appeared neither Adam nor Eve were sinful by nature.* Men do not inherit sin. If man is sinful by nature, why does the devil spend his time working to tempt men to sin?

Most denominationalists believe and teach this damnable doctrine of Calvinism. Most *modern translations* of the Bible are not *translations* at all. Rather, most are nothing more than commentaries on the evils of Calvinism! The NIV is a grand example of Calvinistic doctrine.

The NIV is neither a translation, nor is it a crude paraphrase of these inspired verses of Scripture. The NIV intentionally overflows with damnable Calvinistic doctrines. It warrants no valid consideration in Bible study!

## Comments Regarding Marriage, Divorce, and Remarriage from Romans 7:1-3

---

[31] The Holy Bible, New International Version.

# Commentary on Romans

*1 Know ye not, brethren, (for I speak to them that know the law,) how that the law hath dominion over a man as long as he liveth? 2 For the woman which hath an husband is bound by the law to her husband so long as he liveth; but if the husband be dead, she is loosed from the law of her husband. 3 So then if, while her husband liveth, she be married to another man, she shall be called an adulteress: but if her husband be dead, she is free from that law; so that she is no adulteress, though she be mar-ried to another man.*

Many have struggled with this passage when addressing the subject of remarriage. It is often asserted, one who has divorced a spouse not for fornication may remarry once the other spouse has died. This is a devilish and damnable doctrine.

We submit the following before addressing the subject. We maintain it is only through the death of Christ that one may be released from the burden and guilt and consequences of sin. With this principle we surely all agree. The death of the most righteous individual can in no way negate the guilt or the consequence of *any sin*.

Sin bears consequences. Criminals suffer the consequence of either jail or prison time. One may be released from his incarceration, but he is not released the consequence or guilt of his action. His misconduct required incarceration. After his release, he is still guilty of the crime which he committed. He has, however, paid his proverbial debt to society, but he remains guilty of the crime which caused his imprisonment.

The same is true regarding one who has divorced a spouse for a reason not for fornication (cf. Matt. 19:9). Once one divorces a spouse for a reason other than fornication, he is guilty of doing so—regardless of how long he or his former spouse may live. *If one is put away for any reason other than fornication*, or the spouse who did the putting away for a reason other than fornication "marries" another person, then that individual becomes an adulterer according to the Lord. This forever settles the matter.

Just because one who has been put away (for a reason other

# Commentary on Romans

than fornication) dies, does not release the remaining spouse from the guilt and consequences of an unlawful divorce. In the case under consideration both spouses are guilty of being unlawfully put away. *Neither spouse met the exception permitted by the Lord as dictated in Matthew 19:9.* Neither the original husband or wife, with God's favor, marry another spouse.

However, it is argued that if one spouse in this situation dies, then the remaining spouse is released from the law of the first marriage because there is no living spouse; therefore, the surviving partner cannot be bound to someone who is no longer living. *This is not the issue!* The issue is, and the fact remains, the one who survives is *still guilty* of being divorced for a reason not authorized by the Lord. If not why not?

If it is the case the death of one of the spouses in this situation can release one the from the consequences of sin, then one must conclude the death of one other than Christ can release one from the consequences of sin. As far as the heavens are above the earth is this doctrine from the Lord's mandate. The death of Christ and only the death of Christ can release anyone from the consequences of sin.

## Romans 8:1-8

*1 There is therefore now no condemnation to them which are in Christ Jesus, who walk not after the flesh, but after the Spirit. 2 For the Law of the Spirit of life in Christ Jesus hath made me free from the Law of sin and death. 3 For what the Law could not do, in that it was weak through the flesh, God sending his own Son in the likeness of sinful flesh and for sin, condemned sin in the flesh: 4 That the righteousness of the Law might be fulfilled in us, who walk not after the flesh, but after the Spirit. 5 For they that are after the flesh do mind the things of the flesh; but they that are after the Spirit the things of the Spirit. 6 For to be carnal-ly minded is death; but to be spiritually minded is life and peace. 7 Because the carnal mind is enmity against God: for it is not subject to the Law of God, neither indeed can be. 8 So then they that are in the flesh*

# Commentary on Romans

*cannot please God.*

**Verse 1.** *There is therefore now no condemnation to them which are in Christ Jesus, who walk not after the flesh, but after the Spirit.* Continued emphasis is again in order with respect to the words *therefore* and *wherefore*. Here the apostle uses the word *therefore* showing that which follows in the subsequent verses is a conclusion to chapter 7:15-25.

Paul expressed deliverance from the state of wretchedness in which he found himself as recorded in 7:24 was through Jesus Christ. Here the apostle supplies his inspired conclusion to the matter. *There is therefore now no condemnation to them which are in Christ.* Remaining under the Old Law resulted in spiritual condemnation; however, for those Jews who were in Christ said condemnation was removed, and God's justification was awarded to those who were obedient to the Law of Christ.

The word *now* has reference to the then-current spiritual status in which the obedient Jews were found. *Now* that Christ established His new system and *now* the obedient Jews had given up the Old Law of Moses, and *now* that Jesus Christ had delivered them from the wretchedness in which they found themselves there was no longer condemnation assigned to them.

The phrase, *who walk not after the flesh, but after the Spirit*, identifies exactly those of whom the apostle speaks. Those who *walk after the spirit* are those who walked after the New Law of Christ. Those who walked *after the flesh* were those who remained tethered to the Old Law of Moses. Paul well explained the word *flesh* referred to the Old Law of Moses, and the word *spirit* referred to the New Law of Christ. *It is essential to deeply engrave this in one's mind when delving further into this chapter.*

The apostle declared there was no condemnation under the Law of Christ. Condemnation remained upon those who chose to continue under the Old Law. There was no condemnation in Christ, but there was condemnation under the Law of Moses.

**Verse 2.** *For the Law of the Spirit of life in Christ Jesus hath*

## Commentary on Romans

*made me free from the Law of sin and death.* The *Law of the spirit of the life in Christ* is an inspired statement which contains much. First observe, *the Law of the spirit* refers to the New Law; that is, the New Testament. Second, *the Law of the spirit* is a Law of *life*. It is a Law of life which was contrasted to the Law of death. The Old Law is now a dead Law. The Old Law is not only a dead Law, but it is a Law which resulted in death—spiritual death. Third, *the Law of the spirit* is not only a Law of life; it is a life which is only found *in Christ.*

The *Law of sin and death* refers to the Old Law of Moses. It was a law no longer to be obeyed. Jesus declared: *Behold, your house is left unto you desolate* (Matt. 23:38). By such, Jesus meant the Lord would no longer be in the temple of the Jews, nor would their worship avail anything.

The Old Law of Moses had ended so far as the religious principles and mandates were concerned. Even though the Jews continued to worship by the Old Law they did not enjoy the blessing of the Lord's presence in the temple, nor did they reap the benefit of His blessings.

When the Roman army destroyed the temple and city of Jerusalem in AD 70, that destruction was the final nail in the proverbial coffin of the Mosaical System. When Jesus left the temple, He left it forever desolate (Matt. 23:38). Since that time, the Jews have not been able to keep the Old Law. The Lord abolished the Old Law in a two-fold manner. First, He did so religiously when He nailed it to the cross (Col. 2:14), and secondly in AD 70, which ended the civil system of the Old Law.

The religious side of the Old Law required the Jews to offer sacrifices and numerous other mandates. The civil side required the Jews to execute justice and judgments in the six cities of refuge mandated under the Old Law, cited below.

> Then ye shall appoint you cities to be cities of refuge for you; that the slayer may flee thither, which killeth any person at unawares (Num. 35:11).
>
> And of these cities which ye shall give six cities shall

# Commentary on Romans

*ye have for refuge. Ye shall give three cities on this side Jordan and three cities shall ye give in the land of Canaan, which shall be cities of refuge. These six cities shall be a refuge, both for the children of Israel and for the stranger and for the sojourner among them: that every one that killeth any person unawares may flee thither* (Num. 35:13-15).

*Speak to the children of Israel, saying, Appoint out for you cities of refuge, whereof I spake unto you by the hand of Moses* (Jos. 20:2).

*And unto the children of Gershon, of the families of the Levites, out of the other half tribe of Manasseh they gave Golan in Bashan with her suburbs, to be a city of refuge for the slayer; and Beeshterah with her suburbs; two cities* (Jos. 21:27).

*And out of the tribe of Naphtali, Kedesh in Galilee with her suburbs, to be a city of refuge for the slayer; and Hammothdor with her suburbs and Kartan with her suburbs; three cities* (Jos. 21:32).

Until the Roman army destroyed the city of Jerusalem, the Jews were permitted by the Romans to judge their fellow Jews according to the Law of Moses. Pilate instructed the Jews to take Jesus *and judge him according to your Law* (Jno. 18:31). However, when the Romans destroyed the city of Jerusalem, inclusive of the temple, the civil Law of the Jews was forever ended. From that time forward, no Jew has not been able to keep the Old Law, either religiously or civilly.

So-called Jews today can not trace their lineage back to Abraham, as the Law of Moses required. The genealogical records of the Jewish nation were destroyed by the Roman army in AD 70 when the Roman army destroyed the temple. With those records destroyed, it is no longer possible for anyone who claims to be a Jew to trace his Jewish heritage back to Abraham as the Old Law required.
Further, from the time the Roman army destroyed Jerusalem, no Jew has been able to worship according to the Law of Moses.

# Commentary on Romans

No sacrifices have been made according to the Old Law. There were five different sacrifices required under the Law of Moses. There was *the burnt offering* which is referred to 193 times in the Old Law. *The meal offering* was also required. *The peace offering* was also mandated under the Old Law. *An offering for sins* was required as well. The fifth offering commanded under the Old Law was *the trespass offering.* From the time of the destruction of Jerusalem in AD 70, none of these oblations have been offered according to the Law of Moses.

It is also the case the Old Law required all male Jews were to present themselves in the temple three times each year. *Three times in the year all thy males shall appear before the Lord God* (Exo. 23:17). That the temple is no longer standing, and has not stood since AD 70, eliminates the possibility of the male Jews to *appear before the Lord* as required by the Old Law.

Further, the civil laws regulating the Jews today are not in harmony with the civil laws of the Old Law of Moses. The civil laws of Israel required cities of refuge according to Numbers 35:11-15, noted above. The nation of Israel does not follow the Law of Moses regarding said civil laws. There are no cities of refuge today. Even if the Jews of today had them, they could not comply with the Old Law. The territory now claimed by Israel lacks in the area and places God mandated for the cities of refuge under the Law of Moses. The Jews cannot comply with the Old Law in either spiritually or civilly.

**Verse 3.** *For what the Law could not do, in that it was weak through the flesh, God sending his own Son in the likeness of sinful flesh and for sin, condemned sin in the flesh.* Paul clearly stated there was something the *Law* (of Moses) *could not do!* What was it? Further, we ask *why* could the Law not do that of which the apostle spoke?

First, the Law could not provide complete righteousness. There was righteousness to be had under the Old Law, but it needed to be completed. Paul informed the Jews the righteousness of the Law was *fulfilled in us* (the Jewish converts), as declared in verse 4. Another question is; *how* was the Law *weak through the flesh?* The answer to these questions are recorded for us;

# Commentary on Romans

*For finding fault with them, he saith, Behold, the days come, saith the Lord, when I will make a new covenant with the house of Israel and with the house of Judah* (Heb. 8:8). The Law was not weak because of the Lord's inability to impose a perfect Law. The Law was *weak* through the flesh—that is, through the Jews. In the above-quoted passage, it is well to observe God found *fault with them* (the people), not the Law. The Law was perfect for that which God intended for it to do, which was to bring the Jews to Christ, and it did indeed do so. Consider the following passages.

> *The Lord thy God will raise up unto thee a Prophet from the midst of thee, of thy brethren, like unto me; unto him ye shall hearken; According to all that thou desiredst of the Lord thy God in Horeb in the day of the assembly, saying, Let me not hear again the voice of the Lord my God, neither let me see this great fire any more, that I die not. And the Lord said unto me, They have well spoken that which they have spoken. I will raise them up a Prophet from among their brethren, like unto thee and will put my words in his mouth; and he shall speak unto them all that I shall command him* (Deut. 18:15-18).

> *Wherefore then serveth the Law? It was added because of transgressions, till the seed should come to whom the promise was made; and it was ordained by angels in the hand of a mediator.... Wherefore the Law was our schoolmaster to bring us unto Christ, that we might be justified by faith* (Gal. 3:19, 24).

*And for sin, condemned sin in the flesh.* This passage has caused much confusion and has produced; it seems, as many opinions as there are commentators. However, when one keeps the context of the passage in view the passage is self-explained. The preposition *peri* can mean "on account of" (NKJ) or "because if" (unlike *eis* which means "into" or "unto"). "Because of sin." This refers to the sins of the people (the Jews); the Law made sin known. Sin being made known by the Law resulted in condemnation.

## Commentary on Romans

The phrase is better expressed as: *And because of sin, the Law of Moses* (the flesh) *was the avenue by which God* (under the Old Law) *exposed sin.* It is well to recall the apostle had earlier stated he had not known sin but by the Law (cf. Rom. 7:7).

**Verse 4.** *That the righteousness of the Law might be fulfilled in us, who walk not after the flesh, but after the Spirit.* As noted in the comments of the previous verse, the righteousness of the Old Law of Moses needed to be fulfilled. One could indeed obtain righteousness under the Old Law, as the following example demonstrates: *There was in the days of Herod, the king of Judaea, a certain priest named Zacharias, of the course of Abia: and his wife was of the daughters of Aaron and her name was Elisabeth. And they were both righteous before God, walking in all the commandments and ordinances of the Lord blameless* (Lk. 1:5-6). Further, Paul declared of himself he had obtained the righteousness the Old Law granted. Paul wrote: *Concerning zeal, persecuting the church; touching the righteousness which is in the Law, blameless* (Phil. 3:6).

Even though the parents of John the baptizer and the apostle Paul were found *blameless* under the Old Law and declared to be righteous thereby, their blamelessness and righteousness needed to come to fruition. The fruition and fulfillment of their righteousness was accomplished in prospect by the Law of Christ. Many who lived under the Old Law also acquired such blamelessness and righteousness. The eleventh chapter of the Hebrew epistle proves such to indeed to be the case. If it is the case none could obtain blamelessness or righteousness under the Old Law, then it would be the case none who lived under either the Law of Moses or the Patriarchal Law of the Old Testament could have been, nor were ever, saved.

It has long been argued the sins of those who lived under the Old Law *had their sins rolled forward.* However, there is not one passage of Scripture to support the assertion. The sins of those who lived under the laws of the Old Testament (both Patriarchal and Mosaical) had their sins remitted in prospect. The phrases, *rolled forward,* and, *sins remembered every year,* are nowhere found in the Old or New Testaments. In contrast to this assertion the Hebrew author wrote:

# Commentary on Romans

> For the Law having a shadow of good things to come and not the very image of the things, can never with those sacrifices which they offered year by year continually make the comers thereunto perfect. For then would they not have ceased to be offered? because that the worshipers once purged should have had no more conscience of sins. But in those sacrifices there is a remembrance again made of sins every year. For it is not possible that the blood of bulls and of goats should take away sins. Wherefore when he cometh into the world, he saith, Sacrifice and offering thou wouldest not, but a body hast thou prepared me: In burnt offerings and sacrifices for sin thou hast had no pleasure. Then said I, Lo, I come (in the volume of the book it is written of me,) to do thy will, O God. Above when he said, Sacrifice and offering and burnt offerings and offering for sin thou wouldest not, neither hadst pleasure therein; which are offered by the Law (Heb. 10:1-8).

Sacrifices for sins were made every year, and it was in those sacrifices sin was remembered, not in the minds of those who offered the sacrifices, but by God. The consciences of the worshipers were purged and made pure. With a clear conscience, those of the Old Testament were able to acquire blamelessness and the righteousness of the Old Law. Their consciences were cleared through their sacrifices and their sins were forgiven in prospect. It is not the case the sins of the people were *rolled forward* every year; rather, it is the case the blood of Christ flowed backwards, in retrospect, to remit the sins for which animal blood was shed. The blood of bulls and goats only provided a temporary covering for the sins of those under the Old Law. The blood of those sacrificed bulls and goats did not provide forgiveness from their sins. Only the blood of Christ is able to remit sins. It is also the case the blood of Christ flows forward into the future for those who obeyed and are yet to obey the gospel. Those of the Old Testament had their sins covered by the blood of Christ in retrospect; those who lived after the crucifixion have their sins forgiven in prospect. The blood of Christ flowed and flows in such a way as to cover the times in which men live (in the pres-

# Commentary on Romans

ent) and lived (in the past).

Those *who walk not after* (according to) *the flesh* are those who walk not after the Old Law. Those who walk *after the spirit* are those who walk after the New Law. Indeed, the *New Law* is the Law of Christ which is the New Testament System of faith.

**Verse 5.** *For they that are after the flesh do mind the things of the flesh; but they that are after the Spirit the things of the Spirit.* The meaning of this verse is provided in pristine clarity. The word *flesh* has reference to the Old Law of Moses. The Jews who maintained their desire to and did in fact remain under the Old Law gave way to the things of the Old Law. In contrast, the word *spirit* has reference to the New Law—the Law of Christ. They who are *after the spirit* are those who have obeyed the New Testament System of Christ.

It does one well to keep in mind the Greek texts were written without either capital letters or punctuation. The capitalization of the word *spirit* bears no merit. Translators of the original text assumed the *spirit* as used by Paul referred to the Holy Spirit; thus, they capitalized the word. However, understanding the arguments made by the apostle, and how he used the words *flesh* and *spirit* in metaphorical fashion, well endows the student with how the words are to be contextually defined. It is vital to realize *context always dictates definition.*

A metaphor is a figure is speech in which a term or phrase is applied to something to which it is not literally applicable in order to suggest a resemblance, as in *A mighty fortress is our God*. A metaphor may also be something used, or regarded as being used, to represent something else; an emblem, or a symbol.

Paul uses the words *flesh* and *spirit* metaphorically to represent the Old Law and the New Law. Keeping this in mind through the study of both Romans chapters seven and eight serves the student well and allows for the proper exegetical conclusion to these chapters.

**Verse 6.** *For to be carnally minded is death; but to be spiritually minded is life and peace.* As Paul used the words *flesh* and

# Commentary on Romans

*spirit* metaphorically, he now uses the word *carnal* in the same vein.

For to be Old Lawly-minded—carnally-minded, resulted in spiritual death. However, to be spiritually minded—New Lawly-minded, resulted in spiritual life.

**Verse 7.** *Because the carnal mind is enmity against God: for it is not subject to the Law of God, neither indeed can be.* This verse provides the answer to the question, "Why did the fleshly (Jewish) mind result in spiritual death? *Because,* wrote Paul, *the carnal mind is enmity against God.* The word *enmity* means "to be hostile toward, having hostility; being in opposition to, and having hatred for or toward something or someone." The *carnal mind,* is the Jewish mind. The *Old-lawly* minded Jew was hostile toward the New Law of Christ, and was in opposition to God's will, having a hatred for God's New Law.

The words *for it* have reference to the carnal, *Old-lawly* minded Jews, who refused to be *subject to the Law of God.* It is not at all the case the apostle argued the Jews were not subject to the New Law of Christ. Rather the meaning is the carnally-minded Jew (Old-lawly minded Jew) refused to subject themselves to the New Law of Christ.

The phrase *neither indeed can be* means the carnally-minded Jews could not be subject to God's New Law with the expectation of gaining spiritual life. It also means many Jews could not find it in themselves to bring themselves into subjection to the New Law of Christ.

**Verse 8.** *So then they that are in the flesh cannot please God.* Here the word *so* equates to therefore or wherefore. Verse 8 is the conclusion to verses 1-7. Therefore, they (the Jews who refused to give up the Old Law) were still in the flesh (remaining under the Old Law) and could not please God. Under the Old Law there remained no more sacrifice for sin (Heb. 10:26).

If, as the Calvinist teaches, *the flesh* in these verses refers to the flesh of men, then it is the case no man can please God. Calvinism teaches this very thing for the purpose of promoting the false

# Commentary on Romans

doctrine of irresistible grace. The core intent of Calvinism is to remove man from his accountability to God. But all men shall give an account of himself before God (cf. Rom. 14:12: II Cor. 5:10: Ecc. 12:14).

Why would God appoint *a day, in the which he will judge the world in righteousness by that man whom he hath ordained* if men are already deemed saved or lost according to Calvinism (Acts 17:31)?

## Romans 8:9-17

*9 But ye are not in the flesh, but in the Spirit, if so be that the Spirit of God dwell in you. Now if any man have not the Spirit of Christ, he is none of his. 10 And if Christ be in you, the body is dead because of sin; but the Spirit is life because of righteousness. 11 But if the Spirit of him that raised up Jesus from the dead dwell in you, he that raised up Christ from the dead shall also quicken your mortal bodies by his Spirit that dwelleth in you. 12 Therefore, brethren, we are debtors, not to the flesh, to live after the flesh. 13 For if ye live after the flesh, ye shall die: but if ye through the Spirit do mortify the deeds of the body, ye shall live. 14 For as many as are led by the Spirit of God, they are the sons of God. 15 For ye have not received the spirit of bondage again to fear; but ye have received the Spirit of adoption, whereby we cry, Abba, Father. 16 The Spirit itself beareth witness with our spirit, that we are the children of God: 17 And if children, then heirs; heirs of God and joint-heirs with Christ; if so be that we suffer with him, that we may be also glorified together.*

**Verse 9.** *But ye are not in the flesh, but in the Spirit, if so be that the Spirit of God dwell in you. Now if any man have not the Spirit of Christ, he is none of his.* It seems there is no end of confusion regarding not only this verse, but the entirety of the Roman epistle, especially chapter eight.

The word *but* shows a contrast to verse 8: *So then they that are in the flesh cannot please God.* The apostle declared the Jewish

# Commentary on Romans

converts were not *in the flesh* and Paul has shown the *flesh* is synonymous with the Law of Moses. The meaning of the passage is the converted Jews were no longer *in the flesh* (under the Old Law) but they were *in the spirit* (under the New Law).

The number of those who insist the Holy Spirit personally indwells the Christian in a non-miraculous way is a vast one. However, there is a question which must be posed to those who hold to this doctrine.

In consideration of the apostle's statement, *Now if any man have not the Spirit of Christ, he is none of his*, it is argued by those who hold to the personal indwelling of the Holy Spirit in the saint, that a person receives the personal indwelling at the point of baptism. This position is based solely upon Acts 2:38. *Then Peter said unto them, Repent and be baptized every one of you in the name of Jesus Christ for the remission of sins and ye shall receive the gift of the Holy Ghost.*

If it is the case this doctrine is true, then denying the doctrine would be blasphemous and detrimental to one's eternal welfare which would result in the loss of the soul. If not, why not? Such would be true because the denial rejects the power of God and activity of the Holy Spirit during the act of baptism. Here we pose the following question: "Can man deny any Biblical doctrine and not be in error?" If it is the case that one Bible doctrine may be denied without suffering the consequences of sin, *then it is the case, any biblical doctrine may be denied without the consequence of sin.* Again, if not, why not? Further, If one doctrine of truth can be denied without consequences, any doctrine of truth can be denied. However, those who subscribe to the doctrine of the personal indwelling of the Holy Ghost are not so bold as to make such a claim. Rather, the subscribers to the personal indwelling of the Holy Ghost insist it is not a matter of salvation and allow those who oppose this doctrine latitude and grace. If the matter is not one of salvation, then why insist on the doctrine?

Here we ask another question. Is not every doctrine of the Bible a matter of salvation? If not, why not? It is indeed, strange such assertions are made regarding some Bible doctrines, but are

# Commentary on Romans

seemingly forbidden regarding other Bible doctrines. Are not all Bible doctrines a matters of salvation and equally important? If not, why did the Lord deem them a necessary part of His Word? It is true some doctrines were given for Jews which are not matters of salvation for man today. However, the supposed doctrine of the indwelling of the Holy Spirit, and the non-indwelling of the Holy Spirit *are New Testament doctrines*—both of which cannot be correct. Either one is correct, and the other is not, or both are false. If both are false then it is the case the latter is true. Surely, the foolishness of this can be clearly seen. Both doctrines cannot be true.

Further, those who subscribe to the personal indwelling of the Holy Spirit teach the indwelling of the Holy Spirit is the seal of identity for the saint. If the Holy Spirit is awarded at baptism (Acts 2:38), and if the indwelling of the Holy Spirit is an identifying seal for the Christian (Rom. 8:9); and one denies having received the Holy Spirit at his baptism and one also denies he has the Holy Ghost, then the one who denies the doctrine has denied not one, but two passages of inspiration. Would not such a denial negate their baptism? So what does the phrase, *now if any man have not the Spirit of Christ, he is none of his*, mean?

Keeping the inspired remark of the apostle within the framework in which the apostle made the inspired statement is paramount. The apostle did not limit space in his efforts to show the Jewish converts his use of the words *flesh* and *spirit* are metaphorical. Paul has used the word *flesh* to represent the Old Law, and used the word *spirit* to represent the New Law. The meaning of the phrase is *now if any man have* (has) *not* (obeyed) *the spirit of Christ* (the gospel of the New Testament), *he* (the one who has not obeyed the gospel) *is none of his* (the Lord's and he is not a Christian). This passage has nothing to do with the matter of the personal indwelling of the Holy Ghost. There is no passage which teaches such a doctrine.

**Verse 10.** *And if Christ be in you, the body is dead because of sin; but the Spirit is life because of righteousness.* The word *and* is the conjunction between verses 9 and 10. The verses must remain together to ascertain the intended purpose of the apostle. If it is the case the gospel dwells in you, then you belong to

# Commentary on Romans

Christ and no longer belong to Moses. *And* if it is the case you belong to Christ, then the body of the Law of Moses is dead. The Law of Moses died, which brought about spiritual death to those who remained fettered to it. The Jews who had obeyed the Gospel of Christ died to the Law of Moses, but were given spiritual life under the Law of Christ. It is now in the New Testament System of Christ where righteousness and life are found.

**Verse 11.** *But if the Spirit of him that raised up Jesus from the dead dwell in you, he that raised up Christ from the dead shall also quicken your mortal bodies by his Spirit that dwelleth in you.* To say this passage involves much is an understatement. There is a change in the way Paul uses the word *spirit* in this verse. It must be remembered that *context always dictates definition.*

Paul begins to change his approach in instructing the Jews. The depth of the apostle's instructions begins to increase. Being the inspired logician he was, Paul used that logic to present to the Jews yet another understanding and use of the word *spirit.*

It is of great importance to understand here Paul used is a metonymical statement here. A metonymy is a figure of speech which occurs frequently in the Scriptures and must be understood if one is to interpret the Scriptures correctly. The word *metonymy* is derived from two Greek words—a preposition and a noun. The former indicates change and the latter, name. Combined, they mean "with a change of name." In other words, this figure of speech is one which has a change of name in speaking of a certain event. There are different causes for the employment of this type of language. Regardless of the fundamental reason for the change in phraseology, the idea is a very definite one.

There are four metonymical forms used in the Scriptures. First, there is the general metonymy, as described above. Second, there is the metonymy of the cause, wherein the effect is stated, but the cause is meant. Third there is the metonymy of the effect, which states the cause, but the effect is meant. Last, there is the metonymy of the adjunct, in which "an adverb or adverbial phrase attached to the verb of a clause especially to express a relation of time, place, frequency, degree, or manner." An example of the metonymy of the adjunct is: "Massage therapy."

# Commentary on Romans

Message therapy is an adjunct which means treatment.

In this verse, the metonymy of the cause is used by the apostle. Remember, the effect is stated, but the cause is meant. Paul said, *but if the Spirit of him that raised up Jesus from the dead dwell in you, he that raised up Christ from the dead shall also quicken your mortal bodies by his Spirit that dwelleth in you.* The apostle stated the cause, but the effect was meant. The cause was that Christ was raised up from the dead.

Just as the Holy Spirit was the cause by which Christ was raised from the dead, so it was the case the *Holy Spirit dwelt in* those believing Jews to whom Paul was speaking. But the question is: *How did the Holy Spirit dwell in those obedient Jews?* The metonymy of the cause is used here. The effect was stated, but the cause is meant. The Holy Spirit dwelt in these obedient Jews (the cause) through a miraculous gift awarded (the effect) to these believing Jews through the laying on of the hands of an apostle (cf. Acts 8:18). The same process was used in the Old Testament. Joshua was endowed with the Holy Spirit as well as Moses. Moses wrote: *And Joshua the son of Nun was full of the spirit of wisdom; for Moses had laid his hands upon him: and the children of Israel hearkened unto him, and did as the Lord commanded Moses* (Deut. 34:9).

The same declaration was made by Paul in his address to the church of Galatia. *This only would I learn of you, Received ye the Spirit by the works of the law, or by the hearing of faith* (Gal. 3:2)? Did you receive the gifts of the Holy Spirit from the blessings of the Old Law? Or did you receive the miraculous power to work miracles, speak in tongues, heal, or do other miracles from the blessing of the New Law?

**Verse 12.** *Therefore, brethren, we are debtors, not to the flesh, to live after the flesh.* Paul's meaning here is the Jews were no longer indebted to the Old Law. This verse is the apostle's conclusion to verses 9-11. It is of worth to notice Paul identified these Jewish converts as *brethren.* They were not *brethren* under the Law of Moses, nor were they *brethren* because of their Jewish genealogy; but rather they were *brethren* in the Lord's church.

# Commentary on Romans

They were no longer of the family of Abraham under the Old Law, but were of the new family of God. *Wherefore I desire that ye faint not at my tribulations for you, which is your glory. For this cause I bow my knees unto the Father of our Lord Jesus Christ, Of whom the whole family in heaven and earth is named* (Eph. 3:13-15).

*We are debtors, not to the flesh, to live after the flesh.* It is clear what this passage means. The Jews were no longer indebted to the Law of Moses, but they were indebted to the New Law of Christ. They were no longer to live after the Law of Moses—*the flesh.* They were now to live under the Law of Christ—*the spirit.*

**Verse 13.** *For if ye live after the flesh, ye shall die: but if ye through the Spirit do mortify the deeds of the body, ye shall live.* The Jews who remain under the Old Law were rewarded with spiritual death. The Jews were to mortify themselves from deeds of the Old Law; that is, they were to put the Old Law to death, liberating themselves from it and the works thereof. They could only find spiritual life under the New Law; that acquisition of life required the Jews to no longer work the deeds of the Old Law.

It is good to recall that *there rose up certain of the sect of the Pharisees which believed, saying, that it was needful to circumcise them and to command them to keep the Law of Moses* (Acts 15:5). Regardless of how much or little of the Law of Moses the Jews wished to retain, doing so negated their compliance to the New Law.

**Verse 14.** *For as many as are led by the Spirit of God, they are the sons of God.* The leading of the spirit here is not the leading of the Holy Spirit as many insist. The leading of the spirit here is the avenue by which the converted Jews were to direct their lives. That avenue is the system of the Gospel, nothing more.

If it is the case the leading of the Holy Spirit is intended here, numerous troubles abound. First, unless one is led by the Holy Spirit, he is neither saved or a saint. Only those who are thus *led by the Holy Spirit are the sons of God.* Second, if the Holy Spirit leads, He must do so directly. *The Holy Spirit has never*

# Commentary on Romans

*done anything indirectly.* He cannot do so! Whenever the Holy Spirit acted, His actions were always miraculous. Everything the Godhead does is miraculous. When Christ came to offer Himself as the ultimate sacrifice for sin, He did so through a miraculous event. However, Christ was made incarnate; that is, in the flesh. Thus, the incarnate Christ did things as a man, not by miracle. Neither the Father nor the Holy Spirit were ever made in the likeness of man. All they ever did or will do remains miraculous. *Nowhere in the Scriptures do we read the Holy Spirit ever did anything non-miraculous.*

One may inquire, however, as to how the Father answers prayer. It is best to recall our prayers are offered to the Father through Jesus Christ. It is through *the man Christ Jesus* we have our prayers brought before the throne of the Father. *For there is one God and one mediator between God and men, the man Christ Jesus* (I Tim. 2:5). The Father hears our prayers *through the man Jesus Christ.*

Another difficulty found with this position is: If it is the case the leading of the spirit here is the leading of the Holy Spirit, then it is the case that the Holy Spirit is responsible for our failings and sins. If not, why not? However, some contend the Holy Spirit leads the saint in the right direction, but it is men who fail to follow the path He has dictated. The fallacy of this defense is obvious and is not difficult to resolve. Observe: If it is the case one is directly led by the Holy Spirit, then it is the case the one being led is under the control of the Holy Spirit. We submit the following examples from both the Old and New Testaments.

*And Moses said, Hereby ye shall know that the Lord hath sent me to do all these works; for I have not done them of mine own mind* (Num. 16:28). In this passage it is clear Moses acted not by his own will, but was directed by the Holy Ghost, with whom he could not contend.

The record of Balaam seeking to curse God's people is grossly misunderstood. It is suggested by most that Balaam was a man of God who refused to go contrary to God's mandates for honors and wealth from Balak. The record, however, sets forth the exact opposite.

# Commentary on Romans

*And when Balaam saw that it pleased the Lord to bless Israel, he went not, as at other times, to seek for enchantments, but he set his face toward the wilderness. And Balaam lifted up his eyes, and he saw Israel abiding in his tents according to their tribes; and the spirit of God came upon him. And he took up his parable, and said, Balaam the son of Beor hath said, and the man whose eyes are open hath said: He hath said, which heard the words of God, which saw the vision of the Almighty, falling into a trance, but having his eyes open: How goodly are thy tents, O Jacob, and thy tabernacles, O Israel! As the valleys are they spread forth, as gardens by the river's side, as the trees of lign aloes which the Lord hath planted, and as cedar trees beside the waters. He shall pour the water out of his buckets, and his seed shall be in many waters, and his king shall be higher than Agag, and his kingdom shall be exalted. God brought him forth out of Egypt; he hath as it were the strength of an unicorn: he shall eat up the nations his enemies, and shall break their bones, and pierce them through with his arrows. He couched, he lay down as a lion, and as a great lion: who shall stir him up? Blessed is he that blesseth thee, and cursed is he that curseth thee. And Balak's anger was kindled against Balaam, and he smote his hands together: and Balak said unto Balaam, I called thee to curse mine enemies, and, behold, thou hast altogether blessed them these three times. Therefore now flee thou to thy place: I thought to promote thee unto great honour; but, lo, the Lord hath kept thee back from honour. And Balaam said unto Balak, Spake I not also to thy messengers which thou sentest unto me, saying, If Balak would give me his house full of silver and gold, I cannot go beyond the commandment of the Lord, to do either good or bad of mine own mind; but what the Lord saith, that will I speak?* (Num. 24:1-13).

Baalam was an idolater, he was *not* a worshipper of the Lord. He engaged in pagan enchantments and witchcraft. Even though he made numerous efforts to speak ill of God's people,

## Commentary on Romans

he was restrained by the Holy Spirt and could not do so. Verse two plainly states the Spirit of the God came upon him, which controlled his very speech.

When Baalam said: *If Balak would give me his house full of silver and gold, I cannot go beyond the commandment of the Lord, to do either good or bad of mine own mind*, he was if fact saying he could not speak ill of God's people and curse them because the Holy Spirit not only prevented such, but the Holy Spirit prohibited it and controlled the very tongue of Baalam during the course of the event under consideration (Num. 24:13).

Samuel wrote of King David, saying, *Now these be the last words of David. David the son of Jesse said, and the man who was raised up on high, the anointed of the God of Jacob, and the sweet psalmist of Israel, said, The Spirit of the Lord spake by me, and his word was in my tongue* (II Sam. 23:1-2). When David spoke by inspiration, like all inspired men, he could not but speak that which the Holy Spirit directed. Inspired men were always under the control of the Holy Spirit and could not speak and do as they deemed fitting.

Peter declared: *Knowing this first, that no prophecy of the scripture is of any private interpretation. For the prophecy came not in old time by the will of man: but holy men of God spake as they were moved by the Holy Ghost* (II Pet. 1:20-21). Consider the words of Christ: *But the Comforter, which is the Holy Ghost, whom the Father will send in my name, he shall teach you all things, and bring all things to your remembrance, whatsoever I have said unto you* (Jno. 14:26). *Howbeit when he, the Spirit of truth, is come, he will guide you into all truth: for he shall not speak of himself; but whatsoever he shall hear, that shall he speak: and he will shew you things to come* (Jno. 16:13).

If, then, one is under the control of the Holy Spirit, how can said individual assert his power over the Holy Ghost? Either the Holy Spirit is in full control, or He is not an all-powerful being of the Godhead.

The word *led*, as used in this 14th verse of Romans 8, is a primary verb meaning "properly to lead; by implication to bring, to

# Commentary on Romans

drive, induce, be brought forth, bring (forth), to carry, to keep, or to be led." If it is the case, the Holy Spirit is leading, driving, inducing, bringing forth, carrying, and keeping the Christian, then it is the case the Christian has no power to resist such control. Baalam had no control over the Spirit of God when he attempted to curse the people of God. If it is the case (as the personal indwelling of the Holy Spirit proponents insist) the Christian can refuse, refrain from, and even oppose such a leading of the Holy Spirit, then it is the case the Christian is more powerful than the Holy Ghost. If it is the case the devil wins in the case of a Spirit-led Christian, then it is also the case that Satan is more powerful than the Holy Ghost. Neither men nor the devil are in any way more powerful than the Holy Ghost, the Father, or His Son.

Further, and to the contrary, it is the case the Christian is more powerful than the devil. *Submit yourselves therefore to God. Resist the devil and he will flee from you* (Jas. 4:7). Satan can indeed be resisted and overpowered by the Christian. Therefore, the leading of the spirit as used here can in no way refer to the leading of the Holy Spirit. Saints are to be led by the Gospel. It is the Gospel which is under consideration in Romans 8:14, and it is by the Gospel by which the Christian is to be led. We should remember: Paul has been using the word *spirit* metaphorically representing the New Law, the Gospel of Christ.

Some may object to the things heretofore insisting *the spirits of the prophets are subject to the prophets* (I Cor. 14:32). However, it is essential to realize Paul was speaking of the use of spirtual gifts and not speaking of the Holy Spirit Himself. One endowed with a spiritual gift could misuse his gift or even neglect the use of such. Paul instructed Timothy: *Neglect not the gift that is in thee, which was given thee by prophecy, with the laying on of the hands of the presbytery* (I Tim. 4:14). He also gave instructions to the Corinthians:

> *How is it then, brethren? when ye come together, every one of you hath a psalm, hath a doctrine, hath a tongue, hath a revelation, hath an interpretation. Let all things be done unto edifying. If any man speak in an unknown tongue, let it be by two, or at the most by three, and that by course; and let one interpret. But if*

## Commentary on Romans

*there be no interpreter, let him keep silence in the church; and let him speak to himself, and to God. Let the prophets speak two or three, and let the other judge. If any thing be revealed to another that sitteth by, let the first hold his peace. For ye may all prophesy one by one, that all may learn, and all may be comforted. And the spirits of the prophets are subject to the prophets* (I Cor. 14:26-32).

It is clear from the context here those endowed with gifts of the Holy Spirit could make use of their gift as they saw fit (cf. I Cor. 14:40). The use of spiritual gifts was under the control of the one endowed with said gift.

Those endowed with spiritual (miraculous) gifts were in control of the gifts they were given. It is not at all the case the gifts given to those of the early church controlled the recipient of said gift. Paul wrote to Timothy, saying: *Erastus abode at Corinth: but Trophimus have I left at Miletum sick* (II Tim. 4:20). If the gift controlled the one who had the gift, then why did not Paul heal Trophimus?

**Verse 15.** *For ye have not received the spirit of bondage again.* In the church at Corinth many abused their gifts to receive the praises of fellow saints, but that abuse brought about confusion and disorder, which is why the apostle later said, *Let all things be done decently and in order* (I Cor.14:40). There is within this verse two *spirits* under consideration. One being the *spirit of bondage* and the other *the spirit of adoption.*

Paul's intent here is to sharply contrast the Old Law of Moses to the New Law of Christ. The bondage under consideration refers to the bondage of the Old Law of Moses. The adoption of which Paul speaks refers to the New Law of Christ. Whiteside made the following remarks on this verse:

> Notice the word "again." In becoming children of God we do not again enter into a bondage wherein we serve through fear. The Jew under the law was moved principally through fear and idol worshipers were moved by fear. But not so with the Christian. "But ye

## Commentary on Romans

received the spirit of adoption," or, more exact, "Ye received the spirit of sonship." A Christian is one who has been born again; he is a child of God by birth, rather than by adoption. He serves God, not through a spirit of slavish fear, but through a spirit of filial obedience. "Spirit" as used in this verse does not refer to an individual personal intelligence, but to disposition or attitude. Instead of being moved by fear as slaves, the child of God renders trusting obedience to God and confidently calls upon him as Father. The spirit of fear is displaced by a spirit of reverence, trust and worship. The term "Abba" means "Father." It seems that the two terms are here used for emphasis[32] [sic].

Whiteside made some good observations regarding this verse. We have inserted our comments within parentheses. The *bondage* of which Paul wrote is bondage under the Old Law. *Even so we, when we were children, were in bondage* (to the Old Law) *under the elements* (rudiments and principles) *of the world* (the Old Law): *But now* (under the New Testament), *after that ye have known God, or rather are known of God, how turn ye again to the weak and beggarly elements* (the Old Testament System), *whereunto ye desire again to be in bondage* (Gal. 4:3, 9)?

Agreement is lacking with Whiteside's comments with respect to the word *spirit*. Whiteside stated: "'Spirit' as used in this verse does not refer to an individual personal intelligence, but to disposition or attitude.' To the contrary, the word *spirit* here refers to the Law of Moses. It is important here to note Paul used the word *spirit* in conjunction with the word *bondage*. The bondage under which the Jews were held was the Old Law. Here Paul identifies the Old Law as the *spirit of bondage*[33] [sic].

Consider also: *But before faith came, we were kept under the law, shut up unto the faith which should afterwards be revealed* (Gal. 3:23). It is bondage to be *kept under* something or someone. The Jews were held in *bondage;* that is, they were *kept under* the Old Law until the fullness of time (Gal. 4:4; Col. 2:14).

---

[32] Robertson L. Whiteside.

[33] Ibid.

# Commentary on Romans

The phrase, *the Spirit of adoption, whereby we cry, Abba, Father* also warrants consideration. The *spirit of adoption* is the avenue by which men are adopted by the Father as His children. The Holy Spirit has never adopted anyone! It is one's obedience to the Gospel (*the spirit*) by which one becomes a son of God.

The word *Abba* expresses the idea *God is my Father.* Through obedience of the Gospel one becomes a child of the Father, and it is the avenue by which God's children can indeed call God their Father. Men have either God as their Father, or they have the devil as their father. A comparison of Romans 8:15 and John 8:44 shows such to be the case.

**Verse 16.** *The Spirit itself beareth witness with our spirit, that we are the children of God.* There are four major doctrines set forth from this passage.

First asserted is that the *spirit* which bears witness with our spirit is the Holy Spirit. It is declared the Holy Spirit testifies or serves as a witness on our behalf before the Father one is a child of God. However, this position must be rejected for the following reasons. Paul declared the *spirit itself* bears witness with our spirit. The apostle did not use the word *Himself.* The word *itself* identifies the word *spirit* as an *it* and not a being. While the word can apply to *him, her, or it*, the context of a passage must determine the application of definition. Thus far, the apostle has been using the word *spirit* to refer to the New Testament. Such being the case, the context of the passage disallows for the the words *spirit itself* to apply to the Holy Spirit *Himself.* The phrase *with our spirit* is a prepositional phrase identifying the location of the *spirit.*

Second, if it be the case the Holy Spirit is *with* the spirit of those on behalf of whom He testifies and bears witness, then it is the case the Holy Spirit must do so through His presence *with* the spirit of those for whom He testifies and serves as a witness. This is not plausible for the following reasons. First, there is no passage of inspired text in which the Holy Spirit is mentioned which did not harbor a miracle? *A miracle always occurred when and where the Holy Spirit was present!* When Christ was baptized by John, the Holy Spirit's testimony required His pres-

165

# Commentary on Romans

ence. *And Jesus, when he was baptized, went up straightway out of the water: and, lo, the heavens were opened unto him, and he saw the Spirit of God descending like a dove, and lighting upon him* (Matt. 3:16).

Third, it is argued the *spirit itself,* refers to a miraculous gift awarded to a saint through the laying on of an apostle's hand. This position is entirely plausible and does no damage to the text. Franklin Camp held to this position. Regardless, it must be deduced the first and second positions addressed are neither plausible nor practical.

Fourth, there is the position the *spirit which bears witness* is the Gospel. In that the apostle has awarded no little time and space instructing the Jewish converts they were no longer under the *flesh*—the Old Law, but were rather under the *spirit*—the New Law, he establishes the fact the *spirit which bears witness with our spirit* is the Gospel. This position is a most plausible one.

The fourth is preferred by this author. However, it must be reiterated the third argument is also very plausible. Regardless, the first and second arguments must be given no valid consideration. Those who hold to either the first or second positions have no argument for proof other than *it is something better felt than told.*

**Verse 17.** *And if children, then heirs; heirs of God and joint-heirs with Christ; if so be that we suffer with him, that we may be also glorified together.* The word *and* with which this passage begins is a conjunction which joins the previous verse to this one. The two verses must be considered together. There is a witness to the fact the children of God are indeed His children. The witness was either a miraculous gift of the Holy Spirit, or the witness is the Gospel.

If, then, they are His children, then they are heirs, heirs of God and joint-heirs with Christ. The phrase *joint-heirs* means to be a *co-heir*—that is, by analogy a participant in and with a fellow heir, an heir together with Christ. Children of the Father are awarded an equal share of that which the Son of God has inherited.

# Commentary on Romans

It is indeed a grand blessing to be awarded the same inheritance as the Son of God. Such a blessing should not be considered lightly, but rather relished. Inheritances of men may be good, but the inheritance of God is best. Applause and favors of righteous men may please us well, but the applause and cheers of the Godhead are best. The angels of heaven rejoice when men are made joint-heirs with Christ.

## Romans 8:18-28

*18 For I reckon that the sufferings of this present time are not worthy to be compared with the glory which shall be revealed in us. 19 For the earnest expectation of the creature waiteth for the manifestation of the sons of God. 20 For the creature was made subject to vanity, not willingly, but by reason of him who hath subjected the same in hope, 21 Because the creature itself also shall be delivered from the bondage of corruption into the glorious liberty of the children of God. 22 For we know that the whole creation groaneth and travaileth in pain together until now. 23 And not only they, but ourselves also, which have the firstfruits of the Spirit, even we ourselves groan within ourselves, waiting for the adoption, to wit, the redemption of our body. 24 For we are saved by hope: but hope that is seen is not hope: for what a man seeth, why doth he yet hope for? 25 But if we hope for that we see not, then do we with patience wait for it. 26 Likewise the Spirit also helpeth our infirmities: for we know not what we should pray for as we ought: but the Spirit itself maketh intercession for us with groanings which cannot be uttered. 27 And he that searcheth the hearts knoweth what is the mind of the Spirit, because he maketh intercession for the saints according to the will of God. 28 And we know that all things work together for good to them that love God, to them who are the called according to his purpose.*

**Verse 18.** *For I reckon that the sufferings of this present time are not worthy to be compared with the glory which shall be revealed in us.* The word *reckon* means to suppose, conclude,

# Commentary on Romans

or to deduce. Paul's reckoning was an inspired one and not human surmising.

The *sufferings of this present time* were the sufferings and persecutions through which the church was then going. The Jews were persecuting the church which caused no little suffering for the Lord's people. The apostle had himself been among those who were causing havoc for the church. *As for Saul, he made havoc of the church, entering into every house and haling men and women committed them to prison* (Acts 8:3). *And Saul, yet breathing out threatenings and slaughter against the disciples of the Lord, went unto the high priest and desired of him letters to Damascus to the synagogues, that if he found any of this way, whether they were men or women, he might bring them bound unto Jerusalem* (Acts 9:1-2). *For ye have heard of my conversation in time past in the Jews' religion, how that beyond measure I persecuted the church of God and wasted it: And profited in the Jews' religion above many my equals in mine own nation, being more exceedingly zealous of the traditions of my fathers* (Gal. 1:13-14). Paul also mentioned the *present distress* of persecution as recorded in I Corinthians 7:26.

*The glory which shall be revealed in us* of which the apostle wrote is given address in several passages in the New Testament.

> *Beloved, now are we the sons of God and it doth not yet appear what we shall be: but we know that, when he shall appear, we shall be like him; for we shall see him as he is* (I Jno. 3:2).

> *For our conversation is in heaven; from whence also we look for the Saviour, the Lord Jesus Christ: Who shall change our vile body, that it may be fashioned like unto his glorious body, according to the working whereby he is able even to subdue all things unto himself* (Phil. 3:20-21).

> *So also is the resurrection of the dead. It is sown in corruption; it is raised in incorruption: It is sown in dishonour; it is raised in glory: it is sown in weakness; it is*

# Commentary on Romans

*raised in power: It is sown a natural body; it is raised a spiritual body. There is a natural body and there is a spiritual body* (I Cor. 15:42-44).

*When Christ, who is our life, shall appear, then shall ye also appear with him in glory* (Col. 3:4).

That our natural bodies will be awarded a glorious form at the resurrection is clear. Our appearances will however remain as we are now. The only change that we must put on is immortality.

*And as we have borne the image of the earthy, we shall also bear the image of the heavenly. Now this I say, brethren, that flesh and blood cannot inherit the kingdom of God; neither doth corruption inherit incorruption. Behold, I shew you a mystery; We shall not all sleep, but we shall all be changed, In a moment, in the twinkling of an eye, at the last trump: for the trumpet shall sound and the dead shall be raised incorruptible and we shall be changed. For this corruptible must put on incorruption and this mortal must put on immortality. So when this corruptible shall have put on incorruption and this mortal shall have put on immortality, then shall be brought to pass the saying that is written, Death is swallowed up in victory* (I Cor. 15:49-54).

The changing of the natural body into a spiritual body is inclusive of glorification. It is well to recall Christ *shall change our vile body, that it may be fashioned like unto his glorious body, and we shall be like him* (Phil. 3:21; I Jno. 3:2). This change will result in all physical imperfections being removed and corrected. The blind will see, the deaf will hear, the lame will walk, the weak shall be made strong, and every other physical ailment, handicap, and disfigurement will be corrected.

**Verses 19-23.** *For the earnest expectation of the creature waiteth for the manifestation of the sons of God. For the creature was made subject to vanity, not willingly, but by reason of him who hath subjected the same in hope, Because the creature itself also shall be delivered from the bondage of corruption into*

# Commentary on Romans

*the glorious liberty of the children of God. For we know that the whole creation groaneth and travaileth in pain together until now. And not only they, but ourselves also, which have the firstfruits of the Spirit, even we ourselves groan within ourselves, waiting for the adoption, to wit, the redemption of our body.* These verses have challenged Bible students, scholars, preachers, and elders for eons; and will, without doubt, continue to be a problematic passage of inspired text for generations yet to come.

It must be emphasized with the strongest effort Paul continues to address the Jewish converts in this chapter. Unless this be continuously bannered before the eye of the student, the proper exegesis of the passage cannot be attained. Because the apostle is addressing the Jewish converts, it should be understood the Jews well understood Paul's teaching. The Jews had no issue in realizing the apostle was addressing them in particular. These verses must be approached from a Jewish mindset.

**Verse 19.** *For the earnest expectation of the creature waiteth for the manifestation of the sons of God.* The phrase *earnest expectation* is defined as intense anticipation. What was it, however, which was so intensely anticipated? Who was it or what was it which did the anticipating? The answer to the question of *what* was intensely anticipated is identified as *the manifestation of the sons of God.* The answer to the question regarding *who or what* did the anticipating, it was is the *creature.*

What, though, is the *creature* of which the apostle spoke? The word *creature* is preceded with the definite article *the.* It is of utmost importance to observe the word *creature* is identified as *itself*, as recorded in verse 23. The word *creature* is defined by nearly all Bible students to mean the creature is man. However, the word modifying the word *creature* is not himself, but rather *itself.* Such being the case, it must be realized Paul is speaking of a *thing, he is not speaking of man.* What then is the *thing* of which Paul wrote?

Paul spent no little time comparing and contrasting the Old and the New Laws. The Old Law was the Law of Moses. The New Law is the New Testament. The Old Law has been identified as the *letter*, the *flesh*, and as being *dead.* Further, Paul identified

# Commentary on Romans

the Old Law as *the law of sin and death,* as a *body of death,* and as a *dead body.* The New Law has been identified as the *newness of spirit, the spirit of life,* and *spirit.* Indeed the apostle has used many metaphors to represent the Law of Moses and the Law of Christ.

Here, however, Paul introduces another metaphor to represent the Old Law. Now the word *creature* is used as a metaphor to represent the Old Law. The Old Law was a temporary Law. It was a Law which was to be done away. Even though there was glory found in the Law of Moses, that glory was to come to an end. The glory of the Old Law was fulfilled, and was brought to fruition once Christ came into the world and established the church.

> *But when the fullness of the time was come, God sent forth his Son, made of a woman, made under the law, To redeem them that were under the law, that we might receive the adoption of sons* (Gal. 4:4-5).

> *But if the ministration of death, written and engraven in stones, was glorious, so that the children of Israel could not stedfastly behold the face of Moses for the glory of his countenance; which glory was to be done away: How shall not the ministration of the spirit be rather glorious? For if the ministration of condemnation be glory, much more doth the ministration of righteousness exceed in glory. For even that which was made glorious had no glory in this respect, by reason of the glory that excelleth. For if that which is done away was glorious, much more that which remaineth is glorious* (II Cor. 3:7-11).

Once the Son of God came into the world, the Old Law was no longer glorious; the glory of it was fulfilled and the purpose of the Old Law was completed. The glory of the Old Law was superseded by the New Law of Christ. The Old Law of Moses was now *dead.* The Old Law was the *creature* which prophesied of and *waited* for the revelation of the new glory which was manifested in the sons of God. The sons of God are saints who comprise the body of Christ, not the body of Moses. The body of

# Commentary on Romans

Christ is the church of Christ:

> Now ye are the body of Christ and members in particular (I Cor. 12:27).

> And he is the head of the body, the church: who is the beginning, the firstborn from the dead; that in all things he might have the preeminence (Col. 1:18).

> And hath put all things under his feet and gave him to be the head over all things to the church, which is his body, the fullness of him that filleth all in all (Eph. 1:22-23).

The Jews *were* members of the body of Moses. They *were* members of the *church of Moses.* The church of Moses was established in the wilderness when the Jews came out of Egypt, and were given the Law of Moses at Mount Sinai. Stephen said: *This is that Moses, which said unto the children of Israel, A prophet shall the Lord your God raise up unto you of your brethren, like unto me; him shall ye hear. This is he* (Moses), *that was in the church in the wilderness with the angel* (Christ) *which spake to him in the Mount Sinai and with our fathers: who received the lively oracles to give unto us* (Acts 7:37-38).

The word *waiteth* means "to look for, having a full expectation to find or see the fruition of that which was to be revealed." The church came about and made obedient men sons of God. When the Lord established the New Testament church, the *waiting* of which the apostle spoke was completed, and the sons of God were given place in the Lord's New Testament church through their obedience to the Gospel of Christ.

The word *manifestation* is defined as "the coming about of or the revelation of that which was to be made known." The *manifestation of the sons of God* is the fruition of the establishment of the Lord's church which took place on the day of Pentecost as recorded in Acts 2.

**Verse 20.** *For the creature was made subject to vanity, not willingly, but by reason of him who hath subjected the same in*

# Commentary on Romans

*hope, but by reason of him who hath subjected the same in hope.* The *creature* (the Law of Moses) *was made subject to vanity.* The word *subject* means to be in subjection to. Indeed, the Old Law was in subjection to both the New Law and to Christ. The Law of Moses was a Law of *vanity* meaning it was subject to discontinuation. It was a Law which was, by God's intended design, to die at the time He appointed. The time God appointed was *the fullness of time* of which Paul wrote as recorded in Galatians 4:4.

The phrase *not willingly* refers to the Jews' will—not God's will. It was not the will of the Jews to have the Law of Moses become a *dead* Law. It was not the Jews will to become subject to the New Law of Christ. *But by reason of him who hath subjected the same in hope* shows the opposition of the Jews will to God's will. The *reason* God *subjected* the Old Law to vanity was because the hope of the Old Law was enveloped in the New Law.

*The same* refers to the *creature*—the Old Law was made subject to the New Law. The meaning of the verse is God made the Old Law subjective to the New Law of Christ; not according to the will of the Jews, but according to the will of the Father. The Old Law subjected the Jews to the hope of the New Law. Today, saints are subjected to the same kind of hope. Just as the Old Law contained the hope of bringing forth the New Law, so the New Law contains the hope of heaven for those who live in obedience to the New Law of Christ.

**Verse 21.** *Because the creature itself also shall be delivered from the bondage of corruption into the glorious liberty of the children of God.* This verse explains why the Old Law was made subject to the vanity of which the apostle spoke in verse 20. The word *because* shows why the Old Law was no longer in force.

*The creature itself,* meaning the Old Law and the prophecies thereof, were given deliverance from the spiritual corruption of which Paul wrote here. It is good to again note Paul identifies the word *creature* as an *itself,* and not as a *himself.* The word *corruption* means to perish. The Old Law was to perish, but deliverance from the Old Law was made available though Jesus Christ.

# Commentary on Romans

The phrase *bondage of corruption* refers to being in bondage to the Old Law. The Jews were in bondage to the Old Law so long as the Old Law was in force. Consider the following passages in which Paul speaks of the bondage of the Old Law (comments added).

*And that because of false brethren unawares brought in, who came in privily to spy out our liberty which we have in Christ Jesus, that they might bring us into bondage* [to the Old law] *(Gal. 2:4).*

*Even so we, when we were children, were in bondage under the elements of the world* [the Old Law] *(Gal. 4: 3).*

*But now, after that ye have known God, or rather are known of God, how turn ye again to the weak and beggarly elements, whereunto ye desire again to be in bondage* [to the Old Law] *(Gal. 4:9)?*

*Which things are an allegory: for these are the two covenants; the one from the Mount Sinai, which gendereth to bondage [to the Old Law], which is Hagar (Gal. 4:24). For this Hagar is mount Sinai in Arabia and answereth to Jerusalem which now is and is in bondage* [under the Old Law] *with her children (Gal. 4:25).*

*Stand fast therefore in the liberty wherewith Christ hath made us free and be not entangled again with the yoke of bondage* [to the Old Law] *(Gal. 5:1).*

*And deliver them who through fear of death were all their lifetime subject to bondage* [to the Old Law] *(Heb. 2:15).*

**Verse 22.** *For we know that the whole creation groaneth and travaileth in pain together until now.* To *know* is to properly understand and perceive. Many assert man cannot really know anything. However, truth can be known; it is not in any way subjective. Truth is concrete, it is real, it is not abstract. Only

## Commentary on Romans

through truth can men *know* the things they are commanded to know. The Lord said, *Ye shall know the truth and the truth shall make you free* (Jno. 8:32). Much space could be occupied refuting the foolishness that one cannot really know anything; however, we shall limit ourselves to but a small portion. Those who insist one cannot really know anything have but one question to answer. Are such folks sure beyond any doubt, one cannot really know anything? If they affirm such, they admit they know one cannot know anything. Indeed, the foolishness of such is clear. If they deny such, they again surrender their position. In either case they find themselves foiled by their own folly.

*The whole creation* presented in this passage is of great importance. The word *creature* and the word *creation* of this and the previous verse are the same word in the Greek and used as nouns. The word is defined as creation, creature or ordinance.

In this verse, the noun is modified with the adjective *whole.* That there is a modifying adjective to the noun shows there is something in addition to how the word *creature* was used in the previous verse. The modifying adjective *whole* reveals the word is inclusive of more than was purposed in verse 21. The *whole creation* is in contrast to the *creature.*

It is once again *strongly* emphasized it was to the Jewish converts to whom the apostle was writing. It is also reiterated Paul has been long in reminding the Jews the Law of Moses now stands both in contrast and opposition to the New Law of Christ. Paul had shown the Jews the very Law which they did not want to give up was the very Law which demanded they do so. The apostle constantly contrasted the Old and the New Laws. He has shown the Old Law made numerous prophecies of the New Law and of Christ who brought the New Law. The *creature* as we have noticed in previous verses is the Old Law. Now, however, by adding the adjective *whole,* it needs to be asked: "What is that which Paul intends by adding the modifier?"

The *whole creation* shows Paul not only referred to the Old Law, but to the Patriarchal Law as well. Here, Paul combines the Law of Patriarchs with the Law of Moses, and declared both Laws *groaned and travailed together in pain.* The duration of that

# Commentary on Romans

*groaning and travailing in pain* of the Patriarchal and Mosaical Laws was limited to the time God ordained. How long were the Patriarchal and Mosaical Laws to *groan and travail in pain together?* Paul answers the query with the last words of the verse. The groaning and travailing *together* in pain lasted *until now. Until now* means the New Testament dispensation of Christ. The phrase *until now* also means until the time the church was established. Once the New Law was given, the groanings, travailings, and pains of the Old Testament ceased.

The Patriarchal and Mosaical Laws worked together in prophecy; they worked together in types, in principle, purpose, and theme. Both Laws of the Old Testament worked in unison. Both contained prophecies of the church and of Christ, and they both served man with many types, shadows, and adumbrations of the New Law of Christ.

The words *groaning, travailing,* and *pain* are words which refer to the bearing of a child. The child who was brought forth was in fact Christ. That the Patriarchal Law and those who live under it groaned and travailed is seen in the words of Christ. The Lord declared to the Jews: *Your father Abraham rejoiced to see my day: and he saw it and was glad* (Jno. 8:56). The prophets of the Mosaical Law also spoke of the bringing forth of a child. *For unto us a child is born, unto us a son is given: and the government shall be upon his shoulder: and his name shall be called Wonderful, Counselor, The mighty God, The everlasting Father, The Prince of Peace* (Isa. 9:6). *Therefore the Lord himself shall give you a sign; Behold, a virgin shall conceive and bear a son and shall call his name Immanuel* (Isa. 7:14).

*Together*, the Law of Moses and the Law of the Patriarchs groaned and travailed in pain looking for, hoping to see, and longing for the day when the Christ would come. They looked forward to the day when the Lord would establish His kingdom. That day did indeed come *in the fullness of time* as Paul proclaimed in Galatians 4:4.

There are over three hundred prophecies of the Christ and the church in the Old Testament, found in both the Patriarchal and Mosaical periods. The jelling together of so many prophecies

# Commentary on Romans

with such laser accuracy could only be achieved through God's Divine hand. The first arrow of prophecy was released from the prophetic bow of God in Genesis 3:15. That arrow of prophecy struck the target God intended at the exact time God intended and in the exact place God directed it. Every arrow of prophecy from both the Patriarchal and Mosaical periods found harmonious flight in unison working together, smiting the targets God intended at the time dead-center.

**Verse 23.** *And not only they, but ourselves also, which have the firstfruits of the Spirit, even we ourselves groan within ourselves, waiting for the adoption, to wit, the redemption of our body.* Not only did those of the Patriarchal and Mosaical Laws groan and travail in pain; those who live under the New Law of Christ groan and travail in pain as well. *We,* of this dispensation of the New Testament church groan and long for things yet future. That future event is the *redemption of our body.*

The *we ourselves* of this verse is subjected to three major teachings. Brother Whiteside sets forth two. We shall supply the third.

> But who is referred to in verse 23? and what are the "first-fruits of the Spirit"? It seems to be taken for granted by many commentators that all Christians are here referred to and the "first-fruits of the Spirit" is the same as the "earnest of the Spirit" as mentioned in 2 Cor. 1: 22; 5:5; Eph. 1:13-14. But I cannot see how in any sense the indwelling of the Holy Spirit in the Christian can be called the "first-fruits of the Spirit." It rather seems that the "first-fruits of the Spirit" in the Christian dispensation were the miraculous powers conferred on the apostles. Hence, to encourage Christians to endure their sufferings he reminds them that suffering is the common lot of the whole human family and that even we, the apostles, who have all these miraculous endowments of the Spirit, also groan within ourselves on account of our burdens and afflictions, "waiting for our adoption, to wit, the redemption of our bodies"[34] [sic].

---
[34] Robertson L. Whiteside.

# Commentary on Romans

The third position of this verse teaches those who had the *first-fruits* of the Spirit were those of the early church upon whom an apostle had laid his hands to award such a one with a gift of the Holy Spirit. This is the preferred teaching. We well recall the apostle was speaking to the Jewish converts (of which he was one) and many members of the church at Rome were indeed recipients of such miraculous gifts given by an apostle. *Having then gifts differing according to the grace that is given to us, whether prophecy, let us prophesy according to the proportion of faith; Or ministry, let us wait on our ministering: or he that teacheth, on teaching; Or he that exhorteth, on exhortation: he that giveth, let him do it with simplicity; he that ruleth, with diligence; he that sheweth mercy, with cheerfulness* (Rom. 12:6-8).

*We ourselves groan within ourselves* just as those of the Patriarchal and Mosaical Laws groaned, longing for the coming of the Lord and the New Law. Those of the Old Testament groaned and waited for what God promised; so did they to whom Paul wrote. They were groaning and *waiting for the adoption, to wit, the redemption of our body.* The body of the Mosaical church waited for the *manifestation of the sons of God* as noted in verses 21 and 22. Today the church of the New Testament system of Christ groans and waits for the redemption of our body.

*Our body* can only mean one of two things. First, it may mean the redemption of the physical body of the saint, or the body of Christ—that is, the church. Either is plausible and neither does damage to the text. We prefer the latter.

**Verse 24.** *For we are saved by hope: but hope that is seen is not hope: for what a man seeth, why doth he yet hope for?* The word *hope* is here defined as confidence or expectation.

*We who have the first-fruits* have confidence in this saving *hope.* We have an expectation to be saved through the New Testament system of Christ. Where there is no confidence there is no expectation and where there is no expectation, there is no hope, but all are found in Christ.
**Verse 25.** *But if we hope for that we see not, then do we with patience wait for it.* Two words in this verse should capture one's attention: *see* and *patience.* We first consider the word *see.*

# Commentary on Romans

The word frequently means to possess, to enjoy, suffering, to experience. This is true even in our everyday speech. We see a good time; we see much sorrow; we see much pain. We experience many such things. A person does not hope for what he sees—that is, for what he already has or has experienced. If our redemption was already complete, if there was nothing yet to be desired or expected, there would be no hope. But we desire and expect a glorious future and this hope for full deliverance from the bondage of corruption into the glorious liberty of the children of God causes us to be patient during our period of waiting[35] [sic].

Thayer defines the word *patience* to mean "steadfastness, constancy, endurance, steadfast, sustaining, perseverance."[36] Paul uses the word five times in the Roman letter and the word *patient* twice. We have then a complete perfection of patience provided by the apostle in this epistle.

**Verse 26.** *Likewise the Spirit also helpeth our infirmities: for we know not what we should pray for as we ought: but the Spirit itself maketh intercession for us with groanings which cannot be uttered.* The number of errors touching this verse seems infinite.

Regarding the phrase, *not knowing how to pray as we ought,* it must to be understood Paul wrote this passage during the time when the Holy Spirit was still revealing the New Testament. The early church was lacking in things yet to be revealed. Because revelation was not yet complete, the early church needed inspired teachers, preachers, elders, and instruction. The fullness of revelation being then incomplete made it needful to have inspired men (and women, when necessary) to reveal the truth which was then yet to come. The early church also lacked complete knowledge of what songs or hymns to sing. They lacked knowledge of what needed to be preached. They also lacked knowledge of that for which to pray. Paul stated to the church at Corinth: *What is it then? I will pray with the spirit and I will pray*

---
[35] Robertson L. Whiteside.
[36] Joseph Henry Thayer, D.D.

# Commentary on Romans

*with the understanding also: I will sing with the spirit and I will sing with the understanding also* (I Cor. 14:15). When Paul stated he would sing and pray with the spirit, he meant he would sing and pray as directed by the Holy Spirit. In the early church there were inspired songs and inspired prayers. Once inspiration was complete there was no longer a need for the miraculous gifts, for inspired apostles, elders, teachers, or prophets. Further, there was no longer a need for inspired prayers or inspired songs. Once revelation was completed, the need for such inspired things was removed. This is that about which the apostle spoke when he stated, *we know not how to pray as we ought.*

Until such a time when inspiration was completed the early church needed to be instructed by the Holy Ghost as to how and for what to pray. Contrary to what countless commentators and men proclaim today, saints in the Lord's church do indeed know how to pray. The completion of revelation is that which made such possible. If we in the Lord's church are yet ignorant of for what and how to pray as we ought, then why do saints engage in such? We ask if there will ever be a time in the Lord's church when saints will know how to pray? When inspiration ended, inspired songs and inspired prayers ended. For more on when inspiration ended see notes at the end of the chapter.

Further on, verse 26 it is argued, when one is at loss of words or finds himself unable to express his thoughts adequately; the Holy Spirit comes to the aid of struggling saints in such cases. We are compelled to ask; where in the passage is such a assertion even suggested? Remember, according to the passage it is the *Spirit* which does the *groaning.* If the word *Spirit* refers to the Holy Spirit, then the case *the Holy Spirit must do the groaning* to and before the Father. The argument that the Holy Spirit intercedes on behalf of man's groaning is false. Is not the Holy Spirit capable of communicating with the Father without having to *groan*? We think so! Are we to conclude the Father can understand the groans of the Holy Spirit but not the groanings of the man who He created?

Again we are compelled to further address the argument, as some assert, because we know not how to pray, the Holy Spirit must intercede. However, an elementary reading of the passage

## Commentary on Romans

makes it clear such is not the case. The *groaning* of the verse is performed not by men but by the s*pirit*. Notice, *the spirit itself maketh intercession for us with groanings which cannot be uttered.* The groanings are the groanings of the spirit; this is as clear as inspiration could have written it. Again we insist, if it is the case, the *spirit* under consideration here is the *Holy Spirit,* then it is the case it is the *Holy Spirit* who is involved in the groaning and not the saint.

On the other hand, if it is the case the word *spirit* here refers to the spirit of man, and if it is the case those who insist the Holy Spirit makes intercession for the saints, then it is the case their doctrine is negated. The interceding spirit here must then be something other than the Holy Spirit. It cannot be the case Paul means the Holy Spirit here. The apostolic choice of the word *itself* was not by accident. The word *itself* must refer to an *it,* and not to either the spirit-being of man nor the Holy Spirit. Both the spirit of man and the Holy Spirit are beings, neither is an *it.*

In either case, if it is the spirit of man doing the groaning or, if it is the case the Holy Spirit is doing the groaning, groaning remains nonetheless.

Why would God in His infinite wisdom allow the saint to be in such a quandary as to not know how to pray in the church once revelation was completed? The assertion is foolish. God who is all-powerful and all-knowing seems to lack the ability to resolve the problems associated with the avenue of prayer, according to many. Yet He is able to address any and every other matter imaginable according to these brethren. However, Christ said: *with God all things are possible* (Matt. 19:26). *Is any thing too hard for the Lord* (Gen. 18:14)? Some brethren believe so!

To what then does the word *spirit* refer in this passage? The word is used metonymically. The metonymy here is the metonymy of the effect. The cause is stated, but the effect is meant. The cause was the early church did not know how to nor for what to pray as they ought. Why? The early church did not know how to pray as they ought because revelation was not yet completed. The cause by which the early church prayed was often by a miraculously inspired prayer—that is, by one to whom the spiritual gift of inspired prayer was given. The early church lacked knowl-

# Commentary on Romans

edge regarding the things of the kingdom, which caused understandable frustrations on the part of the early members of the church. Thus, there was the need for the gift of inspired prayers. This is that of which the passage speaks.

The word *groanings* means to sigh with grief. Indeed, the early church grieved because they were lacking in the knowledge of that for which to pray. Remember the disciples of John lacked in their knowledge of that for which they needed to pray. The apostles likewise lacked such knowledge and needed instructions from the Lord regarding this matter (cf. Lk. 11:1).

Countless saints today teach and oftentimes *strongly insist* when one is overwhelmed with grief, the Holy Spirit must then intercede and resolve the matter. *Such a position demands a miracle takes place when one finds it difficult to express his thoughts and feelings to God !* The *groanings* of this verse *do not* represent the frustrations and inadequate feelings of the saints. The *groaning* under consideration is the grief and feeling of frustration which dwelt in the saints of the early church which did not have completed revelation by which to be guided as the church is today. The church today has completed revelation and has the knowledge to pray as it ought. Keeping the passage within the confines to which the apostle fetters it and the time frame of when Paul wrote is essential. Failing to keep things it the time frame in which they belong is one of the most often-committed errors of Bible students.

If our Father needs the Holy Spirit to express the groanings of saints today it would be better to have lived before the Law of Moses was given. *For God heard their groaning, and God remembered his covenant with Abraham, with Isaac, and with Jacob* (Exo. 2:24). *And I have also heard the groaning of the children of Israel, whom the Egyptians keep in bondage; and I have remembered my covenant* (Exo. 6:5). The Law of Moses was not given until Exodus 20—fourteen chapters after Exodus 6:5.

How can it be that the Lord was able to hear and understand the groanings of the descendants of Jacob even before the Old Law was given, but suddenly became sorely ignorant and unable to hear and understand the groanings of saints in the church to-

# Commentary on Romans

day? Amazing!

Further, on not knowing *how to pray as we ought*, it does well to consider the following. When John the baptizer was *preaching in the wilderness of Judea saying, the kingdom of heaven is at hand* (Matt. 3:1), his disciples needed instruction for what to pray. The apostles needed the same from the Lord when they traveled about with Him: *And it came to pass, that, as he was praying in a certain place, when he ceased, one of his disciples said unto him, Lord, teach us to pray, as John also taught his disciples. And he said unto them, When ye pray, say, Our Father which art in heaven, Hallowed be thy name. Thy kingdom come. Thy will be done, as in heaven, so in earth. Give us day by day our daily bread. And forgive us our sins; for we also forgive every one that is indebted to us. And lead us not into temptation; but deliver us from evil* (Lk. 11:1-4).

Just as the disciples of John knew not for what to pray as they ought, so the apostles knew not for what to pray as they ought. Both the disciples of John and Jesus needed instructions; both received such. So also it was the case in the early church. The early church, not having completed inspiration, needed instructions on how to pray (as well as to sing, I Cor. 14:15). This is the proper exegesis of Romans 8:26.

**Verse 27.** *And he that searcheth the hearts knoweth what is the mind of the Spirit, because he maketh intercession for the saints according to the will of God.* It is best to ask just who it is that searches the hearts of men? The answer is provided in the Revelation. *And I will kill her children with death; and all the churches shall know that I am he which searcheth the reins and hearts: and I will give unto every one of you according to your works* (Rev. 2:23). Consider also Paul's letter to Timothy. *For there is one God and one mediator between God and men, the man Christ Jesus* (I Tim. 2:5). For one to insist the Holy Spirit is the intercessor of Romans 8:27 is a miserable failure in recognizing the Revelation and the I Timothy passages given above.

The *he* of Romans 8:27 does not refer to the Holy Spirit, but rather refers to Christ. It is Christ who does the heart-searching and not the Holy Spirit. The words *mediator* and *intercessor* are by

# Commentary on Romans

definition the same. The words are synonymous and cannot refer to different activities as is suggested by those who cling to the position of a personal indwelling of the Holy Spirit. Consider the following passages which clearly identify Christ as the only intercessor who stands between God and man. *Who is he that condemneth? It is Christ that died, yea rather, that is risen again, who is even at the right hand of God, who also maketh intercession for us* (Rom. 8:34). *Wherefore he is able also to save them to the uttermost that come unto God by him, seeing he ever liveth to make intercession for them* (Heb. 7:25). *My little children, these things write I unto you, that ye sin not. And if any man sin, we have an advocate with the Father, Jesus Christ the righteous: And he is the propitiation for our sins: and not for ours only, but also for the sins of the whole world"* (I Jno 2:1-2). We shall provide more on the subject of intercession in prayer later.

**Verse 28.** *And we know that all things work together for good to them that love God, to them who are the called according to his purpose.* Few verses of Scripture have been as grossly perverted as this one. Sad it is so many have for so long so perverted this passage; it seems to be without compare. The word *and* is of the utmost importance, it is a conjunction which ties this verse to the previous one. Just as what Paul declared in verse 27 to be the case, so it is the case with that which is found in this verse. However, it is also inclusive of things the apostle addressed earlier in this chapter.

As observed in verse 27, there was inspired prayer in the first century church which came through the direction of the Holy Spirit by the laying on of an apostle's hands. Because such is indeed the case it is also true all things found in the Old Testament Scriptures *work together for good.*

It is well to recall Paul had discussed the *creature* in connection to the *whole creation* as recorded in verses 19-22. There, it is recalled, the *whole creation* was inclusive of both the Patriarchal Law and the Mosaical Law. Those two Laws were in harmony and worked together for good. Here *all things* which are identified as *working together* are the things of both the Patriarchal Law and Mosaical Law. *All things* — the Patriarchal Law and

# Commentary on Romans

Mosaical Law and the prophecies thereof *worked together for good.* The *good* for which the Laws and prophecies of the Old Testament worked was the bringing about of the New Testament church and the New Testament itself. *All things* here equate to the prophecies of both the Patriarchal and Mosaical Laws of the Old Testament. The *good* mentioned here equates to the New Testament and the establishment of the Lord's church. The passage is not hard to be understood when the student keeps the context of the chapter in order.

Again it is urged upon the reader to recall the apostle is still addressing the Jewish converts. It was imperative for Paul to instill in the minds of the Jewish converts the Law of Moses was now dead, nailed to the cross and forever ended. Paul made many efforts to remind the Jews the very law which they did not wish to give up was the very law which instructed them to do so.

*All things* of both the Patriarchal Law and the Law of Moses contained prophecies of the coming of Christ and His New Covenant—the New Testament. Genesis 12:1-3 and Jeremiah 31:31-34 both attest to this fact. Brother Foy E. Wallace wrote in his commentary on the Revelation the following:

> There are multiple passages in the New Testament gathered around the fact that the types and symbols and prophecies all pointed to Christ and were thus fulfilled. This is why Heb. 1:1,2 declares that God appointed him to be the 'heir of all things' spoken by the prophets; and is why Paul in Eph. 1:10-11 stated that in this dispensation God has gathered together in one 'all things' in Christ; **and why it is in Rom. 8:27-29 the apostle shows that 'all things' of God's plan work together for good, for the redemption of all men who are called according to his purpose in the redemptive plan...**[37] (Emphasis DHC).

That *all things,* good or bad, *work together for good,* as most assert is an amazing error. To suggest God-loving parents who lose a child, or a God-loving father loses his family, that sickness, disease, famine, murder, rape, or even the death of one

---
[37] Foy E. Wallace, Jr.

# Commentary on Romans

not a Christian works for the good of those who love the Lord is truly absurd. It can never be the case the death of anyone not a Christian is anything but sad, yea, even bad. That a parent has a child killed or perhaps traumatically injured leaving the parents with a total invalid in their hands in no way works toward the good of anyone. Such a traumatic occurrence occupies far more time of the parents, and hinders time needed for other duties and responsibilities in the Lord's church. Indeed, such things happen and will continue to happen, but they are in no way good, regardless of how much one may love the Lord.

## Romans 8:29-39

*29 For whom he did foreknow, he also did predestinate to be conformed to the image of his Son, that he might be the firstborn among many brethren. 30 Moreover whom he did predestinate, them he also called: and whom he called, them he also justified: and whom he justified, them he also glorified. 31 What shall we then say to these things? If God be for us, who can be against us? 32 He that spared not his own Son, but delivered him up for us all, how shall he not with him also freely give us all things? 33 Who shall lay any thing to the charge of God's elect? It is God that justifieth. 34 Who is he that condemneth? It is Christ that died, yea rather, that is risen again, who is even at the right hand of God, who also maketh intercession for us. 35 Who shall separate us from the love of Christ? shall tribulation, or distress, or persecution, or famine, or nakedness, or peril, or sword? 36 As it is written, For thy sake we are killed all the day long; we are accounted as sheep for the slaughter. 37 Nay, in all these things we are more than conquerors through him that loved us. 38 For I am persuaded, that neither death, nor life, nor angels, nor principalities, nor pow-ers, nor things present, nor things to come, 39 Nor height, nor depth, nor any other creature, shall be able to separate us from the love of God, which is in Christ Jesus our Lord.*

**Verse 29.** *For whom he did foreknow, he also did predestinate*

# Commentary on Romans

*to be conformed to the image of his Son, that he might be the firstborn among many brethren.* This verse seems to serve the Calvinist well. The assertion set forth, by those who wear the stripes of Calvinism, is God has predestined some unto salvation and some unto eternal peril; and none can change his eternal predestination.

This passage is not hard to understand for those who possess nominal astuteness. It merits mentioning again the context of every passage must be kept in mind to properly ascertain the truth of what any given passage teaches. We have been and will continue to emphasize this matter. The Calvinist teaches the phrase, *for whom he did foreknow,* refers to those whom the Father predetermined unto salvation.

From verse 27 is clear, the *he* identified in the verse is Christ, which was made crystal clear by the apostle John in Revelation 2:23. Christ is the searcher of the hearts of men, and He is the one who intercedes and mediates between God and men. Keeping this in mind we learn verse 29 teaches: *For whom he* (the Father) *did foreknow* (being Christ), *he* (the Father) *also did predestinate to be conformed to the image of his Son, that he* (Christ) *might be the firstborn among many brethren.*

The *he* of verse 29 refers to the Father and not to men. The Father foreordained Christ to be the image of the Father. The Lord said, *I and my Father are one,* Christ also said, *if ye have seen me ye have seen the Father* (Jno. 10:30; 14:9). The word *he* is first person singular, but the Calvinist insists the word is plural. Such is a gross error in both grammar and doctrine.

There is a doctrine of predestination taught in the Scriptures, but it is in no way related to the doctrine taught by Calvinists. Some other passages are provided from which the doctrine of predestination is taught by Calvinists, with comments supplied in parentheses.

1. *Having predestinated us unto the adoption of children by Jesus Christ to himself* (How?), *according to the good pleasure of his will* (which is the Gospel) (Eph. 1:5).

# Commentary on Romans

2. *In whom also we have obtained an inheritance* (How?), *being predestinated* (How?) *according to the purpose of him* (which is the Gospel,) *who worketh all things after the counsel of his own will* (Eph. 1:11).

3. *Elect according to the foreknowledge of God the Father* (How?), *through sanctification of the spirit* (of man), *unto obedience and sprinkling of the blood of Jesus Christ* (on the cross) *Grace unto you and peace, be multiplied* (I Pet. 1:2).

The Calvinistic doctrines of predestination and unconditional election are sister evils. God predestined the one through whom salvation was to come. God also predestined the plan by which salvation would be granted. That plan is the Gospel of Christ. God predestined the destination to which the saved would go. That destination is heaven. God predestined the people who acquired salvation to be rewarded with eternal life in heaven—that is, those who obey *the author and finisher of our faith* (Heb. 5:9). The Lord predestined the author of salvation through His predestined plan unto a predestined destiny, for obedient people.

Suppose invitations are extended to one hundred individuals, but seating is only available for fifty. The first fifty individuals who arrive are predestined to have seating provided. While all are invited and while all may attend, it is not at all the case the first fifty individuals to arrive have been *elected* (predestined) to arrive first. The predestination and election has nothing to do with the attending individuals, rather the predestination and election has reference to the available seating. The same is true regarding the election and predestination of which the Scriptures speak. God has predestinated those who live godly and obediently to His will to be the ones He has elected to save. God has not predestined some to be elected unto salvation and elected some unto damnation.

**Verse 30.** *Moreover whom he did predestinate, them he also called: and whom he called, them he also justified: and whom he justified, them he also glorified.* From this verse it is clear the Father predestined the avenue by which men are predestined. They are predestined to salvation through the avenue by which God calls men—that is, through the Gospel and in no other way.

# Commentary on Romans

Paul forever settled the matter of how God calls man. He wrote: *Whereunto he called you by our gospel, to the obtaining of the glory of our Lord Jesus Christ* (II Thes. 2:14).

Once one has answered the call of the Gospel and remains faithful to it, God then justifies said individual. Without obedience to the call of the Gospel, there is no justification awarded. Once one has been justified by the Father, he is glorified.

**Verses 31-32.** *What shall we then say to these things? If God be for us, who can be against us? He that spared not his own Son, but delivered him up for us all, how shall he not with him also freely give us all things?* The question posed in verse 31 is in rhetoric. Here again it is paramount to recall the audience of the apostle. Paul is still addressing the Jewish converts. There was no logical response the Jews could provide which could refute the arguments made by the apostle. *These things* of which Paul wrote were those *things* which referred to the predestination of God, and the process by which He determined to save man.

On the phrase, *If God be for us, who can be against us*, we ask if it is the case, God is for us, then who shall have success against us? There is no external force or source which has adequate power to conquer the man justified by God. There is, however, an internal force which can do so. That internal force is the individual himself. Men separate themselves from God through their own volition. The prophet Isaiah wrote: *your iniquities have separated between you and your God and your sins have hid his face from you, that he will not hear* (Isa. 59:2). While it is true *that old serpent, which is the devil and Satan*, works to devour us, he cannot do so unless we allow him (Rev. 20:2). The Christian has power over the devil as the Lord's bother declared: *resist the devil and he will flee from you* (Jas. 4:7). Men are drawn away from God *by their own lust* when they allow themselves to be *enticed* (Jas. 1:14).

The assurance Paul gave his Jewish audience as God's children, was they could conquer all that might separate them from God. For God *spared not his own Son, but delivered him up for us all*. Further, Paul declared God had freely given the Jewish converts (yea, all men) *all things* needed to overcome the

# Commentary on Romans

wiles of the Devil.

**Verses 33-34.** *Who shall lay any thing to the charge of God's elect? It is God that justifieth. Who is he that condemneth? It is Christ that died, yea rather, that is risen again, who is even at the right hand of God, who also maketh intercession for us.* These two verses contain both a rhetorical question and the needed reply. The first has suffered much at the hands of the Calvinist.

Once again the Calvinist insists *God's elect,* here and elsewhere, refers to those whom God has predestined and elected unto salvation, which is indeed a long, arduous journey from the truth. This matter has been addressed in the comments of verse 29.

Paul reminds his Jewish audience it is God, not the Old Law of Moses, nor being a descendant of Abraham which justified the Jews before God. God both justifies and sanctifies man, but He does so through obedience to the Gospel of His son and in no other way (cf. Rom. 8:33; Jd. 1).

Because it is Lord who justifies and sanctifies obedient men, it is only logical to conclude condemnation is issued by the Lord as well. The second question posed in these two verses shows it is indeed the Son of God who condemns disobedient men.

The phrase, *it is Christ that died, yea rather, that is risen again*, was especially troublesome for the Sadducees. The resurrection and angels were matters not accepted by them. That Paul emphasizes the resurrected Christ here shows there were many Sadducees who worked hard to influence Jewish converts. To further solidify his message, Paul adds the phrase, *who is even at the right hand of God.* A third point of solidification made by the apostle regarding the resurrected Christ is He *also maketh intercession for us.*

The making of intercession for the saints, as Paul records it here, is essential to address. It is equally essential to recall Paul earlier declared it was Christ *that searcheth the hearts knoweth what is the mind of the Spirit, because he maketh intercession for the saints according to the will of God* (Rom. 8:27). Twice in this

# Commentary on Romans

chapter Paul declared Christ is the intercessor of the saint. How is it countless men and brethren insist the Holy Spirit does the interceding when in fact the apostle makes it undeniably and crystal clear it is Christ who does the interceding on behalf of the saints and not the Holy Spirit?

It is good to hear the Lord's prophet Isaiah regarding the prophecy made concerning the intercession of Christ. This prophecy of Christ's intercession for His children is rarely, if ever, considered and is even more rarely considered to be a prophecy of Christ's intercessory activity. Worse yet, most have not the faintest knowledge of the following prophecy of the statesman prophet: *Therefore will I divide him a portion with the great, and he shall divide the spoil with the strong; because he hath poured out his soul unto death: and he was numbered with the transgressors; and he bare the sin of many, and made intercession for the transgressors* (Isa. 53:12).

Isaiah's prophecy was indeed fulfilled, as seen in the following New Testament passages. Yet it seems as if none are aware of Isaiah's prophecy that Christ would be appointed as the intercessor between man and God. Observe the following passages.

*Who is he that condemneth? It is Christ that died, yea rather, that is risen again, who is even at the right hand of God, who also maketh intercession for us* (Rom. 8:34).

*Wherefore he is able also to save them to the uttermost that come unto God by him, seeing he ever liveth to make intercession for them* (Heb. 7:25).

*For Christ is not entered into the holy places made with hands, which are the figures of the true; but into heaven itself, now to appear in the presence of God for us* (Heb. 9:24).

*My little children, these things write I unto you, that ye sin not. And if any man sin, we have an advocate with the Father, Jesus Christ the righteous* (I Jno. 2:1).

These passages plainly show the prophecy of Isaiah was fulfilled

# Commentary on Romans

in Christ, and only in Christ, not the Holy Spirit.

**Verse 35-37.** *Who shall separate us from the love of Christ? shall tribulation, or distress, or persecution, or famine, or nakedess, or peril, or sword? As it is written, For thy sake we are killed all the day long; we are accounted as sheep for the slaughter. Nay, in all these things we are more than conquerors through him that loved us.* These verses have been wrested, warped, writhed, and wrenched by so many for so long there seems there is no end to the number of students who have no understanding of the passage.

The Calvinist once again stands center stage with his gross eror. *Who shall separate us from the love of Christ?* The Calvinst insists no one can do so. Not man, not the devil, nor any other creature inclusive of self. It is impossible to fall from the grace the Lord has granted, so the Calvinist teaches. None, it is argued, can take it away. The Calvinist sweetens his damnable doctrine wrongfully citing the Lord, wherein He said: *And I give unto them eternal life; and they shall never perish, neither shall any man pluck them out of my hand. My Father, which gave them me, is greater than all; and no man is able to pluck them out of my Father's hand* (Jno. 10:28-29). The doctrine sounds sweet and is favorably agreeable to the Calvinist, but the idea lacks Biblical foundation. Calvinists fails to realize man himself can indeed remove himself from the Lord's care, protection, and His hand. Revelation 3:16 informs the Bible student the Lord can spew one out. Paul told the church of Galatia that those who returned to the Old Law had *fallen from grace* (Gal. 5:4). We wonder just who it was that caused some of the Jewish converts of Galatia to return to the Old Law and cause their fall from grace? Is the Calvinist willing to affirm it was the Lord's doing? We think not.

*Who shall separate us from the love of Christ?* Most students are of the mindset the Lord will in no way deny man His love. It is felt by most God never ceases to love anyone. *The apostle is not speaking of God's love for man, but rather Paul is speaking about man's love for God.* Who shall separate us from our love for God? is the purpose of the question posed. Neither *tribulation, or distress, or persecution, or famine, or nakedness, or per-*

# Commentary on Romans

*il, or sword* can separate man form his love for God, but man himself can. There are two things not mentioned in this passage which can separate man from God: 1) sin, and 2) self. *Behold, the Lord's hand is not shortened, that it cannot save; neither his ear heavy, that it cannot hear: But your iniquities have separated between you and your God, and your sins have hid his face from you, that he will not hear* (Isa. 59:1-2).

It is well to note *the sufferings of this present time* recorded in verse 18 would cause many to depart from the truth, but such departures were only accomplished by the individuals who refused to stand up to the test of the distress and tribulation through which the church was then going. Verse 36 refers to the martyrdom many of the church suffered, which is quoted from Psalm 44:22.

In the face of all the things the church was then suffering there was victory to be had; thus, verse 37 expressed the assurance the justified and sanctified children of God they were *more than conquerors.* The victory they were to enjoy was *through Christ* that so loved them and not through the Old Law.

**Verses 38-39.** *For I am persuaded, that neither death, nor life, nor angels, nor principalities, nor powers, nor things present, nor things to come, Nor height, nor depth, nor any other creature, shall be able to separate us from the love of God, which is in Christ Jesus our Lord.* These verses are merely additional things Paul adds to the list he provided in verse 35.

Paul said he was persuaded nothing external of the Christian had power enough to separate anyone from the love the Christian is to have for the Lord. As stated before, the love about which Paul wrote is the love the saint is to have for God and not the love God has for man.

God the Father can, will, and does cease to love those who insist on sin and iniquity, as He told Israel: *All their wickedness is in Gilgal: for there I hated them: for the wickedness of their doings I will drive them out of mine house, I will love them no more: all their princes are revolters* (Hos. 9:15). *Keep yourselves in the love of God, looking for the mercy of our Lord Jesus Christ unto*

# Commentary on Romans

*eternal life* (Jd. 21).

That God never ceases to love anyone causes a serious question to be raised. Does God intend to send anyone to hell? If so, whom? Does the Lord plan on sending one to hell whom men say he never ceases to love? Is it not the case only those who fail to obtain God's love, or those who have surrendered it will find their place among those who weep and gnash their teeth?

## When Did Inspiration End?

The question posed is not trivial, but merits much consideration. It has long been held by most students, miracles and inspiration ended when the last one to whom an apostle had given a spiritual gift died. This view is far from the true. It can in no any way be affirmed. To the contrary, the Scripture sets forth detailed and clear information as to when inspiration—the miraculous age ended. That this question be answered is of the utmost importance when one studies the Scripture.

We pose the following question: *What was the work of the Holy Spirit?* The answer to this question is four-fold. First, the work of the Holy Spirit was to reveal truth to those through whom God determined. David *said the Spirit of the Lord spake by me His word was on my tongue* (II Sam. 23:2). Peter declared of the Old Testament prophets that *prophecy came not in old time by the will of man: but holy men of God spake as they were moved by the Holy Ghost* (II Pet. 1:21). The word *moved* means to have been *carried along* by the Holy Ghost. Jesus informed the apostles that they would be endowed by the Holy Spirit when He would come upon them. Jesus said to the twelve: *Howbeit when he, the Spirit of truth, is come, he will guide you into all truth* (Jno. 16:13). Men of the Old and New Testaments were inspired for the purpose of revealing truth.

Second, the work of the Holy Spirit was to glorify Christ: *He shall glorify me: for he shall receive of mine, and shall shew it unto you* (Jno. 16:14).

A third work of the Holy Spirit was *reprove the world of sin, and of righteousness, and of judgment:* As the Lord declared as recorded in John 16:8.

# Commentary on Romans

The fourth work of the Holy Spirit was to confirm the word He revealed to those He inspired. Why should anyone believe that a man called Jesus had been raised from the dead? Acts 8:5-8 explains the reason people believed the Gospel.

*5 Then Philip went down to the city of Samaria, and **preached Christ** unto them. 6 And the people with one accord gave heed unto those things which Philip spake, **hearing and seeing the miracles** which he did. 7 For unclean spirits, crying with loud voice, came out of many that were possessed with them: and many taken with palsies, and that were lame, were healed. 8 And there was great joy in that city* (emph. DHC).

The prophet Daniel was informed by the Holy Ghost that the New Covenant would be confirmed by the the same. Daniel was also informed as to how long the confirmation of the New Covenant would last. *And he shall confirm the covenant with many for one week: and in the midst of the week he shall cause the sacrifice and the oblation to cease, and for the overspreading of abominations he shall make it desolate, even until the consummation, and that determined shall be poured upon the desolate* (Dan. 9:27).

Our focus here is the confirmation of the covenant of which the prophet spoke *and* the duration of that confirmation. The confirmation of that covenant was to be for *one week.* But how long is the *one week* of which Daniel wrote? The answer is determined by the events Daniel declared would unfold during this *one week* period.

Daniel stated that *in the midst of the week he shall cause the sacrifice and the oblation to cease....* The sacrifices and oblations of the Mosaical Law ended when Christ was crucified. Christ put an end to the Old Law and the sacrifices required under the Old Law. The sacrifice of Christ was *in the midst of the week* of the confirmation of which Daniel was told. The word *midst* indicates the middle. In the middle of the week of confirmation of the new covenant Christ was crucified. The balance of the week was yet to be fulfilled. Thus, until the week of confir-

# Commentary on Romans

mation was complete, the new covenant of which both Jeremiah and Daniel spoke would continue being confirmed.

Christ was crucified *in the midst of the week.* Christ was about 35 (33½, to be more precise) when He was crucified. The week under consideration spoken of by Daniel lasted for 70 years. Inspiration ended in the year AD 70, when Jerusalem was destroyed by Titus under the decree of Nero. New Testament inspiration began prior to AD 1., the year generally recognized as the one in which the Lord was born.

Prior to Christ's birth, three individuals became inspired as the New Covenant of which Jeremiah and Daniel spoke began being revealed. Mary and Elizabeth became inspired after the birth of Jesus was announced. Zechariah spoke by inspiration after John was born and his tongue was loosed. Simeon and Anna spoke by inspiration shortly after the birth of Jesus (usually referred to as AD 1). The confirmation of the New Testament continued until AD 70 and ceased as instantly as it began.

There are two objections to this exegesis. The first is that the week of confirmation of which Daniel spoke is a literal one-week period. However, if the one week of covenant confirmation is one literal week, then multiple issues arise. First, Daniel stated that the crucifixion was to be in the midst of the one-week period of the covenant confirmation. If the one week is literal, then Christ was crucified 3½ days into the one literal week. That would allow but 3½ days of the supposed literal one week for the rest of the confirmation of the New Covenant to be completed. This of course would mean that all the books of the New Testament would have to have been written and confirmed within 3½ days. Further, Paul could not have made so much as even the first missionary journey within such a small time frame.

A second objection asserts that the one week on covenant confirmation, of which Daniel spoke, is figurative of a seven-year period. This objection is refuted with the same argument given above. If the one week is a period of seven years, then the problem of an insufficient amount of time to execute all the missionary journeys of Paul still remains. This also means all the books of the New Testament would had to have been completed and

# Commentary on Romans

confirmed by the year AD 37, just 3½ years after Christ was crucified. Paul's journeys and the completion of the New Testament could not have occurred in such a short period of time.

In that the one week period is a figurative period of 70 years, there remains 37 years from the crucifixion of Christ for the New Covenant to have confirmation completed. This well allows sufficient time for the travels of Paul to take place.

It does one well to understand the counting process of time and years as dictated by Moses as recorded in Leviticus 25:1-22. The one week of covenant confirmation of which Daniel spoke as recorded in Daniel 9:27 can only be a period of seventy years.

We are informed as to when inspiration both began and ceased. Inspiration only confirmed the New Covenant for one week—70 years. Every book of the New Testament was written and confirmed before AD 70, inclusive of the Revelation. The crucifixion of Christ was in the midst of the week of the confirmation of the New Covenant. Again, the week under consideration of Daniel 9:27 can only mean a period of seventy years beginning prior to the year AD 1, the year Christ was born.

The counting of time of Daniel's prophecy is given Divine commentary in Leviticus.

> And thou shalt number seven sabbaths of years unto thee, seven times seven years; and the space of the seven sabbaths of years shall be unto thee forty and nine years. Then shalt thou cause the trumpet of the jubilee to sound on the tenth day of the seventh month, in the day of atonement shall ye make the trumpet sound throughout all your land. And ye shall hallow the fiftieth year, and proclaim liberty throughout all the land unto all the inhabitants thereof: it shall be a jubilee unto you; and ye shall return every man unto his possession, and ye shall return every man unto his family. A jubilee shall that fiftieth year be unto you: ye shall not sow, neither reap that which groweth of itself in it, nor gather the grapes in it of thy vine undressed. For it is the jubilee: it shall be holy unto you: ye shall eat the

# Commentary on Romans

*increase thereof out of the field* (Lev. 25:8-12).

It cannot be the case the Revelation to John was written in AD 96. AD 96 is 26 years removed from the period of the confirmation of the covenant of which Daniel wrote and clearly pinpointed. The study of every book of the New Testament, inclusive of the Revelation, will bear a better and proper understanding of what the inspired authors intended, as directed by the Holy Spirit, when one understands the *one week* period of confirmation spoken of by Daniel.

Why is it that brethren fail to understand the age of miracles, *the work of the Holy Spirit, and the confirmation of the new covenant ended as abruptly as it began?*

Remember the words of David, who sought the Lord not to take the Holy Spirit (inspiration) from him (II Sam. 23:2). God saw fit to put an end to visions prophecies and miracles as quickly as they began. For about 400 years there were no prophets after Malachi. After Malachi, just when and how did inspiration of the Old Testament end? *It ended instantly* after Malachi completed his inspired work. It is not plausible to separate the one week of covenant confirmation from the crucifixion of Christ, as mentioned in the same passage.

# Commentary on Romans

## Romans 9:1-5

*1 I say the truth in Christ, I lie not, my conscience also bearing me witness in the Holy Ghost: 2 That I have great heaviness and continual sorrow in my heart. 3 For I could wish that myself were accursed from Christ for my brethren, my kinsmen according to the flesh: 4 Who are Israelites; to whom pertaineth the adoption and the glory and the covenants and the giving of the law and the service of God and the promises; 5 Whose are the fathers and of whom as concerning the flesh Christ came, who is over all, God blessed for ever. Amen.*

**Verse 1.** *I say the truth in Christ, I lie not, my conscience also bearing me witness in the Holy Ghost. I say the truth in Christ.* This is the most solemn oath man can make. Such an oath calls for the seal of Christ upon it. It is an oath which is not only observed in heaven, but one that has upon it a Divine seal. Oaths must not be made lightly. Oaths made are fettered to the souls of those who make them.

Obedience to the gospel is an oath taken; an oath which has declared one's undivided, and unwavering dedication to the Lord and his church. This oath of obedience is one which has both rewards and consequences latched to it. The rewards are eternal as are the consequences. Any oath merits serious, somber, solemn, and grave consideration before utterance. The Lord expressed it well when He said, *If any man come to me and hate not his father and mother and wife and children and brethren and sisters, yea and his own life also, he cannot be my disciple. And whosoever doth not bear his cross and come after me, cannot be my disciple. For which of you, intending to build a tower, sitteth not down first and counteth the cost, whether he have sufficient to finish it? Lest haply, after he hath laid the foundation and is not able to finish it, all that behold it begin to mock him* (Lk. 14:26-29).

*I lie not.* Three witnesses attested to Paul having spoken the truth. First, Christ served as his witness. Second, the conscience of the apostle was witness to him. Third, the Holy Ghost

# Commentary on Romans

was called as a witness on behalf of the apostle. The Lord declared: *in the mouth of two or three witnesses every word may be established.* Paul indeed provided the number of needed witnesses, as the Lord directed (Matt. 18:16).

*My conscience also bearing me witness in the Holy Ghost.* Barnes wrote of the words, *My conscience:* "Conscience is that act or judgment of the mind by which we decide on the lawfulness or unlawfulness of our actions and by which we instantly approve or condemn them. It exists in every man and is a strong witness to our integrity or to our guilt"[38] [sic] .

A man's conscience either acquits or condemns him, and it must be clear in order to win the Lord's favor. Even when one is in error, the conscience must be clear. Paul persecuted the church, but did so with a good conscience—even though his conduct was bad. *And Paul, earnestly beholding the council, said, Men and brethren, I have lived in all good conscience before God until this day* (Acts 23:1). While Paul's conduct was ill toward the church before his conversion, his conscience was clear, but he was still wrong. The apostle was not haunted by an evil conscience because of his past; he was troubled because of his conduct. He wrote to the church of Galatia, saying: *For ye have heard of my conversation in time past in the Jews' religion, how that beyond measure I persecuted the church of God and wasted it* (Gal. 1:13). Even so, the apostle's conscience was clear, based upon his Jewish dedication. Paul believed, as did most Jews, he was doing the Lord's will in his efforts to squelch the spread of the Gospel.

**Verses 2-3.** *That I have great heaviness and continual sorrow in my heart. For I could wish that myself were accursed from Christ for my brethren, my kinsmen according to the flesh.* Paul had Christ, his conscience, and the Holy Ghost as witnesses to testify for himself. They testified Paul had a great and continuous sorrow in his heart for his fellow Jews. Paul would rather suffer eternal damnation than to have his fellow Jews suffer it. The love Paul had for his fellow Jew was a supreme and unequaled love. *I could wish that myself were accursed from Christ for my brethren, my kinsmen according to the flesh.*

---
[38] Albert Barnes.

# Commentary on Romans

*For scarcely for a righteous man will one die: yet peradventure for a good man some would even dare to die* (Rom. 5:7). Paul was willing to die for those who were garbed with strong hatred for himself and Christ. The apostle donned the mantle of sainthood supremely well. All saints must work diligently toward the same of character as Paul. Paul wrote: *Be ye followers of me, even as I also am of Christ* (I Cor. 11:1).

**Verses 4-5.** *Who are Israelites; to whom pertaineth the adoption and the glory and the covenants and the giving of the law and the service of God and the promises; Whose are the fathers and of whom as concerning the flesh Christ came, who is over all, God blessed for ever. Amen.* Paul's brethren were descendants of Jacob, whom God named Israel. They had been adopted as God's special and chosen people. Whiteside comments:

> "The glory perhaps includes all the manifestations of God's care for them, including also the Shekinah, the emblem of his presence in the Holy of Holies. From Abraham onward God had made covenants with no other people, nor had he given laws to any other people. As the laws were God-given, they were perfectly suited to their needs"[39] [sic].

Clarke authored the following comments on verses four and five, which are worthy of consideration. All emphasis is his.

**Who are Israelites** – Descendants of Jacob, a man so highly favored of God and from whom he received his name *Israel—a prince of God*, Gen. 32:28; from which name his descendants were called *Israelites* and separated unto God for his glory and praise. Their very name of *Israelites* implied their very high dignity; they were a *royal nation; princes of the most high God*[40] [sic].

**The adoption** – The Israelites were all taken into the *family* of God and were called his *sons* and *firstborn*, Exo. 4:22; Deut. 14:1; Jer. 31:9; Hos. 11:1; and this

---
[39] Robertson L. Whiteside.
[40] Adam Clarke.

# Commentary on Romans

adoption took place when God made the covenant with them at Horeb[41] [sic].

**The glory** – The manifestation of God among them; principally by the *cloud* and *pillar* and the *Shekinah*, or Divine presence, appearing between the cherubim over the mercy-seat. These were peculiar to the Jews; no other nation was ever thus favoured[42] [sic].

**The covenants** – The covenants made with Abraham, both that which relates to the *spiritual seed* and that which was peculiar to his *natural descendants*, Gal. 3: 16,17; which covenants were afterwards renewed by Moses, Deut. 29:1. Some suppose that the *singular* is here put for the plural and that by *covenants* we are to understand the d*ecalogue*, which is termed ברית *ber-ith*, or *covenant*, Deut. 4:13. But it is more likely that the apostle alludes to the great *covenant* made with Abraham and to its various *renewals* and *extensions* at different times afterwards, as well as to its twofold design—the grant of the *land of Canaan* and the rest that remains for the people of God[43] [sic].

**The giving of the law** – The revelation of God by God himself; contains a system of moral and political precepts. This was also peculiar to the Jews; for to no other nation had he ever given a revelation of his will.[44]

**The service** – Λατρεια. The particular ordinances, rites and ceremonies of their religious worship and especially the sacrificial system, so expressive of the sinfulness of sin and the holiness of God[45] [sic].

**The promises** – The land of Canaan and the blessings of the Messiah and his kingdom; which promises had been made and often repeated to the patriarchs and to

---

[41] Adam Clarke
[42] Ibid.
[43] Ibid.
[44] Ibid.
[45] Ibid.

# Commentary on Romans

the prophets[46] [sic].

Paul closes these verses with the word *amen*. The oath Paul had taken upon himself was one with which he assured his fellow Jews his word was true. Looking at the words with which Paul opened his oath, *I say the truth in Christ, I lie not*, and the word with which he closed his oath, *Amen*, solidifies the testimony and oath of which he spoke in verse one.

*Who are Israelites?* The question is not one from which the apostle seeks an answer. Rather, the question is posed to inform the Jewish converts the Israelites of which Paul speaks are the true Israelites.

It is the intent of the apostle in these verses to rebut the Jewish assertion they were entitled to salvation. The Jews assumed, because their religious system was given by the Lord, there would be no end to it. The Jews believed the Messiah, of which the prophets spoke, would set up an earthly kingdom under the monarchy of the Messiah. The apostles themselves were among those who believed the Messiah's kingdom was to be an earthly one. Just before the Lord's ascension from Bethany, when the apostles and Christ *were come together, they asked of him, saying, Lord, wilt thou at this time restore again the kingdom to Israel* (Acts 1:6)?

Paul realized it was needful to refute the Jewish addiction the Kingdom of God was to be physical. The apostle found it necessary to dismantle these prejudices and errors of the Jews.
The Israelites took much pride in their descent from Abraham, and they relied upon that descent for their acceptance with God. Paul pointed out it is one thing to be *of Israel,* but it was quite another thing to be *Israel* (that is) to possess the qualities and character of the true Israel. Under the Law of Moses pedigree was a great value, but under the Law of Christ the valued pedigree was being a Christian, not a Jew.

## Romans 9:6-17

6 *Not as though the word of God hath taken none ef-*

---
[46] Adam Clarke

# Commentary on Romans

*fect. For they are not all Israel, which are of Israel: 7 Neither, because they are the seed of Abraham, are they all children: but, In Isaac shall thy seed be called. 8 That is, They which are the children of the flesh, these are not the children of God: but the children of the promise are counted for the seed. 9 For this is the word of promise, At this time will I come and Sara shall have a son. 10 And not only this; but when Rebecca also had conceived by one, even by our father Isaac; 11 (For the children being not yet born, neither having done any good or evil, that the purpose of God according to election might stand, not of works, but of him that calleth;) 12 It was said unto her, The elder shall serve the younger. 13 As it is written, Jacob have I loved, but Esau have I hated. 14 What shall we say then? Is there unrighteousness with God? God forbid. 15 For he saith to Moses, I will have mercy on whom I will have mercy and I will have compassion on whom I will have compassion. 16 So then it is not of him that willeth, nor of him that runneth, but of God that sheweth mercy. 17 For the scripture saith unto Pharaoh, Even for this same purpose have I raised thee up, that I might shew my power in thee and that my name might be declared throughout all the earth.*

**Verses 6-7.** *Not as though the word of God hath taken none effect. For they are not all Israel, which are of Israel: Neither, because they are the seed of Abraham, are they all children: but, In Isaac shall thy seed be called.* "The condition of fleshly Israel, though not clearly stated in verses 1-5, was, nevertheless, implied. But the fact that fleshly Israel had rejected Christ and was therefore anathema from Christ, did not show that the Word of God—the promise to Abraham—had come to nought. Verse 7 shows that the promise made to Abraham is the Word of God that Paul had in mind. Even though fleshly Israel had rejected Christ, there was yet a spiritual Israel and the promise was fulfilled in them. Paul's language in these verses shows that the promise made to Abraham terminated in spiritual Israel. They do greatly err who think the promise to Abraham is yet to be fulfilled in fleshly Israel. Blood descent from Abraham does not entitle one to share in the promise. Verse 7 explains that neither be-

# Commentary on Romans

cause they are Abraham's seed, are they all children, but in Isaac his seed was to be called. In verses 6 and 7, Paul begins to show the Jews that they had no right to complain, even if God did reject them for another people. In working out his plans, God had rejected the other sons of Abraham and selected Isaac through whom the promised seed should come. Other illustrations Paul gives later"[47] [sic].

Isaiah wrote: *So shall my word be that goeth forth out of my mouth: it shall not return unto me void, but it shall accomplish that which I please and it shall prosper in the thing whereto I sent it* (Isa. 55:11). Regardless of how man responds to God's Word, His Word always accomplishes the task whereunto He sends it. Men either accept God's it and obey it or reject it and disobey. Those who obey reap the benefits God promises to give. The same word of promise also holds the promise of consequences upon those who reject the Word of the Lord. The same water that saved Noah and his family was the same water that destroyed those who refused to obey God. The same sunshine that softens butter is the same sunshine that hardens clay. God's word is either accepted or rejected based upon the condition of heart into which it is sown. What does Paul mean when he says, *For they are not all Israel, which are of Israel?*

It is needful to understand the Israel of which Paul speaks first is physical Israel. The second use of Israel refers to spiritual Israel. The spiritual Israel under consideration is the church. The Lord said to the apostles: *Verily I say unto you, That ye which have followed me, in the regeneration when the Son of man shall sit in the throne of his glory, ye also shall sit upon twelve thrones, judging the twelve tribes of Israel* (Matt. 19:28). The church is identified as the twelve tribes of Israel in this passage. James, the Lord's brother, understood the church was the new twelve tribes of Israel. James so identified them in James 1:1.

The body of Christ—that is, His church—is the Israel of God today, but it is a spiritual Israel. Physical Israel will never be restored as an earthly nation. The kingdom of God is spiritual and *not of this world* (Jno. 18:36).

---
[47] Robertson L. Whiteside.

# Commentary on Romans

Just because one was a direct descendant of Abraham did not make him part of spiritual Israel, the true *seed of Abraham*. The spiritual Israel under consideration is comprised of both Jews and Gentiles. Isaiah wrote: *And it shall come to pass in the last days, that the mountain of the Lord's house shall be established in the top of the mountains and shall be exalted above the hills; and all nations shall flow unto it. And many people shall go and say, Come ye and let us go up to the mountain of the Lord, to the house of the God of Jacob; and he will teach us of his ways and we will walk in his paths: for out of Zion shall go forth the Law and the word of the Lord from Jerusalem* (Isa. 2:2-3).

The phrases, *all nations shall flow unto it* and *many people,* refer to Gentile nations to whom the Gospel was to be preached. Luke wrote: *For the promise is unto you and to your children and to all that are afar off, even as many as the Lord our God shall call* (Acts 2:39). Paul later declared of the Gospel: *it is the power of God unto salvation to every one that believeth; to the Jew first and also to the Greek* (Rom. 1:16).

The Israel of God, the church of Christ, is made up of both Jew and Gentile. The partition between the Jews and Gentiles was removed in Christ. *For he is our peace, who hath made both one and hath broken down the middle wall of partition between us* (Eph. 2:14).

The name Israel refers to the spiritual state of God's people. The name Jacob reflects the natural state. For this reason the church of Christ is the Israel of God. Paul further solidified the matter when he said that *there is neither Jew nor Greek...for ye are all one in Christ Jesus* (Gal. 3:28).

**Verse 8.** *That is, They which are the children of the flesh, these are not the children of God: but the children of the promise are counted for the seed.* Understanding the above comments make the meaning of this verse easy to grasp. Notice how Paul contrasts the *children of the flesh* to *the children of God.*

The Lord longs for **spiritual** children not **physical** ones. If God were pleased with physical children, He could create as many as would please Him. John addressed this matter in His disserta-

# Commentary on Romans

tion with the Jews when He said: *And think not to say within yourselves, We have Abraham to our father: for I say unto you, that God is able of these stones to raise up children unto Abraham* (Matt. 3:9). Obedience to the Law of Christ made one an Israelite of God, not one's lineage to Abraham. The Jews were called in Abraham's seed, not through the seed of Moses nor the Law of Moses.

**Verses 9-13.** *For this is the word of promise, At this time will I come and Sara shall have a son. And not only this; but when Rebecca also had conceived by one, even by our father Isaac; (For the children being not yet born, neither having done any good or evil, that the purpose of God according to election might stand, not of works, but of him that calleth;) It was said unto her, The elder shall serve the younger. As it is written, Jacob have I loved, but Esau have I hated.* Isaac was the child of promise given by God to Abraham and Sarah. Christians are the children of promise under the New Testament System of Christ. Peter and the other apostles declared: *For the promise is unto you and to your children and to all that are afar off, even as many as the Lord our God shall call* (Acts 2:39). Whiteside comments:

> In choosing Jacob, God chose his descendants; and every Jew gloried in that choice. But the selection of Jacob and the rejection of Esau had nothing to do with their salvation. If it had pertained to their salvation, there would have been no point in mentioning the fact that the younger was selected instead of the older; for even the most dogmatic predestinarian would not say that the oldest son is the natural heir of salvation and all the other sons reprobates. The fact is that the selection of Jacob was the selection of a people rather than an individual. Had it been the election to salvation, then the nations descending from Jacob were all elected to salvation and Esau's descendants were all lost. Jehovah's language to Rebekah shows plainly that he was speaking of the descendants of Jacob and Esau rather than of them as individuals: "Two nations are in thy womb and two peoples shall be separated from thy bowels: and the one people shall be stronger than the other people; and the elder shall serve the younger"

# Commentary on Romans

(Gen. 25:23). Nor does the statement that the elder shall serve the younger apply to Jacob and Esau as individuals, for as individuals Jacob came nearer serving Esau. However, it did come to pass that the descendants of Esau served the descendants of Jacob (1 Chr. 18:12,13)[48] [sic].

God was not unjust in selecting Jacob over Esau, as some of the the Jews contended. God made a choice; His choice was made before either Jacob or Esau were born, God's choice did not make God unrighteous. He chose to save the Jews through Christ, and not through Moses or the Old Law. The Jews were persuaded that, because Paul argued salvation was in Christ and not Moses, God was unjust. Paul, however, negated the Jewish objection in verses 14-15. Just because God makes a choice, does not warrant the conclusion the selection of one over another is an injustice. God chose Abel rather than Cain. God chose Jacob over Esau. God chose Mary over some other virgin. His choices were not unjust, as many of the Jews insisted.

**Verses 14-15.** *What shall we say then? Is there unrighteousness with God? God forbid. For he saith to Moses, I will have mercy on whom I will have mercy and I will have compassion on whom I will have compassion.* There was no unrighteousness with God in the selection He had made. If God selected Isaac and Jacob because they would be the best instruments through which to work out his plans, and the Jews gloried in these selections, why should they think that it would be out of harmony with God's nature to reject the Jews because of unbelief and accept the Gentiles who did believe? Even though God had rejected the Jewish nation as such, they had the same opportunity as did the Gentiles to become children of God. Whiteside adds the following comments on verse 15:

> It seems that Moses had grown somewhat discouraged on account of the waywardness of the children of Israel and showed a reluctance to go on, unless God would show him some special favors. Was this a gentle reminder to Moses? God had shown mercy to his people in spite of all that Pharaoh could do and he could and

---
[48] Robertson L. Whiteside.

## Commentary on Romans

would, continue to show them mercy even should Moses become discouraged. No one can keep God from showing mercy to whom he will. But to whom will he show mercy? "He that covereth his transgressions shall not prosper; but whoso confesseth and forsaketh them shall obtain mercy" (Prov. 28:13). And all the objections and efforts of the Jews would not keep him from having mercy on the Gentiles who turned to him. "Let the wicked forsake his way and the unrighteous man his thoughts; and let him return unto Jehovah and he will have mercy upon him; and to our God, for he will abundantly pardon" (Isa. 55:7)[49] [sic].

Every choice made by the Father is a just one. The same mercy God extended to Jacob was extended to Esau. The same grace offered to Isaac was offered to Ishmael. The same salvation offered to the Jews was offered to the Gentile. That God chose one above another to work toward His purpose does not negate His mercy, grace, peace, blessings, or salvation to another. The Father chose Christ to serve as his only begotten Son through whom salvation was to come. Could the Father not have chosen the Holy Spirit to serve as the same? The Father chose the Holy Spirit to reveal all truth; could he not have chosen Christ for the task? Is the Father unjust because he chose Christ for the work of salvation?

**Verse 16.** *So then it is not of him that willeth, nor of him that runneth, but of God that sheweth mercy.* The *him that willeth* and *him that runneth* as mentioned here has reference to man and not to the Father. The word *but* shows the contrast between the one who *willeth* and the one that *runneth*.

*So then it is not of him.* It is vital to properly ascertain the meaning of this phrase: what is not *of him*? The word *it* refers to something, but what? The *it* under consideration refers to the mercy and compassion noted in verse 15. Mercy and compassion were not so readily issued by the Jews to the Gentiles, but God issued His mercy and compassion upon all men, Jew and Gentile.

---

[49] Robertson L. Whiteside

# Commentary on Romans

Calvinists travel far on the road of the damnable doctrine of predestination using these verses as a basis from which to devise such foolishness. *It is not in him,* so the Calvinist contends—meaning man, who either wills or runs to acquire salvation. God has chosen to show mercy and compassion when, where, and upon whom He pleases, and man has no control over his eternal destiny. One is either predestined to salvation or damnation. This doctrine is of course devilish, damnable, and a demonic diatribe against God's Word.

**Verse 17.** *For the scripture saith unto Pharaoh, Even for this same purpose have I raised thee up, that I might shew my power in thee and that my name might be declared throughout all the earth.* God made the choice to work out His will through Pharaoh. That God chose to work through Pharaoh did not make God unjust. Pharaoh was unjust and ungodly before God chose him; therefore, God chose to work through him. God used Pharaoh because He knew his heart, God knew the king would not submit to Him even though many miracles would be worked through Moses and Aaron to persuade him to be obedient to the Lord. All the miracles God worked through Moses and Aaron in Egypt were avenues by which the Lord made it possible for Pharaoh to be obedient to God's will.

God also showed His power in Pharaoh throughout all the earth, as verse 17 states. As a result, the name of the Lord was declared throughout the earth, as seen in Joshua 2:1-11.

> *And Joshua the son of Nun sent out of Shittim two men to spy secretly, saying, Go view the land, even Jericho. And they went and came into an harlot's house, named Rahab and lodged there. And it was told the king of Jericho, saying, Behold, there came men in hither to night of the children of Israel to search out the country. And the king of Jericho sent unto Rahab, saying, Bring forth the men that are come to thee, which are entered into thine house: for they be come to search out all the country. And the woman took the two men and hid them and said thus, There came men unto me, but I wist not whence they were: And it came to pass about the time of shutting of the gate, when it*

# Commentary on Romans

*was dark, that the men went out: whither the men went I wot not: pursue after them quickly; for ye shall overtake them. But she had brought them up to the roof of the house and hid them with the stalks of flax, which she had laid in order upon the roof. And the men pursued after them the way to Jordan unto the fords: and as soon as they which pursued after them were gone out, they shut the gate. And before they were laid down, she came up unto them upon the roof; And she said unto the men, I know that the Lord hath given you the land and that your terror is fallen upon us and that all the inhabitants of the land faint because of you. For we have heard how the Lord dried up the water of the Red sea for you, when ye came out of Egypt; and what ye did unto the two kings of the Amorites, that were on the other side Jordan, Sihon and Og, whom ye utterly destroyed. And as soon as we had heard these things, our hearts did melt, neither did there remain any more courage in any man, because of you: for the Lord your God, he is God in heaven above and in earth beneath* (Jos. 2:1-11).

Consider also the words of the prophet Habakkuk:

*The burden which Habakkuk the prophet did see. O Lord, how long shall I cry, and thou wilt not hear! even cry out unto thee of violence, and thou wilt not save! Why dost thou shew me iniquity, and cause me to behold grievance? for spoiling and violence are before me: and there are that raise up strife and contention. Therefore the law is slacked, and judgment doth never go forth: for the wicked doth compass about the righteous; therefore wrong judgment proceedeth. Behold ye among the heathen, and regard, and wonder marvellously: for I will work a work in your days, which ye will not believe, though it be told you. For, lo, I raise up the Chaldeans, that bitter and hasty nation, which shall march through the breadth of the land, to possess the dwellingplaces that are not theirs. They are terrible and dreadful: their judgment and their dignity shall proceed of themselves. Their horses also are swifter than the*

# Commentary on Romans

leopards, and are more fierce than the evening wolves: and their horsemen shall spread themselves, and their horsemen shall come from far; they shall fly as the eagle that hasteth to eat. They shall come all for violence: their faces shall sup up as the east wind, and they shall gather the captivity as the sand. And they shall scoff at the kings, and the princes shall be a scorn unto them: they shall deride every strong hold; for they shall heap dust, and take it. Then shall his mind change, and he shall pass over, and offend, imputing this his power unto his god. Art thou not from everlasting, O Lord my God, mine Holy One? we shall not die. O Lord, thou hast ordained them for judgment; and, O mighty God, thou hast established them for correction. Thou art of purer eyes than to behold evil, and canst not look on iniquity: wherefore lookest thou upon them that deal treacherously, and holdest thy tongue when the wicked devoureth the man that is more righteous than he? And makest men as the fishes of the sea, as the creeping things, that have no ruler over them? They take up all of them with the angle, they catch them in their net, and gather them in their drag: therefore they rejoice and are glad. Therefore they sacrifice unto their net, and burn incense unto their drag; because by them their portion is fat, and their meat plenteous. Shall they therefore empty their net, and not spare continually to slay the nations? I will stand upon my watch, and set me upon the tower, and will watch to see what he will say unto me, and what I shall answer when I am reproved. And the Lord answered me, and said, Write the vision, and make it plain upon tables, that he may run that readeth it. For the vision is yet for an appointed time, but at the end it shall speak, and not lie: though it tarry, wait for it; because it will surely come, it will not tarry. Behold, his soul which is lifted up is not upright in him: but the just shall live by his faith. Yea also, because he transgresseth by wine, he is a proud man, neither keepeth at home, who enlargeth his desire as hell, and is as death, and cannot be satisfied, but gathereth unto him all nations, and heapeth unto him all people (Hab. 1:1-

# Commentary on Romans

2:5).

In short, God's prophet was questioning the Lord as to why He chose to use a nation far more wicked than the Israelites to punish them. The Lord later declared, in the work of the prophet, that Babylon would receive their punishment in due time, as God saw fit. The key point there is that the just would live by faith. He would help Israel conquer in the days of Joshua because the nation was faithful. Likewise, he would punish His people when they lacked faith.

## Romans 9:18-33

*18 Therefore hath he mercy on whom he will have mercy and whom he will he hardeneth. 19 Thou wilt say then unto me, Why doth he yet find fault? For who hath resisted his will? 20 Nay but, O man, who art thou that repliest against God? Shall the thing formed say to him that formed it, Why hast thou made me thus? 21 Hath not the potter power over the clay, of the same lump to make one vessel unto honour and another unto dishonour? 22 What if God, willing to shew his wrath and to make his power known, endured with much longsuffering the vessels of wrath fitted to destruction: 23 And that he might make known the riches of his glory on the vessels of mercy, which he had afore prepared unto glory, 24 Even us, whom he hath called, not of the Jews only, but also of the Gentiles? 25 As he saith also in Hosea, I will call them my people, which were not my people; and her beloved, which was not beloved. 26 And it shall come to pass, that in the place where it was said unto them, Ye are not my people; there shall they be called the children of the living God. 27 Esaias also crieth concerning Israel, Though the number of the children of Israel be as the sand of the sea, a remnant shall be saved: 28 For he will finish the work and cut it short in righteousness: because a short work will the Lord make upon the earth. 29 And as Esaias said before, Except the Lord of Sabaoth had left us a seed, we had been as Sodom and been made like unto Gomorrah. 30 What shall we say then? That*

# Commentary on Romans

*the Gentiles, which followed not after righteousness, have attained to righteousness, even the righteousness which is of faith. 31 But Israel, which followed after the law of righteousness, hath not attained to the law of righteousness. 32 Wherefore? Because they sought it not by faith, but as it were by the works of the law. For they stumbled at that stumbling-stone; 33 As it is written, Behold, I lay in Zion a stumbling-stone and rock of offence: and whosoever believeth on him shall not be ashamed.*

As often noted, Calvinists find numerous passages to promote the damnable doctrines of predestination and unconditional election; this passage is among them. Calvinists lack the knowledge to properly ascertain truth and the ability to properly understand context. Such flaws result in a total failure to exegete the Scriptures properly. When proper exegesis is discarded, proper conclusions are never acquired. *Context always dictates definition*, yet context never seems to find a place in the Calvinistic mind. Calvinists have always failed to adorn themselves with the good garments of sound Biblical, hermeneutics and the apparel of logic in their Bible studies. Satan has long tailored colorful costumes of confusion and deceit to prey on the minds of the simple. Calvinists have been swift to adorn themselves with the garments of the wicked one's wardrobe rather than don the doctrine of God. They have long garbed themselves in uniforms of debauchery and deception. The text now under consideration is no different; it too has been warped and wrenched by those *that are unlearned and unstable.*

Whiteside wrote the following in order to call attention to the ever present need to properly and appropriately keep matters in context.

> Introductory Note: 'In chapter 9, Paul enters on a new train of thought, which he continues to the close of the eleventh chapter. He has developed his theme that the gospel is God's power for saving men and has shown that only through obedience to the gospel can men be saved, whether they be Jews or Gentiles. This would naturally lead to certain questions concerning the Jew-

## Commentary on Romans

ish nation. 'The theme of 1:16,17 has been worked out; it has been shown that the gospel is a power of God unto salvation for them that believe, a power needed by Gentile and Jew alike, guaranteed on condition of faith and in response to faith by the love of God and adequate to man's needs as shown in history and in individual experience; and a brief description has been given of the actual state of the Christian in Christ and of the certainty and splendor of his hope, resting upon the love of God. Naturally at this point the question of the Jews arises; they were the typical instance of a people brought into close and peculiar relation to God and they therefore afford a crucial case of God's dealings with such. How then did it come to pass that they rejected the gospel? What is their present state? their future destiny? and how does this affect Christians? The answer is found in the conditions under which God selects men for the executing of his purposes. It is important to bear in mind that the selection throughout is regarded as having reference not to the final salvation of persons, but to the execution of the purpose of God. Underlying the whole section is the special object of Saint Paul to justify himself in preaching the gospel to the Gentiles (Cambridge Greek Testament)"[50] [sic].

Whiteside's observations are astute and serve the student well. The studious eye must be well targeted on the intent of the apostle. Again, we issue the continued necessity to keep all matters in proper context.

**Verse 18.** *Therefore hath he mercy on whom he will have mercy and whom he will he hardeneth.* This verse serves as a conclusion to the previous verses. It is the Lord's will to have mercy upon those who obey Him, and it is the Lord's will to harden the hearts of those who refuse to submit to His will. *And for this cause God shall send them strong delusion, that they should believe a lie: That they all might be damned who believed not the truth, but had pleasure in unrighteousness* (II Thes. 2:11-12). God sends *strong delusions* to those who have no love for the

---
[50] Robertson L. Whiteside.

# Commentary on Romans

truth. Why would God send *strong delusions* to those who are predestined to damnation if Calvinism is true?

God would not have to harden the hearts of men who are *predestined* to condemnation. If the Calvinistic doctrine of predestination is true, it would be superfluous for the Lord to harden the hearts of those He has determined to condemn. On the contrary, if the doctrine of predestination is true regarding the *saved elect*, it would be of no use for the Lord to cause those predestined to salvation to have their hearts softened. Men are hardened in heart through their own doings. God's way, word, will, and wishes for men are the same for all men. The Lord is *not willing that any should perish, but that all should come to repentance* (II Pet. 3:9). Man is drawn away of *his own lust* (Jas. 1: 14).

The plagues God placed upon the Egyptians caused Pharaoh to harden his heart while it weakened the will of his servants. *And Moses and Aaron came in unto Pharaoh and said unto him, Thus saith the Lord God of the Hebrews, How long wilt thou refuse to humble thyself before me? let my people go, that they may serve me.... And Pharaoh's servants said unto him, How long shall this man be a snare unto us? let the men go, that they may serve the Lord their God: knowest thou not yet that Egypt is destroyed* (Exo. 10:3, 7)?

Paul wrote: *Now the Spirit speaketh expressly, that in the latter times some shall depart from the faith, giving heed to seducing spirits and doctrines of devils; Speaking lies in hypocrisy; having their conscience seared with a hot iron* (I Tim. 4:1-2). The seared conscience has the brand of Satan upon it. It has been scarred and hardened and has become immune to tenderness and touch. Satan always keeps the branding iron of the conscience ready and white-hot. Satan wishes to use it on everyone; however, his success is dependent on the wayward heart. The application of the devil's branding iron upon the one's conscience is always self-inflicted. When men refuse to walk in the pathways of righteousness and goodness, they sear their own consciences. *Thus saith the Lord, Stand ye in the ways and see and ask for the old paths, where is the good way and walk therein and ye shall find rest for your souls. But they said, We will not*

# Commentary on Romans

*walk therein* (Jer. 6:16). Why would God require the Jews to amend their ways if He had already determined to condemn them? How is it so many insist the Lord involves Himself in such frivolous work?

We find it of interest the phrase used by Jeremiah, *ye shall find rest for your souls*, was echoed by Christ when He said: *Come unto me, all ye that labour and are heavy laden, and I will give you rest* (Jer. 6:16: Matt. 11:28).

**Verse 19.** *Thou wilt say then unto me, Why doth he yet find fault? For who hath resisted his will?* The Jews reasoned, if God had mercy on the Israelites while they were in Egypt, why is He finding fault with them now? Further, the Jews argued, if the Lord hardened the hearts of others, why does He then find fault with them?

Indeed, the Jews who posed such questions to the apostle were divisive ones. They were unwilling to surrender to God's New Covenant. Even though Jeremiah prophesied God would establish a New Covenant and the Jews were to comply with it, they refused it when it came to fruition (Jer. 31:31-34).

**Verses 20-21.** *Nay but, O man, who art thou that repliest against God? Shall the thing formed say to him that formed it, Why hast thou made me thus? Hath not the potter power over the clay, of the same lump to make one vessel unto honour and another unto dishonour?* These verses may seem to be the apostle's answer to the questions posed in verse 19; however, these verses are more of a rebuke to the Jews who insisted on such questions. The questions posed in verse 19 are charges levied in the form of questions. The questions were not honest ones, but designed to charge Paul with blasphemy and were further designed to charge God with injustice.

Paul wrote: *For who hath known the mind of the Lord, that he may instruct him? But we have the mind of Christ* (I Cor. 2:16). The following passages set forth the same idea: *Can a man be profitable unto God, as he that is wise may be profitable unto himself* (Job 22:2)? *Shall he that contendeth with the Almighty instruct him? he that reproveth God, let him answer it* (Job 40:2).

# Commentary on Romans

*Who hath directed the Spirit of the Lord, or being his counselor hath taught him? With whom took he counsel and who instructed him and taught him in the path of judgment and taught him knowledge and shewed to him the way of understanding* (Isa. 40: 13-14)?

Numerous references to the potter and the clay are used in the Scriptures to illustrate God's power over his people.

*Then I went down to the potter's house and, behold, he wrought a work on the wheels. And the vessel that he made of clay was marred in the hand of the potter: so he made it again another vessel, as seemed good to the potter to make it. Then the word of the Lord came to me, saying, O house of Israel, cannot I do with you as this potter? saith the Lord. Behold, as the clay is in the potter's hand, so are ye in mine hand, O house of Israel* (Jer. 18:3-6).

*But now, O Lord, thou art our father; we are the clay and thou our potter; and we all are the work of thy hand* (Isa. 64:8).

*The Lord hath made all things for himself: yea, even the wicked for the day of evil* (Pro. 16:4).

*That this is a rebellious people, lying children, children that will not hear the law of the Lord* (Isa. 30:9). *I have spread out my hands all the day unto a rebellious people, which walketh in a way that was not good, after their own thoughts* (Isa. 65:2). The Jews were children of rebellion under the Old Law, but under the New Law they were more so. Paul demonstrated how the Jews had no right to either question God or charge Him with mercilessness or injustice.

**Verse 22.** *What if God, willing to shew his wrath and to make his power known, endured with much longsuffering the vessels of wrath fitted to destruction.* This is yet another point in Paul's reply to the questions of verse 19. If God wills to show His wrath against sin and His power to punish sin, why should any object? To say God is not willing to do so is to accuse Him of being indif-

# Commentary on Romans

ferent to sin. *God's wrath is revealed from heaven against all ungodliness and unrighteousness of men* (Rom. 1:18).

Yet the Lord is not willing *that any should perish, but that all should come to repentance* (II Pet. 3:9). Because God is *not willing any should perish,* He provides all men opportunity to repent. God was longsuffering with Pharaoh's rebellion and with the nation of Israel. God's longsuffering is a manifestation of God's mercy and goodness. Many take advantage of the Lord's longsuffering so they may indulge in more sin; however, the day of God's wrath will come. Years ago, I asked a young teen why he had not yet obeyed the gospel? His reply was: *There are still some things want to do I can't do as a Christian.* Sadly, the lad drowned in eighteen inches of water about one month later, never having obeyed the gospel.

Paul addressed the Jews in chapter two, saying: *or despisest thou the riches of his goodness and forbearance and long-suffering, not knowing that the goodness of God leadeth thee to repentance? but after thy hardness and impenitent heart treasurest up for thyself wrath in the day of wrath and revelation of the righteous judgment of God; who will render to every man according to his works* (Rom. 2:4-6). Peter says:

> *Wherefore, beloved, seeing that ye look for such things, be diligent that ye may be found of him in peace, without spot, and blameless. And account that the longsuffering of our Lord is salvation; even as our beloved brother Paul also according to the wisdom given unto him hath written unto you; As also in all his epistles, speaking in them of these things; in which are some things hard to be understood, which they that are unlearned and unstable wrest, as they do also the other scriptures, unto their own destruction* (II Pet. 3: 14-16).

**Verses 23-24.** *And that he might make known the riches of his glory on the vessels of mercy, which he had afore prepared unto glory, Even us, whom he hath called, not of the Jews only, but also of the Gentiles?* Much space has been given in earlier comments refuting Calvinism, little shall be awarded here.

# Commentary on Romans

Calvinism insists God has selected some unto mercy and glory—salvation, but such is not at all the context of the passage.

Ponder the following: God made known some things. What did He make known? According to this passage, He made known the riches of His glory, which were upon the vessels of mercy. As to what each of these matters refers is the crux of our inquiry. What are the riches of God's glory? They include salvation, as the following verses demonstrate: *Or despisest thou the riches of his goodness and forbearance and longsuffering; not knowing that the goodness of God leadeth thee to repentance* (Rom. 2:4)? *In whom we have redemption through his blood, the forgiveness of sins, according to the riches of his grace* (Eph. 1:7). *The eyes of your understanding being enlightened; that ye may know what is the hope of his calling and what the riches of the glory of his inheritance in the saints* (Eph. 1:18). *That in the ages to come he might shew the exceeding riches of his grace in his kindness toward us through Christ Jesus* (Eph. 2:7). *That he would grant you, according to the riches of his glory, to be strengthened with might by his Spirit in the inner man* (Eph. 3:16).

The vessels of mercy here are in contrast to the vessels of wrath of verse 22. Men are vessels of wrath or mercy. *But the Lord said unto him, Go thy way: for he is a chosen vessel unto me, to bear my name before the Gentiles and kings and the children of Israel* (Acts 9:15). *That every one of you should know how to possess his vessel in sanctification and honour* (I Thes. 4:4). *If a man therefore purge himself from these, he shall be a vessel unto honour, sanctified and meet for the master's use and prepared unto every good work* (II Tim. 2:21). *Likewise, ye husbands, dwell with them according to knowledge, giving honour unto the wife, as unto the weaker vessel and as being heirs together of the grace of life; that your prayers be not hindered* (I Pet. 3:7). Vessels of mercy are those who acquire God's mercy. Vessels of wrath are those upon whom God's wrath is poured. Pharaoh served as a vessel of wrath through his own choosing, not because the Lord predestined him to do so.

There is yet a third question to consider, which is: To what does the phrase, *which he had afore prepared unto glory,* refer? The

# Commentary on Romans

vessels of mercy are those upon whom God's mercy is bestowed because of obedience to the Lord's will. Upon the obedient, God's mercy is poured out; upon those of wrath, the Lord pours out His wrath. He has determined blessing of mercy be awarded to the obedient, and His wrath upon the disobedient.

Paul continues responding to the Jews who contended with the apostle about God's will. If God wills to show His wrath against sin why should any object? If God wills to award obedient men with mercy, would any object? The Jews objected to the mercy of God being awarded to the Gentile, but Paul refutes the objection in the remainder of the chapter.

**Verses 24-25.** *Even us, whom he hath called, not of the Jews only, but also of the Gentiles? As he saith also in Hosea, I will call them my people, which were not my people; and her beloved, which was not beloved.* Paul refers to the prophet Hosea in this passage. *And I will sow her unto me in the earth; and I will have mercy upon her that had not obtained mercy; and I will say to them which were not my people, Thou art my people; and they shall say, Thou art my God* (Hos. 2:23).

Paul assured the Jewish converts the call of the Gospel was for both the Jew and the Gentile; he did the same in chapter one in verses fifteen through seventeen.

**Verse 26.** *And it shall come to pass, that in the place where it was said unto them, Ye are not my people; there shall they be called the children of the living God.* Paul had arduous work in convincing the Jews God always intended for mercy and salvation be granted to the Gentiles under the New Covenant.

The Jews also needed convincing God removed the middle barrier between the Jew and the Gentile. The apostle settled this matter when he wrote:

> *For he is our peace, who hath made both one and hath broken down the middle wall of partition between us; Having abolished in his flesh the enmity, even the law of commandments contained in ordinances; for to make in himself of twain one new man, so making*

# Commentary on Romans

peace; And that he might reconcile both unto God in one body by the cross, having slain the enmity thereby: And came and preached peace to you which were afar off and to them that were nigh. For through him we both have access by one Spirit unto the Father. Now therefore ye are no more strangers and foreigners, but fellow citizens with the saints and of the household of God* (Eph. 2:14-19).

**Verses 27-29.** *Isaiah also crieth concerning Israel, Though the number of the children of Israel be as the sand of the sea, a remnant shall be saved: For he will finish the work and cut it short in righteousness: because a short work will the Lord make upon the earth. And as Esaias said before, Except the Lord of Sabaoth had left us a seed, we had been as Sodom and been made like unto Gomorrah.* The following passage relates to these verses:

> *And it shall come to pass in that day, that the remnant of Israel and such as are escaped of the house of Jacob, shall no more again stay upon him that smote them; but shall stay upon the Lord, the Holy One of Israel, in truth. The remnant shall return, even the remnant of Jacob, unto the mighty God. For though thy people Israel be as the sand of the sea, yet a remnant of them shall return: the consumption decreed shall overflow with righteousness. For the Lord God of hosts shall make a consumption, even determined, in the midst of all the land* (Isa. 10:20-23).

There were no righteous men to be found in Sodom and Gomorrah; because of their total wickedness, God utterly destroyed them. The whole nation of Israel would have been destroyed in captivity had not there been some righteous Jews there. When Lot was delivered from the cities of Sodom and Gomorrah, he was a righteous man—despite the offer he made concerning his daughters! Consider carefully the words of the passage most brethren would cite:

> *And turning the cities of Sodom and Gomorrah into ashes condemned them with an overthrow, making*

222

# Commentary on Romans

> *them an ensample unto those that after should live ungodly; And delivered just Lot, vexed with the filthy conversation of the wicked: (For that righteous man dwelling among them, in seeing and hearing, vexed his righteous soul from day to day with their unlawful deeds)* (II Pet. 2:6-8).

That Lot was declared righteous cannot be denied; this passage clearly proclaims **when** he was righteous—while living among them. John Lillie describes Lot as a man "beset on all hands by the most flagrant abominations, and without the sympathy or support of neighbors or kindred like-minded with himself, maintained faith in God, and led a sober and righteous life."[51]

Lot tried to counteract the evil intentions of the men of Sodom. Genesis 19:1 tells us: *And there came two angels to Sodom at even; and Lot sat in the gate of Sodom: and Lot seeing them rose up to meet them; and he bowed himself with his face toward the ground.* Adam Clarke comments on this verse: "Probably, in order to prevent unwary travellers from being entrapped by his wicked townsmen, he waited at the gate of the city to bring the strangers he might meet with to his own house...." [sic].[52]

> *But before they lay down, the men of the city, even the men of Sodom, compassed the house round, both old and young, all the people from every quarter: And they called unto Lot and said unto him, Where are the men which came in to thee this night? bring them out unto us, that we may know them. And Lot went out at the door unto them and shut the door after him, And said, I pray you, brethren, do not so wickedly. Behold now, I have two daughters which have not known man; let me, I pray you, bring them out unto you and do ye to them as is good in your eyes: only unto these men do nothing; for therefore came they under the shadow of my roof. And they said, Stand back. And they said again, This one fellow came in to sojourn and he will needs be a judge: now will we deal worse with thee, than with them. And they pressed sore upon the man,*

---

[51] John Lillie.
[52] Adam Clarke.

# Commentary on Romans

*even Lot, and came near to break the door. But the men put forth their hand and pulled Lot into the house to them and shut to the door. And they smote the men that were at the door of the house with blindness, both small and great: so that they wearied themselves to find the door* (Gen. 19:4-11).

When Lot challenged the wickedness of the men, they turned on him immediately, determined to thwart any kind of righteousness that he might seek to impose on them. So perverse and steadfast were they that continued to try to carry out their plan even though they were blind!

But how can Lot be called *righteous* when he offered his own daughters to be sexually abused? First, hospitality was a high priority in those days. He was honor-bound to protect the visitors under his roof. If they were emissaries from another land, such a heinous insult would surely have brought war upon Sodom. Second, he may have thought that illicit but natural sex was better than the illicit abomination of homosexuality. Third, because he knew what the men were like, he may have thought they would have rejected the offer and been somewhat mollified for his having made it. He was wrong. Furthermore, he was acting in the face of a crisis—not according to his usual logic. The event does show that a righteous man is not necessarily a perfect one.

**Verses 30-33.** *What shall we say then? That the Gentiles, which followed not after righteousness, have attained to righteousness, even the righteousness which is of faith. But Israel, which followed after the law of righteousness, hath not attained to the law of righteousness. Wherefore? Because they sought it not by faith, but as it were by the works of the law. For they stumbled at that stumbling-stone; As it is written, Behold, I lay in Zion a stumbling-stone and rock of offence: and whosoever believeth on him shall not be ashamed.* When a man is forgiven and his sins blotted out, he is righteous.

Men attain righteousness when they, through faith, become obedient to the Lord Jesus Christ. The Gentiles became righteous by their obedience to the gospel. *But thanks be to God, that, whereas ye were servants of sin, ye became obedient from the*

# Commentary on Romans

*heart to that form of teaching whereunto ye were delivered; and being made free from sin, ye became servants of righteousness* (Rom. 6:17-18).

Verse 31. **The** Israelites professed adherence to the Law of Moses, but they did not keep that law. Instead, therefore, of being righteous, they were sinners—transgressors of the law they professed to follow. Verses 32-33: The law could not make righteous the one who had transgressed it. The only hope, therefore, of the Jew, as well as of the Gentile, is to attain righteousness through faith in the Lord Jesus Christ; but because He was not what they expected in the Messiah, the Jews rejected Him—to them He was a stone of stumbling. "We preach Christ crucified, unto the Jews a stumbling-block" (I Cor.1:23). But those who did believe in Christ were not put to shame, as men are when they find that they have been deceived into following a false leader. "And blessed is he, whosoever shall find no occasion of stumbling in me" (Matt.11:6). Jesus fails no one who puts his trust in him; he is not slack concerning his promises[53] [sic].

Paul had much work in addressing the problems of the church at Rome. The Jewish converts did much to convince the Gentile converts the Law of Moses was to be kept in conjunction with the Law of Christ.

It is good to again emphasize that which Luke wrote: *But there rose up certain of the sect of the Pharisees which believed, saying, That it was needful to circumcise them, and to command them to keep the law of Moses* (Acts 15:5).

## Romans 10:1-21

*1 Brethren, my heart's desire and prayer to God for Israel is that they might be saved. 2 For I bear them record that they have a zeal of God, but not according to knowledge. 3 For they being ignorant of God's righteousness and going about to establish their own right-*

---
[53] Robertson L. Whiteside.

# Commentary on Romans

eousness, have not submitted themselves unto the righteousness of God. 4 For Christ is the end of the Law for righteousness to every one that believeth. 5 For Moses describeth the righteousness which is of the Law, That the man which doeth those things shall live by them; 6 But the righteousness which is of faith speaketh on this wise, Say not in thine heart, Who shall ascend into heaven? (that is, to bring Christ down from above: 7 Or, Who shall descend into the deep? (that is, to bring up Christ again from the dead.) 8 But what saith it? The word is nigh thee, even in thy mouth and in thy heart: that is, the word of faith, which we preach. 9 That if thou shalt confess with thy mouth the Lord Jesus and shalt believe in thine heart that God hath raised him from the dead, thou shalt be saved. 10 For with the heart man believeth unto righteousness; and with the mouth confession is made unto salvation. 11 For the scripture saith, Whosoever believeth on him shall not be ashamed. 12 For there is no difference between the Jew and the Greek: for the same Lord over all is rich unto all that call upon him. 13 For whosoever shall call upon the name of the Lord shall be saved. 14 How then shall they call on him in whom they have not believed? and how shall they believe in him of whom they have not heard? and how shall they hear without a preacher? 15 And how shall they preach, except they be sent?16 But they have not all obeyed the gospel. For Esaias saith, Lord, who hath believed our report? 17 So then faith cometh by hearing, and hearing by the word of God. 18 But I say, Have they not heard? Yes verily, their sound went into all the earth and their words unto the ends of the world. 19 But I say, Did not Israel know? First Moses saith, I will provoke you to jealousy by them that are no people and by a foolish nation I will anger you. 20 But Esaias is very bold and saith, I was found of them that sought me not; I was made manifest unto them that asked not after me. 21 But to Israel he saith, All day long I have stretched forth my hands unto a disobedient and gain-saying people.

# Commentary on Romans

**Verse 1.** *Brethren, my heart's desire and prayer to God for Israel is, that they might be saved.* Recalling it is still Jewish converts the apostle is addressing, this verse casts a bright beacon from the heart of the apostle for his Jewish brethren. *Brethren,* as the apostle declares, *my heart's desire and prayer to God for Israel is, that they might be saved.* The use of the word *brethren* here is of great importance. Jews disobedient to the Gospel considered Paul to be apostate from the Law of Moses and were intent on killing him. Here, Paul is addressing Jewish converts and assured them his desire and prayer for the unbelieving Jews was for their salvation.

For all Israel, Paul prayed and hoped for their salvation. The phrase, *that they might be saved,* reflects the reality Paul possessed knowing all Israel—the whole Jewish nation—would not obey the Gospel and acquire salvation. Paul prayed his fellow Jews would believe and repent unto the obedience of the Gospel. As a Pharisee, Paul lived in rigid strictness to the Law of Moses (cf. Acts 26:5). He reminded his fellow Jews, *which knew me from the beginning, if they would testify, that after the most straitest sect of our religion I lived a Pharisee* (Acts 26:5). Such a reminder served as a prompting cue assuring the Jews, as a Pharisee, Paul well understood the arduousness involved in obeying the Gospel of Christ and leaving the Law of Moses.

**Verses 2-3.** *For I bear them record that they have a zeal of God, but not according to knowledge. For they being ignorant of God's righteousness and going about to establish their own righteousness, have not submitted themselves unto the righteousness of God.* The bearing of the record by the apostle for his fellow Jews was something he was well qualified to do. Paul was well aware of the intense exertions put forth by the Jews to remain married to the Law of Moses. However, Paul, demonstrated the Jews failed in doing so. These verses are a commentary on chapter two. In chapter one, Paul informed the Gentile converts they went about to set forth their own system of righteousness but failed. In chapter two, the apostle informed the Jewish converts they failed as well.

Here, Paul shows such efforts resulted in the Jews being disobedient to the prophecies and promises of the Old Law; in so

# Commentary on Romans

doing they did not submit *themselves unto the righteousness of God.* The righteousness of God here refers not to the Gospel only, but also to the prophecies which pointed to the Gospel of the New Testament System. The Jews refused to submit to the New Law of Christ prophesied in the Old Law. They failed in both cases.

**Verses 4-5.** *For Christ is the end of the Law for righteousness to every one that believeth. For Moses describeth the righteousness which is of the Law, That the man which doeth those things shall live by them.* Christ was the sole purpose of the New Law. Paul wrote: *Wherefore the Law was our schoolmaster to bring us unto Christ, that we might be justified by faith* (Gal. 3:24). Two matters of great importance are embedded within this passage. First, the Law was designed to bring the Jews to Christ. Second, justification was granted by the system of faith under Christ and not under the Old Law of Moses.

To better understand the phrase, *the end of,* consider its use elsewhere. *Now the end of the commandment is charity out of a pure heart and of a good conscience and of faith unfeigned* (I Tim. 1:15). *Receiving the end of your faith, even the salvation of your souls* (I Pet. 1:9). *For to this end Christ both died and rose and revived, that he might be Lord both of the dead and living* (Rom. 14:9). The phrase, *the end of,* means for the purpose of.

Verse five refers to the words of Moses: *Ye shall therefore keep my statutes and my judgments: which if a man do, he shall live in them: I am the Lord* (Lev. 18:5).

These words were spoken in answer to the objections made by the Jews. The apostle appeals to Moses, both in regard to the righteousness of the Law and of faith. The Law here is in contrast to faith. The Law refers to the New Law; faith refers to the system of the Gospel under Christ. Paul argued those who refused to obey Christ had in fact refused to obey the Law of Moses. James noted; *For whosoever shall keep the whole Law and yet offend in one point, he is guilty of all* (Jas. 2:10).

Moses informed the Jews that *the Lord thy God will raise up unto thee a prophet from the midst of thee, of thy brethren, like un-*

# Commentary on Romans

*to me; unto him ye shall hearken* (Deut. 18:15). The Jews, for the most part, refused to accept the prophet once He came. That prophet was indeed Christ.

**Verses 6-9.** *But the righteousness which is of faith speaketh on this wise, Say not in thine heart, Who shall ascend into heaven? (that is, to bring Christ down from above: Or, Who shall descend into the deep? (that is, to bring up Christ again from the dead.) But what saith it? The word is nigh thee, even in thy mouth and in thy heart: that is, the word of faith, which we preach; That if thou shalt confess with thy mouth the Lord Jesus and shalt believe in thine heart that God hath raised him from the dead, thou shalt be saved.* Paul makes use of *personification,* a figure of speech wherein human characteristics are given to the inanimate. If righteousness itself could speak, what would it say?

*For this commandment which I command thee this day, it is not hidden from thee, neither is it far off. It is not in heaven, that thou shouldest say, Who shall go up for us to heaven and bring it unto us, that we may hear it and do it? Neither is it beyond the sea, that thou shouldest say, Who shall go over the sea for us and bring it unto us, that we may hear it and do it? But the word is very nigh unto thee, in thy mouth and in thy heart, that thou mayest do it* (Deut. 30:11-14).

The intended meaning is Moses exhorted the Jews unto obedience. He assured the Jews the commands of the Lord were reasonable, plain, intelligible, and must be obeyed. Proper obedience to the Law of Moses demanded the Jews to recognize and obey the Messiah once He came.

**Verses 10-11.** *For with the heart man believeth unto righteousness; and with the mouth confession is made unto salvation. For the scripture saith, Whosoever believeth on him shall not be ashamed.* It is well to observe the number of times Paul uses the phrases, *as it is written, the scripture saith,* or *Moses describeth.* Such phrases should serve the student as a strong reminder; it is indeed the Jews to whom the apostle was speaking. It would be of little use to make numerous references to the Law of Moses if Paul were addressing the Gentiles. We continue to

# Commentary on Romans

belabor this point because Paul did.

*The word is nigh thee* should not be difficult to ascertain. The *word* which was *nigh* unto the Jews was the word of salvation. Confessing Jesus to be the Son of God was the beginning point for the Jews regarding their salvation. Confession alone does not make one a child of God! Jesus said, *The time is fulfilled and the kingdom of God is at hand: repent ye and believe the gospel* (Mk. 1:15). The Lord also said, *I said therefore unto you, that ye shall die in your sins: for if ye believe not that I am he, ye shall die in your sins* (Jno. 8:24).

**Verses 12-13.** *For there is no difference between the Jew and the Greek: for the same Lord over all is rich unto all that call upon him. For whosoever shall call upon the name of the Lord shall be saved.* Under the New Law of Christ there was no distinction between Jew and Gentile. God was working out his greater plan —the plan in which Jew and Gentile would have the same standing before Jehovah. But the Law of Moses—all things Jewish— had to be taken out of the way before the Jew and Gentile could be brought together into one body (cf. Eph. 2:13-18). In Paul's writings, he made numerous arguments showing the Law of Moses ended. However, some of the Jewish converts failed to realize the Jews no longer had any advantage over the Gentiles. Paul demonstrated God no longer made a distinction between Jew and Gentile; thus, Paul's preaching to the Gentiles made these Jews deeply bitter toward the apostle. The Jews refused to recognize the riches of God's grace were just as abundant for the Gentiles, as for the Jew. *Whosoever shall call upon the name of the Lord*—Jew or Gentile—*shall be saved.* The saving of the Gentiles was detestable to the Jews. However, Paul had clearly proven such was God's will, and the Old Testament prophets often declared such would come to pass.

Paul was an apostle to the Gentiles; his time preaching to them was the Lord's way of instructing Paul the Gospel was for the Gentile as well as the Jew. Paul, being the staunch Pharisee he was, made giving up the Old Law far more difficult. That the Lord chose him to go to the Gentiles was perhaps a more difficult thing for him to accept. Surely these things well prepared and qualified him to inform the Jews the Gospel was indeed for both

# Commentary on Romans

Jew and Gentile.

Verse 13 is a quote from Isaiah. *Therefore thus saith the Lord God, Behold, I lay in Zion for a foundation a stone, a tried stone, a precious corner stone, a sure foundation: he that believeth shall not make haste* (Isa. 28:16). To believe in Christ is to recognize Him for whom and what He is—to put our full trust in Him; to confess Him is to pledge our allegiance to Him. Verbal declaration alone is worthless; we must acknowledge Him by word and deed as our Lord—our Prophet, Priest, and King, as well as our Savior. This type of confession, coupled with obedience ultimately brings one to eternal life.

Salvation is now offered through the Gospel to all, whether Jew or Gentile. This was a great blow to the Jew. It is now, *whosoever believeth on him shall not be confounded* (I Pet. 2:6). When we put our trust or confidence in men, they often betray that confidence, and we are put to shame or *confounded.* However, we can put our full confidence in Christ, and give Him our best service without fearing He will betray us or put us to shame. We can glory in Him now and forever more.

Verse 13 is awarded additional comment as this portion of our text continues. Paul quoted Joel 2:32 and in so doing reminded the Jews the Gospel of Jesus Christ is for *whosoever.* The word *whosoever* means either Jew or Gentile. On the day of Pentecost when the church was established, Peter and the rest of the apostles quoted the prophecy of Joel 2:28-32. Paul declared the same message. There was no contradiction in the message the other apostles and Paul preached. The Gospel is the same for both the Jew and the Gentile (cf. Gal. 3:28).

**Verses 14-15.** *How then shall they call on him in whom they have not believed? and how shall they believe in him of whom they have not heard? and how shall they hear without a preacher? And how shall they preach, except they be sent? as it is written, How beautiful are the feet of them that preach the gospel of peace and bring glad tidings of good things!* These verses serve as the answer to the question Paul knew the Jews would have asked. *How then shall they call?* was a question of the Jews. In contrast to God calling man, as Paul set forth in II Thessalonians

# Commentary on Romans

2:14, we have here **how** men call on the Lord. God calls men through the Gospel; men call on God through obedience to the Gospel. How could the Jews, who did not believe in Christ as the Messiah, call on Him in whom they did not believe? They could not. None can call on the Lord without proper obedient belief in Christ.

Here we again remind the reader Paul often presented questions he knew his Jewish brethren would ask; then he answers their queries. In these verses the apostle asked four questions of his Jewish brethren.

First, *how shall men call upon the Lord?* Second, *how can one believe in Christ of whom they had not heard?* Third, *how can one hear* what God demands without the preaching of the Gospel? Fourth, *how can one expect the preaching of the Gospel to be executed without a preacher having been sent?* The responses to the questions Paul posed are rhetorical ones. First, none can call upon the Messiah without first believing in the Messiah. Second, none can expect to believe in Christ if they have never heard of Him.

Third, none can expect the preaching of the Gospel to take place unless a preacher is sent. This was the case during the first days of the church when inspired teachers and preachers were required. Today, one can come to a knowledge of the truth and obey it without having a preacher. There are numerous cases where such has occurred. This author's grandfather, e.g., studied and memorized New Testament Scriptures for two years before obeying the Gospel without the aid of a teacher or preacher.

The fourth of Paul's questions warrants more inclusive commentary. Paul was preaching the Gospel during the time of inspiration. Today men hear it through preaching or reading the inspired Scriptures—not from inspired men. In the first century many preachers were under the direction of the Holy Spirit, by whom they were often instructed where to proclaim the Gospel. Numerous examples are recorded in the Scriptures.

> *And as they went through the cities, they delivered them the decrees for to keep, that were ordained of the*

# Commentary on Romans

*apostles and elders which were at Jerusalem. And so were the churches established in the faith and increased in number daily. Now when they had gone throughout Phrygia and the region of Galatia and were forbidden of the Holy Ghost to preach the word in Asia, After they were come to Mysia, they assayed to go into Bithynia: but the Spirit suffered them not. And they passing by Mysia came down to Trees. And a vision appeared to Paul in the night; There stood a man of Macedonia and prayed him, saying, Come over into Macedonia and help us. And after he had seen the vision, immediately we endeavored to go into Macedonia, assuredly gathering that the Lord had called us for to preach the gospel unto them* (Acts 16:4-10).

*And the angel of the Lord spake unto Philip, saying, Arise and go toward the south unto the way that goeth down from Jerusalem unto Gaza, which is desert. And he arose and went: and, behold, a man of Ethiopia, an eunuch of great authority under Candace queen of the Ethiopians, who had the charge of all her treasure and had come to Jerusalem for to worship, Was returning and sitting in his chariot read Esaias the prophet. Then the Spirit said unto Philip, Go near and join thyself to this chariot. And Philip ran thither to him and heard him read the prophet Isaiah and said, Understandest thou what thou readest? And he said, How can I, except some man should guide me? And he desired Philip that he would come up and sit with him. The place of the scripture which he read was this, He was led as a sheep to the slaughter; and like a lamb dumb before his shearer, so opened he not his mouth: In his humiliation his judgment was taken away: and who shall declare his generation? for his life is taken from the earth. And the eunuch answered Philip and said, I pray thee, of whom speaketh the prophet this? of himself, or of some other man? Then Philip opened his mouth and began at the same scripture and preached unto him Jesus. And as they went on their way, they came unto a certain water: and the eunuch said, See, here is water; what doth hinder me to be baptized? And Philip*

## Commentary on Romans

*said, If thou believest with all thine heart, thou mayest. And he answered and said, I believe that Jesus Christ is the Son of God. And he commanded the chariot to stand still: and they went down both into the water, both Philip and the eunuch; and he baptized him. And when they were come up out of the water, the Spirit of the Lord caught away Philip, that the eunuch saw him no more: and he went on his way rejoicing. But Philip was found at Azotus: and passing through he preached in all the cities, till he came to Caesarea* (Acts 8:26-40).

Peter was also directed by the Lord to go to the house of Cornelius as recorded in Acts 10. But today, Gospel preachers do not preach *by* inspiration. Today, they *proclaim* what was inspired back then. Only Gospel preachers preach the Gospel. Denominational preachers preach denominationalism.

The preaching of the Gospel is a spiritual blessing. Only those in Christ have access to the preaching of the Gospel. *Blessed be the God and Father of our Lord Jesus Christ, who hath blessed us with all spiritual blessings in heavenly places in Christ* (Eph. 1:3). *So then faith cometh by hearing and hearing by the word of God* (Rom. 10:17). Faith comes by hearing the Word of God—not by denominational doctrine!

The phrase about *beautiful feet* comes from the prophet Isaiah. *How beautiful upon the mountains are the feet of him that bringeth good tidings, that publisheth peace; that bringeth good tidings of good, that publisheth salvation; that saith unto Zion, Thy God reigneth* (Isa. 52:7)!

The Lord considers the feet of those who faithfully proclaim the Gospel of exceeding value. However, men usually do not. The Lord informed the apostles and those of the limited commission they would often not be well received. *And whatsoever house ye enter into, there abide and thence depart. And whosoever will not receive you, when ye go out of the city, shake off the very dust from your feet for a testimony against them* (Lk. 9:4-5).

The Lord further illustrated the point, as recorded by John. Je-

## Commentary on Romans

sus *riseth from supper and laid aside his garments; and took a towel and girded himself. After that he poureth water into a basin, and began to wash the disciples' feet, and to wipe them with the towel wherewith he was girded. Then cometh he to Simon Peter: and Peter saith unto him, Lord, dost thou wash my feet?* (Jno. 13:4-6). Though the lesson of this text is humility, one can see the deep respect the Lord has for those who proclaim the Gospel.

**Verse 16.** *But they have not all obeyed the gospel. For Isaiah saith, Lord, who hath believed our report?* This verse presents much with regarding Biblical belief, which is necessarily fettered to obedience. Biblical belief and obedience cannot be separated. Consider the words of Peter, who in his first epistle wrote: *Unto you therefore which believe he is precious: but unto them which be disobedient, the stone which the builders disallowed, the same is made the head of the corner* (2:7). Paul noted not all who had heard the Gospel of Christ had obeyed it. Most reject it today; most will continue to reject it.

**Verse 17.** *So then faith cometh by hearing, and hearing by the word of God.* Here the word *so* is an adverb of manner, revealing how faith comes. Godly-approved faith comes only by the hearing of God's Word. Hearing must be united with obedience. When one rightly and gladly hears the word of God, he accepts and obeys it. On the day of Pentecost, when the Gospel was declared by Peter and the rest of the apostles, there were a few who *gladly received his word* and *were baptized: and the same day there were added unto them about three thousand souls* (Acts 2:41). The Gospel must be listened to intently, received readily, obeyed hastily, and continued in steadfastly.

Those of Berea displayed a grand and notable character through their willingness to hear the preaching of Paul and Silas. *And the brethren immediately sent away Paul and Silas by night unto Berea: who coming thither went into the synagogue of the Jews. These were more noble than those in Thessalonica, in that they received the word with all readiness of mind and searched the scriptures daily, whether those things were so* (Acts 17:10-11).

Consider the qualities of behavior possessed by those of Berea.

# Commentary on Romans

First, they received the Word presented. Second, they did so with a readiness of mind. Third, they searched the Scriptures as presented. These three qualities proved them worthy of nobility as declared by inspiration. The same nobility awarded to the Bereans is awarded to men today who follow their example.

**Verse 18.** *But I say, Have they not heard? Yes verily, their sound went into all the earth and their words unto the ends of the world.* The Jews of every nation under heaven heard the Gospel preached within the lifetime of the apostles.

> *And when the day of Pentecost was fully come, they were all with one accord in one place. And suddenly there came a sound from heaven as of a rushing mighty wind and it filled all the house where they were sitting. And there appeared unto them cloven tongues like as of fire and it sat upon each of them. And they were all filled with the Holy Ghost and began to speak with other tongues, as the Spirit gave them utterance. And there were dwelling at Jerusalem Jews, devout men, out of every nation under heaven. Now when this was noised abroad, the multitude came together and were confounded, because that every man heard them speak in his own language. And they were all amazed and marvelled, saying one to another, Behold, are not all these which speak Galileans? And how hear we every man in our own tongue, wherein we were born? Parthians and Medes and Elamites and the dwellers in Mesopotamia and in Judaea and Cappadocia, in Pontus and Asia, Phrygia and Pamphylia, in Egypt and in the parts of Libya about Cyrene and strangers of Rome, Jews and proselytes, Cretes and Arabians, we do hear them speak in our tongues the wonderful works of God* (Acts 2:1-11).

The Jews present on Pentecost came from sixteen different nations, which are identified in Acts 2:9-11. The phrase, *their sound went into all the earth and their words unto the ends of the world* means exactly that. Paul informed the Colossian church of this fact when he wrote: *If ye continue in the faith grounded and settled and be not moved away from the hope of*

# Commentary on Romans

*the gospel, which ye have heard and which was preached to every creature which is under heaven* (Col. 1:23).

**Verse 19.** *But I say, Did not Israel know? First Moses saith, I will provoke you to jealousy by them that are no people and by a foolish nation I will anger you.* The passage cited by Paul is from Deuteronomy 32:21, which expresses God would place upon the Jews the consequences of favoring the Gentiles to provoke the Jews to jealousy.

The idea of *provoking the Jews unto jealousy* was in the sense of driving them to emulation. The calling of the Gentiles to obey the Gospel was as an avenue by which the Jews would be motivated to obey the Gospel and obtain salvation.

**Verses 20-21.** *But Esaias is very bold and saith, I was found of them that sought me not; I was made manifest unto them that asked not after me. But to Israel he saith, All day long I have stretched forth my hands unto a disobedient and gainsaying people.* Once more Paul refers to the inspired pen of Isaiah in these two verses which are found in Isaiah 65:1-2.

Consider a few thoughts regarding the words of Isaiah. First, Isaiah declared the Lord was to be found by some not seeking Him. Second, the phrase, *all day long,* means "without ceasing." God was constant in His calling of the Jews to obey Him. Third, the outstretched arms of the Lord portray Him as willing, well ready to receive and welcome His people.

In this chapter, Paul begins to strongly solidify the argument the Gospel is for all—Jew and Gentile. The Gospel is all-powerful and sufficient to save all men. As the apostle approaches the end of his address to the Jews, he begins to incorporate the Gentiles. Not many verses hence, the apostle's full attention will once again be focused upon the Gentiles.

## Romans 11:1-6

*1 I say then, Hath God cast away his people? God forbid. For I also am an Israelite, of the seed of Abraham, of the tribe of Benjamin. 2 God hath not cast away his*

# Commentary on Romans

*people which he foreknew. Wot ye not what the scripture saith of Elias? how he maketh intercession to God against Israel, saying, 3 Lord, they have killed thy prophets, and digged down thine altars; and I am left alone, and they seek my life. 4 But what saith the answer of God unto him? I have reserved to myself seven thousand men, who have not bowed the knee to the image of Baal. 5 Even so then at this present time also there is a remnant according to the election of grace. 6 And if by grace, then is it no more of works: otherwise grace is no more grace. But if it be of works, then is it no more grace: otherwise work is no more work.*

An overview of these verses is fitting before addressing each independently. The Jews who opposed Paul claimed he was teaching God had now rejected the Jews. Paul, however, would not have promoted a doctrine which denied his own salvation. He gives himself as an example that the rejection of the Jewish nation had nothing to do with the salvation of individual Jews. *For I am also an Israelite, of the seed of Abraham, of the tribe of Benjamin.* God had never denied any obedient Jew salvation. The Lord did not cast off his people, as the many Jews insisted.

Paul used Elijah's complaint against God and His reply to the prophet to solidify his argument. For the most part Israel had forsaken the Lord and were no longer acceptable to Him. God informed the prophet there were yet seven thousand in Israel whom He recognized as faithful. There have always been a faithful few upon whom the Lord could depend. The same is true in the Lord's church today. Many in congregations simply occupy space in pews, with their names on membership roles rather than in the Lamb's *Book of Life.* Church attendance is not the same thing as *living by faith.*

The Jews who obeyed the Gospel were among a new remnant of God's people. The Old Law, so far as its religious functions were concerned, was now defunct. The civil system of the Old Law was be brought to an end by the Roman army in AD 70.

The way of salvation was now through the Gospel system of Christ, not the Old Law. Under the new system, there is no dis-

# Commentary on Romans

tinction between Jew and Gentile. The Jews did not favorably respond to no longer being God's chosen people, as Paul taught. God, under the Gospel of Christ, made no distinction between the Jews and Gentiles; they were now one in Christ. Paul argued the same matter with the Jews of Galatia. He wrote: *But before faith came, we were kept under the Law, shut up unto the faith which should afterwards be revealed. Wherefore the Law was our schoolmaster to bring us unto Christ, that we might be justified by faith. But after that faith is come, we are no longer under a schoolmaster. For ye are all the children of God by faith in Christ Jesus* (Gal. 3:23-26).

The Jews believed being a Jew made them exempt from the penalty of sin. To the contrary, Paul declared no amount of works under any law can blot out sins. Forgiveness is subject to grace regardless of how many conditions of a law one may meet. Forgiveness has always been a matter of God's applied grace. One may keep Spiritual Law and stand justified on his own merit, but God's grace is still needed. There is no grace when man merits justification by works only. Paul wrote of the Jews: *Wherefore? Because they sought it not by faith, but as it were by the works of the Law. For they stumbled at that stumbling stone* (Rom. 9:32). *Knowing that a man is not justified by the works of the law, but by the faith of Jesus Christ, even we have believed in Jesus Christ, that we might be justified by the faith of Christ and not by the works of the law: for by the works of the law shall no flesh be justified* (Gal. 2:16).

**Verse 1.** *I say then, Hath God cast away his people? God forbid. For I also am an Israelite, of the seed of Abraham, of the tribe of Benjamin.* Here the apostle answers an unasked question enveloped in the minds of his Jewish brethren. Paul assured the Jews that God had not *cast away* His people. If so, he too stood among those cast away. The apostle calls upon his pedigree and heritage to set forth proof that if God had not *cast away his people.* Paul used three arguments to solidify his case: First, he was an Israelite. Second, he was of the seed of Abraham. Third, he was of the tribe of Benjamin, from which the first king of Israel came. The importance of these three matters was of great value to Paul's argument.

# Commentary on Romans

**Verse 2-3.** *God hath not cast away his people which he foreknew. Wot ye not what the scripture saith of Elias? How he maketh intercession to God against Israel, saying, Lord, they have killed thy prophets and digged down thine altars; and I am left alone and they seek my life.* Paul continued his response, emphasizing, God had not at all *cast away His people"*of which the Jews accused Paul of teaching.

Paul refers to the prophet Elijah to solidify his argument for his fellow Jews. The apostle asked; *Wot ye not what the scripture saith of Elias?* Paul then quotes from I Kings: *And he said, I have been very jealous for the Lord God of hosts: for the children of Israel have forsaken thy covenant, thrown down thine altars and slain thy prophets with the sword; and I, even I only, am left; and they seek my life, to take it away.... And he said, I have been very jealous for the Lord God of hosts: because the children of Israel have forsaken thy covenant, thrown down thine altars and slain thy prophets with the sword; and I, even I only, am left; and they seek my life, to take it away* (I Kings 19:10, 14).

**Verse 4.** *But what saith the answer of God unto him? I have reserved to myself seven thousand men, who have not bowed the knee to the image of Baal.* Just as there was a remnant of faithful Jews in the days of Elijah, so was there a remnant of faithful Jews during the first century. Some Jews recognized and accepted the Messiah once He arrived. Andrew was one of first two apostles who recognized the Lord as the Messiah.

> *Again the next day after John stood and two of his disciples; And looking upon Jesus as he walked, he saith, Behold the Lamb of God! And the two disciples heard him speak and they followed Jesus. Then Jesus turned and saw them following and saith unto them, What seek ye? They said unto him, Rabbi, (which is to say, being interpreted, Master,) where dwellest thou? He saith unto them, Come and see. They came and saw where he dwelt and abode with him that day: for it was about the tenth hour. One of the two which heard John speak and followed him, was Andrew, Simon Peter's brother. He first findeth his own brother Simon and saith unto him, We have found the Messias, which is,*

# Commentary on Romans

*being interpreted, the Christ. And he brought him to Jesus. And when Jesus beheld him, he said, Thou art Simon the son of Jonah: thou shalt be called Cephas, which is by interpretation, A stone. The day following Jesus would go forth into Galilee and findeth Philip and saith unto him, Follow me. Now Philip was of Bethsaida, the city of Andrew and Peter. Philip findeth Nathanael and saith unto him, We have found him, of whom Moses in the Law and the prophets, did write, Jesus of Nazareth, the son of Joseph* (Jno. 1:35-45).

Once the Lord was recognized as the Messiah, there was no hesitancy to follow Him by those who wished to be part of the remnant to which Paul referred in the following verse.

**Verse 5.** *Even so then at this present time also there is a remnant according to the election of grace.* Some have made much about that which the phrase *this present time* refers. *This present time* means exactly that. It was the time in which Paul wrote; it was a time when the Gospel was being revealed by inspiration; it was the time when the Old Law had died; it was a time the Jews wished not to see, nor did the Jews believe such a time would ever come. The remnant of faithful Jews obeyed the Gospel did so having understood the prophecy of Moses where he wrote:

> *The Lord thy God will raise up unto thee a Prophet from the midst of thee, of thy brethren, like unto me; unto him ye shall hearken; According to all that thou desiredst of the Lord thy God in Horeb in the day of the assembly, saying, Let me not hear again the voice of the Lord my God, neither let me see this great fire any more, that I die not. And the Lord said unto me, They have well spoken that which they have spoken. I will raise them up a Prophet from among their brethren, like unto thee and will put my words in his mouth; and he shall speak unto them all that I shall command him. And it shall come to pass, that whosoever will not hearken unto my words which he shall speak in my name, I will require it of him* (Deut. 18:15-19).

# Commentary on Romans

Total apostasy has never occurred among God's people. He has always had a faithful few to stand in the gap and hold onto the ways of the Lord. Just as in the days of Elijah there was a remnant; there will always be a remnant who serve the Lord as mandated. God did not *cast off* His people as the Jews charged, but God did and does cast off those who insisted on rebellion.

God's grace has always been awarded to those who are part of a faithful remnant. Neither the Law of Moses nor the works thereof could endow one with God's grace as the Jews contended. Rather, the grace of God is awarded based upon obedience from the heart. Paul had previously contended for such when he wrote: *But God be thanked, that ye were the servants of sin, but ye have obeyed from the heart that form of doctrine which was delivered you* (Rom. 6:17). The Jews, most often, did not obey the Lord, but when they did, obedience was seldom from the heart. An example of the obedience of the Jews minus the heart was recorded by Isaiah.

> *Hear, O heavens, and give ear, O earth: for the Lord hath spoken, I have nourished and brought up children, and they have rebelled against me. The ox knoweth his owner, and the ass his master's crib: but Israel doth not know, my people doth not consider. Ah sinful nation, a people laden with iniquity, a seed of evildoers, children that are corrupters: they have forsaken the Lord, they have provoked the Holy One of Israel unto anger, they are gone away backward. Why should ye be stricken any more? ye will revolt more and more: the whole head is sick, and the whole heart faint. From the sole of the foot even unto the head there is no soundness in it; but wounds, and bruises, and putrifying sores: they have not been closed, neither bound up, neither mollified with ointment. Your country is desolate, your cities are burned with fire: your land, strangers devour it in your presence, and it is desolate, as overthrown by strangers. And the daughter of Zion is left as a cottage in a vineyard, as a lodge in a garden of cucumbers, as a besieged city. Except the Lord of hosts had left unto us a very small remnant, we should have been as Sodom, and we*

# Commentary on Romans

*should have been like unto Gomorrah. Hear the word of the Lord, ye rulers of Sodom; give ear unto the law of our God, ye people of Gomorrah. To what purpose is the multitude of your sacrifices unto me? saith the Lord: I am full of the burnt offerings of rams, and the fat of fed beasts; and I delight not in the blood of bullocks, or of lambs, or of he goats. When ye come to appear before me, who hath required this at your hand, to tread my courts? Bring no more vain oblations; incense is an abomination unto me; the new moons and sabbaths, the calling of assemblies, I cannot away with; it is iniquity, even the solemn meeting. Your new moons and your appointed feasts my soul hateth: they are a trouble unto me; I am weary to bear them. And when ye spread forth your hands, I will hide mine eyes from you: yea, when ye make many prayers, I will not hear: your hands are full of blood. Wash you, make you clean; put away the evil of your doings from before mine eyes; cease to do evil; Learn to do well; seek judgment, relieve the oppressed, judge the fatherless, plead for the widow. Come now, and let us reason together, saith the Lord: though your sins be as scarlet, they shall be as white as snow; though they be red like crimson, they shall be as wool. If ye be willing and obedient, ye shall eat the good of the land* (Isa. 1:1-19).

Obedience must come from the heart to be acceptable to the Father. The Jews had great difficulty accepting that God did not award grace through the Old Law. Such is Paul's argued case in verse six.

**Verse 6.** *And if by grace, then is it no more of works: otherwise grace is no more grace. But if it be of works, then is it no more grace: otherwise work is no more work.* Paul demonstrated grace was awarded not by the works of the Old Law, but rather God's grace has always been awarded to those who obeyed God from the heart and not through parroted oratory or obligation. *Whosoever is of a willing heart, let him bring it, an offering of the Lord* (Exo. 35:5b).

243

# Commentary on Romans

Many in the church today attend worship because they are *supposed to* or because they *have to*—not because they want, wish, or are permitted to. How much greater would the church be if every member had the desire to attend rather than feeling the obligation to do so? Attendance of Bible study and worship are precious opportunities; they are not chores for those who love the Lord. God has no appreciation for those who regard any assembly as a chore or as an obligation. God's grace is given to those who love the Lord, but it is not awarded to those who "*obey*" because of *obligation!* Those who attend under such criteria are not at all involved in worship. They are involved in sin!

## Romans 11:7-11

> 7 What then? Israel hath not obtained that which he seeketh for; but the election hath obtained it and the rest were blinded 8 (According as it is written, God hath given them the spirit of slumber, eyes that they should not see and ears that they should not hear;) unto this day. 9 And David saith, Let their table be made a snare and a trap and a stumblingblock and a recompence unto them: 10 Let their eyes be darkened, that they may not see and bow down their back alway. 11 I say then, Have they stumbled that they should fall? God forbid: but rather through their fall salvation is come unto the Gentiles, for to provoke them to jealousy.

**Verses 7-8.** *What then? Israel hath not obtained that which he seeketh for; but the election hath obtained it and the rest were blinded. (According as it is written, God hath given them the spirit of slumber, eyes that they should not see and ears that they should not hear;) unto this day.* Paul begins to summarize his arguments concerning the nation of Israel and God's dealings with them in these verses. The question, *what then,* means, "What is the spiritual state of Israel?" The answer to the inquisition is set forth in the next phrase of the verse with three points. Paul's first answer to the question is, *Israel hath not obtained that which he seeketh for.* The nation of Israel sought salvation and the blessings of God, but they did so according to their will.

# Commentary on Romans

Paul had previously written: *Brethren, my heart's desire and prayer to God for Israel is, that they might be saved. For I bear them record that they have a zeal of God, but not according to knowledge. For they being ignorant of God's righteousness and going about to establish their own righteousness, have not submitted themselves unto the righteousness of God* (Rom. 10:1-3).

The second answer to Paul's question stands in contrast to his first. Paul noted, *but the election hath obtained it.* The word *but* of the second reply establishes the contrast to the first. *The election*—the church—had obtained that for which it was not seeking. Many of the Jews did obtain God's saving grace through obedience to the Gospel of Christ; most did not.

Paul explains why in the third installment of his answer: *And the rest were blinded* by the truth of the Gospel. The spiritual blindness of disobedient Jews is found numerous times in the Old Testament, as in the passages that follow:

> *Yet the Lord hath not given you an heart to perceive and eyes to see and ears to hear, unto this day* (Deut. 29:4).

> *And he said, Go and tell this people, Hear ye indeed, but understand not; and see ye indeed, but perceive not. Make the heart of this people fat and make their ears heavy and shut their eyes; lest they see with their eyes and hear with their ears and understand with their heart and convert and be healed* (Isa, 6:9-10).

> *For the Lord hath poured out upon you the spirit of deep sleep and hath closed your eyes: the prophets and your rulers, the seers hath he covered* (Isa. 29:10).

Both the Lord and Paul spoke of the spiritual blindness of the Jews, as the following two passages show:

> *Therefore speak I to them in parables: because they seeing see not; and hearing they hear not, neither do they understand. And in them is fulfilled the prophecy of Esaias, which saith, By hearing ye shall hear and*

# Commentary on Romans

*shall not understand; and seeing ye shall see and shall not perceive: For this people's heart is waxed gross and their ears are dull of hearing and their eyes they have closed; lest at any time they should see with their eyes and hear with their ears and should understand with their heart and should be converted and I should heal them* (Matt. 13:13-15).

*And when we came to Rome, the centurion delivered the prisoners to the captain of the guard: but Paul was suffered to dwell by himself with a soldier that kept him. And it came to pass, that after three days Paul called the chief of the Jews together: and when they were come together, he said unto them, Men and brethren, though I have committed nothing against the people, or customs of our fathers, yet was I delivered prisoner from Jerusalem into the hands of the Romans. Who, when they had examined me, would have let me go, because there was no cause of death in me. But when the Jews spake against it, I was constrained to appeal unto Caesar; not that I had ought to accuse my nation of. For this cause therefore have I called for you, to see you and to speak with you: because that for the hope of Israel I am bound with this chain. And they said unto him, We neither received letters out of Judaea concerning thee, neither any of the brethren that came shewed or spake any harm of thee. But we desire to hear of thee what thou thinkest: for as concerning this sect, we know that every where it is spoken against. And when they had appointed him a day, there came many to him into his lodging; to whom he expounded and testified the kingdom of God, persuading them concerning Jesus, both out of the Law of Moses and out of the prophets, from morning till evening. And some believed the things which were spoken and some believed not. And when they agreed not among themselves, they departed, after that Paul had spoken one word, Well spake the Holy Ghost by Esaias the prophet unto our fathers, Saying, Go unto this people and say, Hearing ye shall hear and shall not understand; and seeing ye shall see and not perceive: For*

# Commentary on Romans

*the heart of this people is waxed gross and their ears are dull of hearing and their eyes have they closed; lest they should see with their eyes and hear with their ears and understand with their heart and should be converted and I should heal them. Be it known therefore unto you, that the salvation of God is sent unto the Gentiles and that they will hear it. And when he had said these words, the Jews departed and had great reasoning among themselves* (Acts 28:16-29).

**Verses 9-10.** *And David saith, Let their table be made a snare and a trap and a stumblingblock and a recompence unto them: Let their eyes be darkened, that they may not see and bow down their back alway.* The passage quoted by Paul here is from Psalm 69:22-23. Whiteside comments:

> "Their table was put for their religious food. Instead of being led to Christ by the Law they were entrapped by their blind adherence to the Law; they were caught as in a snare. And their blind adherence to the Law would be their recompense and that would amount to condemnation. Their rejection of Christ and their blind devotion to the Law was their ruin. Paul said such people judged themselves unworthy of eternal life (Acts 13:46). In clinging to the Law and rejecting Christ, the Jews were wearing a yoke which they were not able to bear (Acts 15:10). Their course brought upon themselves the destruction of their nation and hard servitude"[54] [sic].

The following passages also relate to bondage:

> *And that because of false brethren unawares brought in, who came in privily to spy out our liberty which we have in Christ Jesus, that they might bring us into bondage. Even so we, when we were children, were in bondage under the elements of the world. But now, after that ye have known God, or rather are known of God, how turn ye again to the weak and beggarly elements, whereunto ye desire again to be in bondage?*

---
[54] Robertson L. Whiteside.

# Commentary on Romans

*Which things are an allegory: for these are the two covenants; the one from the mount Sinai, which gendereth to bondage, which is Agar. For this Agar is mount Sinai in Arabia and answereth to Jerusalem which now is and is in bondage with her children. Stand fast therefore in the liberty wherewith Christ hath made us free and be not entangled again with the yoke of bondage* (Gal. 2:4; 4:3, 9, 24-25; 5:1).

*And deliver them who through fear of death were all their lifetime subject to bondage.... While they promise them liberty, they themselves are the servants of corruption: for of whom a man is overcome, of the same is he brought in bondage* (Heb. 2:15: II Pet. 2:19).

Paul's exhortation for the Jewish converts to; *stand fast therefore in the liberty wherewith Christ hath made us free,* as noted in Galatians 5:1, means to stand fast in their liberation from the bondage of the Old Law, and maintain the freedom found under the Law of Christ.

**Verse 11.** *I say then, Have they stumbled that they should fall? God forbid: but rather through their fall salvation is come unto the Gentiles, for to provoke them to jealousy.* As Paul did in the previous verses, he does here. He poses a question for the Jews and responds; *I say then, Have they stumbled that they should fall?* The fall of the Jews was the result of their having stumbled over Christ as the chief cornerstone. Both David and Isaiah prophesied Christ was to be the cornerstone upon whom the Jews should build themselves. *The stone which the builders refused is become the head stone of the corner* (Psa. 118:22). *Therefore thus saith the Lord God, Behold, I lay in Zion for a foundation a stone, a tried stone, a precious corner stone, a sure foundation: he that believeth shall not make haste* (Isa. 28:16). Peter also made reference to the prophet Isaiah in his first epistle wherein he wrote: *Wherefore also it is contained in the scripture, Behold, I lay in Zion a chief corner stone, elect, precious: and he that believeth on him shall not be confounded. Unto you therefore which believe he is precious: but unto them which be disobedient, the stone which the builders disallowed, the same is made the head of the corner* (I Pet. 2:6-7).

# Commentary on Romans

The Law of Moses was a partition between the Jews and Gentiles, but in Christ that wall was broken down. Paul addressed the Gentile converts in Ephesus on this matter:

> Wherefore remember, that ye being in time past Gentiles in the flesh, who are called uncircumcision by that which is called the Circumcision in the flesh made by hands; That at that time ye were without Christ, being aliens from the commonwealth of Israel and strangers from the covenants of promise, having no hope and without God in the world: But now in Christ Jesus ye who sometimes were far off are made nigh by the blood of Christ. For he is our peace, who hath made both one and hath broken down the middle wall of partition between us; Having abolished in his flesh the enmity, even the Law of commandments contained in ordinances; for to make in himself of twain one new man, so making peace; And that he might reconcile both unto God in one body by the cross, having slain the enmity thereby: And came and preached peace to you which were afar off and to them that were nigh. For through him we both have access by one Spirit unto the Father. Now therefore ye are no more strangers and foreigners, but fellowcitizens with the saints and of the household of God; And are built upon the foundation of the apostles and prophets, Jesus Christ himself being the chief corner stone (Eph. 2:11-20).

For the Jews, the breaking down of *the middle wall of partition* was devastating. It was not a comfortable matter for the Jews to accept the end of the Old Law. Paul further declared Christ had *abolished in his flesh the enmity, even the Law of commandments contained in ordinances; for to make in himself of twain one new man, so making peace; And that he might reconcile both unto God in one body by the cross, having slain the enmity thereby* (Eph. 2:15-16).

The middle wall—the Old Law—which divided the Jews from the Gentiles was authored by Christ, but it was to come to an end at the time God appointed. In Christ there was peace between the Jews and the Gentiles. In Christ, the Jews and Gentiles were

## Commentary on Romans

made one body. The one body of the Jews and Gentiles was a place of spiritual peace between them. No longer was there a dividing Law; all men were to become one in Christ.

The refusal of many Jews to obey the Gospel prompted Paul and Barnabas to turn their efforts to the Gentiles.

> And when the Jews were gone out of the synagogue, the Gentiles besought that these words might be preached to them the next Sabbath. Now when the congregation was broken up, many of the Jews and religious proselytes followed Paul and Barnabas: who, speaking to them, persuaded them to continue in the grace of God. And the next sabbath day came almost the whole city together to hear the word of God. But when the Jews saw the multitudes, they were filled with envy and spake against those things which were spoken by Paul, contradicting and blaspheming. Then Paul and Barnabas waxed bold and said, It was necessary that the word of God should first have been spoken to you: but seeing ye put it from you and judge yourselves unworthy of everlasting life, lo, we turn to the Gentiles. For so hath the Lord commanded us, saying, I have set thee to be a light of the Gentiles, that thou shouldest be for salvation unto the ends of the earth (Acts 13:42-47).

### Romans 11:12-24

> 12 Now if the fall of them be the riches of the world and the diminishing of them the riches of the Gentiles; how much more their fullness? 13 For I speak to you Gentiles, inasmuch as I am the apostle of the Gentiles, I magnify mine office: 14 If by any means I may provoke to emulation them which are my flesh and might save some of them. 15 For if the casting away of them be the reconciling of the world, what shall the receiving of them be, but life from the dead? 16 For if the firstfruit be holy, the lump is also holy: and if the root be holy, so are the branches. 17 And if some of the branches be broken off and thou, being a wild olive

## Commentary on Romans

*tree, wert graffed in among them and with them partakest of the root and fatness of the olive tree; 18 Boast not against the branches. But if thou boast, thou bearest not the root, but the root thee. 19 Thou wilt say then, The branches were broken off, that I might be graffed in. 20 Well; because of unbelief they were broken off and thou standest by faith. Be not highminded, but fear: 21 For if God spared not the natural branches, take heed lest he also spare not thee. 22 Behold therefore the goodness and severity of God: on them which fell, severity; but toward thee, goodness, if thou continue in his goodness: otherwise thou also shalt be cut off. 23 And they also, if they abide not still in unbelief, shall be grafted in: for God is able to graft them in again. 24 For if thou wert cut out of the olive tree which is wild by nature and wert grafted contrary to nature into a good olive tree: how much more shall these, which be the natural branches, be grafted into their own olive tree?*

**Verse 12.** *Now if the fall of them be the riches of the world and the diminishing of them the riches of the Gentiles; how much more their fullness?* Paul ended his address to the Jewish converts and begins his discussion with the Gentiles. The word *now* establishes this fact when one considers the clarity of verse 13.

*The fall of them* means the fall of disobedient Jews. Paul issues a strong and stern warning to the Gentile converts in these verses. The apostle informed the Gentiles the disobedient Jews were cut off from the true olive tree. Such allowed obedient Gentiles to be grafted as wild branches. The culmination of Paul's warning to the Gentiles is found in verse 21.

The *fall* of the Jews made it possible for the Gentiles to be grafted into the branches of salvation. *The riches of the world* means the riches of salvation to the world of the Gentiles. Paul spoke of the *riches* of God's grace twice in his letter to the Ephesians. *In whom we have redemption through his blood, the forgiveness of sins, according to the riches of his grace* (Eph. 1:7). *That in the ages to come he might shew the exceeding riches of his grace in his kindness toward us through Christ Jesus* (Eph. 2:7).

# Commentary on Romans

The *diminishing of them* means the deterioration of the riches God gave first to the Jews. The Jews allowed them to spoil and decay; the Gentiles were then granted access to His grace. The Jews' rejection and loss of God's riches and grace was complete and full. Premillennialism teaches that the *fullness* here means a complete and full restoration of Israel as a nation over which Christ will reign on earth for one thousand years in Jerusalem on David's throne. To the contrary, the *fullness* refers to the *fullness* or complete destruction of the Jews as a nation—*not their restoration as a nation*. The destruction of Jerusalem in AD 70 was the fullness about which Paul had written. The refusal of the Jews to acknowledge Jesus as the Messiah accelerated their destruction, which was described by the Lord: *For then shall be great tribulation, such as was not since the beginning of the world to this time, no, nor ever shall be* (Matt. 24:21).

**Verse 13-14.** *For I speak to you Gentiles, inasmuch as I am the apostle of the Gentiles, I magnify mine office: If by any means I may provoke to emulation them which are my flesh and might save some of them.*

> Paul was discussing at length the fate of the Jews, he would not have Gentile Christians think he was forgetting the Gentile people. He had been chosen as an apostle of the Gentiles and he gloried in that ministry. He demonstrated that he was sent of God by the miracles he performed. He hoped that his preaching to the Gentiles and his miracles among them would stir some of the Jews to such a pitch of jealousy that they would so investigate the testimony concerning the Christ as to become believers in Jesus as the Christ. By so doing he would be an instrument in saving those who believed his preaching. By teaching, backed up by a godly life, any Christian may be an agent in saving others[55] [sic].

That the apostle is now addressing the Gentile converts cannot be denied. The apostle is clear, his audience plainly identified, and his message is without obscurity. His motive was that he

---
[55] Robertson L. Whiteside.

# Commentary on Romans

might *provoke to emulation them which are my flesh and might save some of them* meaning the Jews.

*Emulation* means "to excite unto jealousy." Paul wrote: *Some indeed preach Christ even of envy and strife; and some also of good will: The one preach Christ of contention, not sincerely, supposing to add affliction to my bonds: But the other of love, knowing that I am set for the defense of the gospel. What then? notwithstanding, every way, whether in pretense, or in truth, Christ is preached; and I therein do rejoice, yea and will rejoice* (Phil. 1:15-18). Paul's words of the Philippians passage addressed the **motive** of those who preached, not the **method**.

However, Paul was neither promoting nor condoning *the end justifies the means.* The apostle earlier refuted such, saying, *And not rather, (as we be slanderously reported and as some affirm that we say,) Let us do evil, that good may come? whose damnation is just* (Rom. 3:8).

**Verse 15.** *For if the casting away of them be the reconciling of the world, what shall the receiving of them be, but life from the dead?* The casting away of the Jews did not award the whole world with salvation; it awarded the opportunity of it. The receiving of Jews does not mean the Jews would be restored as a nation, nor unto spiritual reconciliation as Premillennialism teaches.

Reconciliation is offered to all men. The Jews had (and still have) opportunity to be saved through the same process as the Gentiles had and have: that is, through obedience to the Gospel. All the Jews of whom Paul then spoke were dead in their sins, just as the Gentiles. Through obedience to the Gospel, all men are awarded opportunity to gain God's saving grace and favor. When one obeys, he is resurrected from the death of sin and awarded life in Christ.

The chosen people of God today are neither Jews nor Gentiles; rather, the chosen of God are those who have obeyed the Gospel and remain faithful to it. *For as many of you as have been baptized into Christ have put on Christ. There is neither Jew nor Greek, there is neither bond nor free, there is neither male nor female: for ye are all one in Christ Jesus* (Gal. 3:27-28).

# Commentary on Romans

***Verse 16-17.*** *For if the firstfruit be holy, the lump is also holy: and if the root be holy, so are the branches. And if some of the branches be broken off and thou, being a wild olive tree, wert grafted in among them and with them partakest of the root and fatness of the olive tree.* No little confusion envelops these verses. Most commentators utilize much space referring to Old Testament passages which address the subject of firstfruits and the other terms offered in this passage. There are four matters for consideration here in this verse: the *firstfruit,* the *lump,* the *root,* and the *branches.* All four terms work together and need not be addressed individually. Often students become so deeply lost in defining words they fail to grasp the message intended.

These verses summarized simply means the Jews, who were once God's chosen, were to be a holy people—a holy nation—but because of their apostasy they were cut off. As branches, they were to bear holy fruit; their failure to do so resulted in God pruning them from the natural olive tree. The apostle informed the Gentiles that some of the natural branches of the olive tree were cut off. The Gentiles, as wild olive branches, were awarded opportunity to be grafted into the natural tree. However, a strong warning was issued to the Gentile converts not to think they could not be cut off. Note verse 21: *For if God spared not the natural branches, take heed lest he also spare not thee.*

***Verses 18-21.*** *Boast not against the branches. But if thou boast, thou bearest not the root, but the root thee. Thou wilt say then, The branches were broken off, that I might be grafted in. Well; because of unbelief they were broken off and thou standest by faith. Be not highminded, but fear: For if God spared not the natural branches, take heed lest he also spare not thee.* Paul simply warns the Gentile converts: if God cut off the Jews as natural branches, the Gentiles could suffer the same fate.

> From what was said in verses 11 and 12, the Gentile Christian might conclude that the Jews were rejected for the definite purpose of granting salvation to the Gentiles. The rejection of the Jews, which resulted from their sins, did hasten the preaching of the gospel to the Gentiles; they were not arbitrarily rejected for the

# Commentary on Romans

special benefit of Gentiles. The term '*unbelief*' here stands for all their sin and rebellion. In reality they cut themselves loose from all relations with God. By their faith the Gentile Christians stood in God's favor. They did not obtain God's favor through God's partiality to them, nor through any merit of their own, but by grace through faith in the Lord Jesus Christ. Jews could obtain that favor in the same way. There were therefore neither grounds nor occasion for their glorying over the Jews. Besides, these Gentile Christians might also be broken off from God's favor, as a result of unbelief. By a natural birth all Jews had been God's people—they had been born into covenant relationship with God; but that covenant ended at the cross and that left the Jews in the same condition as the Gentiles: For they continued not in my covenant and I regarded them not, saith the Lord" (Heb. 8:9). This should be a warning to Gentile Christians—in fact to all members of the New Covenant, whether Jews or Gentiles; "for if God spared not the natural branches, neither will he spare thee." This shows conclusively that Christians may conduct themselves in such way as to sever themselves from God's favor[56] [sic].

**Verses 22-23.** *Behold therefore the goodness and severity of God: on them which fell, severity; but toward thee, goodness, if thou continue in his goodness: otherwise thou also shalt be cut off. And they also, if they abide not still in unbelief, shall be grafted in: for God is able to graft them in again.* Saving obedient men through their faith, and the cutting off of the disobedient shows both the mercy and justice of God. God's goodness and severity is likewise seen through such action of the Lord. *Behold then the goodness and severity of God.*

God dealt severely with the Jews because they fell through unbelief. His goodness would be extended to the Gentile Christians so long as they did not fall through unbelief. In his goodness and in his severity God is neither tyrannical nor whimsical; the display of either his goodness or severity depends on man's atti-

---
[56] Robertson L. Whiteside.

## Commentary on Romans

tude toward him. Let us not get a onesided view of God. "God is love" (1 John 4:8). It is equally true that "our God is a consuming fire" (Heb. 12:29). Because of unbelief the Jews had been cut off from God's favor. Their only hope therefore was to come back to God through faith in Christ. Any among them could be grafted again into God's favor, "if they continue not in their unbelief." God was able to graft them in again; the only hindering cause was their unbelief[57] [sic].

**Verse 24.** *For if thou wert cut out of the olive tree which is wild by nature and wert grafted contrary to nature into a good olive tree: how much more shall these, which be the natural branches, be grafted into their own olive tree?* A wild tree is unpruned and untended; its fruit lacks in quality compared to the cultured tree. The Gentiles were likewise: their fruit would be far superior once grafted into the tended natural tree.

We now consider the phrase *how much more shall these, which be the natural branches, be grafted into their own olive tree?* This speaks to the fact, as God was able to graft in wild branches—Gentiles, He could again graft in the natural branches. As branches of the true vine the Christian is to bear much fruit. The Lord said; *Every branch in me that beareth not fruit he taketh away: and every branch that beareth fruit, he purgeth it, that it may bring forth more fruit* (Jno. 15:2).

### Romans 11:25-36

*25 For I would not, brethren, that ye should be ignorant of this mystery, lest ye should be wise in your own conceits; that blindness in part is happened to Israel, until the fulness of the Gentiles be come in. 26 And so all Israel shall be saved: as it is written, There shall come out of Zion the Deliverer and shall turn away ungodliness from Jacob: 27 For this is my covenant unto them, when I shall take away their sins. 28 As concerning the gospel, they are enemies for your sakes: but as touching the election, they are beloved for the fathers' sakes. 29 For the gifts and calling of God are*

---

[57] Robertson L. Whiteside.

# Commentary on Romans

*without repentance. 30 For as ye in times past have not believed God, yet have now obtained mercy through their unbelief: 31 Even so have these also now not believed, that through your mercy they also may obtain mercy. 32 For God hath concluded them all in unbelief, that he might have mercy upon all. 33 O the depth of the riches both of the wisdom and knowledge of God! how unsearchable are his judgments and his ways past finding out! 34 For who hath known the mind of the Lord? or who hath been his counselor? 35 Or who hath first given to him and it shall be recompensed unto him again? 36 For of him and through him and to him, are all things: to whom be glory for ever. Amen.*

**Verse 25.** *For I would not, brethren, that ye should be ignorant of this mystery, lest ye should be wise in your own conceits; that blindness in part is happened to Israel, until the fullness of the Gentiles be come in.* Paul wanted the Gentiles to be aware of the cutting off of the natural branches from the metaphorical olive tree, and the grafting in of the wild branches.

The *mystery* under consideration is the mystery of the spiritual blindness of the Jews and their refusal to accept Jesus as the Messiah. Because Paul intended the Gentiles to understand the *mystery* and not be *ignorant* of it, establishes the fact the revelation—making known of the mystery—was indeed understood by the Gentile converts based on the subsequent verses of the apostle's comments. The mystery of this verse, simply stated, was the hardening of heart of the Jews.

*Lest ye should be wise in your own conceits.* The converted Gentiles had been behaving themselves in an untoward manner against the Jewish converts. Here the apostle strongly warns the Gentiles to cease such behavior.

On the phrase, *that blindness in part is happened to Israel,* we note that the spiritual blindness of Israel was not a total blindness of all the Jews. The phrase is a qualifying statement; it does not demand the conclusion all Israel had blinded their eyes. The spiritual blindness of Israel as a nation was only partial.

# Commentary on Romans

Some of the Jews had obeyed the Gospel and became enlightened. Adam Clarke commented this phrase, saying:

> Partial blindness, or blindness to a *part of them*; for they were not *all* unbelievers: several thousands of them had been converted to the Christian faith; though the *body* of the nation, and especially its *rulers*, civil and spiritual, continued opposed to Christ and his doctrine[58] [sic].

The phrase, *until the fullness of the Gentiles be come in* has warmed the heart of many Calvinistic Premillennialists. Ninety-five percent of the religious world holds to some form of Premillennialism. The doctrine is false and damnable. Countless debates, both oral and written, have addressed this devilish dogma, and the Scriptures have always destroyed the doctrine.

Some have conjectured the *fullness of the Gentiles* refers to a time when the Gentiles fully reject the Lord. Others insist the phrase means the total acceptance of the Gospel by the Gentiles. It is clear the two are diametrically opposed. Both cannot be true, but both can be and are indeed wrong. Before offering our comments on what the phrase means, consider the following comments of Albert Barnes.

> The word "fullness" in relation to the Jews is used in Rom. 11:12. It means until the abundance or the great multitude of the Gentiles shall be converted. The word is not used elsewhere in respect to the Gentiles; and it is difficult to fix its meaning definitely. It doubt-less refers to the future spread of the gospel among the nations; to the time when it may be said that the great mass, the abundance of the nations, shall be converted to God. At present, they are, as they were in the times of the apostle, idolaters, so that the mass of mankind are far from God. But the Scriptures have spoken of a time when the gospel shall spread and prevail among the nations of the earth; and to this the apostle refers. He does not say, however, that the Jews may not be converted until all the Gentiles be-

---
[58] Adam Clarke.

# Commentary on Romans

come Christians; for he expressly supposes Rom. 11: 12-15 that the conversion of the Jews will have an important influence in extending the gospel among the Gentiles. Probably the meaning is, that this blindness is to continue until great numbers of the Gentiles shall be converted; until the gospel shall be extensively spread; and then the conversion of the Jews will be a part of the rapid spread of the gospel, and will be among the most efficient and important aids in completing the work. If this is the case, then Christians may labor still for their conversion. They may seek that in connection with the effort to convert the pagan; and they may toil with the expectation that the conversion of the Jews and Gentiles will not be separate, independent, and distinct events; but will be inter-mingled, and will be perhaps simultaneous. The word "fullness" may denote such a general turning to God, without affirming that each individual shall be thus converted to the Christian faith[59] [sic].

It is assumed by some that *the fullness of the Gentiles* means that all Gentiles will be finally converted to Christ, and that will be followed by the conversion of the whole Jewish race. Some kingdom advocates interpret *"the fullness of the Gentiles"* as the full count of the Gentiles; that is, when the Lord gathered out of the Gentiles the full number he wants for rulers in the supposed future kingdom, then evangelism among them will cease, and the Jews will then turn to Christ[60] [sic].

The phrase, *the fullness of the Gentiles*, means the full and complete provocation of the Jews unto *jealousy* and *emulation*, as Paul declared in verses 11 and 14.

**Verse 26.** *And so all Israel shall be saved: as it is written, There shall come out of Zion the Deliverer and shall turn away ungodliness from Jacob:* Premillennialists warm themselves much by the devil's fire of Calvinism regarding this verse. Barnes further wrote: "That is, in this manner; or when the great abundance of

---

[59] Albert Barnes.

[60] Robertson L. Whiteside.

# Commentary on Romans

the Gentiles shall be converted, then all Israel shall be saved"[61] [sic].

As far as is the east is from the west is this doctrine from the truth. Consider a few logical arguments against Barnes' comments. First, if such be the case for the nation of Israel, then it is the case the salvation of an untold number of Jews is dependent on the obedience of an untold number of the Gentiles. Second, Paul declared: *There is neither Jew nor Greek, there is neither bond nor free, there is neither male nor female: for ye are all one in Christ Jesus* (Gal. 3:28). Paul's declaration negates the argument there are Jews today. No one who claims to be a Jew today can prove such. The temple of the Jews no longer exists in which the priests were to serve. The garments of the High Priest have no longer been passed to a successor as mandated by the Law of Moses. The Ark of the Covenant no longer exists, having been destroyed by the Roman army in AD 70. Further, the vessels of gold which were used in the temple are no longer in existence.

Consider the following reasons why we insisted the Roman army captured the Ark of the Covenant, destroying it and the vessels of gold which were used in the temple. The Mosaical Law required these items be used in the temple. If they remained in Babylon after the captivity of the Jews during that time, then it would be the case the restoration of the Jews to Jerusalem and their worship in the new temple lacked these things, and the priests and High Priest could not comply with the Law of Moses. Further, it would be the case the Lord was not able to worship as the Law of Moses required.

> *Then Darius the king made a decree, and search was made in the house of the rolls, where the treasures were laid up in Babylon. And there was found at Achmetha, in the palace that is in the province of the Medes, a roll, and therein was a record thus written: In the first year of Cyrus the king the same Cyrus the king made a decree concerning the house of God at Jerusalem, Let the house be builded, the place where they offered sacrifices, and let the foundations thereof be*

---
[61] Albert Barnes.

# Commentary on Romans

*strongly laid; the height thereof threescore cubits, and the breadth thereof threescore cubits; With three rows of great stones, and a row of new timber: and let the expenses be given out of the king's house: And also let the golden and silver vessels of the house of God, which Nebuchadnezzar took forth out of the temple which is at Jerusalem, and brought unto Babylon, be restored, and brought again unto the temple which is at Jerusalem, every one to his place, and place them in the house of God* (Ezra 6:1-5).

No so-called Jew can today comply with the Old Law as God mandated. The Jews were required by the Old Law to have a record of their genealogy back to Abraham. The Jews today cannot comply with the sacrifices mandated by the Old Law. Further, there is no record of the Levitical priesthood or a genealogy of the High Priest. Whats more is the Jews do not have a High Priest today.

These are but a few reasons why anyone who claims to be a Jew cannot prove such—and why no so-called Jew can comply with the Old Law, as God dictated. The Law of Moses has forever ended. Paul wrote: *Blotting out the handwriting of ordinances that was against us, which was contrary to us, and took it out of the way, nailing it to his cross* (Col. 2:14).

*And so all Israel shall be saved: as it is written, There shall come out of Zion the Deliverer and shall turn away ungodliness from Jacob.* The word *so* is an adverb of manner. The same manner by which the Gentiles were to be saved is the same manner by which Israel would be saved. The manner of salvation by which all Israel and all the Gentiles were to be saved is by obedience to the Gospel of the New Testament.

*As it is written.* It is always needful to inquire where things are written when inspiration tells us *it is written.* Here Paul refers to the prophet Isaiah: *And the Redeemer shall come to Zion, and unto them that turn from transgression in Jacob, saith the Lord* (Isa. 59:20). "The Deliverer is Christ Jesus. 'Jacob' here stands for the descendants of Jacob. Jesus came to turn away ungodliness from Jacob, and did that for all who accepted him. They

# Commentary on Romans

were to turn from their ungodliness—their impiety, or irreverence, and he would take away their sins, and that was his covenant with them"[62] [sic].

**Verse 27.** *For this is my covenant unto them, when I shall take away their sins.* This verse is a continuation of the passage which Paul quoted from Isaiah. *As for me, this is my covenant with them, saith the Lord; My spirit that is upon thee, and my words which I have put in thy mouth, shall not depart out of thy mouth, nor out of the mouth of thy seed, nor out of the mouth of thy seed's seed, saith the Lord, from henceforth and for ever* (Isa. 59:21). The covenant of which Isaiah spoke and which Paul cited is the New Covenant of which Jeremiah wrote (31:31-34).

**Verse 28.** *As concerning the gospel, they are enemies for your sakes: but as touching the election, they are beloved for the fathers' sakes.* The unbelieving Jews were indeed *"enemies"* of Christ, and His church. Adam Clarke wrote:

> The unbelieving Jews, with regard to the Gospel which they have rejected, are at present enemies to God, and aliens from his kingdom, under his Son Jesus Christ, on account of that extensive grace which has overturned their *peculiarity*, by admitting the Gentiles into his Church and family: but with regard to the original purpose of *election*, whereby they were chosen and separated from all the people of the earth to be the peculiar people of God, *they are beloved for the fathers' sake*; he has still favor in store for them on account of their *forefathers* the *patriarchs*[63] [sic].

God never issued a *purpose of election* for any, as asserted by Barnes. *They,* the *enemies* of the Gospel refers to the unbelieving Jews. The rejection of the Gospel by the Jews proved to be a blessing to the Gentiles providing them the avenue by which they too might be partakers of the heavenly gift of salvation through Jesus Christ. The phrase, *they are enemies for your sakes,* means, for your (the Gentiles') advantage. The rejection

---

[62] Robertson L. Whiteside.

[63] Adam Clarke.

# Commentary on Romans

of the Gospel by the Jews made the preaching of it to the Gentiles possible.

The phrase, *but as touching the election*, is likewise abused by those who don the damnable doctrine of Calvinism. The *election* here refers to the nation of the Jews; elected by God, through whom the Messiah was to come. Moses wrote: *The Lord did not set his love upon you, nor choose you, because ye were more in number than any people; for ye were the fewest of all people* (Deut. 7:7). *Only the Lord had a delight in thy fathers to love them, and he chose their seed after them, even you above all people, as it is this day* (Deut. 10:15). Only in this way were the Jews God's *election.* The Jews were *beloved for the fathers' sakes.*

**Verse 29.** *For the gifts and calling of God are without repentance.* Here the words, *gifts of God*, refer to salvation and eternal life. Holiness, righteousness, and obedience to the Father are wages men often forfeit. Both holy and sinful living have rewards attached to them. Paul said: *For the wages of sin is death; but the gift of God is eternal life through Jesus Christ our Lord* (Rom. 6:23). He further said: *For by grace are ye saved through faith; and that not of yourselves: it is the gift of God* (Eph. 2:8).

The *calling of God* is accomplished only through obedience of the Gospel. Man receives no *direct calling* from God. Those who assert they *received their calling* by some small, still voice charge the Lord with falsehoods. Paul declared: *Whereunto he called you by our gospel, to the obtaining of the glory of our Lord Jesus Christ* (II Thes. 2:14). The prophet Isaiah spoke unto the children of Israel, saying, *I have not spoken in secret, in a dark place of the earth...* (Isa. 45:19a). Jesus said: *I spake openly to the world; I ever taught in the synagogue, and in the temple, whither the Jews always resort; and in secret have I said nothing* (Jno. 18:20). In both the Old and New Testaments, Deity denies secretly calling any man unto and into the work of God. Further, the Holy Spirit has called no one unto obedience or an office of any sort. Man is called by the Gospel and only by the Gospel unto the obedience (cf. II Thes.2:14).

# Commentary on Romans

On the phrase, *without repentance,* it is needful to understand what the word *repentance* means. Here the word means to regret or to have remorse. Paul used the word *repent* in two differing ways in his letter to the church at Corinth. He wrote: *For godly sorrow worketh repentance to salvation not to be repented of: but sorrow of the world worketh death* (II Cor. 7:10). The first word in this passage means regret or remorse. The second means to change—a reversal. Godly sorrow leads one to change his life for the better; which is not to be regretted, but worldly sorrow results in spiritual death. Worldly sorrow is a sorrow for having been caught in an evil. Godly sorrow brings about obedience. Barnes noted the following:

> Without repentance—This does not refer to man, but to God. It does not mean that God confers his favors on man without his exercising repentance, but that God does not repent, or change, in his purposes of bestowing his gifts on man. What he promises he will fulfill; what he purposes to do, he will not change from or repent of. As he made promises to the fathers, he will not repent of them, and will not depart from them; they shall all be fulfilled; and thus it was certain that the ancient people of God, though many of them had become rebellious, and had been cast off, should not be forgotten and abandoned. This is a general proposition respecting God, and one repeatedly made of him in the Scriptures; see Num 23:19, "God is not a man, that he should lie; neither the son of man, that he should repent: hath he not said, and shall he not do it? hath he spoken, and shall he not make it good?" Eze 24:14; I Sa 15:29; Psa 89:35-36; Tit 1:2; Heb 6:18; Jam 1:17. It follows from this...[64] [sic].

> God had selected the fathers, Abraham, Isaac, and Jacob, and their descendants as the line through which the Christ would come, and he had not repented of that selection; and even though these descendants had so sinned as to be broken off from his favor, they were beloved on account of the fathers, and not on their own

---

[64] Albert Barnes.

# Commentary on Romans

account[65] [sic].

**Verses 30-31.** *For as ye in times past have not believed God, yet have now obtained mercy through their unbelief: Even so have these also now not believed, that through your mercy they also may obtain mercy.* Just as the Jews were disobedient to the Old Law, so the Gentiles were disobedient to the Patriarchal Law. Paul addressed this matter in verses 10 and 11; see comments thereon.

**Verse 32.** *For God hath concluded them all in unbelief, that he might have mercy upon all.* Here Paul argues both Jew and Gentile were children of unbelief. Because of the disobedience of *them all—they all* (both Jew and Gentile) stood in need of God's mercy.

Paul argued this point in chapter 3 wherein he wrote; *What then? Are we better than they? No, in on wise: for we have before proved both Jews and Gentiles, that they are all under sin* (Rom. 3:9). *Even the righteousness of God which is by faith of Jesus Christ unto all and upon all them that believe: for there is no difference: For all have sinned, and come short of the glory of God* (Rom. 3:22-23). The word *all* in these verses refers to the Jews and the Gentiles.

**Verses 33-36.** *O the depth of the riches both of the wisdom and knowledge of God! how unsearchable are his judgments, and his ways past finding out! For who hath known the mind of the Lord? or who hath been his counselor? Or who hath first given to him, and it shall be recompensed unto him again? For of him, and through him, and to him, are all things: to whom be glory for ever. Amen.* Some have suggested these verses serve as a song of adoration and praise by the apostle to the Lord; for His awarding man an avenue by which he can acquire salvation. Just from where such a conclusion comes we are not told.

It is far beyond man's ability to counsel God regarding the Father's scheme of redemption; His ways are *past finding out.* It does indeed seem to be the case, as Paul makes use of an apostrophe in these verses. An *apostrophe* is an exclamatory

---
[65] Robertson L. Whiteside.

# Commentary on Romans

figure of speech which occurs when a speaker or writer changes his present audience, and directs his attention to a third unmentioned or non-present individual or party.

How sublime are these words! They refer to the provisions for salvation as revealed in the gospel, including God's use of men and nations in the development of this plan of salvation, as had been set forth in this letter, and not merely, as some think, to what was said in verses 30 and 31. In the Bible use of the term "knowledge of God" that phrase does not refer to what God knows, but to what is known, or may be known, about him; that is, it refers to the things revealed about him and his plans. Here are some examples of the use of the phrase: "Then shalt thou understand the fear of Jehovah, and find the knowledge of God" (Prov. 2:5). "...there is no truth, nor goodness, nor knowledge of God in the land" (Hosea 4:1). "Some have no knowledge of God" (1 Cor. 15:34). Paul prayed that the Colossians be "increasing in the knowledge of God" (Col. 1:9-10). "But grow in the grace and knowledge of our Lord and Savior Jesus Christ" (2 Pet 3:18). (See also Hosea 6:6; 2 Cor. 10:5; 2 Pet. 1:2-3, 8). In not one passage does the phrase refer to what God knows, any more than the phrase "knowledge of mathematics" refers to what mathematics knows. No uninspired man could search out and discern the judgments of God, nor trace out his ways down through the ages as he used men and nations in working out his plans and purposes. And no one can know the mind of God, save as he reveals it. By man's unaided powers he cannot find out these glorious things. "But unto us God revealed them through the Spirit: for the Spirit searcheth all things. yea, the deep things of God. For who among men knoweth the things of a man, save the spirit of the man, which is in him? Even so the things of God none knoweth, save the Spirit of God. But we received, not the spirit of the world, but the Spirit which is from God; that we might know the things that were freely given to us of God. Which things also we speak, not in words which man's wisdom teacheth, but which the Spirit

# Commentary on Romans

teacheth" (1 Cor. 2:9-13). Only as God reveals himself may we know his mind. And no one has ever given anything to God, so as to bring God under obligation to recompense him; for all things are of him, through him, and unto him. We cannot therefore enrich him by giving him that which is already his; but we can, with Paul, say, "To him be glory for ever"[66] [sic].

## Romans 12:1-8

*1 I beseech you therefore, brethren, by the mercies of God, that ye present your bodies a living sacrifice, holy, acceptable unto God, which is your reasonable service. 2 And be not conformed to this world: but be ye transformed by the renewing of your mind, that ye may prove what is that good, and acceptable, and perfect, will of God. 3 For I say, through the grace given unto me, to every man that is among you, not to think of himself more highly than he ought to think; but to think soberly, according as God hath dealt to every man the measure of faith. 4 For as we have many members in one body, and all members have not the same office: 5 So we, being many, are one body in Christ, and every one members one of another. 6 Having then gifts differing according to the grace that is given to us, whether prophecy, let us prophesy according to the proportion of faith; 7 Or ministry, let us wait on our ministering: or he that teacheth, on teaching; 8 Or he that exhorteth, on exhortation: he that giveth, let him do it with simplicity; he that ruleth, with diligence; he that sheweth mercy, with cheerfulness.*

Paul now turns his attention to both the Jews and the Gentiles. He had addressed chapter 1 to the Gentile converts, chapter 2 to the Jewish saints, and chapter 3 to both. In chapters 4:1-11:11 the apostle addressed the Jewish Christians. The remaining verses of chapter 11 were directed to both the Jews and the Gentiles. The remainder of the epistle is directed toward both audiences. Though both Jew and Gentile saints are intended for the most part, there are, at times, arguments Paul makes which

---
[66] Robertson L. Whiteside.

# Commentary on Romans

have deeper meanings for the Jews and other times for the Gentiles.

It is good to recall, under both the Patriarchal and Mosaical laws, animal sacrifices were mandated by the Lord. The sacrifices the Lord required were well detailed under each respective law. All sacrifices were to be without spots or blemishes. The Lord never authorized the sacrificing of any animal which was less than the best anyone had or was blemished in any way. The sacrifices of those who lived under the laws of the Old Testament were considered gifts to the Lord.

Sacrifices brought to the Lord were to be living and healthy. The Lord never accepted dead sacrifices from those who lived under the laws of the Old Testament, nor does He accept less today. While most are familiar with the sacrifices of the Law of Moses, it seems less are familiar with the sacrifices of the Patriarchal law. Below are listed a sampling of them.

*And Abel, he also brought of the firstlings of his flock and of the fat thereof. And the Lord had respect unto Abel and to his offering* (Gen. 4:4).

*And Noah builded an altar unto the Lord; and took of every clean beast, and of every clean fowl, and offered burnt offerings on the altar* (Gen. 8:20).

*After these things the word of the Lord came unto Abram in a vision, saying, Fear not, Abram: I am thy shield, and thy exceeding great reward. And Abram said, Lord God, what wilt thou give me, seeing I go childless, and the steward of my house is this Eliezer of Damascus? And Abram said, Behold, to me thou hast given no seed: and, lo, one born in my house is mine heir. And, behold, the word of the Lord came unto him, saying, This shall not be thine heir; but he that shall come forth out of thine own bowels shall be thine heir. And he brought him forth abroad, and said, Look now toward heaven, and tell the stars, if thou be able to number them: and he said unto him, So shall thy seed be. And he believed in the Lord; and he counted*

# Commentary on Romans

*it to him for righteousness. And he said unto him, I am the Lord that brought thee out of Ur of the Chaldees, to give thee this land to inherit it. And he said, Lord God, whereby shall I know that I shall inherit it? And he said unto him, Take me an heifer of three years old, and a she goat of three years old, and a ram of three years old, and a turtledove, and a young pigeon. And he took unto him all these, and divided them in the midst, and laid each piece one against another but the birds divided he not. And when the fowls came down upon the carcasses, Abram drove them away. And when the sun was going down, a deep sleep fell upon Abram; and, lo, an horror of great darkness fell upon him. And he said unto Abram, Know of a surety that thy seed shall be a stranger in a land that is not theirs, and shall serve them; and they shall afflict them four hundred years; And also that nation, whom they shall serve, will I judge: and afterward shall they come out with great substance. And thou shalt go to thy fathers in peace; thou shalt be buried in a good old age. But in the fourth generation they shall come hither again: for the iniquity of the Amorites is not yet full. And it came to pass, that, when the sun went down, and it was dark, behold a smoking furnace, and a burning lamp that passed between those pieces* (Gen. 15:1-17).

*Then Jacob offered sacrifice upon the mount, and called his brethren to eat bread: and they did eat bread, and tarried all night in the mount* (Gen. 31:54).

Sacrifices made to the Lord must have the heart emotionally involved and strongly affixed to them. When the heart feels no sacrifice, God is not pleased. King David well understood this fact. David once occasioned to pride himself in the number of soldiers of his army and went contrary to God's command.

*And David's heart smote him after that he had numbered the people. And David said unto the Lord, I have sinned greatly in that I have done: and now, I beseech thee, O Lord, take away the iniquity of thy servant; for I have done very foolishly.... And Gad came that day to*

# Commentary on Romans

*David, and said unto him, Go up, rear an altar unto the Lord in the threshingfloor of Araunah the Jebusite. And David, according to the saying of Gad, went up as the Lord commanded. And Araunah looked, and saw the king and his servants coming on toward him: and Araunah went out, and bowed himself before the king on his face upon the ground. And Araunah said, Wherefore is my Lord the king come to his servant? And David said, To buy the threshingfloor of thee, to build an altar unto the Lord, that the plague may be stayed from the people. And Araunah said unto David, Let my Lord the king take and offer up what seemeth good unto him: behold, here be oxen for burnt sacrifice, and threshing instruments and other instruments of the oxen for wood. All these things did Araunah, as a king, give unto the king. And Araunah said unto the king, The Lord thy God accept thee. And the king said unto Araunah, Nay; but I will surely buy it of thee at a price: neither will I offer burnt offerings unto the Lord my God of that which doth cost me nothing. So David bought the threshingfloor and the oxen for fifty shekels of silver. And David built there an altar unto the Lord, and offered burnt offerings and peace offerings. So the Lord was intreated for the land, and the plague was stayed from Israel* (II Sam. 24:10,18-25).

David's attitude is well displayed in verse 24. When offering the things of sacrifice, David refused the kind generosity of Araunah and said; *neither will I offer burnt offerings unto the Lord my God of that which doth cost me nothing.* There are four attitudes of giving and sacrifice provided in this verse. The first of which is one that sets forth the attitude, *I will not offer.* Second, *I will not offer unto the Lord* is an attitude possessed by many. Third, and most common among many saints is the attitude which declares; *I will not offer unto the Lord of that which costs me.* Last, the only acceptable attitude is portrayed for the saint who insists, *I will not offer unto the Lord of that which costs me nothing.*

When one offers unto the Lord that which costs him nothing, he has offered nothing. One's giving must be sacrificial if one ex-

# Commentary on Romans

pects his offering to be accepted by the Lord. The morning meal well illustrates the difference between an offering and sacrifice. For a chicken, it is an offering; for a pig it is a sacrifice.

**Verse 1.** *I beseech you therefore, brethren, by the mercies of God, that ye present your bodies a living sacrifice, holy, acceptable unto God, which is your reasonable service.* First, note the apostle begs the saints *by the mercies of God* in their sacrifices unto Him.

*The mercies of God* "constituted a reason why they should present their bodies a living sacrifice.[67]

The word "mercies" here denotes favor shown to the undeserving, or kindness, compassion, etc. The plural is used in imitation of the Hebrew word for mercy, which has no singular. The word is not often used in the New Testament; see 2 Co 1:3, where God is called *"the Father of mercies";* Phi 2:1; Col 3:12; Heb 10:28[68] [sic].

The phrase, *that ye present your bodies*, is vast in application. The word *present* is wide and broad in definition and scope. The word means "to *stand* beside, to exhibit, volunteer, submit, to be at hand and ready to aid, to assist, bring forth, to bring before, to give presently, to prove, provide, shew, stand before, to yield, to place beside or near, to set at hand, to place a person or thing at one's disposal, to show, to bring to, bring near, to bring into one's fellowship or intimacy." Not only do these descriptive words and phrases portray the scope of the word, but the intent goes further. As saints, we are to offer our lives as a a gift to the Lord. As the Lord awarded man with *the gift of eternal life,* so must saints award God with the gift of their lives and service (Rom. 6:23). With such a broad spectrum adhering to this phrase, it serves the saint best to exhaust himself in the performing of these things.

*A living sacrifice* is intended—not one dead in sin or filled with complacency—rather, a life fervent in spirit and dedication. The

---
[67] Albert Barnes.
[68] Adam Clarke.

## Commentary on Romans

word *life* is broad in scope: "to live, breathe, be among the spiritually living, not the spiritually dead, to enjoy a real spiritual life, to have true life and worthy of the name of God, to be active, a blessing to the church—the kingdom of God—to pass through life in the manner of serving God, living and acting in a manner becoming to the Christian, to be in full vigor in one's Christian living, to be fresh, strong, efficient, active, powerful, and efficacious in the church." Saints too often exhaust themselves in everything but the work of the church, leaving the work for the faithful few. This author's father often said: *ten percent of the congregation does ninety percent of the work.*

The word *holy* is defined as "sacred, pure, and blameless." Saints are to conduct themselves accordingly:

*Because it is written, Be ye holy; for I am holy* (I Pet. 1:16).

*And ye shall be holy unto me: for I the Lord am holy, and have severed you from other people, that ye should be mine* (Lev. 20:26).

*And ye shall be unto me a kingdom of priests, and an holy nation. These are the words which thou shalt speak unto the children of Israel* (Exo. 19:6).

*But ye are a chosen generation, a royal priesthood, an holy nation, a peculiar people; that ye should shew forth the praises of him who hath called you out of darkness into his marvelous light* (I Pet. 2:9).

*And thou shalt make a plate of pure gold, and grave upon it, like the engravings of a signet, Holiness to the Lord* (Exo. 28:36).

*And they made the plate of the holy crown of pure gold, and wrote upon it a writing, like to the engravings of a signet, Holiness to the Lord* (Exo. 39:30).

On the phrase, *acceptable unto God,* it is vital we realize the sacrifice and the presentation of ourselves to God must be pleasing to Him. The word *acceptable* is here used as an adjective describing the noun *holy.* Isaiah wrote:

# Commentary on Romans

*To what purpose is the multitude of your sacrifices unto me? saith the Lord: I am full of the burnt offerings of rams, and the fat of fed beasts; and I delight not in the blood of bullocks, or of lambs, or of he goats. When ye come to appear before me, who hath required this at your hand, to tread my courts? Bring no more vain oblations; incense is an abomination unto me; the new moons and sabbaths, the calling of assemblies, I cannot away with; it is iniquity, even the solemn meeting. Your new moons and your appointed feasts my soul hateth: they are a trouble unto me; I am weary to bear them. And when ye spread forth your hands, I will hide mine eyes from you: yea, when ye make many prayers, I will not hear: your hands are full of blood. Wash you, make you clean; put away the evil of your doings from before mine eyes; cease to do evil* (Isa. 1:11-16).

Many believe they serve the Lord only through obedience to the Lord's commands, but unless the heart is acceptable with the Lord there is no acceptance of service from the Lord. Of the numerous things mentioned by Isaiah, the Lord mandated them all. However, the heart of the people was not where it should have been, which resulted in God having a great disgust with the people to the degree God hated their efforts. The same is true today; parroted compliance is not joyful and desirous obedience. Without the heart in one's service, there is no obedience or hope of gaining God's approval.

We also have in this verse the phrase, *which is your reasonable service.* Of the many things presented regarding our service, sacrifice and living are both reasonable. Doing less is unreasonable and unacceptable with the Lord. For many, it seems, the Lord is far too unreasonable for requiring such things from His children. A sad comment was once made by a member of the Lord's church (with whom this author once studied) who declared; *I didn't think God expected so much.*

The word *reasonable* pertains to logic, especially spiritual logic; it applies to the soul and the saving of it. It is illogical to do less than God has demanded and described for His children. If one

# Commentary on Romans

loves the Lord, he will keep His commandments (Jno. 14:15).

**Verse 2.** *And be not conformed to this world: but be ye transformed by the renewing of your mind, that ye may prove what is that good, and acceptable, and perfect, will of God.* This verse contains a command; it is neither a suggestion nor a recommendation. Salvation depends upon man's obedience to all of God's Laws. None of them may be set aside or considered void.

Here an antithesis stands—the command to *be not conformed to this world* is contrasted to being *transformed.* Conformity is good when it is to God's Word, but it is a great evil when one conforms to the things and ways of the world, including behavior, dress, habits, peers, speech, and appearance. Paul instructed the church at Thessalonica to *abstain from all appearance of evil* (I Thes. 5:22).

The word *conformed* means to fashion alike; that is, conform to the same pattern, to fashion self according to. The word also is defined as to conform one's self in mind and character to another's pattern, to fashion one's self according to. Here the word is in the verb form which shows continuous action on the part of those who engage in such conduct.

Prior obedience to the Gospel, a person walked in the ways of the world: *Wherein in time past ye walked according to the course of this world, according to the prince of the power of the air, the spirit that now worketh in the children of disobedience* (Eph. 2:2). Saints must recall Christ *gave himself for our sins, that he might deliver us from this present evil world, according to the will of God and our Father* (Gal. 1:4). Matthew Henry wrote:

> Conversion and sanctification are the renewing of the mind, a change not of the substance, but of the qualities of the soul. It is the same with making a new heart and a new spirit—new dispositions and inclinations, new sympathies and antipathies; the understanding enlightened, the conscience softened, the thoughts rectified; the will bowed to the will of God, and the affections made spiritual and heav-enly: so that the man is not what he was—old things are

# Commentary on Romans

passed away, all things are become new; he acts from new principles, by new rules, with new designs. The mind is the acting ruling part of us; so that the renewing of the mind is the renewing of the whole man, for out of it are the *issues of life*, Pro. 4:23[69] [sic].

Some Christians, like the children of Israel, want to copy the ways and practices of other people. This Paul forbids. His language also bans our drifting into the customs prevailing about us; and Christians will drift into the customs of other religious people, if they do not study the Bible, and make it their guide in speech and action. The Christian should make the Bible his guide, and give no thought as to whether it makes him like or unlike others. ...as children of obedience, not fashioning yourselves according to your former lusts in the time of your ignorance: but like as he who called you is holy, be ye yourselves also holy in all manner of living (1 Pet. 1:14,15). Saints are to fashion themselves according to the life of Christ and the gospel, not the world. "But be ye transformed." This demands a radical change in the thinking and the conduct of those who become Christians. The Greek word here rendered "transformed" is rendered transfigured in Matt. 17:2 and Mark 9:2. The Christian is made responsible for this change; the change is not brought about suddenly. "Though our outward man is decaying, yet our inward man is renewed day by day" (2 Cor. 4:16). This transformation can be brought about only by renewing the mind, the inward man, day by day. No one can transform his character while holding to the same old stock of ideas and ideals[70] [sic].

The antithesis of not being *conformed* for the saint is to be *transformed,* which means "to change into another form, to transform, to transfigure, just as Christ's appearance was changed and was resplendent with divine brightness on the mount of transfiguration. It is a metamorphic change, a complete and total change, a transfiguration, a transformation. The word is likewise in the verb

---
[69] Matthew Henry.

[70] Robertson L. Whiteside.

# Commentary on Romans

form demanding continuous action on the part of the Christian."

*The renewing of your mind*—that is, the one who departs from the ways of the world, and obeys the gospel must renew his mind. Many definitions have been awarded to the word *repent*, one of which expresses the idea of thinking differently and responding in kind through one's actions. A grand definition of the word *repentance* insists the word means a change of mind which results in a change of life. A penitent mind is a mind changed, it is truly a mind renewed—renewed unto and for the service of God.

The word *your* may seem superfluous on which to comment; however, in the construction of this phrase used by the apostle the word is in the genitive case which marks a noun as being the possessor of another noun. Placing the modifying noun *your* in the genitive case indicates that two nouns *your* and *mind* are related and cannot be separated.

The whole of the phrase, *by the renewing of your mind*, is in the instrumental case, which is used to indicate the noun *mind*, which is the instrument or means by or with which the Christian achieves or accomplishes the goal desired or dictated. The renewing of the mind for the saint must be desired in order for one to achieve the dictated instruction on inspiration.

On the phrase, *that ye may prove,* observe the burden of proof lies upon the Christian, not on the Lord. In addition to this verse, Paul uses the word *prove* in four additional passages. *I speak not by commandment, but by occasion of the forwardness of others, and to prove the sincerity of your love* (II Cor. 8:8). *Examine yourselves, whether ye be in the faith; prove your own selves. Know ye not your own selves, how that Jesus Christ is in you, except ye be reprobates* (II Cor. 13:5)? *But let every man prove his own work, and then shall he have rejoicing in himself alone, and not in another* (Gal. 6:4). *Prove all things; hold fast that which is good* (I Thes. 5:21). Notice, in each of these passages the burden of proof falls upon the saint. The Christian is to prove many things—yea, *all things*—as noted in the latter passage.

## Commentary on Romans

So far as the passage under consideration is concerned, there are three specific things which the saint must *prove*. First, saints are to *prove* that which is *good*. The word *good* is broad in scope and includes the following: "of good constitution or nature, useful, salutary, good, pleasant, agreeable, joyful, happy, excellent, distinguished, upright, honorable, properly beautiful, chiefly good, literally or morally, valuable or virtuous, for good use, that which is better, fair, honest, meet— fitting and worthy."

Second, Paul instructs the Christian to *prove* that which is *acceptable*. The word means agreeable and well pleasing.

Third, the saint is to *prove* the *perfect*. The word *perfect* means to be brought to its end, finished, wanting nothing necessary to completeness, consummate human integrity and virtue of men, full grown, adult, of full age, mature, complete in labor, growth, mental and moral character, of full age.

It is the duty of every Christian to *prove* these things, to do so in such a way that it shines as a guiding light to others, both to saints and those of the world. The Lord commanded the apostles: *Let your light so shine before men, that they may see your good works, and glorify your Father which is in heaven* (Matt. 5:16). Saints must do likewise.

The *will of God* is *good, acceptable, and perfect*, but the saint bears the duty of proving it. The word *will* expresses what one wishes or has determined shall be done. The purpose of God is to bless mankind through Christ. That which God wishes to be done by the Christian are His commands, precepts, desires, and pleasure.

**Verse 3.** *For I say, through the grace given unto me, to every man that is among you, not to think of himself more highly than he ought to think; but to think soberly, according as God hath dealt to every man the measure of faith.* Here Paul asserts his apostleship and Divine right to speak on behalf of the Lord. Jesus said to the apostles: *He that heareth you heareth me; and he that despiseth you despiseth me; and he that despiseth me despiseth him that sent me* (Lk. 10:16). This assured the apostles they had Divine authority to speak on behalf of the Lord—by

# Commentary on Romans

inspiration. Christ informed Ananias of the authority which was to be given unto Paul after he obeyed the Gospel.

> *And there was a certain disciple at Damascus, named Ananias; and to him said the Lord in a vision, Ananias. And he said, Behold, I am here, Lord. And the Lord said unto him, Arise, and go into the street which is called Straight, and inquire in the house of Judas for one called Saul, of Tarsus: for, behold, he prayeth, And hath seen in a vision a man named Ananias coming in, and putting his hand on him, that he might receive his sight. Then Ananias answered, Lord, I have heard by many of this man, how much evil he hath done to thy saints at Jerusalem: And here he hath authority from the chief priests to bind all that call on thy name. But the Lord said unto him, Go thy way: for he is a chosen vessel unto me, to bear my name before the Gentiles, and kings, and the children of Israel: For I will shew him how great things he must suffer for my name's sake* (Acts 9:10-16).

Paul charged brethren in the church at Corinth, who were endowed with the gift of the discerning of spirits, to put his apostleship to the test—that is, to use their spiritual gift to either confirm or denounce his inspired apostolic authority. Paul insisted: *If any man think himself to be a prophet, or spiritual, let him acknowledge that the things that I write unto you are the commandments of the Lord* (I Cor. 14:37). We supply these comments in light of the fact there are countless folks who deny the apostleship of Paul, thus excluding all his epistles from the New Testament. Not a few so-called *saints* have also tethered themselves to this evil.

The phrase, *for I say*, is an apostolic one, showing the saints of the church of Rome that Paul was indeed authorized to speak on behalf of the Lord. This is an essential matter to consider, for in verses 6-8 the apostle speaks of some of the spiritual gifts with which some in the church at Rome were endowed. Paul confirmed his authority saying, *through the grace given unto me*, meaning he spoke by inspiration.

# Commentary on Romans

Paul often found it necessary to defend his apostleship. To the church of Ephesus Paul wrote; *Unto me, who am less than the least of all saints, is this grace given, that I should preach among the Gentiles the unsearchable riches of Christ* (Eph. 3:8).

Near the close of this Roman epistle, Paul said: *Nevertheless, brethren, I have written the more boldly unto you in some sort, as putting you in mind, because of the grace that is given to me of God* (Rom. 15:15). Also, to the church of Corinth, Paul wrote: *According to the grace of God which is given unto me, as a wise masterbuilder, I have laid the foundation, and another buildeth thereon. But let every man take heed how he buildeth thereupon* (I Cor. 3:10).

We recall from chapter 11 Paul's chiding of both the Jews and the Gentiles because of the spirit of haughtiness which had arisen amongst them. The Jews were the natural branches which were cut off, which resulted in the grafting in of the Gentiles. The Jews contended (because they were Jews) they were in fact accepted by God on that ground alone. The Gentiles were subject to the same haughtiness by their having been awarded the opportunity to obey the Gospel. Because of such dangers, Paul wrote *to every man that is among you,* meaning Jew and Gentile. They were *not to think of himself more highly than he ought to think.* The phrase *more highly* means "to overly esteem one's self, to *be vain, or arrogant."*

Instead of thinking more highly than they ought to of themselves, they were *to think* soberly, which requires one "to be of sound mind, to be in one's right mind, to exercise self-control, to put a moderate estimate upon one's self, think of one's self soberly, and to curb one's passions." Neither Jews nor Gentiles were to be as Theudas who went about *boasting himself to be somebody* (Acts 5:36).

To the phrase, *according as God hath dealt to every man the measure of faith,* many Calvinists have tethered themselves. Calvinists assert God has measured out to each one of the *"elect"* a degree of faith, each one's measure or portion of faith being different. To some men God awards more, to others less.

# Commentary on Romans

*The measure of faith* under consideration here has reference to the spiritual gifts Paul identified in verses 6-8. The Lord *measured* spiritual gifts unto whom He willed. However, the spiritual gifts *measured* unto the recipients thereof required both the prayer of an apostle and the laying on of their hands.

> *Now when the apostles which were at Jerusalem heard that Samaria had received the word of God, they sent unto them Peter and John: Who, when they were come down, prayed for them, that they might receive the Holy Ghost: (For as yet he was fallen upon none of them: only they were baptized in the name of the Lord Jesus.) Then laid they their hands on them, and they received the Holy Ghost. And when Simon saw that through laying on of the apostles' hands the Holy Ghost was given, he offered them money* (Acts 8:14-18).

The word *dealt* means "to divide, to separate into parts, cut into pieces, to distribute a thing among people, to bestow or to impart upon one. The purpose of such a dividing or imparting is clarified in the following verse.

**Verse 4.** *For as we have many members in one body, and all members have not the same office.* The church does indeed have many members, but Paul's intent here is to emphasize that both Jews and Gentiles make up the one body of the church. In *one body* they both serve the Lord and the church of which they are part. *For ye are all the children of God by faith in Christ Jesus. For as many of you as have been baptized into Christ have put on Christ. There is neither Jew nor Greek, there is neither bond nor free, there is neither male nor female: for ye are all one in Christ Jesus* (Gal. 3:26-28). In the Lord's church, pedigree, heritage, gender, education, affluence, or status is of no value.

Paul used the phrase *one body* to first emphasize unity among the saints and, second, the oneness of the church. The Jews and Gentiles were to be unified in one and only *one body.* This *one body* is the Lord's church. *And hath put all things under his feet, and gave him to be the head over all things to the church, which is his body, the fullness of him that filleth all in all* (Eph. 1:

# Commentary on Romans

22-23). *There is one body, and one Spirit, even as ye are called in one hope of your calling* (Eph. 4:4). *And he is the head of the body, the church: who is the beginning, the firstborn from the dead; that in all things he might have the preeminence* (Col. 1:18).

*And all members have not the same office.* The word *office* refers to the doing of a thing. The word is feminine which should instill in the Christian the gender of the Lord's church. The Lord's church is His bride, and she must be about her proper business. While the context of Paul's narrative refers to the spiritual gifts with which some of the early church possessed the principle may be applied to the use of one's talents. Not everyone bears the same talents or skills of another. Some may bear similar talents, others different talents. Some may have the talent to lead singing while others do not. One may be talented in the realm of teaching or other needed things, but every one has the ability to serve in some *office.* There is no option in the Lord's church to do nothing.

**Verse 5.** *So we, being many, are one body in Christ, and every one members one of another.* The word *so* equates to *even so* or, better said, *even though.* This verse is conclusive to the previous one. Even as we are numerous in our members we are all part of one body—the body of Christ—His church. Even though we are of one body, we serve as individuals. We are to work in unity, unison, and complete harmony serving the Lord. As members in the Lord's church, we must also serve one another. The spiritual gifts enjoyed by many of the early church were for the edification on one another. Paul was troubled with the same difficulties in the church at Corinth. He laments:

> *Now there are diversities of gifts, but the same Spirit. And there are differences of administrations, but the same Lord. And there are diversities of operations, but it is the same God which worketh all in all. But the manifestation of the Spirit is given to every man to profit withal. For to one is given by the Spirit the word of wisdom; to another the word of knowledge by the same Spirit; To another faith by the same Spirit; to another the gifts of healing by the same Spirit; To*

# Commentary on Romans

*another the working of miracles; to another prophecy; to another discerning of spirits; to another divers kinds of tongues; to another the interpretation of tongues: But all these worketh that one and the selfsame Spirit, dividing to every man severally as he will. For as the body is one, and hath many members, and all the members of that one body, being many, are one body: so also is Christ* (I Cor. 12:4-12).

As all Christians are one body in Christ, and members one of another, no member should think himself to be above another. The word "office" in verse 4 refers to function. Each member of the body of Christ has an office, a function, just as does each member of our own body, and is an essential part of the body. It is a sobering thought. Paul dwells on this same illustration in greater length in 1 Cor. 12:12-27[71][sic].

**Verses 6-8.** *Having then gifts differing according to the grace that is given to us, whether prophecy, let us prophesy according to the proportion of faith; Or ministry, let us wait on our ministering: or he that teacheth, on teaching; Or he that exhorteth, on exhortation: he that giveth, let him do it with simplicity; he that ruleth, with diligence; he that sheweth mercy, with cheerfulness.*

The age of spiritual gifts ended in AD 70, as prophesied in Daniel 9:24-27 and Zechariah 13:1-7, and confirmed by Paul in I Corinthians 13:8-10. It is best to recall Paul is addressing both Jewish and Gentile converts here. The early church was in need of spiritual (miraculous) gifts in the first century because Divine Revelation was not then completed. Once inspiration completed, the work of revealing God's Word, the miraculous age ended as instantly as it began.

It has long been argued the miraculous age ended when the last living individual who was endowed with a miraculous gift died. Strong opposition is taken against this assertion. First, there is no evidence to prove this position, either internally or externally.

Second, brethren fail to realize the miraculous age of the New

---
[71] Robertson L. Whiteside.

# Commentary on Romans

Testament began instantly when deemed necessary by the Holy Spirit. There was a period of about four hundred years between the days of Malachi and the time when Christ was born. There were no inspired prophets during that time. Such being the case, it is needful to remind the reader once the New Testament era began, the Holy Spirit once again activated both men and women with miraculous endowments.

Before the birth of Christ, we read of only, Zechariah, Elizabeth, and Mary speaking by inspiration, revealing matters about both John the baptizer and the Lord. Christ was born in the year 1. The year Christ was born the Holy Spirit endowed other men and women (Simeon and Anna) to speak prophetically about Jesus.

Why do men, who regard the Bible as truth, have no trouble understanding that the Holy Spirit suddenly **began** to endow men and women with inspired revelation but have great difficulty realizing that just as suddenly He **ended** the age of miracles and inspiration as quickly as He started it? *The age of miracles ended as instantly as it began.* There is not one element of evidence to indicate otherwise.

The inspiration of the apostles began instantly, and it ended instantly, as did all spiritual endowments. All miracles and inspiration ended in AD 70. Why folks accept the instant beginning of the miraculous but fail to accept the end (the cessation of the miraculous) is amazing.

Further, it is good to recall the audience of the apostle here and why he finds it necessary to address the matter at hand. The Jews and Gentiles in the church at Rome were at odds one with the other, and the apostle was working toward the unity needed within the congregation there. Both Jewish and Gentile converts were endowed with spiritual (miraculous) gifts, as is observed in these verses. Paul instructed both Jewish and Gentile converts to use those gifts for the betterment of the congregation. As the congregation of Rome grew it became needful to have additional spiritual gifts. This explains why, in part, Paul returned to the congregations he established during his missionary journeys. It also explains why he wished to pass through Rome on his intended journey to Spain. He had told them: *For I long to see*

# Commentary on Romans

*you, that I may impart unto you some spiritual gift, to the end ye may be established* (Rom. 1:11).

Paul identifies seven spiritual gifts possessed by the church at Rome. The list is not inclusive of all spiritual gifts given by the laying on of the apostles' hands, but it is inclusive of the ones possessed in Rome (Acts 8:18). Paul encouraged brethren in Rome to use their spiritual gifts as they were instructed.

The first gift identified by the apostle is the gift of prophecy. The word *prophecy* means "to give a discourse emanating from Divine inspiration, declaring the purpose of God, whether by reproving and admonishing the wicked, comforting the afflicted, or revealing things hidden. It also includes the foretelling of future events, but is not at all restricted to it.

Next, the gift of ministry mentioned. Its definition includes "the ministration of those who render to others Christian affections—especially those who help meet the needs of others by the collection of or the distribution of charities."

Teaching was among the spiritual gifts possessed by some of the Roman saints. The word means "to teach by inspiration, to hold discourse with others in order to instruct them, to deliver inspired didactic discourses and discharge the office of a teacher, conduct one's self as a teacher."

Paul then lists the gift of exhortation, which involves being able "to admonish, to beg, entreat, beseech, to strive, to appease by entreaty, to console, to encourage and strengthen by consolation, to comfort by inspiration." The early church needed such exhortation because early church members were lacking in knowledge of that in which they needed exhortation.

The gift of giving follows exhortation, but why would the early church need an inspired gift of giving? Consider, under the Old Laws of the Patriarchal and Mosaical dispensations, giving was most often the offering of animal sacrifices. There were monetary offerings, but these were most often reserved for the building and maintenance of the physical structures of the tabernacle and temples. Animal sacrifices offered were used, for the most

# Commentary on Romans

part, to supply sustenance for the priests. Under the New Law of Christ animal sacrifices were no longer offered. The church, therefore, needed direction and instruction regarding monetary giving. Those who were endowed with this gift could then instruct others in proper giving under the New Law of Christ.

The gift of ruling is applicable to the leadership—the elders of a congregation. The early church needed inspired elders to oversee the flock of God. Consider Paul's admonition to the elders of the church at Ephesus. Luke recorded Paul's instruction to them and reminded them they were to *take heed therefore unto yourselves, and to all the flock, over the which the Holy Ghost hath made you overseers, to feed the church of God, which he hath purchased with his own blood* (Acts 20:28). In the church at Jerusalem the oversight was in the hands of the apostles, but where congregations existed in which no apostles were present, inspired elders were necessary. *Now when the apostles which were at Jerusalem heard that Samaria had received the word of God, they sent unto them Peter and John* (Acts 8:14).

The last spiritual gift listed is the gift of mercy. Why would mercy be a needed spiritual gift in the early church? We note mercy means to have mercy on, to help one afflicted or seeking aid, to help the afflicted, to bring help to the wretched. However, the act of the mercy extended here was by Divine guidance. There were times in the early church it would be especially needful given the attitude many of the Jewish converts had toward the Gentile converts. The reverse was also true. With the inspired gift of mercy there was no difficulty in deciphering situations which required such mercy.

Each spiritual gift listed in these verses has attached an emotional involvement required by the possessor of the respective gift. The gift of prophecy must be exercised proportionally. Overbearing brethren are detrimental to the Lord's church. Peter warned of such elders who would perhaps be unruly *lords over God's heritage* (I Pet. 5:3).

Elders are pastors of a local congregation. They are also identified as bishops, shepherd, presbyters. These words are always used in the plural form. No one pastor, elder, bishop, shepherd,

# Commentary on Romans

or presbyter was ever appointed over any one congregation. The denominational world, however, has deemed it fitting to appoint a *pastor* over their local congregations, which is a direct violation of Scripture. For the qualifications of pastors, elders, bishops, or presbyters; see I Timothy 3:1-7 and Titus 1:5-11. In I Peter 5:1 and 13, Peter stated he was one of the elders of the local congregation of Babylon. We set forth these matters for there are some in the Lord's church who have adopted the doctrine of having one individual assigned as the *pastor* of their local congregation. Some have even assigned to themselves the title of the *parson*. The word pastor, in its strongest definition literally means "one who is an elder of a local congregation who also serves as the local evangelist." Again, no congregation may have one *pastor,* elder, bishop, presbyter, or shepherd. There must always be a plurality of men appointed to the office.

The gift of ministering required a *waiting on*. *Waiting on* means "to do so instrumentality. The one endowed with the gift of ministering was to serve as the instrument by and through whom the service was to be executed."

The inspired teacher was to serve not simply as a teacher, but a teacher of sound doctrine, as the word is defined. Today saints and elders must *be able by sound doctrine both to exhort and to convince the gainsayers* (Titus 1:9).

The gift of exhortation was to be executed by much entreaty—begging. Begging men to obey God is not a foolish activity.

Giving was to be done in simplicity. *Simplicity* means "singleness of mind, sincerity of heart, mental honesty. It must be a virtue free from hypocrisy, not self seeking, openness of heart, manifesting itself by generosity." Consider Ananias and Sapphira: *But a certain man named Ananias, with Sapphira his wife, sold a possession, And kept back part of the price, his wife also being privy to it, and brought a certain part, and laid it at the apostles' feet. But Peter said, Ananias, why hath Satan filled thine heart to lie to the Holy Ghost, and to keep back part of the price of the land? Whiles it remained, was it not thine own? and after it was sold, was it not in thine own power? why hast thou conceived this thing in thine heart? thou hast not lied unto men,*

# Commentary on Romans

*but unto God* (Acts 5:1-4).

Ruling was to be done with eagerness and earnestness, to accomplish the desired goal. Elders of the church today do best whey follow suit.

Mercy is to be "executed with and from a cheerful heart, in readiness of mind, goodly zeal of spirit, and strong eagerness." Saints do well to eagerly extend mercy where it is warranted.

## Romans 12:9-21

*9 Let love be without dissimulation. Abhor that which is evil; cleave to that which is good. 10 Be kindly affectioned one to another with brotherly love; in honour preferring one another; 11 Not slothful in business; fervent in spirit; serving the Lord; 12 Rejoicing in hope; patient in tribulation; continuing instant in prayer; 13 Distributing to the necessity of saints; given to hospitality. 14 Bless them which persecute you: bless, and curse not. 15 Rejoice with them that do rejoice, and weep with them that weep. 16 Be of the same mind one toward another. Mind not high things, but condescend to men of low estate. Be not wise in your own conceits. 17 Recompense to no man evil for evil. Provide things honest in the sight of all men. 18 If it be possible, as much as lieth in you, live peaceably with all men. 19 Dearly beloved, avenge not yourselves, but rather give place unto wrath: for it is written, Vengeance is mine; I will repay, saith the Lord. 20 Therefore if thine enemy hunger, feed him; if he thirst, give him drink: for in so doing thou shalt heap coals of fire on his head. 21 Be not overcome of evil, but overcome evil with good.*

**Verse 9.** *Let love be without dissimulation. Abhor that which is evil; cleave to that which is good.* Three commands are set forth this verse. Paul keeps his attention toward both Jews and Gentiles. These commands are universally applicable to the Lord's church.

## Commentary on Romans

First, we have the order of *love* listed. This must be a brotherly love of strong affection, wishing for the best for one's fellow man, especially the brethren. It must be a love of benevolence and warm affection. *Agape*, in the original, is the same love of which Christ spake and other writers of the New Testament echoed:

> For God so loved the world, that he gave his only begotten Son, that whosoever believeth in him should not perish, but have everlasting life (Jno. 3:16).

> A new commandment I give unto you, That ye love one another; as I have loved you, that ye also love one another. By this shall all men know that ye are my disciples, if ye have love one to another (Jno. 13:34-35).

> This is my commandment, That ye love one another, as I have loved you (Jno. 15:12).

> These things I command you, that ye love one another (Jno. 15:17).

> Owe no man any thing, but to love one another: for he that loveth another hath fulfilled the law (Rom. 13:8).

> For, brethren, ye have been called unto liberty; only use not liberty for an occasion to the flesh, but by love serve one another (Gal. 5:13).

> With all lowliness and meekness, with longsuffering, forbearing one another in love (Eph. 4:2).

> And the Lord make you to increase and abound in love one toward another, and toward all men, even as we do toward you (I Thes. 3:12).

> But as touching brotherly love ye need not that I write unto you: for ye yourselves are taught of God to love one another (I Thes. 4:9).

> And let us consider one another to provoke unto love and to good works (Heb. 10:24).

# Commentary on Romans

*Seeing ye have purified your souls in obeying the truth through the Spirit unto unfeigned love of the brethren, see that ye love one another with a pure heart fervently* (I Pet. 1:22).

*Finally, be ye all of one mind, having compassion one of another, love as brethren, be pitiful, be courteous* (I Pet. 3:8).

*Honor all men. Love the brotherhood. Fear God. Honor the king* (I Pet. 2:17).

*For this is the message that ye heard from the beginning, that we should love one another* (I Jno. 3:11).

*And this is his commandment, That we should believe on the name of his Son Jesus Christ, and love one another, as he gave us commandment* (I Jno. 3:23).

*Beloved, let us love one another: for love is of God; and every one that loveth is born of God, and knoweth God* (I Jno. 4:7).

*Beloved, if God so loved us, we ought also to love one another. No man hath seen God at any time. If we love one another, God dwelleth in us, and his love is perfected in us* (I Jno. 4:11-12).

*And now I beseech thee, lady, not as though I wrote a new commandment unto thee, but that which we had from the beginning, that we love one another* (II Jno. 5).

The word *dissimulation* is defined as "unfeigned, undisguised, sincere and without hypocrisy. Love tailored with insincerity is hypocrisy." Saints are commanded to love the brethren. *For scarcely for a righteous man will one die: yet peradventure for a good man some would even dare to die* (Rom. 5:7). *Hereby perceive we the love of God, because he laid down his life for us: and we ought to lay down our lives for the brethren* (I Jno. 3:16). Second is the command to *abhor that which is evil.* The word

# Commentary on Romans

*abhor* is strong and means "to have an intense dislike for, to have a horror of something, a phobia about a thing or person, and a strong and deep hated for." Saints must actively *abhor* all that is evil. The Christian must *abstain from all appearance of evil* (I Thes. 5:22). Appearance is "the external or outward appearance, a form, figure, or shape." No matter in which form evil which appears, it is a matter from which saints abstain.

Barnes claims: "The word *evil* has reference to malice, or unkindness, rather than to evil in general. The apostle is exhorting love, and kindness; to all people."[72] Clarke adds: "Hate sin as you would hate that hell to which it leads."[73] Evil must be repulsive to every saint, that repulsion must not be concealed, but outwardly expressed. Paul wrote concerning evil works: *And have no fellowship with the unfruitful works of darkness, but rather reprove them* (Eph. 5:11). Abhorrence of evil requires a strong exposing of it, not mere objection.

Paul set forth two negatives in this verse, but now issues the antithetical positive to *cleave to that which is good.* The word *cleave* means "to glue together, cement, fasten together, to join or fasten firmly together, to join one's self securely to." The word is a verb which demands a continuous positive aggressive action and character. Matthew Henry commented:

> *Abhor that which is evil, cleave to that which is good.* God hath shown us what is good: these Christian duties are enjoined; and that is evil which is opposite to them. Now observe, [1.] We must not only not do evil, but we must *abhor that which is evil.* We must hate sin with an utter and irreconcilable hatred, have an antipathy to it as the worst of evils, contrary to our new nature, and to our true interest—hating all the appearances of sin, even the garment spotted with the flesh. [2.] We must not only do that which is good, but we must cleave to it. It denotes a deliberate choice of, a sincere affection for, and a constant perseverance in, that which is good. "So cleave to it as not to be allured nor affrighted from it, cleave *to him that is good,* even

---

[72] Albert Barnes.

[73] Adam Clarke.

# Commentary on Romans

to the Lord (Act 11:23), with a dependence and acquiescence." It is subjoined to the precept of brotherly love, as directive of it; we must love our brethren, but not love them so much as for their sakes to commit any sin, or omit any duty; not think the better of any sin for the sake of the person that commits it, but forsake all the friends in the world, to cleave to God and duty[74] [sic].

Often, saints leave that which is good rather than cleave to it. What is *good*? *Good* is "that which is of great constitution or nature, that which is useful, pleasant, agreeable, joyful, happy, excellent, distinguished as upright, and honorable to God."

**Verse 10.** *Be kindly affectioned one to another with brotherly love; in honour preferring one another.* "The word *affectioned* used here occurs no where else in the New Testament. It properly denotes tender affection, such as what subsists between parents and children; and it means that Christians should have similar feelings toward each other, as belonging to the same family, and as united in the same principles and interests"[75] [sic].

The words, *kindly affectioned*, are one in the original which means the reciprocal tenderness of parents and children. As the parent loves the child, so the child loves the parent. As the parent tends to the needs of the child, so the child depends upon the parent. As a babe, the child is unaware of his dependency, but as the child grows in understanding he begins to grasp his need for the parent. As brethren, we must grow in our understanding of the need we have one for another. Though we are many, we are *one body in Christ and every one members one of another* (Rom. 12:5). As members of Christ and His church *of whom the whole family in heaven and earth is named*, saints must conduct themselves accordingly (Eph. 3:15).

**Verse 11.** *Not slothful in business; fervent in spirit; serving the Lord.* In this verse three matters are enjoined upon the Christian, just as in verse nine. First, the Christian is warned of slothfulness. Second, the exhortation of fervency is enjoined last;

---
[74] Matthew Henry.
[75] Albert Barnes.

# Commentary on Romans

serving the Lord is mandatory.

The charge is that we be *not slothful in business.* Slothfulness is "to be sluggish, backward, indolent, irksome or tardy in one's duties. The word also refers to those who are slow, idle, and destitute of promptness of mind and activity"[76] [sic]. The Lord has reserved a space for those who don slothfulness.

> *Then he which had received the one talent came and said, Lord, I knew thee that thou art an hard man, reaping where thou hast not sown, and gathering where thou hast not strawed: And I was afraid, and went and hid thy talent in the earth: lo, there thou hast that is thine. His lord answered and said unto him, Thou wicked and slothful servant, thou knewest that I reap where I sowed not, and gather where I have not strawed: Thou oughtest therefore to have put my money to the exchangers, and then at my coming I should have received mine own with usury. Take therefore the talent from him, and give it unto him which hath ten talents. For unto every one that hath shall be given, and he shall have abundance: but from him that hath not shall be taken away even that which he hath. And cast ye the unprofitable servant into outer darkness: there shall be weeping and gnashing of teeth* (Matt. 25:24-30).

Solomon warned against inventing excuses for slothfulness:

> *The hand of the diligent shall bear rule: but the slothful shall be under tribute* (Pro. 12:24).

> *The slothful man roasteth not that which he took in hunting: but the substance of a diligent man is precious* (Pro. 12:27).

> *The way of the slothful man is as an hedge of thorns: but the way of the righteous is made plain* (Pro. 15:19).

> *He also that is slothful in his work is brother to him that*

---
[76] Albert Barnes.

# Commentary on Romans

*is a great waster* (Pro. 18:9).

*A slothful man hideth his hand in his bosom, and will not so much as bring it to his mouth again* (Pro. 19:24).

*The desire of the slothful killeth him; for his hands refuse to labour* (Pro. 21:25).

*The slothful man saith, There is a lion without, I shall be slain in the streets* (Pro. 22:13).

*I went by the field of the slothful, and by the vineyard of the man void of understanding* (Pro. 24:30).

*The slothful man saith, There is a lion in the way; a lion is in the streets* (Pro. 26:13).

*As the door turneth upon his hinges, so doth the slothful upon his bed* (Pro. 26:14).

*The slothful hideth his hand in his bosom; it grieveth him to bring it again to his mouth* (Pro. 26:15).

Being busy with the things of the world is detrimental; busying oneself in the lord's vineyard serves a Christian best.

*And a certain man of the sons of the prophets said unto his neighbour in the word of the Lord, Smite me, I pray thee. And the man refused to smite him. Then said he unto him, Because thou hast not obeyed the voice of the Lord, behold, as soon as thou art departed from me, a lion shall slay thee. And as soon as he was departed from him, a lion found him, and slew him. Then he found another man, and said, Smite me, I pray thee. And the man smote him, so that in smiting he wounded him. So the prophet departed, and waited for the king by the way, and disguised himself with ashes upon his face. And as the king passed by, he cried unto the king: and he said, Thy servant went out into the midst of the battle; and, behold, a man turned aside, and brought a man unto me, and said, Keep this*

# Commentary on Romans

> *man: if by any means he be missing, then shall thy life be for his life, or else thou shalt pay a talent of silver. And as thy servant was busy here and there, he was gone. And the king of Israel said unto him, So shall thy judgment be; thyself hast decided it. And he hasted, and took the ashes away from his face; and the king of Israel discerned him that he was of the prophets. And he said unto him, Thus saith the Lord, Because thou hast let go out of thy hand a man whom I appointed to utter destruction, therefore thy life shall go for his life, and thy people for his people. And the king of Israel went to his house heavy and displeased, and came to Samaria* (I Kings 20:35-43).

While one may busy himself in many matters, he may often busy himself too much. As the Lord busied Himself in the work of His Father, so must the Christian busy himself in the same. The Lord said, *I must be about my Father's business* (Lk. 2:49). Those who insist they are too busy to involve themselves in the Lord's work are indeed too busy! It is an ill thing to be too busy regarding our Father's business. None in the Lord's church are exempt from serving as profitable laborers. The Lord declared he would cast *the unprofitable servant into outer darkness: there shall be weeping and gnashing of teeth* (Matt. 25:30).

> *But what think ye? A certain man had two sons; and he came to the first, and said, Son, go work to day in my vineyard. He answered and said, I will not: but afterward he repented, and went. And he came to the second, and said likewise. And he answered and said, I go, sir: and went not* (Matt. 21:28-30).

> *And it came to pass, that, as they went in the way, a certain man said unto him, Lord, I will follow thee whithersoever thou goest. And Jesus said unto him, Foxes have holes, and birds of the air have nests; but the Son of man hath not where to lay his head. And he said unto another, Follow me. But he said, Lord, suffer me first to go and bury my father. Jesus said unto him, Let the dead bury their dead: but go thou and preach the kingdom of God. And another also said, Lord, I will*

# Commentary on Romans

*follow thee; but let me first go bid them farewell, which are at home at my house. And Jesus said unto him, No man, having put his hand to the plough, and looking back, is fit for the kingdom of God* (Lk. 9:57-62).

Those who have things to do before doing the Lord's work have placed the things of the world above the Lord and His church. Such brethren have more regard for their treasures than for the brethren, the church, and the Lord. They wish more for possessions or pleasures than for salvation for themselves or for those yet lost. Entertainment ranks higher than evangelism. Slothfulness is a great evil and does much harm to the soul of the saint.

Being *fervent in spirit* follows slothfulness. Fervency of spirit is the antithesis of slothfulness. Being fervent is to be of a seething attitude, fiery in action, and heated in conduct. Saints are to work fervently in the best activities. The word *spirit* is disposition or influence which fills and governs the soul.

Jeremiah, the prophet of old, possessed fervency of spirit even though he felt compelled to cease his preaching. He suffered much at the hands of the disobedient Israelites of his day which caused him to cry: *For since I spake, I cried out, I cried violence and spoil; because the word of the Lord was made a reproach unto me, and a derision, daily. Then I said, I will not make mention of him, nor speak any more in his name. But his word was in mine heart as a burning fire shut up in my bones, and I was weary with forbearing, and I could not stay* (Jer. 20:8-9).

*Jesus, who gave himself for us, that he might redeem us from all iniquity, and purify unto himself a peculiar people, zealous of good works* deserves fervency of spirit from every saint (Tit. 2:14). How can one offer little unto the Lord and expect much? How can saints expect to run with the world and expect blessings of righteousness? Saints must have strong passions, desires, wills, and a fiery zeal for the church and the work thereof. Less is not accepted by the Lord.

Christians must be busy *serving the Lord.* Service to the Lord requires being a slave. Being a slave to the Lord means to serve willfully, do service, to obey, and cheerfully submit. A servant of

# Commentary on Romans

the Lord surrenders himself to the Lord's will. Servants of Christ are those whose service is used in extending and advancing His cause. As servants of Christ we must always consider His eyes are upon us and we are accountable to Him for all we do, be it in word or in deed. Paul wrote: *And whatsoever ye do in word or deed, do all in the name of the Lord Jesus, giving thanks to God and the Father by him* (Col. 3:17). *And whatsoever ye do, do it heartily, as to the Lord, and not unto men* (Col. 3:23).

Weak-handed, weak-headed, and weak-hearted Christians will stand before the Lord empty-handed, empty-headed, and empty-hearted. *Watch ye, stand fast in the faith, quit you like men, be strong* (I Cor. 16:13).

**Verse 12.** *Rejoicing in hope; patient in tribulation; continuing instant in prayer.* The call to rejoice in hope is here issued. In hope of what? *In hope of eternal life, which God, that cannot lie, promised before the world began* (Titus 1:2). *That being justified by his grace, we should be made heirs according to the hope of eternal life* (Titus 3:7). *We are saved by hope: but hope that is seen is not hope: for what a man seeth, why doth he yet hope for* (Rom. 8:24). Without hope there is no salvation. "The Christian must be industrious in the Lord's service; otherwise he has no hope. Hope sustains men in all their undertakings; and to the Christian, hope of future bliss brings joy and happiness even in his tribulations and difficulties."[77]

Those of the world are without hope. Paul wrote: *That at that time ye were without Christ, being aliens from the commonwealth of Israel, and strangers from the covenants of promise, having no hope, and without God in the world* (Eph. 2:12). Hope is an often-discussed matter, which is found in 121 verses of Scripture and used 130 times. Hope must dwell in every saint. As Christians, Peter commanded us to *sanctify the Lord God in your hearts: and be ready always to give an answer to every man that asketh you a reason of the hope that is in you with meekness and fear* (I Pet. 3:15).

Christ is the hope of the world. He is the hope of salvation and the hope of all who would seek eternal life. Without Christ, hope

---
[77] By Robertson L. Whiteside.

# Commentary on Romans

is nonexistent; *For the hope which is laid up for you in heaven, whereof ye heard before in the word of the truth of the gospel* (Col. 1:5). *if ye continue in the faith grounded and settled, and be not moved away from the hope of the gospel, which ye have heard, and which was preached to every creature which is under heaven; whereof I Paul am made a minister* (Col. 1:23).

Saints must also be *patient in tribulation*. *Patience* means "to remain, to tarry behind, to abide, not recede or flee, to preserve, and when under misfortunes and trials hold fast to one's faith in Christ, to endure, bear bravely and calmly in the face of ill treatments." When Jeremiah became weary in his service to God, the Lord asked him; *If thou hast run with the footmen, and they have wearied thee, then how canst thou contend with horses? and if in the land of peace, wherein thou trustedst, they wearied thee, then how wilt thou do in the swelling of Jordan* (Jer. 12:5)? Often saints feel as if things could be no worse, but things often degenerate to even lower states of despair.

*Tribulation* means "pressing, pressing together, pressure, oppression, affliction, distress, straits or difficulties." In all of these things the Christian is to remain patient. None of these should provoke one to separate himself from the Lord. *Tribulations* do not leave us without comfort. Paul wrote:

> *Blessed be God, even the Father of our Lord Jesus Christ, the Father of mercies, and the God of all comfort; Who comforteth us in all our tribulation, that we may be able to comfort them which are in any trouble, by the comfort wherewith we ourselves are comforted of God. For as the sufferings of Christ abound in us, so our consolation also aboundeth by Christ. And whether we be afflicted, it is for your consolation and salvation, which is effectual in the enduring of the same sufferings which we also suffer: or whether we be comforted, it is for your consolation and salvation. And our hope of you is steadfast, knowing, that as ye are partakers of the sufferings, so shall ye be also of the consolation* (II Cor. 1:3-7).

Further, James declared: "*My brethren, count it all joy when ye*

# Commentary on Romans

*fall into divers temptations; Knowing this, that the trying of your faith worketh patience. But let patience have her perfect work, that ye may be perfect and entire, wanting nothing"* (Jas. 1:2-4).

> *Who shall separate us from the love of Christ? shall tribulation, or distress, or persecution, or famine, or nakedness, or peril, or sword? As it is written, For thy sake we are killed all the day long; we are accounted as sheep for the slaughter. Nay, in all these things we are more than conquerors through him that loved us. For I am persuaded, that neither death, nor life, nor angels, nor principalities, nor powers, nor things present, nor things to come, Nor height, nor depth, nor any other creature, shall be able to separate us from the love of God, which is in Christ Jesus our Lord* (Rom. 8:35-39).

**Verse 13.** *Distributing to the necessity of saints; given to hospitality.* Compulsion again drives us to remind the reader that the apostle is addressing both Jewish and Gentile converts. We continue to press this issue because Paul did.

Divisiveness among the Jews and Gentiles in the early church was a matter which required much attention. We are aware of the Jews' disposition who contended that, because they were God's chosen race, their salvation was sealed. Paul continuously refuted that objection and relentlessly informed the Jews that, because of their rejection of Christ and His gospel, their conduct prompted the grafting in of the Gentiles as a wild olive branch. However, the Gentiles could not afford to become high-minded about the matter; Paul gave them strong warning.

This divisiveness between the Jews and Gentiles is also observed in other passages. Paul addressed this matter, saying:

> *For as we have many members in one body, and all members have not the same office: So we, being many, are one body in Christ, and every one members one of another* (Rom. 12:4-5).

> *Now I beseech you, brethren, by the name of our Lord*

# Commentary on Romans

> *Jesus Christ, that ye all speak the same thing, and that there be no divisions among you; but that ye be perfectly joined together in the same mind and in the same judgment. For it hath been declared unto me of you, my brethren, by them which are of the house of Chloe, that there are contentions among you* (I Cor. 1:10-11).

> *That there should be no schism in the body; but that the members should have the same care one for another* (I Cor. 12:25).

On the phrase, *distributing to the necessity of saints,* there is much to consider. The Lord spoke of famines which would precede the days of the destruction of Jerusalem.

> *And Jesus answered and said unto them, Take heed that no man deceive you. For many shall come in my name, saying, I am Christ; and shall deceive many. And ye shall hear of wars and rumors of wars: see that ye be not troubled: for all these things must come to pass, but the end is not yet. For nation shall rise against nation, and kingdom against kingdom: and there shall be famines, and pestilences, and earthquakes, in divers places. All these are the beginning of sorrows* (Matt. 24:4-8).

Agabus prophesied of the famine which would soon arise in the days of the early church:

> *And in these days came prophets from Jerusalem unto Antioch. And there stood up one of them named Agabus, and signified by the Spirit that there should be great dearth throughout all the world: which came to pass in the days of Claudius Caesar. Then the disciples, every man according to his ability, determined to send relief unto the brethren which dwelt in Judaea: Which also they did, and sent it to the elders by the hands of Barnabas and Saul* (Acts 11:27-30).

Paul, being aware of the prophecy of Agabus, made great efforts

## Commentary on Romans

to gather funds to purchase substance for the stricken saints of Jerusalem. In this epistle Paul wrote:

> Whensoever I take my journey into Spain, I will come to you: for I trust to see you in my journey, and to be brought on my way thitherward by you, if first I be somewhat filled with your company. But now I go unto Jerusalem to minister unto the saints. For it hath pleased them of Macedonia and Achaia to make a certain contribution for the poor saints which are at Jerusalem. It hath pleased them verily; and their debtors they are. For if the Gentiles have been made partakers of their spiritual things, their duty is also to minister unto them in carnal things (Rom. 15:24-27).

Before Paul's second journey to Corinth, he reminded the saints to establish a treasury which he should receive from them and take to the saints of Jerusalem who were troubled by the famine then present. Paul wrote:

> Now concerning the collection for the saints, as I have given order to the churches of Galatia, even so do ye. Upon the first day of the week let every one of you lay by him in store, as God hath prospered him, that there be no gatherings when I come. And when I come, whomsoever ye shall approve by your letters, them will I send to bring your liberality unto Jerusalem (I Cor. 16:1-3).

Paul had given the same command to the churches of Galatia. In his second epistle to the Corinthians, Paul spoke highly of the churches of Macedonia for their abundant and generous giving on behalf of the saints affected by the famine in Jerusalem.

> Moreover, brethren, we do you to wit of the grace of God bestowed on the churches of Macedonia; How that in a great trial of affliction the abundance of their joy and their deep poverty abounded unto the riches of their liberality. For to their power, I bear record, yea, and beyond their power they were willing of themselves; Praying us with much entreaty that we would

# Commentary on Romans

*receive the gift, and take upon us the fellowship of the ministering to the saints. And this they did, not as we hoped, but first gave their own selves to the Lord, and unto us by the will of God. Insomuch that we desired Titus, that as he had begun, so he would also finish in you the same grace also* (II Cor. 8:1-6).

Distributing to the needs of the brethren is a duty enjoined upon every member of the Lord's church. Understanding the famines of which the Lord spoke as recorded in Matthew 24, one may better grasp Paul's comment to the church at Galatia: *As we have therefore opportunity, let us do good unto all men, especially unto them who are of the household of faith* (Gal. 6:10).

Paul instructed the saints at Rome to be *given to hospitality*. This was a very necessary command when so many Christians were being banished, persecuted, and martyred. The word *hospitality* is a verb which requires action. It must be furnished when it is sought. Christians are to seek opportunities of aiding those who stand in need. Barnes suggested:

> This expression means that they should readily and cheerfully entertain strangers. This is a duty which is frequently enjoined in the Scriptures, Heb 13:2, "Be not forgetful to entertain strangers, for thereby many have entertained angels unawares;" 1 Pe 4:9, "Use hospitality one to another without grudging." Paul makes this especially the duty of a Christian bishop; 1 Ti 3:2, "A bishop then must...be given to hospitality;" Tit 1:8. Hospitality is especially enjoined by the Saviour, and its exercise commanded; Mat 10:40, Mat 10:42, "He that receiveth you receiveth me, etc." The waver of hospitality is one of the charges which the Judge of mankind will allege against the wicked, and on which he will condemn them; Mat 25:43, "I was a stranger, and ye took me not in." It is especially commended to us by the example of Abraham Gen 18:1-8, and of Lot Gen 19:1-2, who thus received angels unawares[78] [sic].

---

[78] Albert Barnes.

# Commentary on Romans

Pursuing hospitality and the duty of entertaining strangers was a necessary virtue in the early church when famine was rampant. Persecutions against the early church resulted in saints being dragged from their homes, bound and reserved for persecution and martyrdom. Before his conversion, Paul himself was party so such evils against the church. *And Saul was consenting unto his death. And at that time there was a great persecution against the church which was at Jerusalem; and they were all scattered abroad throughout the regions of Judaea and Samaria, except the apostles. And devout men carried Stephen to his burial, and made great lamentation over him. As for Saul, he made havoc of the church, entering into every house, and haling men and women committed them to prison* (Acts 8:1-3).

**Verse 14.** *Bless them which persecute you: bless, and curse not.* Persecutions against the church are inevitable. Jesus said: *Blessed are ye, when men shall revile you, and persecute you, and shall say all manner of evil against you falsely, for my sake. Rejoice, and be exceeding glad: for great is your reward in heaven: for so persecuted they the prophets which were before you* (Matt. 5:11-12). "Persecutions are the common lot of Christians. 'Yea, and all that would live godly in Christ Jesus shall suffer persecution' (2 Tim. 3:12). It is living godly as a Christian that brings persecution. It is not personal enmity; it is enmity against Christ"[79] [sic].

The word *persecute* is broad in scope. It is defined as "to make, to run or flee, put to one to flight, drive one away, to run swiftly in order to catch a person or thing, to run after, to pursue in a hostile manner, to in any way whatsoever harass, trouble, or molest, to mistreat, to cause one to suffer." Saints not persecuted often lack in a good broadcasting of their Christian light.

The words *bless, and curse not* complete this verse. Blessings for the good of our foes must be called down on their behalf. The Lord said: *But I say unto you, Love your enemies, bless them that curse you, do good to them that hate you, and pray for them which despitefully use you, and persecute you* (Matt. 5:44). He further said: *Bless them that curse you, and pray for them which despitefully use you* (Lk. 6:28).

---
[79] Robertson L. Whiteside

# Commentary on Romans

"It is living godly as a Christian that brings persecution. It is not personal enmity; it is enmity against Christ. This should cause the Christian to pity the persecutor for his blind rage. The greatest blessing we can confer upon the persecutor is to lead him to be a Christian"[80] [sic].

The mandate to *bless and curse not* is forced by the imperative mood used by the apostle. The command is twofold—positive and negative in duty. The command is obligatory and a must; therefore, it should be executed with all diligence. Barnes says:

> Bless only; or continue to bless, however long or aggravated may be the injury. Do not be provoked to anger, or to cursing, by any injury, persecution, or reviling. This is one of the most severe and difficult duties of the Christian religion; and it is a duty which nothing else but religion will enable people to perform. To curse denotes properly to devote to destruction. Where there is power to do it, it implies the destruction of the object. Thus, the fig-tree that was cursed by the Saviour soon withered away: Mar 11:21. Thus, those whom God curses will be certainly destroyed; Mat 25:41. Where there is not power to do it, to curse implies the invoking of the aid of God to devote to destruction. Hence, it means to imprecate; to implore a curse from God to rest on others; to pray that God would destroy them. In a larger sense still, it means to abuse by reproachful words; to calumniate; or to express oneself in a violent, profane, and outrageous manner. In this passage it seems to have special reference to this"[81] [sic].

**Verse 15.** *Rejoice with them that do rejoice, and weep with them that weep.* Christians are to be empathetic and sympathetic with the brethren. Sharing gladness when the occasion calls for it or mourning when the need arises is always comforting.

"If a fellow-Christian has a righteous cause for rejoicing, we should rejoice with him. Too often we envy the good fortune of others. And we should enter into full sympathy with others in their

---

[80] Robertson L. Whiteside.

[81] Albert Barnes.

## Commentary on Romans

sorrows"[82] [sic]. Saints are to "take a lively interest in the prosperity of others. Let it be a matter of rejoicing to you when you hear of the health, prosperity, or happiness of any brother"[83] [sic]. "Christians should arduously labour after a compassionate or sympathizing mind. Let your heart feel for the distressed; enter into their sorrows, and bear a part of their burdens. It is a fact, attested by universal experience, that by sympathy a man may receive into his own affectionate feelings a measure of the distress of his friend, and that his friend does find himself relieved in the same proportion as the other has entered into his griefs"[84] [sic]. The picture of the phrase is better expressed as, rejoicing with the rejoicing, weeping with the weeping.

**Verse 16.** *Be of the same mind one toward another. Mind not high things, but condescend to men of low estate. Be not wise in your own conceits.* Passages abound in the Scriptures which promote unity and like-mindedness. David declared: *Behold, how good and how pleasant it is for brethren to dwell together in unity* (Psa. 133:1)!

Jesus prayed for like-mindedness and unity among the apostles and the saints. *Neither pray I for these alone, but for them also which shall believe on me through their word; That they all may be one; as thou, Father, art in me, and I in thee, that they also may be one in us: that the world may believe that thou hast sent me* (Jno. 17:20-21).

Paul constrained the brethren to dwell in unity. *Now the God of patience and consolation grant you to be like-minded one toward another according to Christ Jesus* (Rom. 15:5). He charged the church at Corinth to obtain and remain in unity. *Now I beseech you, brethren, by the name of our Lord Jesus Christ, that ye all speak the same thing, and that there be no divisions among you; but that ye be perfectly joined together in the same mind and in the same judgment* (I Cor. 1:10). The brethren of Philippi were enjoined unto it. *Let this mind be in you, which was also in Christ Jesus* (Phil. 2:5). There are numerous approaches to this verse, which Barnes demonstrates:

---

[82] Robertson L. Whiteside: 1945.

[83] Adam Clarke.

[84] Ibid.

## Commentary on Romans

This passage has been variously interpreted. "Enter into each other's circumstances, in order to see how you would yourself feel." Chrysostom. "Be agreed in your opinions and views." Stuart. "Be united or agreed with each other." Flatt; compare Phi 2:2; 2 Co 13:11. A literal translation of the Greek will give somewhat a different sense, but one evidently correct. "Think of, that is, regard, or seek after the same thing for each other; that is, what you regard or seek for yourself, seek also for your brethren. Do not have divided interests; do not be pursuing different ends and aims; do not indulge counter plans and purposes; and do not seek honors, offices, for yourself which you do not seek for your brethren, so that you may still regard yourselves as brethren on a level, and aim at the same object." The Syriac has well rendered the passage: "And what you think concerning yourselves, the same also think concerning your brethren; neither think with an elevated or ambitious mind, but accommodate yourselves to those who are of humbler condition;" compare 1 Pet. 3:8[85] [sic].

**Mind not high things** – Be not ambitious; affect nothing above your station; do not court the rich nor the powerful; do not pass by the poor man to pay your court to the great man; do not affect titles or worldly distinctions; much less sacrifice your conscience for them. The attachment to high things and high men is the vice of little, shallow minds. However, it argues one important fact, that such persons are conscious that they are of no worth and of no consequence in themselves, and they seek to render themselves observable and to gain a little credit by their endeavors to associate themselves with men of rank and fortune, and if possible to get into honorable employments; and, if this cannot be attained, they affect honorable Titles.[86] [sic].

James and others throughout the Bible have written:

---

[85] Albert Barnes.
[86] Ibid.

# Commentary on Romans

*My brethren, have not the faith of our Lord Jesus Christ, the Lord of glory, with respect of persons. For if there come unto your assembly a man with a gold ring, in goodly apparel, and there come in also a poor man in vile raiment; And ye have respect to him that weareth the gay clothing, and say unto him, Sit thou here in a good place; and say to the poor, Stand thou there, or sit here under my footstool: Are ye not then partial in yourselves, and are become judges of evil thoughts? Hearken, my beloved brethren, Hath not God chosen the poor of this world rich in faith, and heirs of the kingdom which he hath promised to them that love him? But ye have despised the poor. Do not rich men oppress you, and draw you before the judgment seats? Do not they blaspheme that worthy name by the which ye are called? If ye fulfill the royal law according to the scripture, Thou shalt love thy neighbour as thyself, ye do well: But if ye have respect to persons, ye commit sin, and are convinced of the law as transgressors* (Jas. 2:1-9).

*Be not wise in your own conceits. Woe unto them that are wise in their own eyes, and prudent in their own sight* (Isa. 5:21)!

*For if a man think himself to be something, when he is nothing, he deceiveth himself* (Gal. 6:3).

*Wherefore let him that thinketh he standeth take heed lest he fall* (I Cor. 10:12).

*Pride goeth before destruction, and an haughty spirit before a fall* (Pro. 16:18).

Both the Jews and Gentiles were in danger of this peril. The pride of the Jews in their heritage made them subject to this fall. The haughtiness of the Gentiles having been grafted into the olive tree put them in the same danger. Paul warns both of the dangers of ill attitudes and of conceit.

# Commentary on Romans

**Verse 17.** *Recompense to no man evil for evil. Provide things honest in the sight of all men.* This may be one of the most difficult precepts of Christianity, but the law of Christ on the subject is unyielding. It is a solemn demand made on all saints, and it must be obeyed. The world's philosophy toward those who have caused ill toward one is to *get even.*

Returning evil for evil settles nothing, but usually makes bad matters worse. Besides, to return evil for evil puts one in the class of evil doers. Spite work is of the devil. Even men of the world look upon retaliation as beneath the dignity of a gentleman, and therefore not honorable. "There is a common standard of honor which Christians must by no means ignore." When a Christian so far forgets himself as to violate the world's standard of honor, he loses his influence for good. And this does not mean that we must be men-pleasers. The Greek word for "take thought" means to pre-think—to think before you adopt a certain course of action. The Christian lowers himself in the estimation of men when he engages in things that the world thinks beneath the Christian profession; he also disobeys Paul's injunction[87] [sic].

*Provide things honest in the sight of all men.* The word rendered *provide* means "to think properly, rightly meditate beforehand. Make it a matter of previous thought, of settled plan, or design." This direction would make things a matter of principle and fixed purpose to do what is right; and not to leave it to the fluctuations of feeling or to the influence of excitement.

Not only is it the case things must be provided in honesty, but honest things must be provided. Ill-gotten gain is a sin from which saints must refrain. Extortion, embezzlement, gambling, theft, and like gains are detrimental to the soul. Paul wrote: *Providing for honest things, not only in the sight of the Lord, but also in the sight of men* (II Cor. 8:21).

The word *honest* refers to "things which are beautiful, chiefly good and morally acceptable, that which is valuable and virtu-

---
[87] Robertson L. Whiteside.

## Commentary on Romans

ous, better things, fair and good things, and worthy things." The Lord knows when things are obtained through devilish means. There are nearly one hundred passages of Scripture wherein "the eyes of the Lord" are given mention. Such being the case, it is best to provide honest things and do so honestly. The providing of things honest is for the benefit of a need for one's self and others. One does much harm to himself when things are provided through iniquity.

*In the sight of all men* is the charge issued by Paul. While God sees all, saints must also consider the eyes of men, both of the sinner and the saint, when making provisions for those in need. Jesus said, *Let your light so shine before men, that they may see your good works, and glorify your Father which is in heaven* (Matt. 5:16).

It is before *men* saints must let their light shine. The word *they* refers to mankind, specifically, those of the world. The glorification of the Father here is often understood as a glorification awarded to the Father by the good works done by the Christian. However, the glorification of the Father is executed by those *men* who see the good works of the Christian. The Christian must be doing good works for the express purpose of giving the Father the glory, whether said glorification comes from the good works performed by the saint or from "*men*" of the world.

**Verse 18.** *If it be possible, as much as lieth in you, live peaceably with all men.* Peace is a treasure among any peoples and merits pursuit. Peter said: *For he that will love life, and see good days, let him refrain his tongue from evil, and his lips that they speak no guile: Let him eschew evil, and do good; let him seek peace, and ensue it* (I Pet. 3:10-11). Peace is a good treasure worthy of pursuit; it serves brethren best when it is achieved.

Times exist when living peaceably with others is not possible. In such cases it is best to separate. Some possess ill will against the Lord's church; they cannot be numbered among those who prefer peace. These men are as Jude described:

> *These are murmurers, complainers, walking after their own lusts; and their mouth speaketh great swelling*

# Commentary on Romans

*words, having men's persons in admiration because of advantage.* But, beloved, remember ye the words which were spoken before of the apostles of our Lord Jesus Christ; How that they told you there should be mockers in the last time, who should walk after their own ungodly lusts. These be they who separate themselves, sensual, having not the Spirit (Jd. 16-19).

Christians should strive especially to be at peace among themselves. And we should do our best, without sacrificing truth and duty, to be at peace with all men. We should not be meddlers in other men's affairs; but if we preach the truth, rebuke, and exhort, somebody will not like it. It is impossible therefore to be at peace with all men. Neither Jesus nor Paul could be at peace with the enemies of Christ. We must contend earnestly for the faith—we must fight the good fight of faith[88] [sic].

Regarding the phrase, *if it be possible,* Barnes wrote:

> If it can be done. This expression implies that it could not always be done. Still it should be an object of desire; and we should endeavor to obtain it. As much as lieth in you – This implies two things: (1) We are to do our utmost endeavors to preserve peace, and to appease the anger and malice of others. (2) We are not to "begin" or to "originate" a quarrel. So far as "we" are concerned, we are to seek peace. But then it does not always depend on us. Others may oppose and persecute us; they will hate religion, and may slander, revile, and otherwise injure us; or they may commence an assault on our persons or property. For "their" assaults we are not answerable; but we are answerable for our conduct toward them; and on no occasion are we to commence a warfare with them. It may not be "possible" to prevent their injuring and opposing us; but it is possible not to begin a contention with them; and "when they" have commenced a strife, to seek peace, and to evince a Christian spirit. This command doubt-

---
[88] Robertson L. Whiteside.

# Commentary on Romans

less extends to everything connected with strife; and means that we are not to "provoke" them to controversy, or to prolong it when it is commenced; see Psa 34:14; Mat 5:9, Mat 5:39-41; Heb 12:14. If all Christians would follow this command, if they would never "provoke" to controversy, if they would injure no man by slander or by unfair dealing, if they would compel none to prosecute them in law by lack of punctuality in payment of debts or honesty in business, if they would do nothing to irritate, or to prolong a controversy when it is commenced, it would put an end to no small part of the strife that exists in the world[89] [sic].

*With all men.* Be they sinner or saint matters not. Brethren especially must live peaceably with one another—and not divide when the differences between them are matters of opinion.

*And some days after Paul said unto Barnabas, Let us go again and visit our brethren in every city where we have preached the word of the Lord, and see how they do. And Barnabas determined to take with them John, whose surname was Mark. But Paul thought not good to take him with them, who departed from them from Pamphylia, and went not with them to the work. And the contention was so sharp between them, that they departed asunder one from the other: and so Barnabas took Mark, and sailed unto Cyprus; And Paul chose Silas, and departed, being recommended by the brethren unto the grace of God* (Acts 15:36-40).

It was not a matter of doctrine which caused Paul and Barnabas to part company; it was a matter of opinion. It serves us well to realize we are forbidden to make matters of opinion matters of doctrine. Opinions vary; doctrine does not. Doctrine is not subjective or abstract. It is real and concrete, there are no variables attached to it.

**Verse 19.** *Dearly beloved, avenge not yourselves, but rather give place unto wrath: for it is written, Vengeance is mine; I will repay, saith the Lord.* Retaliation and revenge are driven by ven-

---
[89] Albert Barnes

# Commentary on Romans

dettas. To engage in either is thievery from the Lord, for vengeance belongs to Him. To engage in them is to take upon one's self that which is reserved for the Father. While saints may *rob God of tithes and offerings,* they may also rob God of other things (Mal. 3:8). The Lord is often robbed of our time, our talents, our service, and numerous other things. How is it that so many deem it fitting to take God's law into their own hands?

*Dearly beloved* is a term of strong endearment, which shows Paul's genuine love for the saints at Rome. "This expression of tenderness was especially appropriate in an exhortation to peace. It reminded them of the affection and friendship which ought to subsist among them as brethren"[90] [sic]. "Paul's addressing them as 'beloved' would remind them that they should feel the same way toward one another. That feeling would promote peace and good fellowship among them, for people do not indulge in strife and harsh words with those they love"[91] [sic].

*Avenge not* yourselves. Not even the Lord did so. *Who, when he was reviled, reviled not again; when he suffered, he threatened not; but committed himself to him that judgeth righteously* (I Pet. 2:23). *He was oppressed, and he was afflicted, yet he opened not his mouth: he is brought as a lamb to the slaughter, and as a sheep before her shearers is dumb, so he openeth not his mouth* (Isa. 53:7). *And when he was accused of the chief priests and elders, he answered nothing. Then said Pilate unto him, Hearest thou not how many things they witness against thee? And he answered him to never a word; insomuch that the governor marvelled greatly* (Matt. 27:12-14).

It is a hard thing to remain passive in the face of wrongs committed against us, even ones legal in nature. Paul wrote: *Now therefore there is utterly a fault among you, because ye go to law one with another. Why do ye not rather take wrong? why do ye not rather suffer yourselves to be defrauded* (I Cor. 6:7)? On the phrase *but rather give place unto wrath,* Matthew Henry provides the following comments:

---

[90] Albert Barnes.
[91] Robertson L. Whiteside.

# Commentary on Romans

This is a hard lesson to corrupt nature; and therefore he subjoins, [1.] A remedy against it: *Rather give place unto wrath.* Not to our own wrath; to give place to this is to give place to the devil, Eph 4:26, Eph 4:27. We must resist, and stifle, and smother, and suppress this; but, *First,* To the wrath of our enemy. "Give place to it, that is, be of a yielding temper; do not answer wrath with wrath, but with love rather. *Yielding pacifies great offenses,* Ecc 10:4. Receive affronts and injuries, as a stone is received into a heap of wool, which gives way to it, and so it does not rebound back, nor go any further." So it explains that of our Saviour (Mat 5:39), *Whosoever shall smite thee on thy right cheek, turn to him the other also.* Instead of meditating how to revenge one wrong, prepare to receive another. When men's passions are up, and the stream is strong, let it have its course, lest by an unseasonable opposition it be made to rage and swell the more. When others are angry, let us be calm; this is a remedy against revenge, and seems to be the genuine sense. But, *Secondly,* Many apply it to the wrath of God: "Give place to this, make room for him to take the throne of judgment, and let him alone to deal with thine adversary"[92] [sic].

The *wrath* unto which the saint is to give way means "to give God His due in executing His justice. Give place unto the Lord and His wrath, He will avenge all those who bid it. Giving place unto wrath is unto God's wrath—not the wrath of men. Let the Lord execute His wrath, saints must not execute their own."

*For it is written, Vengeance is mine; I will repay, saith the Lord.* There is nothing which escapes the eyes of God. He will reward the righteous with blessings and He will reward the wicked with His wrath. He does so at His leisure and not ours. Patience is therefore, required by those who suffer at the hands of wicked men. *It is written,* Paul tells us wrath and vengeance are the Lord's, be it far from the saint to take it from Him. Those who steal the wrath of God shall themselves be rewarded with it. *To me belongeth vengeance, and recompence; their foot shall slide in due time: for the day of their calamity is at hand, and the*

---
[92] Matthew Henry

# Commentary on Romans

*things that shall come upon them make haste* (Deut. 32:35). *Vengeance belongeth unto me; I will recompense, saith the Lord.*

> Paul's citation of the passage did not change its meaning nor its application. This phrase does not refer to the vengeance God will take on sinners at the final judgment. Under the law of Moses, God took vengeance on evildoers by the agency of chosen authorities. Later, Paul will show how such is to be done. Instead of taking personal vengeance on an enemy, give him food and drink as his needs may require. If there is any degree of manhood in him, this course will fill him with shame and remorse—figuratively it will heap coals of fire on his head, and may entirely melt down his enmity. If it does not do this, it will make him feel uncomfortable, in that he has no evil thing he can say about you. By following the course outlined in verses 19 and 20, the Christian overcomes evil with good; if he seeks with his own hands to inflict punishment on an enemy, he is overcome of evil—he himself becomes evil"[93] [sic].

The phrase, *saith the Lord*, forever settles the matter as to whom all wrath and vengeance belong. The phrase, *thus saith the Lord*, occurs in 430 verses and is used 2,856 times in the Scriptures. Indeed men ought to give way unto what the Lord has said.

**Verse 20.** *Therefore if thine enemy hunger, feed him; if he thirst, give him drink: for in so doing thou shalt heap coals of fire on his head.* This is a quotation from Solomon who wrote; *If thine enemy be hungry, give him bread to eat; and if he be thirsty, give him water to drink: For thou shalt heap coals of fire upon his head, and the Lord shall reward thee* (Pro. 25:21-22).

> Do not withhold from any man the offices of mercy and kindness; you have been God's enemy, and yet God fed, clothed, and preserved you alive: do to your enemy as God has done to you. If your enemy be hungry,

---

[93] Robertson L. Whiteside

# Commentary on Romans

feed him; if he be thirsty, give him drink: so has God dealt with you. And has not a sense of his goodness and longsuffering towards you been a means of melting down your heart into penitential compunction, gratitude, and love towards him? How know you that a similar conduct towards your enemy may not have the same gracious influence on him towards you? Your kindness may be the means of begetting in him a sense of his guilt; and, from being your fell enemy, he may become your real friend[94] [sic]!

**Verse 21.** *Be not overcome of evil, but overcome evil with good.* This phrase is present passive imperative; meaning "to conquer, stop being conquered by evil things or men. Overcome evil with good, keep on conquering evil with the good. Drown evil with good and in the good."

Do not allow evil to overcome you; rather overcome evil with, by, and through the good one should do. Saints are often overtaken in faults, as Paul informed us in Galatians 6:1. However, being overtaken, as Paul warned, means to be overtaken by surprise. In the Romans' passage, the overcoming of which Paul writes is one in which the saint engages by intent and design. Falling into a fault is vastly different from intentionally entering into one. Saints must not design such against another.

When saints overcome evil with good, they heap fires of coals upon those who are evil toward them. Further, the Lord repays evil men who cast vengeance against the saints. Evil men accrue severe penalties for their evil deeds. The best revenge Christians may take against their adversaries is to do good unto them; in that, *God is not unrighteous to forget your work and labour of love, which ye have shewed toward his name, in that ye have ministered to the saints, and do minister* (Heb. 6:10).

## Romans 13:1-10

*1 Let every soul be subject unto the higher powers. For there is no power but of God: the powers that be are ordained of God. 2 Whosoever therefore resisteth*

---
[94] Adam Clarke.

# Commentary on Romans

*the power, resisteth the ordinance of God: and they that resist shall receive to themselves damnation. 3 For rulers are not a terror to good works, but to the evil. Wilt thou then not be afraid of the power? do that which is good, and thou shalt have praise of the same: 4 For he is the minister of God to thee for good. But if thou do that which is evil, be afraid; for he beareth not the sword in vain: for he is the minister of God, a revenger to execute wrath upon him that doeth evil. 5 Wherefore ye must needs be subject, not only for wrath, but also for conscience sake. 6 For this cause pay ye tribute also: for they are God's ministers, attending continually upon this very thing. 7 Render therefore to all their dues: tribute to whom tribute is due; custom to whom custom; fear to whom fear; honour to whom honour. 8 Owe no man any thing, but to love one another: for he that loveth another hath fulfilled the law. 9 For this, Thou shalt not commit adultery, Thou shalt not kill, Thou shalt not steal, Thou shalt not bear false witness, Thou shalt not covet; and if there be any other commandment, it is briefly comprehended in this saying, namely, Thou shalt love thy neighbour as thyself. 10 Love worketh no ill to his neighbour: therefore love is the fulfilling of the law.*

Albert Barnes composed the following six observations, all of which have been italicized.

*In the seven first verses of this chapter, the apostle discusses the subject of the duty which Christians owe to civil government; a subject which is extremely important, and at the same time exceedingly difficult. There is no doubt that he had express reference to the special situation of the Christians at Rome; but the subject was of so much importance that he gives it a "general" bearing, and states the great principles on which all Christians are to act. The circumstances which made this discussion proper and important were the following:*

*(1) The Christian religion was designed to extend*

# Commentary on Romans

*throughout the world. Yet it contemplated the rearing of a kingdom amid other kingdoms, an empire amid other empires. Christians professed supreme allegiance to the Lord Jesus Christ; he was their Lawgiver, their Sovereign, their Judge. It became, therefore, a question of great importance and difficulty, "what kind'" of allegiance they were to render to earthly magistrates.*

*(2) The kingdoms of the world were then "pagan" kingdoms. The laws were made by pagans, and were adapted to the prevalence of paganism. Those kingdoms had been generally founded in conquest, and blood, and oppression. Many of the monarchs were blood-stained warriors; were unprincipled men; and were polluted in their private, and oppressive in their public character. Whether Christians were to acknowledge the laws of such kingdoms and of such men, was a serious question, and one which could not but occur very early. It would occur also very soon, in circumstances that would be very affecting and trying. Soon the hands of these magistrates were to be raised against Christians in the fiery scenes of persecution; and the duty and extent of submission to them became a matter of very serious inquiry.*

*(3) Many of the early Christians were composed of Jewish converts. Yet the Jews had long been under Roman oppression, and had borne the foreign yoke with great uneasiness. The whole pagan magistracy they regarded as founded in a system of idolatry; as opposed to God and his kingdom; and as abomination in his sight. With these feelings they had become Christians; and it was natural that their former sentiments should exert an influence on them after their conversion. How far they should submit, if at all, to heathen magistrates, was a question of deep interest; and there was danger that the "Jewish" converts might prove to be disorderly and rebellious citizens of the empire.*

*(4) Nor was the case much different with the "Gentile"*

# Commentary on Romans

*converts. They would naturally look with abhorrence on the system of idolatry which they had just forsaken. They would regard all as opposed to God. They would denounce the "religion" of the pagans as abomination; and as that religion was interwoven with the civil institutions, there was danger also that they might denounce the government altogether, and be regarded as opposed to the laws of the land.*

*(5) There "were" cases where it was right to "resist" the laws. This the Christian religion clearly taught; and in cases like these, it was indispensable for Christians to take a stand. When the laws interfered with the rights of conscience; when they commanded the worship of idols, or any moral wrong, then it was their duty to refuse submission. Yet in what cases this was to be done, where the line was to be drawn, was a question of deep importance, and one which was not easily settled. It is quite probable, however, that the main danger was, that the early Christians would err in "refusing" submission, even when it was proper, rather than in undue conformity to idolatrous rites and ceremonies.*

*(6) In the "changes" which were to occur in human governments, it would be an inquiry of deep interest, what part Christians should take, and what submission they should yield to the various laws which might spring up among the nations. The "principles" in which Christians should act are settled in this chapter*[95] *[sic].*

Paul here speaks of civil governments, human governments. These injunctions apply to all men, especially to all Christians, in all times and places; but there was then a special need for such teaching. Christianity was new, and was regarded by some as antagonistic to human governments. There was likely to be such a notion among Christians. The Jews were especially averse to being subject to the Roman government, and Jews who became Christians would likely hold to their former prejudice against being subject to Rome. And

---
[95] Albert Barnes.

# Commentary on Romans

converts from heathenism might feel that, having confessed Jesus Christ as their king, they were not subject to any other government. Hence the special need for Paul's plain and emphatic teaching. To make such submission to earthly governments seem more reasonable and necessary he informs them that all power is of God, and that civil governments are ordained of God. He who denies this fact denies the voice of inspiration. The fact that governments sometimes turn out bad, and do unjust things, does not prove Paul's statement to be untrue. The devil sometimes controls the actions of governments, but that does not prove that all governments belong to the devil. The devil sometimes gets into churches and causes them to do evil and unjust things, but that does not prove that the devil owns and controls all churches. The design of civil government is to promote the security and the well-being of its citizens; and there would be no security of life and property, if there were no human governments. And so obedience to civil authorities is a fundamental requirement of the gospel. "Put them in mind to be in subjection to rulers, to authorities, to be obedient, to be ready unto every good work" (Tit. 3:1). "Be subject to every ordinance of man for the Lord's sake: whether to the king, as supreme; or unto governors, as sent by him for vengeance on evil-doers and for praise to them that do well. For so is the will of God, that by well-doing ye should put to silence the ignorance of foolish men" (1 Pet. 2:13-15). One can scarcely imagine a government that would be worse than none. In all he says, Paul assumed that governments would carry out their God-appointed mission. Of course, if a government demands that a Christian must do anything against the will of God, he must obey God rather than man. Aside from this one thing, the Christian should be the best of all citizens; for "the powers that be are ordained of God"[96] [sic].

**Verse 1.** *Let every soul be subject unto the higher powers. For there is no power but of God: the powers that be are ordained of*

---
[96] Robertson L. Whiteside.

# Commentary on Romans

God. *Every soul* of society is regulated by the laws of the land in which they live. The Jews, in their efforts to entrap the Lord, tempted Him, saying: *Tell us therefore, What thinkest thou? Is it lawful to give tribute unto Caesar, or not? But Jesus perceived their wickedness, and said, Why tempt ye me, ye hypocrites? Shew me the tribute money. And they brought unto him a penny. And he saith unto them, Whose is this image and superscription? They say unto him, Caesar's. Then saith he unto them, Render therefore unto Caesar the things which are Caesar's; and unto God the things that are God's* (Matt. 22:17-21).

The *higher powers* refers to those in authority, not simply rulers of kingdoms. Even those to whom authority has been delegated must be given subjection when the mandates of the laws do not conflict with the Laws of God.

*For there is no power but of God: the powers that be are ordained of God.* Powers—human governments, are "*ordained*" by God. The word *ordained,* as defined by W. E. Vine, means, "ordained to be the Judge of men."[97] God has appointed powers and offices unto men. However, it must be realized God allows men to serve themselves with detriment if men wish and want for things evil. God often gives men that for which they lust and pine. He did so in the days of Samuel.

> *And it came to pass, when Samuel was old, that he made his sons judges over Israel. Now the name of his firstborn was Joel; and the name of his second, Abiah: they were judges in Beersheba. And his sons walked not in his ways, but turned aside after lucre, and took bribes, and perverted judgment. Then all the elders of Israel gathered themselves together, and came to Samuel unto Ramah, And said unto him, Behold, thou art old, and thy sons walk not in thy ways: now make us a king to judge us like all the nations. But the thing displeased Samuel, when they said, Give us a king to judge us. And Samuel prayed unto the Lord. And the Lord said unto Samuel, Hearken unto the voice of the people in all that they say unto thee: for they have not rejected thee, but they have rejected me, that I should*

---
[97] W.E. Vine.

# Commentary on Romans

*not reign over them. According to all the works which they have done since the day that I brought them up out of Egypt even unto this day, wherewith they have forsaken me, and served other gods, so do they also unto thee. Now therefore hearken unto their voice: howbeit yet protest solemnly unto them, and shew them the manner of the king that shall reign over them. And Samuel told all the words of the Lord unto the people that asked of him a king. And he said, This will be the manner of the king that shall reign over you: He will take your sons, and appoint them for himself, for his chariots, and to be his horsemen; and some shall run before his chariots. And he will appoint him captains over thousands, and captains over fifties; and will set them to ear his ground, and to reap his harvest, and to make his instruments of war, and instruments of his chariots. And he will take your daughters to be confectioneries, and to be cooks, and to be bakers. And he will take your fields, and your vineyards, and your olive yards, even the best of them, and give them to his servants. And he will take the tenth of your seed, and of your vineyards, and give to his officers, and to his servants. And he will take your menservants, and your maidservants, and your goodliest young men, and your asses, and put them to his work. He will take the tenth of your sheep: and ye shall be his servants. And ye shall cry out in that day because of your king which ye shall have chosen you; and the Lord will not hear you in that day. Nevertheless the people refused to obey the voice of Samuel; and they said, Nay; but we will have a king over us; That we also may be like all the nations; and that our king may judge us, and go out before us, and fight our battles. And Samuel heard all the words of the people, and he rehearsed them in the ears of the Lord. And the Lord said to Samuel, Hearken unto their voice, and make them a king. And Samuel said unto the men of Israel, Go ye every man unto his city* (I Sam. 8:1-22).

The continued rebellion of the Jews provoked God to send the nation of Israel into the Babylonian captivity of which Jeremiah

# Commentary on Romans

prophesied. *And this whole land shall be a desolation, and an astonishment; and these nations shall serve the king of Babylon seventy years. And it shall come to pass, when seventy years are accomplished, that I will punish the king of Babylon, and that nation, saith the Lord, for their iniquity, and the land of the Chaldeans, and will make it perpetual desolations.... For thus saith the Lord, That after seventy years be accomplished at Babylon I will visit you, and perform my good word toward you, in causing you to return to this place* (Jer. 25:11-12; 29:10).

God, through the prophet Hosea, said to the nation of Israel: *I gave thee a king in mine anger, and took him away in my wrath* (Hos. 13:11). Nations rise and fall but God's hand is always in it.

Brethren have long taught God ordained three Divine institutions, but such *is not* the case. The Lord instituted marriage—that is, the home, and He instituted the church, but *He did not* institute nations or kingdoms. Consider the first organized city—nation—of which the Scriptures speak.

*And Cain went out from the presence of the Lord, and dwelt in the land of Nod, on the east of Eden. And Cain knew his wife; and she conceived, and bare Enoch: and he builded a city, and called the name of the city, after the name of his son, Enoch* (Gen. 4:16-17). After the city of Enoch was built we read of numerous other cities and nations which men built—all of which were established by wicked men.

> *And Cush begat Nimrod: he began to be a mighty one in the earth. He was a mighty hunter before the Lord: wherefore it is said, Even as Nimrod the mighty hunter before the Lord. And the beginning of his kingdom was Babel, and Erech, and Accad, and Calneh, in the land of Shinar. Out of that land went forth Asshur, and builded Nineveh, and the city Rehoboth, and Calah, And Resen between Nineveh and Calah: the same is a great city. And Mizraim begat Ludim, and Anamim, and Lehabim, and Naphtuhim, And Pathrusim, and Casluhim, (out of whom came Philistim,) and Caphtorim. And Canaan begat Sidon his firstborn, and Heth, And the Jebusite, and the Amorite, and the Girgasite, And*

# Commentary on Romans

*the Hivite, and the Arkite, and the Sinite, And the Arvadite, and the Zemarite, and the Hamathite: and afterward were the families of the Canaanites spread abroad. And the border of the Canaanites was from Sidon, as thou comest to Gerar, unto Gaza; as thou goest, unto Sodom, and Gomorrah, and Admah, and Zeboim, even unto Lasha. These are the sons of Ham, after their families, after their tongues, in their countries, and in their nations* (Gen. 10:8-20).

Of the city built by Cain and the cities and kingdoms built by those mentioned in Genesis 10, there is no record God ordained any of them. It is well to realize Paul declared *God ordained the powers—rulers of nations—but He did not ordain the nations. The only nation God ordained was the nation of Israel.* Israel, however, rebelled against the Lord which resulted in their final fall in AD 70. The church is the Lord's kingdom which God ordained before the beginning of time, but He did not ordain any earthly nation besides the nation of Israel.

**Verse 2.** *Whosoever therefore resisteth the power, resisteth the ordinance of God: and they that resist shall receive to themselves damnation.* So long as the laws of a nation are in harmony with the principles of God's Law, men—especially saints—are to subject themselves thereunto. When the laws of the land stand in opposition to godliness, the powers in them must be opposed by the Christian.

When men oppose the laws of the land and the powers thereof, which are in harmony with Divine principles, they bring upon themselves the wrath of both God and the powers that be. "Because these powers are ordained of God, the one who resisteth—takes his stand against—the power resists the ordinance of God. To resist the government does not simply mean to fail sometimes to obey a law; it is to take a stand against the government—to defy the authority of the government. To do this is to array oneself against both God and the government, and in so doing brings upon himself the judgment of both "[98] [sic]. These things are true so long as the laws of the land are not contrary to God's Laws and principles.

---
[98] Robertson L. Whiteside.

# Commentary on Romans

**Verse 3.** *For rulers are not a terror to good works, but to the evil. Wilt thou then not be afraid of the power? do that which is good, and thou shalt have praise of the same:* For good works one suffers not at the hands of those who are in power.

Governments are permitted by God to exercise punishments upon violators. Liberally-minded men and brethren who oppose the death penalty insist such is *legalized murder.* However, the Scriptures teach to the contrary.

The phrase, *put to death*, is found 348 times in the Scriptures. The phrase, *shall surely be put to death*, is found 215 times. The penalty of death for particular crimes against both God or man is a Divinely-established principle. Those who oppose this principle oppose the principle of God; such is detrimental to society, the church, and souls. God has ordained the powers that be to establish laws by which any given society must be governed. With ordained authority, governments establish penalties for crimes committed against them. In that God has allocated such power to governments, men ought to *be afraid of the power* which God has bestowed upon the authorities of the nations. When men *do that which is good,* they shall *have praise of the same.* The *same* refers to the ordained powers God authorized.

Paul was stating the proper functions of civil governments. His statements are a guide to the duties and imitations of governments, and a rebuke to those who overstep the bounds of their proper functions. Governments sometimes fail to function within their proper limits, just as churches sometimes fail to function as they should. The failure of a church to function as it should does not prove that the devil originated it, nor that all churches are owned and controlled by the devil; neither does a persecuting government prove that the devil controls all governments. No human government is perfect, and certainly the Roman government was far from perfection; but try to imagine the fate of the early Christians and of all other decent people, had there been no government at all. All governments are pleased with law-abiding citizens. The trouble was, the Roman government had some laws concerning relig-

## Commentary on Romans

ion, which Christians could not obey; and this caused the trouble. Monsters of cruelty like Nero made it hard on Christians. Civil governments were meant to be ministers of God for the good of the people; but they sometimes swerve from their God-appointed mission, and become instruments of cruelty. The sword, as here used, is a symbol of power—the power, or authority, to inflict the death penalty. The death penalty for certain crimes is one of God's fundamental requirements. Long before the law of Moses was given God said to Noah, "Whoso sheddeth man's blood, by man shall his blood he shed: for in the image of God made he man" (Gen. 9:6). This decree of God has always had to be carried out in a legal way; otherwise it would be murder "He beareth not the sword in vain; for he is a minister of God, an avenger for wrath to him that doeth evil." No person should therefore take vengeance with his own hands"[99] [sic].

Peter provided inspired commentary on this matter. *Submit yourselves to every ordinance of man for the Lord's sake: whether it be to the king, as supreme; Or unto governors, as unto them that are sent by him for the punishment of evildoers, and for the praise of them that do well. For so is the will of God, that with well doing ye may put to silence the ignorance of foolish men* (I Pet. 2:13-15). Solomon informed us that *the fear of a king is as the roaring of a lion: whoso provoketh him to anger sinneth against his own soul* (Pro. 20:2).

**Verse 4.** *For he is the minister of God to thee for good. But if thou do that which is evil, be afraid; for he beareth not the sword in vain: for he is the minister of God, a revenger to execute wrath upon him that doeth evil.* He refers to the one in power. He serves as *minister to God,* in society for the good of men and society.

The governing power which bears the sword of punishment over a nation does not wield said sword vainly, nor is it without just cause. The governments of nations appoint those who are to serve as "*a revenger to execute wrath upon him that doeth evil.*"

---
[99] Robertson L. Whiteside.

# Commentary on Romans

He that *beareth the sword* is God's "vindictive minister, to execute wrath; to inflict punishment upon the transgressors of the law"[100] [sic].

> While vengeance belongs to God He executes "his vengeance" by means of subordinate agents. It belongs to him to take vengeance by direct judgments, by the plague, famine, sickness, or earthquakes; by the appointment of magistrates; or by letting loose the passions of people to prey upon each other. When a magistrate inflicts punishment on the guilty, it is to be regarded as the act of God taking vengeance "by him;" and on this principle only is it right for a judge to condemn a man to death. It is not because one man has by nature any right over the life of or because "society" has any right collectively which it has not as individuals; but because "God" gave life, and because he has chosen to take it away when crime is committed by the appointment of magistrates, and not by coming forth himself visibly to execute the laws[101] [sic].

**Verse 5.** *Wherefore ye must needs be subject, not only for wrath, but also for conscience sake.* The word *wherefore* serves as the conclusion to the arguments set forth by Paul in verses one through four. Because the ordained powers established by the Lord do not *bear the sword in vain,* it behooves all men to subject themselves to the laws of the land in which they live.

Paul gives two reasons for the saints to subject themselves unto the powers ordained by God. First, saints should do so because honorable conduct in society prevents the *wrath* of magistrates and authorities from befalling the saints. Second, saints do well in subjecting themselves to the powers that be *for conscience sake.*

The wrath of earthly authorities is the human side of the matter. The sake of the conscience is from the spiritual perspective. Man must bear a clean and clear conscience before God. However, the clearness of the conscience of the saint must be in

---
[100] Adam Clarke.
[101] Albert Barnes.

# Commentary on Romans

harmony with the Laws of God. The conscience is not his only guide, but it is a vital component to man's justification before God.

Barnes wrote: "As a matter of conscience, or of 'duty to God,' because 'he' has appointed it, and made it necessary and proper. A good citizen yields obedience because it is the will of God; and a Christian makes it a part of his religion to maintain and obey the just laws of the land; see Mat 22:21; compare Ecc 8:2, 'I counsel them to keep the king's commandments, and 'that in regard of the oath of God'"[102] [sic]. Context is always crucial in the study of the Scripture; consider this assessment.

> It is of *Magistracy in general*, considered as a divine ordinance, that this is spoken: and the statement applies equally to all forms of government, from an unchecked despotism—such as flourished when this was written, under the Emperor Nero—to a pure democracy. The inalienable right of all subjects to endeavor to alter or improve the form of government under which they live is left untouched here. But since Christians were constantly charged with turning the world upside down, and since there certainly were elements enough in Christianity of moral and social revolution to give plausibility to the charge, and tempt noble spirits, crushed under misgovernment, to take redress into their own hands, it was of special importance that the pacific, submissive, loyal spirit of those Christians who resided at the great seat of political power, should furnish a visible refutation of this charge[103] [sic].

**Verse 6.** *For this cause pay ye tribute also: for they are God's ministers, attending continually upon this very thing.* Tribute has reference to the annual tax levied upon houses, lands, and persons. Perhaps a better understanding of the passage would be to say; *for this cause ye pay taxes.* The *cause* is the bearer of the sword—the ordained powers are God's ministers.

The Christian must pay his taxes; the officers of the

---

[102] Albert Barnes

[103] Robert Jamieson, A.R. Fausset, and David Brown,

# Commentary on Romans

government must be paid, "for they are ministers of God's service." No Christian should try to avoid paying his just share of government expenses; it is common honesty, as well as a Christian duty. Our Lord taught the Jews to pay their taxes (Matt. 22:15-22). "Render to all their dues"; or, Pay to all what you owe. Pay tribute and custom to whom they are due. Tribute—direct taxes on a person and his property; custom is revenue levied on imports and trades. So long as we live in the flesh, even if all people were Christians, we need civil governments; for there are things that must be done, that the church as a body is not authorized to do[104] [sic].

Attending continually upon this very thing means "to be earnest towards, to be constantly and diligent in, to attend to assiduously; adhere closely to the paying of one's tribute unto governments. The Lord himself paid his tribute as required by the Roman government.

> *And when they were come to Capernaum, they that received tribute money came to Peter, and said, Doth not your master pay tribute? He saith, Yes. And when he was come into the house, Jesus prevented* (went before; dhc) *him, saying, What thinkest thou, Simon? of whom do the kings of the earth take custom or tribute? of their own children, or of strangers? Peter saith unto him, Of strangers. Jesus saith unto him, Then are the children free. Notwithstanding, lest we should offend them, go thou to the sea, and cast an hook, and take up the fish that first cometh up; and when thou hast opened his mouth, thou shalt find a piece of money: that take, and give unto them for me and thee* (Matt. 17:24-27).

**Verses 7-8.** *Render therefore to all their dues: tribute to whom tribute is due; custom to whom custom; fear to whom fear; honour to whom honour. Owe no man any thing, but to love one another: for he that loveth another hath fulfilled the law.* Render therefore to all their dues, especially to magistrates, and to all

---
[104] Robertson L. Whiteside.

# Commentary on Romans

with whom we have to do. Below are two pertinent analyses.

To be just is to give to all their due, to give everyone his own. What we have we have as stewards; others may have an interest in, and must have their dues. "Render to God his due in the first place, to yourselves, to your families, your relations, to the commonwealth, to the church, to the poor, to those that you have dealings with in buying, selling, exchanging, etc. Render to all their dues; and that readily and cheerfully, not tarrying till you are by law compelled to it. He specifies, 1. Due taxes: *Tribute to whom tribute is due, custom to whom custom.* Most of the countries where the gospel was first preached were subject at this time to the Roman yoke, and were made provinces of the empire. He wrote this to the Romans, who, as they were rich, so they were drained by taxes and impositions, to the just and honest payment of which they are here pressed by the apostle. Some distinguish between tribute and custom, understanding by the former constant standing taxes, and by the latter those which were occasionally required, both of which are to be faithfully and conscientiously paid as they become legally due. Our Lord was born when his mother went to be taxed; and he enjoined the payment of tribute to Caesar. Many, who in other things seem to be just, yet make no conscience of this, but pass it off with a false ill-favored maxim, that it is no sin to cheat the king, directly contrary to Paul's rule, *Tribute to whom tribute is due.* 2. Due respect: *Fear to whom fear, honour to whom honour.* This sums up the duty which we owe not only to magistrates, but to all superiors, parents, masters, all that are over us in the Lord, according to the fifth commandment: *Honour thy father and mother.* Compare Lev 19:3, *You shall fear every man his mother and his father;* not with a fear of amazement, but a loving, reverent, respectful, obediential fear. Where there is not this respect in the heart to our superiors, no other duty will be paid aright. 3. Due payment of debts (Rom 13:8): "*Owe no man any thing;*" that is, do not continue in any one's debt, while you are able to pay it, further

## Commentary on Romans

than by, at least, the tacit consent of the person to whom you are indebted. Give every one his own. Do not spend that upon yourselves, which you owe to others. "The *wicked borroweth, and payeth not again,* Psa 37:21. Many that are very sensible of the trouble think little of the sin of being in debt.[105]

If a man pays promptly according to contract, he owes nothing. "Render to all their dues"—pay what is due. When therefore the time comes to meet an obligation, meet it promptly. But the obligation to love one another is always due, and is never fully paid; it is a perpetual debt. "Owe no man anything, save to love one another: for he that loveth the other hath fulfilled the law." But the law is not fulfilled by mere sentiment, or feeling, but by deeds of helpfulness; and it means, as well, refraining from doing any harm. It means that one must refrain from doing the evil things mentioned in verse 9. "For this"—this is the sum of fulfilling the law of love, namely, refrain from the evils mentioned, and love your neighbor as yourself; really it is all summed in the one command: "Thou shalt love thy neighbor as thyself." And we love our neighbor as ourselves when we treat him as well as we would have him treat us. If a man loves his neighbor as himself, he will not do him any harm, but always good[106] [sic].

*Love one another: for he that loveth another hath fulfilled the law.* Dissension was a constant issue between the Jews and Gentiles in the early church. Paul charged the brethren at Rome that love must *be without dissimulation* (Rom. 12:9).

The subject of love is much addressed in the Scriptures. *For all the law is fulfilled in one word, even in this; Thou shalt love thy neighbour as thyself* (Gal. 5:14). *And the Lord make you to increase and abound in love one toward another, and toward all men, even as we do toward you* (I Thes. 3:12). *And let us consider one another to provoke unto love and to good works* (Heb. 10:24). *Let brotherly love continue* (Heb. 13:1). Honor *all*

---
[105] Matthew Henry.
[106] Robertson L. Whiteside.

# Commentary on Romans

men. Love the brotherhood. Fear God. Honor the king (I Pet. 2: 17). Finally, be ye all of one mind, having compassion one of another, love as brethren, be pitiful, be courteous (I Pet. 3:8). For this is the message that ye heard from the beginning, that we should love one another (I Jno. 3:11). We know that we have passed from death unto life, because we love the brethren. He that loveth not his brother abideth in death (I Jno. 3:14). And this is his commandment, That we should believe on the name of his Son Jesus Christ, and love one another, as he gave us commandment (I Jno. 3:23). Beloved, let us love one another: for love is of God; and every one that loveth is born of God, and knoweth God (I Jno. 4:7). Beloved, if God so loved us, we ought also to love one another (I Jno. 4:11). Hear the conclusion of this matter; By this shall all men know that ye are my disciples, if ye have love one to another (Jno. 13:35). These things I command you, that ye love one another (Jno. 15:17). If a man say, I love God, and hateth his brother, he is a liar: for he that loveth not his brother whom he hath seen, how can he love God whom he hath not seen (I Jno. 4:20)?

Words of anger are often the deepest roots of division among brethren. We do best when we refrain from offending brethren. Solomon said: *A brother offended is harder to be won than a strong city: and their contentions are like the bars of a castle* (Pro. 18:19). Consider the words of a song we sing.

Angry words! O let them never, From the tongue unbridled slip, May the heart's best impulse ever, Check them ere they soil the lip.

**Refrain:** Love one another thus saith the Savior, Children obey the Father's blest command, Love each other, love each other, 'Tis' the Father's blest command.

Love is much too pure and holy, Friendship is too sacred far, For a moment's reckless folly, Thus to desolate and mar. [Refrain]

Angry words are lightly spoken, Bitterest thoughts are rashly stirred, Brightest links of life are broken, By a single angry word. [Refrain].[107]

---
[107] Words and Music; Horatio R. Palmer.

# Commentary on Romans

*Keep yourselves in the love of God, looking for the mercy of our Lord Jesus Christ unto eternal life (Jd., v. 21).*

**Verses 9-10.** *For this, Thou shalt not commit adultery, Thou shalt not kill, Thou shalt not steal, Thou shalt not bear false witness, Thou shalt not covet; and if there be any other commandment, it is briefly comprehended in this saying, namely, Thou shalt love thy neighbour as thyself. Love worketh no ill to his neighbour: therefore love is the fulfilling of the law.* Five principles of the Ten Commandments of the Law are set forth in this verse. The forbidding of adultery, murder, thievery, false witnessing, and covetousness were part of the Law of Moses.

While God's Law has changed, His principles have not. *Every principle* of the Law of Moses was included in the Patriarchal Law, and they are also set forth in the New Testament. God changed His worship practices when Christ ushered in the Law of the New Testament, but He did not change His principles.

"The words '*or this'* is the sum of fulfilling the law of love, namely, refrain from the evils mentioned, and love your neighbor as yourself; really it is all summed in the one command: 'Thou shalt love thy neighbor as thyself.' And we love our neighbor as ourselves when we treat him as well as we would have him treat us. If a man loves his neighbor as himself, he will not do any of these things to his fellow man"[108] [sic].

Concerning the matter of love, Paul wrote love; *doth not behave itself unseemly, seeketh not her own, is not easily provoked, thinketh no evil* (I Cor. 13:5). 1 Corinthians 13 is Paul's inspired commentary on the matter of love. It behooves every saint to tend well the matter as the apostle declared therein. Jesus said: *Ye have heard that it hath been said, Thou shalt love thy neighbour, and hate thine enemy. But I say unto you, Love your enemies, bless them that curse you, do good to them that hate you, and pray for them which despitefully use you, and persecute you; That ye may be the children of your Father which is in heaven: for he maketh his sun to rise on the evil and on the good, and sendeth rain on the just and on the unjust* (Matt. 5:43-45).

---

[108] Robertson L. Whiteside.

# Commentary on Romans

## Romans 13:11-14

*11 And that, knowing the time, that now it is high time to awake out of sleep: for now is our salvation nearer than when we believed. 12 The night is far spent, the day is at hand: let us therefore, the day is at hand: and let us put on the armor of light. 13 Let us walk honestly, as in the day; not in rioting and drunkenness, not in chambering and wantonness, not in strife and envying. 14 But put ye on the Lord Jesus Christ, and make not provision for the flesh, to fulfill the lusts thereof.*

There is much for consideration in these verses. It seems as if there is no end to the provision of misguided commentaries. We risk over-indulgence reminding the reader context is essential in the study of Scripture. Before truth can be ascertained from any inspired passage the context must be ascertained, established, and regarded as the standard by which the meaning of any given passage may be achieved. Context, context, context are the first three rules of exegesis. Hermeneutics is crucial: a valid hermeneutical approach is not optional; it is an absolute essential!

These verses have as their focus the destruction of Jerusalem which occurred in AD 70. The Lord spoke of the destruction of Jerusalem in Matthew 24, Mark 13, and Luke 21. In each of those inspired chapters, the Lord made clear the destruction of Jerusalem was the topic of His discourse. Before considering these verses, we pose the following questions. First, why did Paul say, *for now is our salvation nearer than when we believed*? What did Paul mean? Second, the apostle said *the day is at hand* —what day? Answering these questions must be acquired through the process of induction. When ascertaining truth proper exegesis must include *induction, deduction, reduction, and production*. *Inducing* refers to gathering all the information from every passage which addresses the subject under consideration. Complete induction must come before one can responsibly *deduce*—reach a proper deduction about the given topic. One must then *reduce* the induced information to the contextual settings in which the subject matter is found. Only then can the student reach the proper conclusions; then he can *produce* the intended purpose of the author.

# Commentary on Romans

Consider the following passages from which countless errors have been promoted. These plainly address warnings against the then-living Jewish generation and the Lord's stern warnings regarding the total destruction of the city of Jerusalem. Premillennialists have long insisted these verses refer to the *sign of the times* of the end of the world. If it is the case, as the Lord stated, no man can know when the end of the world is to occur (and it is), why do so many make endless efforts to determine the very thing they and the Lord, insisted cannot be done? Amazing!

Peter wrote: *But the end of all things is at hand: be ye therefore sober, and watch unto prayer* (I Pet. 4:7). The things at hand refers to the destruction of Jerusalem, not the end of the world. Further, Jesus said: *And, behold, I come quickly; and my reward is with me, to give every man according as his work shall be* (Rev. 22:12). The Lord was addressing the subject of the destruction of Jerusalem here as He also did when He said: *He which testifieth these things saith, Surely I come quickly. Amen. Even so, come, Lord Jesus* (Rev. 22:20).

James wrote: *Be ye also patient; stablish your hearts: for the coming of the Lord draweth nigh. Grudge not one against another, brethren, lest ye be condemned: behold, the judge standeth before the door* (Jas. 5:8-9). If the comments of James have reference to the end of the world, then it is the case James was given more information about the end of the world than the Lord Himself had. Such an assertion is far beyond the borders of sound reasoning.

Paul exhorted the church at Philippi: *Let your moderation be known unto all men. The Lord is at hand* (Phil. 4:5). This too has reference to the destruction of Jerusalem; otherwise, Paul, like James, was awarded more information about the matter than the Lord.

Last, we consider the words of the Hebrews' author who wrote: *Not forsaking the assembling of ourselves together, as the manner of some is; but exhorting one another: and so much the more, as ye see the day approaching* (Heb. 10:25). It has long been argued *the day approaching* refers to the Lord's Day—Sunday. However, the day must refer to the day of the destruction of

# Commentary on Romans

Jerusalem. There are nineteen passages of Scripture in which the Lord spoke of the things which would happen to the then-living generation. Below are several pertinent passages.

> Verily I say unto you, All these things shall come upon this generation (Matt. 23:36).

> Verily I say unto you, This generation shall not pass, till all these things be fulfilled (Matt. 24:34).

> And he sighed deeply in his spirit, and saith, Why doth this generation seek after a sign? verily I say unto you, There shall no sign be given unto this generation (Mk. 8:12).

> Whosoever therefore shall be ashamed of me and of my words in this adulterous and sinful generation; of him also shall the Son of man be ashamed, when he cometh in the glory of his Father with the holy angels (Mk. 8:38).

> Verily I say unto you, that this generation shall not pass, till all these things be done (Mk. 13:30).

> And the Lord said, Whereunto then shall I liken the men of this generation? and to what are they like (Lk. 7:31)?

> And when the people were gathered thick together, he began to say, This is an evil generation: they seek a sign; and there shall no sign be given it, but the sign of Jonas the prophet. For as Jonas was a sign unto the Ninevites, so shall also the Son of man be to this generation. The queen of the south shall rise up in the judgment with the men of this generation, and condemn them: for she came from the utmost parts of the earth to hear the wisdom of Solomon; and, behold, a greater than Solomon is here. The men of Nineveh shall rise up in the judgment with this generation, and shall condemn it: for they repented at the preaching of Jonas; and, behold, a greater than Jonas is here (Lk.

# Commentary on Romans

11:29-32).

*That the blood of all the prophets, which was shed from the foundation of the world, may be required of this generation; From the blood of Abel unto the blood of Zacharias, which perished between the altar and the temple: verily I say unto you, It shall be required of this generation* (Lk. 11:50-51).

*And the lord commended the unjust steward, because he had done wisely: for the children of this world are in their generation wiser than the children of light* (Lk. 16:8).

*But first must he suffer many things, and be rejected of this generation* (Lk. 17:25).

*Verily I say unto you, This generation shall not pass away, till all be fulfilled* (Lk. 21:32).

The destruction of Jerusalem is a subject not lightly addressed by the Lord. Make notice of the number of times the Lord used the phrase *this generation* in the passages provided.

In Acts 2, Luke wrote: *And with many other words did he testify and exhort, saying, Save yourselves from this untoward generation* (Acts 2:40). The apostles made use of the same words spoken by Christ *this generation.* The then living generation to whom the apostles preached on the Day of Pentecost were clearly identified as *this generation;* such was by not accident. When the first gospel sermon was presented by the apostles on the day of Pentecost, it was inclusive of many matters.
The inspired record states: *and with many other words did he testify and exhort.* The *many other* matters addressed by the apostles included such things mentioned in verse 42. The apostles' doctrine, fellowship, breaking of bread, and prayers were included in the preaching of the twelve. They preached the crucifixion of Christ, they proclaimed the outpouring of the Holy Ghost, and they preached the necessity of repentance and baptism. However, such was not the extent of the preaching of the apostles on the Day of Pentecost. They preached the need to

# Commentary on Romans

not only save their souls by obedience to the Gospel, but the apostles charged the Jews with saving themselves *from this untoward generation* (the generation then living).

*This untoward generation* mentioned refers to the *generation* of which the Lord spoke, as quoted above. It was *this generation* (the then-living generation) of the Jews which needed salvation from the destruction of Jerusalem brought about by the Roman Empire. If it is the case the phrase, *this generation*, applies to the *now*-living generation, when will the salvation of such ever be realized? To which generation will the passage apply? When will *this generation* come to fruition?

It is of great importance to realize the reasons Peter and the rest of the apostles quoted from the prophet Joel on that day when the Gospel was first proclaimed. The verses below are followed with added comments in brackets.

> *But Peter, standing up with the eleven, lifted up his voice, and said unto them, Ye men of Judaea, and all ye that dwell at Jerusalem, be this known unto you, and hearken to my words: For these are not drunken, as ye suppose, seeing it is but the third hour of the day. But this is that which was spoken by the prophet Joel; And it shall come to pass in the last days,* [of the Jewish dispensation] *saith God, I will pour out of my Spirit upon all flesh: and your sons and your daughters shall prophesy, and your young men shall see visions, and your old men shall dream dreams: And on my servants and on my handmaidens I will pour out in those days of my Spirit; and they shall prophesy: And I will shew wonders in heaven* [the sky] *above* [consider Matt. 24:27-30], *and signs in the earth beneath; blood, and fire, and vapour of smoke: The sun* [during the day] *shall be turned into darkness,* [by the Roman soldiers on their horses] *and the moon into* [the color of] *blood* [distorted by the dust-filled air caused by the Roman army], *before that great and notable day of the Lord come* [AD 70]: *And it shall come to pass, that whosoever shall call on the name of the Lord shall be saved* [from the destruction of Jerusalem in AD 70]

# Commentary on Romans

(Acts 2:14-21).

We again note that Luke informed us Peter and rest of the apostles made reference to *this generation* during their preaching of the first Gospel sermon on the Day of Pentecost. *And with many other words did he testify and exhort, saying, Save yourselves from this untoward generation* (Acts 2:40).

The phrase, *this generation*, occurs 41 times in the New Testament. Of those 41 times Christ used it 40 times. Luke recorded the phrase once in Acts 2 wherein the apostles used it on the Day of Pentecost. Peter and the rest of the apostles used the phrase to remind the Jews to save themselves from the then-living generation which was to suffer the consequences of their rebellion against the Lord's anointed Christ. In every passage in which Christ used the phrase, *this generation*, He was addressing the destruction of Jerusalem or the condemnation which was to come upon the disobedient Jews—their rejection of the Gospel. See notes at the end of the chapter.

**Verse 11.** *And that, knowing the time, that now it is high time to awake out of sleep: for now is our salvation nearer than when we believed.* The words, *and that*, mean "in that ye know." The verse literally means: *And in that ye know the time of our salvation* (from the destruction of Jerusalem) *is nearer than when we when we first believed* —and obeyed the gospel it is time indeed to awake out of spiritual sleep.

*Knowing the time* has reference to *the time* of the destruction of Jerusalem of which Christ spoke in Matthew 24, Mark 13, and Luke 21. The Lord taught the apostles there would be clear *signs* of warning as to when the destruction of Jerusalem would begin. *So likewise ye, when ye shall see all these things, know that it is near, even at the doors* (Matt. 24:33; cf. Mk. 13:29).

The apostles asked the Lord: *Tell us, when shall these things be? and what shall be the sign when all these things shall be fulfilled* (Mk. 13:4)? The Lord said: *And then shall appear the sign of the Son of man in heaven: and then shall all the tribes of the earth mourn, and they shall see the Son of man coming in the clouds of heaven with power and great glory* (Matt. 24:30).

# Commentary on Romans

The context of the Lord's dissertations concerns the destruction of Jerusalem. Failing to keep the contexts of Matthew 24, Mark 13, and Luke 21 in their proper settings leads to colossal errors. Premillennialists have so wrested these chapters that it is beyond comprehension. Sadly, countless brethren have followed suit. Peter wrote of both Paul's writings *and other Scriptures* the willfully ignorant twist, wrench, and warp so greatly it is impossible for them to ascertain truth (II Pet. 3:16).

*For now is our salvation nearer than when we believed.* Salvation from what? If it is the case Paul is speaking of one's spiritual, eternal salvation; then why did he speak of *knowing the time?* Is it not a foregone conclusion every faithful Christian draws *nearer* to eternal salvation as each day passes? Indeed, it is, however, Paul was speaking of salvation from the destruction of Jerusalem in AD 70.

While we have good respect for brother Whiteside we must *strongly contend* with his comments on this passage. He wrote:

And this additional matter, "knowing the season"— knowing the character of the time in which they lived— it was time for them to arouse from their indifference and lethargy. Few Christians are ever as wide awake as they should be. "Wherefore he saith, Awake thou that sleepest, and arise from the dead, and Christ shall shine upon thee" (Eph. 5:14). "Salvation nearer." **This seems to refer to their eternal salvation; for they were already in possession of salvation in Christ from their alien sins. As time passes eternal salvation comes nearer. It is now nearer than when we first believed**[109] [sic] (emph. DHC).

It is clear that the context of this verse deals with the salvation of Christians from the destruction of Jerusalem. Further, if it is the case the salvation under consideration refers to spiritual salvation; it must be the case salvation comes long after one obeys the Gospel. Spiritual salvation is acquired upon one's obedience to the Gospel which includes submission to baptism. Acts 2:38, I Peter 3:21, and Mark 16:15-16 all declare salvation—spiritual salvation from sin is acquired at baptism.

---

[109] Robertson L. Whiteside.

# Commentary on Romans

Some insist the second coming of the Lord is the topic Paul intends, but such an assertion demands the conclusion Paul was awarded more information about the second coming of Christ than Christ Himself had. On this phrase Barnes wrote: "The reference is apparently to the Lord's second coming, rather than to future glory."[110] This doctrine must be rejected.

The phrase, *it is high time to awake out of sleep,* means the hour has come. The word *awake* means "to collect one's faculties; to waken, to arouse from sleep, to arise from sitting or lying, from disease, from death; or from obscurity, inactivity, lift up, raise again, rear up, arise or to stand up." *Out of sleep* means "to rise from spiritual inactivity and lethargy. No longer endowed with insensibility to the doctrines and duties of religion."[111] Spiritual sleep is "a fatal indifference to eternal things."[112]

Compulsion drives us to comment on the Peter's inspired words in his first epistle before delving further into the text. Consider the following verses with comments provided.

*Yet if any man suffer as a Christian* [because of the persecution then present against the church], *let him not be ashamed; but let him glorify God on this behalf. For the time is come* [for the beginning of the destruction of Jerusalem] *that judgment* [persecutions] *must begin at the house of God* [the church]: *and if it first begin at us* [Christians], *what shall the end be of them* [the Jews] *that obey not the gospel of God? And if the righteous* [the saints] *scarcely be saved* [from the destruction of Jerusalem], *where shall the ungodly and the sinner* [the disobedient Jews] *appear? Wherefore let them* [the Christians] *that suffer according to the will of God commit the keeping of their souls to him in well doing, as unto a faithful Creator* (I Pet. 4:16-19).

**Verse 12.** *The night is far spent, the day is at hand: let us therefore, the day is at hand:, and let us put on the armor of light.* *The night* means the spiritual darkness in which the unbelieving Jews chose to remain. It was the period of time between the establishment of the church, and the destruction of Jerusalem so

---
[110] Albert Barnes.
[111] Adam Clarke.
[112] Robert Jamieson, A.R. Fausset, and David Brown.

# Commentary on Romans

declared by the Lord. Night is when men sleep and rest in tranquility, when peace envelops their space.

The twilight of the Old Law had come, and the dawn of the new day of the church began to shine on the day of Pentecost. The shadows of the moonlight age grew dark and the light of that night was fading quickly. The spiritual law of Moses ended at the cross of Christ (Col. 2:14). Now the civil law of Moses would also cease as AD 70 was now close at hand.

The Patriarchal age was the starlight age, the Mosaical age was the moonlight age, and the Christian age is the sunlight age. The moonlight age of Moses was coming to its civil end; Paul was warning the early church of the eminent destruction of Jerusalem.

The time was not so far away when the destruction of Jerusalem would begin. Jesus identified the time as: *When ye therefore shall see the abomination of desolation, spoken of by Daniel the prophet, stand in the holy place, (whoso readeth, let him understand)* (Matt. 24:15).

Paul says at the close of this letter: *And the God of peace shall bruise Satan under your feet shortly. The grace of our Lord Jesus Christ be with you. Amen* (Rom. 16:20). This verse echoes what we have here. Notice Paul's use of the word *shortly*. It is used in twelve verses in the New Testament and is defined as: soon, briefly, or swiftly. The word cannot apply to distant future events. Paul said in Romans 13:12 that *the day is at hand* which means near, and he used the word *shortly* in Romans 16:20. Only those who wrest the Scriptures in an effort make these words and phrases mean distant or far into the future.

*The day is at hand*—what day? The day of salvation from the destruction of Jerusalem. There can be no other day under consideration. If this refers to the Lord's second coming, then, again, it is the case Paul was endowed with more information about the Lord's second coming than the Lord Himself. Such is indeed a fruition of foolishness.

The *last days* had indeed come, but what are the *last days*? The

# Commentary on Romans

number of those believe and teach the *last days* equates to the last times of the world is beyond counting. Sadly, countless members of the Lord's church also contend for the same. However, the phrase *last days* does not refer to such time.

There are six passages which record the *last days* all of which we shall observe. We shall insert in bold text, where needed, the phrase **of Judaism**, meaning the last days of the Old Law, the religious system of the Old Law, the civil system of the Old Law, and all things pertaining to the Law of Moses. We shall also provide comments afterward.

*And it shall come to pass in the last days* **of Judaism,** *that the mountain of the Lord's house shall be established in the top of the mountains, and shall be exalted above the hills; and all nations shall flow unto it* (Isa. 2:2). The Lord's church was indeed established during the *last days* of Judaism.

*But in the last days* **of Judaism,** *it shall come to pass, that the mountain of the house of the Lord shall be established in the top of the mountains, and it shall be exalted above the hills; and people shall flow unto it* (Mic. 4:1). This passage is a prophecy of Micah, who was contemporary with Isaiah.

*And it shall come to pass in the last days* **of Judaism,** *saith God, I will pour out of my Spirit upon all flesh: and your sons and your daughters shall prophesy, and your young men shall see visions, and your old men shall dream dreams* (Acts 2:17). The apostles did indeed see the Spirit poured out in the *last days* of Judaism.

*This know also, that in the last days* **of Judaism,** *perilous times shall come* (II Tim. 3:1). In the *last days* **of Judaism** perilous times of earthquakes and famines did come to pass, as the Lord declared in Matthew 24, Mark 13, and Luke 21.

*Hath in these last days* **of Judaism** *spoken unto us by his Son, whom he hath appointed heir of all things, by whom also he made the worlds* (Heb. 1:2). The Lord began His preaching in the *last days* of Judaism.

# Commentary on Romans

*Knowing this first, that there shall come in the last days* **of Judaism,** *scoffers, walking after their own lusts* (II Pet. 3:3). Scoffers of the New Law of Christ walked after their own lusts of the Old Law, in the *last days* of Judaism.

In addition to these clear passages, there are more that have reference to the *last days* of Judaism.

*Who verily was foreordained before the foundation of the world, but was manifest in* **these last times** *for you* (I Pet. 1:20).

*Little children,* **it is the last time***: and as ye have heard that Antichrist shall come, even now are there many Antichrists; whereby we know that* **it is the last time** (I Jno. 2:18).

The phrase, *in these last times*, is found twice, and the phrase, *it is the last time,* once. It is as clear as inspiration could have made it! The *last times* and the *last days* were the days of the end of all things Mosaical. For men to contend we are **now** *in the last time* or that we **now** live in the *last days* does not harmonize with the Scripture and rejects the message of the inspired authors .

Many argue that the Christian dispensation is the *last times* or the *last days*. Those who contend for said position err, neither knowing nor understanding what inspiration plainly teaches. The *last times* and the *last days* were the ending days of Judaism—nothing more, nothing less.

**Verses 13-14.** *Let us walk honestly, as in the day; not in rioting and drunkenness, not in chambering and wantonness, not in strife and envying. But put ye on the Lord Jesus Christ, and make not provision for the flesh, to fulfill the lusts thereof.* Verses 13-14 are mandates set forth by Paul which bear negative and positive charges. Negative aspects come first, and the positive emphasis follows. Paul, in keeping with his style and manner, forgets not to encourage the brethren in their Christian walk. This was true especially in light of the matter at hand.

The *walk* here means to live, conduct, or behave properly. The conduct of the saint must be honest and morally upright. Chris-

# Commentary on Romans

tians do themselves much hurt when they act otherwise. Christians must realize the Lord sees all *as in the day.* He is not blinded by the cover of darkness. Places of sin most often open their doors in the night. Men who frequent places of strong drink —drunkenness, ill repute—chambering and unbridled lusts— wantonness, are not adorned with the spiritual clothing of which the Lord approves. They have not *put on the Lord Jesus Christ* nor prepared themselves for the time when they must give an account of their deeds. *For we must all appear before the judgment seat of Christ; that every one may receive the things done in his body, according to that he hath done, whether it be good or bad* (II Cor. 5:10). *So then every one of us shall give account of himself to God* (Rom. 14:12). *For God shall bring every work into judgment, with every secret thing, whether it be good, or whether it be evil* (Ecc. 12:14).

No Christian should be guilty of unseemly conduct. Love does not behave itself unseemly (1 Cor. 13:5): A Christian man should be a gentleman—a gentle man. He should not stumble, as if he were walking in the dark; he should walk uprightly, as in the day. But if he does not walk in the light of the gospel, he is sure to stumble. He should not be guilty of revelling and drunkenness; the two usually go together. To revel is to engage in hilarious conduct, and the drunkard usually does that. "Not in chambering"—not in unchaste conduct with the opposite sex; and wantonness—lewdness. Strife and jealousy usually grow out of such conduct. Verse 14 is in contrast with verse 13. Instead of indulging in such things as mentioned in verse 13, we are to clothe ourselves with the characteristics manifested by our Lord while he was in the flesh—put ourselves completely under his authority, and let him always be our guide. We are to make his life our life[113] [sic].

The phrase, *not in strife and envying*, means the saint must not involve himself in wrangling or contention. He must not have an attitude of uncontrolled excitement nor endow himself with fierceness or indignation. Further, he must not be envious or conten-

---
[113] Robertson L. Whiteside.

# Commentary on Romans

tious; he must not seek rivalry or promote jealousy.

*Putting on,* or being clothed with Jesus Christ, signifies receiving and believing the Gospel—and consequently taking its maxims for the government of life, having the mind that was in Christ. The ancient Jews frequently use the phrase, putting on the *shechinah* (meaning the feminine aspect of the Divine, DHC) or Divine majesty, to signify the soul's being clothed with immortality, and rendered fit for glory. To be clothed with a person is a Greek phrase, signifying to assume the interests of another—to enter into his views, to imitate him, and be wholly on his side.

The charge to *make not provision for the flesh* refers not to food, clothing, and shelter; rather, the intention here is *making provisions for* fleshly lusts and desires. Such is made clear when considering the last words of the passage, *to fulfill the lusts thereof.* The word *lusts* means forbidden lust. Many men have unquenchable thirsts and lusts, *rioting and drunkenness, chambering and wantonness.*[114]

Additionally, concerning making provisions for the flesh, Jesus taught:

*Therefore I say unto you, Take no thought for your life, what ye shall eat, or what ye shall drink; nor yet for your body, what ye shall out on. Is not the life more than meat, and the body more than raiment? Behold the fowls of the air: for they sow not, neither do they reap, nor gather into barns; yet your heavenly Father feedeth them. Are ye not much better than they? Which of you by taking thought can add one cubit unto his stature? And why take ye thought for raiment? Consider the lilies of the field, how they grow; they toil not, neither do they spin: And yet I say unto you, That even Solomon in all his glory was not arrayed like one of these. Wherefore, if God so clothe the grass of the field, which to day is, and to morrow is cast into the*

---

[114] Adam Clarke.

# Commentary on Romans

*oven, shall he not much more clothe you, O ye of little faith? Therefore take no thought, saying, What shall we eat? Or, What shall we drink? Or, Wherewithal shall we be clothed? (For after all these things do the Gentiles seek:) for your heavenly Father knoweth that ye have need of all these things. But seek ye first the kingdom of God, and his righteousness, and all these things shall be granted unto you. Take therefore no thought fo to morrow: for the morrow shall take thought for the things of itself. Sufficient unto the day is the evil thereof (Matt. 6:25-34).*

David wrote: *I have been young, and now am old; yet have I not seen the righteous forsaken, not his seed begging bread* (Ps. 37:25). Righteous men need not seek for things physical, but physical men often seek for things spiritual.

## Chapter End Notes

Every passage involving the phrase, *this generation*, is provided below. The fact is that the Lord spoke the phrase every time save one. The one passage in which the Lord did not make use of the phrase is found in Acts 2:40, in which Peter used it when he preached the first Gospel sermon. Thus he reminded the Jews to prevent the loss of their lives once the fall of Jerusalem began. The Lord warned the generation then living—*this generation,* to be aware of the coming destruction of Jerusalem. Christ, having warned the Jews so many times of the pending fall of Jerusalem should have been a strong motivation for the Jews who heard the apostles preach that message on the Day of Pentecost. Observe each of the passages in light of the context in which each is found.

Acts 2:38 is the salvation from sin, but verse 40 is the salvation from the destruction of Jerusalem. The prophet Joel made this crystal clear: *And I will shew wonders in the heavens and in the earth, blood, and fire, and pillars of smoke. The sun shall be turned into darkness, and the moon into blood, before the great and the terrible day of the Lord come. And it shall come to pass, that whosoever shall call on the name of the Lord shall be delivered* (Joel 2:30-32a). For this reason Peter quoted the prophecy

# Commentary on Romans

of Joel on the day of Pentecost (Acts 2:19-21).

> *But whereunto shall I liken this generation? It is like unto children sitting in the markets, and calling unto their fellows* (Matt. 11:16).

> *The men of Nineveh shall rise in judgment with this generation, and shall condemn it: because they repented at the preaching of Jonas; and, behold, a greater than Jonas is here. The queen of the south shall rise up in the judgment with this generation, and shall condemn it: for she came from the uttermost parts of the earth to hear the wisdom of Solomon; and, behold, a greater than Solomon is here* (Matt. 12:41-42).

> *Then goeth he, and taketh with himself seven other spirits more wicked than himself, and they enter in and dwell there: and the last state of that man is worse than the first. Even so shall it be also unto this wicked generation* (Matt. 12:45).

> *Verily I say unto you, All these things shall come upon this generation* (Matt. 23:36).

> *Verily I say unto you, This generation shall not pass, till all these things be fulfilled* (Matt. 24:34).

> *And he sighed deeply in his spirit, and saith, Why doth this generation seek after a sign? verily I say unto you, There shall no sign be given unto this generation* (Mk. 8:12).

> *Whosoever therefore shall be ashamed of me and of my words in this adulterous and sinful generation; of him also shall the Son of man be ashamed, when he cometh in the glory of his Father with the holy angels* (Mk. 8:38).

> *Verily I say unto you, that this generation shall not pass, till all these things be done* (Mk. 13:30).

# Commentary on Romans

*And the Lord said, Whereunto then shall I liken the men of this generation? and to what are they like* (Lk. 7:31)?

*And when the people were gathered thick together, he began to say, This is an evil generation: they seek a sign; and there shall no sign be given it, but the sign of Jonas the prophet. For as Jonas was a sign unto the Ninevites, so shall also the Son of man be to this generation. The queen of the south shall rise up in the judgment with the men of this generation, and condemn them: for she came from the utmost parts of the earth to hear the wisdom of Solomon; and, behold, a greater than Solomon is here. The men of Nineveh shall rise up in the judgment with this generation, and shall condemn it: for they repented at the preaching of Jonas; and, behold, a greater than Jonas is here* (Lk. 11:29-32).

*That the blood of all the prophets, which was shed from the foundation of the world, may be required of this generation; From the blood of Abel unto the blood of Zacharias, which perished between the altar and the temple: verily I say unto you, It shall be required of this generation* (Lk. 11:50-51).

*And the lord commended the unjust steward, because he had done wisely: for the children of this world are in their generation wiser than the children of light* (Lk. 16:8).

*But first must he suffer many things, and be rejected of this generation* (Lk. 17:25).

*Verily I say unto you, This generation shall not pass away, till all be fulfilled* (Lk. 21:32).

In Acts 2:40 we have the charge to the Jews by Peter and the rest of the apostles to save themselves from the destruction which was to soon fall upon the great city of the Jews. *And with*

# Commentary on Romans

*many other words did he testify and exhort, saying, Save yourselves from this untoward generation* (Acts 2:40).

Surely one can see the intention of the apostles when they proclaimed the need to save themselves from the then living generation. Notice the salvation under consideration here is the salvation from the then-living generation—not a past generation nor a future generation but *this generation*—the one then living to whom the apostles then spoke.

When the apostles were handed the *keys to the kingdom,* as promised by the Lord, they unlocked the doors of the kingdom and opened them widely on the day of Pentecost. They unsheathed the *sword of the Spirit* with determined dedication, never to sheath it again (cf. Matt. 16:18-19; Eph. 6:17). The apostles wielded the *sword of the Spirit* with unrelenting power and surgical precision, which *pricked* the hearts of about three thousand souls on the Day of Pentecost (Acts 2:37).

The doctrine of Premillennialism falls hard against and upon the sword of God and will die a slow but sure death. To insist *this generation,* to whom the Lord spoke, is to be applied to generations yet future is folly, foolish, and false. The doctrines of Premillennialists are a devilish, damnable, and detestable diatribe. The doctrine is untrue, unacceptable, unrighteous, and unholy. Indeed the *unstable and unlearned wrest* the Scriptures as Peter declared in II Peter 3:16.

## Romans 14:1-9

*1 Him that is weak in the faith receive ye, but not to doubtful disputations. 2 For one believeth that he may eat all things: another, who is weak, eateth herbs. 3 Let not him that eateth despise him that eateth not; and let not him which eateth not judge him that eateth: for God hath received him. 4 Who art thou that judgest another man's servant? to his own master he standeth or falleth. Yea, he shall be holden up: for God is able to make him stand. 5 One man esteemeth one day above another: another esteemeth every day alike. Let every man be fully persuaded in his own mind. 6 He that*

# Commentary on Romans

*regardeth the day, regardeth it unto the Lord; and he that regardeth not the day, to the Lord he doth not regard it. He that eateth, eateth to the Lord, for he giveth God thanks; and he that eateth not, to the Lord he eateth not, and giveth God thanks. 7 For none of us liveth to himself, and no man dieth to himself. 8 For whether we live, we live unto the Lord; and whether we die, we die unto the Lord: whether we live therefore, or die, we are the Lord's. 9 For to this end Christ both died, and rose, and revived, that he might be Lord both of the dead and living.*

Whiteside suggests that

> in this chapter and in 1 Cor., chapters 8 and 10:14-33, Paul discusses the matter of eating meat; but in the main the points of emphasis in the two letters are different. In Corinthians he warns brethren against eating meat under circumstances that might lead others to eat certain meat in honor of an idol, but the main point in this fourteenth chapter is somewhat different. The Christian Jews, at least, many of them, had not entirely broken away from the Law of Moses. They observed certain days, and were disposed to condemn the Gentile Christians for not doing so. They would not eat meat that the law declared unclean. Some ate only herbs, lest they might eat meat that had been dedicated to an idol. The Gentile Christians would consider their conduct as foolishness. Perhaps some Gentile converts, having been used to eating certain meats dedicated to idols, feared to eat any meat, lest they honor an idol in so doing. All these matters were grounds for a lot of criticisms and strife[115] [sic].

The church at Rome had many troubles, not unlike congregations today. Opinions vary on countless subjects, but it is essential to bear in mind that opinions are not standards by which the church is to be regulated. One may hold to the opinion Paul's thorn in the flesh were the Pharisees who continued to trouble him on every side. Another may be of the opinion Paul's thorn

---
[115] Robertson L. Whiteside.

# Commentary on Romans

involved the Sadducees—or perhaps he had poor vision. While others might hold to other opinions, it must be realized opinions apply to those who subscribe to them. Doctrine, however, applies to the universal church and is that by which the saints must govern themselves. Sadly, many in the church have such strong opinions that they dictate them as doctrine.

**Verse 1.** *Him that is weak in the faith receive ye, but not to doubtful disputations.* The Jews had no little trouble in surrendering to the New Testament system of Christ, and in many things held to the Law of Moses.

Just as in the church of Corinth experienced contentions, so it was the case in the church of Rome: *Now I beseech you, brethren, by the name of our Lord Jesus Christ, that ye all speak the same thing, and that there be no divisions among you; but that ye be perfectly joined together in the same mind and in the same judgment. For it hath been declared unto me of you, my brethren, by them which are of the house of Chloe, that there are contentions among you* (I Cor. 1:10-11).

**Verse 2.** *For one believeth that he may eat all things: another, who is weak, eateth herbs.* The Jewish converts in the church at Rome believed the eating of certain meats was forbidden, holding to the Law of Moses. Peter was troubled with the same matter as is seen in the book of Acts.

> *There was a certain man in Caesarea called Cornelius, a centurion of the band called the Italian band, A devout man, and one that feared God with all his house, which gave much alms to the people, and prayed to God alway. He saw in a vision evidently about the ninth hour of the day an angel of God coming in to him, and saying unto him, Cornelius. And when he looked on him, he was afraid, and said, What is it, Lord? And he said unto him, Thy prayers and thine alms are come up for a memorial before God. And now send men to Joppa, and call for one Simon, whose surname is Peter: He lodgeth with one Simon a tanner, whose house is by the sea side: he shall tell thee what thou oughtest to do. And when the angel which spake unto*

# Commentary on Romans

*Cornelius was departed, he called two of his household servants, and a devout soldier of them that waited on him continually; And when he had declared all these things unto them, he sent them to Joppa. On the morrow, as they went on their journey, and drew nigh unto the city, Peter went up upon the housetop to pray about the sixth hour: And he became very hungry, and would have eaten: but while they made ready, he fell into a trance, And saw heaven opened, and a certain vessel descending unto him, as it had been a great sheet knit at the four corners, and let down to the earth: Wherein were all manner of fourfooted beasts of the earth, and wild beasts, and creeping things, and fowls of the air. And there came a voice to him, Rise, Peter; kill, and eat. But Peter said, Not so, Lord; for I have never eaten any thing that is common or unclean. And the voice spake unto him again the second time, What God hath cleansed, that call not thou common* (Acts 10:1-15).

After the vision observed by Peter, he still found it difficult to surrender to the Divine instruction given to him. Paul confronted Peter about the matter of not eating things forbidden by the Law of Moses and Peter's eating with the Jews only. Paul told him *before them all, If thou, being a Jew, livest after the manner of Gentiles, and not as do the Jews, why compellest thou the Gentiles to live as do the Jews* (Gal. 2:14b)?

**Verse 3.** *Let not him that eateth despise him that eateth not; and let not him which eateth not judge him that eateth: for God hath received him.* "Many Jewish Christians held that the Law of Moses was still in force. They could not always be sure that the meat bought in the market was not from an animal which the law declared unclean, nor could they be sure that it had not been dedicated to an idol. They therefore ate herbs"[116] [sic].

**Verse 4.** *Who art thou that judgest another man's servant? to his own master he standeth or falleth. Yea, he shall be holden up: for God is able to make him stand.* Many Christians in the early church owned slaves—servants—as it is stated in the pas-

---
[116] Robertson L. Whiteside.

# Commentary on Romans

sage. Barnes comments: "That is, who gave you this right to sit in judgment on others; compare Luk 12:14. There is reference here particularly to the 'Jew,' who on account of his ancient privileges, and because he had the Law of God, would assume the prerogative of 'judging' in the case, and insist on conformity to his own views; see Acts 15. The doctrine of this Epistle is uniformly, that the Jew had no such privilege, but that in regard to salvation he was on the same level with the Gentile"[117] [sic].

All men are subject to the judgment of God, who causes one to stand or fall, based on obedience. Saints must judge doctrinal matters, but they are forbidden to do so in matters of opinions.

**Verses 5-6.** *One man esteemeth one day above another: another esteemeth every day alike. Let every man be fully persuaded in his own mind. He that regardeth the day, regardeth it unto the Lord; and he that regardeth not the day, to the Lord he doth not regard it. He that eateth, eateth to the Lord, for he giveth God thanks; and he that eateth not, to the Lord he eateth not, and giveth God thanks.* Paul's audience and purpose must be kept in mind. Differences between Jewish and Gentile converts were at times strong. Some Jews more readily surrendered the things pertaining to the Old Law of Moses, while others relentlessly kept themselves addicted to it.

Paul addresses the problem forthrightly in these verses. The *one man* who esteemed *one day above another* refers to the Jewish convert who wished to keep certain days reverenced, as mandated according to the Law of Moses. The *another* (man who) esteemed *every day alike* refers to the Gentile convert. Below are comments by Barnes and Whiteside.

> Another "esteemeth—That is, the Gentile" Christian. Not having been brought up amidst the Jewish customs, and not having imbibed their opinions and prejudices, they would not regard these days as having any special sacredness. The appointment of those days had a special reference "to the Jews." They were designed to keep them as a separate people, and to prepare the nation for the "reality," of which their rites were

---
[117] Albert Barnes.

# Commentary on Romans

but the shadow. When the Messiah came, the passover, the feast of tabernacles, and the other special festivals of the Jews, of course vanished, and it is perfectly clear that the apostles never intended to inculcate their observance on the Gentile converts[118] [sic].

The leaders of a church could not adopt these Jewish holidays and demand that all the members observe them. The Judaizing teachers had got in their work among the churches of Galatia, which led Paul to say, "Ye observe days, and months, and seasons, and years. I am afraid of you, lest by any means I have bestowed labor upon you in vain" (Gal. 4:10,11). If the leaders should set any such days to be observed by the church, the members should not submit to such an arrangement. "Let no man judge you in meat, or in drink, or in respect of a feast day or a new moon or a sabbath day" (Col. 2:16)[119] [sic].

These verses have been bludgeoned, blundered, battered, and beaten by countless commentators to justify what the Scriptures do not teach nor intend. So called *Christian holidays* have been awarded the proverbial stamp of approval based on gross perversions on these verses. Christmas, Easter, Palm Sunday, Ash Wednesday, and other holidays are not , and never were, Biblical mandates. Historical research of each of these so-called religious holidays will show they all find their roots in Catholicism. There are no religious holidays saints are required to honor. The New Testament mentions not one holiday ordained by inspired men or God. Saints are required to assemble to worship the Lord on the first day the week to reverence, respect, rightfully regard, and remember the Lord's death. Every religious holiday is dictated by man. Holidays are not in and of themselves sinful; but when one dictates holidays must be kept for the purpose of rendering homage to Deity, such is contrary to the teaching of the New Testament and is therefore sinful.

It must be understood the context of these verses refers to the differences between the Jewish and Gentile converts in the early

---

[118] Albert Barnes.

[119] Robertson L. Whiteside.

# Commentary on Romans

church. When one takes a text out of context, he makes it a pretext. There is not one day reserved to reverence the birth of Christ, His resurrection, His entry into Jerusalem, or other such occasion. Saints are to remember the Lord's death on the first day of the week by participating in the partaking of the Lord's Supper. This is the only day reserved unto the Lord which saints must observe which must be done upon the first day of every week.

**Verses 7-8.** *For none of us liveth to himself, and no man dieth to himself. For whether we live, we live unto the Lord; and whether we die, we die unto the Lord: whether we live therefore, or die, we are the Lord's.* Man is not the dictator of standards, rules, or guidelines in either spiritual or moral matters. Such a philosophy is humanistic—it is humanism. Humanism is the philosophy which insists men must take a non-theistic stance in life which must be centered on human agency looking only to science rather than revelation (inspiration) from a supernatural source (God) to understand the world.

Every society must be regulated by Divine Law. When men allow humanists to dictate doctrines for society, they step far off the pathway of godliness into the field of folly, foolishness, and devilish destruction. Twice Solomon said: *There is a way which seemeth right unto a man, but the end thereof are the ways of death* (Pro. 14:12; 16:25). Jeremiah declared: *Lord, I know that the way of man is not in himself: it is not in man that walketh to direct his steps* (Jer. 10:23).

The Jews were no longer bound to the Law of Moses, the Gentiles were no longer subject to the Patriarchal Law; both were all one in Christ and no longer lived under the old religious systems to which they were formerly married. Both were now married to Christ (Rom. 7:4). Paul clearly declared such when he wrote: *There is neither Jew nor Greek, there is neither bond nor free, there is neither male nor female: for ye are all one in Christ Jesus* (Gal. 3:28).

**Verse 9.** *For to this end Christ both died, and rose, and revived, that he might be Lord both of the dead and living.* The phrase, *to this end*, means "for the purpose of." Christ died for the pur-

# Commentary on Romans

pose of making us—Jew and Gentile—one in Christ. Christ prayed to this end when he uttered the words; *Neither pray I for these alone, but for them also which shall believe on me through their word; That they all may be one; as thou, Father, art in me, and I in thee, that they also may be one in us: that the world may believe that thou hast sent me* (Jno. 17:20-21).

Paul wrote of the death of Christ, saying it was the avenue by which He *abolished in his flesh the enmity, even the law of commandments contained in ordinances; for to make in himself of twain one new man, so making peace* (Eph. 2:15).

Christ *rose,* as Paul stated, meaning He was resurrected from the dead. The activities of Christ to make all men one was threefold. First, Christ died; second, He rose from the dead; and, third, He *revived,* which literally means "to live again." Christ did not merely rise from the dead, He *revived* Himself. He fully recovered, and He rose from the dead to die no more. When Lazarus came from the tomb, the Lord said, *Loose him, and let him go* (Jno. 11:44). Lazarus emerged in his burial clothing. Jesus came from the tomb without His burial garments. Lazarus would have to be donned with burial clothing again; Christ never again was to wear such because He was to die no more.

The phrase, *both of the dead and living,* means those saints who had already died and those yet living. When Jesus said, *God is not the God of the dead, but of the living* (Matt. 22:32), He meant the spiritually living and not the spiritually dead. In contrast, He said; *And as touching the dead, that they rise: have ye not read in the book of Moses, how in the bush God spake unto him, saying, I am the God of Abraham, and the God of Isaac, and the God of Jacob?* The Lord meant Abraham, Isaac, and Jacob were spiritually alive, living in the Hadean realm of paradise (Mk. 12:26).

## Romans 14:10-18

*10 But why dost thou judge thy brother? or why dost thou set at nought thy brother? for we shall all stand before the judgment seat of Christ. 11 For it is written, As I live, saith the Lord, every knee shall bow to me,*

# Commentary on Romans

*and every tongue shall confess to God. 12 So then every one of us shall give account of himself to God. 13 Let us not therefore judge one another any more: but judge this rather, that no man put a stumblingblock or an occasion to fall in his brother's way. 14 I know, and am persuaded by the Lord Jesus, that there is nothing unclean of itself: but to him that esteemeth any thing to be unclean, to him it is unclean. 15 But if thy brother be grieved with thy meat, now walkest thou not charitably. Destroy not him with thy meat, for whom Christ died. 16 Let not then your good be evil spoken of: 17 For the kingdom of God is not meat and drink; but righteousness, and peace, and joy in the Holy Ghost. 18 For he that in these things serveth Christ is acceptable to God, and approved of men.*

These verses have long been misused to justify *situation ethics.* The philosophy of situational ethics was pioneered by Joseph Fletcher (1905-1991). Fletcher taught that every law, rule, principle, ideal, and norm is only contingent and valid if it happens to serve *love.* In certain circumstances, laws may be broken or ignored if a different course will result in a better and more loving outcome. Fletcher's philosophy is Humanistic. Humanism teaches what is right for one may not be right for another and vice-versa. Both philosophies are diametrically opposed to Biblical teaching. They enthrone man above God. Both assault godiness and moral virtues. Both are damnable and blasphemous. Men who live by either or both shall die in sin.

**Verse 10.** *But why dost thou judge thy brother? or why dost thou set at nought thy brother? for we shall all stand before the judgment seat of Christ.* It is not at all the case judgments are forbidden. The context of this passage must be reserved in order to ascertain the proper exegesis. The subject under consideration is the eating of certain meats or the refusal thereof.

Jewish converts who were burdened in conscience by the eating of many of the meats consumed by the Gentile converts were quick to pass the judgment of condemnation on the Gentiles because of some of the meats they ate. The Jews "who believed they should observe the days required in the law, and refused to

# Commentary on Romans

eat meats prohibited by the law, would condemn [the Gentiles, DHC] as sinners those who did not do likewise; and those who ate meat and refused to observe certain days would count as foolish and unworthy of consideration those who did not eat meat and observed days"[120] [sic].

It is truly amazing how nearly every saint considers his brother as the one weaker in the faith, while considering himself as the stronger one. The *meat-eating* Gentiles considered the *non-meat-eating* Jews as weaker in the faith, and the non-meat-eating Jews considered the Gentile converts the weaker ones. The problem was no small matter for the Roman congregation. It was for this reason Paul reminded the saints that *we shall all stand before the judgment seat of Christ.* Christ would judge the brethren regarding such matters. However, the judgment Christ will impose, will not be based upon the eating of meats or the refusal to do so. The judgment imposed by the Lord would be based upon the attitude and frame of mind with which the saints of Rome judged one another.

Judgments must be garbed with mercy and righteousness. Where judgment is passed without mercy, mercy is not awarded. Judgments not clothed with righteousness result in righteousness denied. The Lord said: *Judge not, that ye be not judged. For with what judgment ye judge, ye shall be judged: and with what measure ye mete, it shall be measured to you again* (Matt. 7:1-2). Further, the Lord mandated the employment of righteousness in judging. *Judge not according to the appearance, but judge righteous judgment* (Jno. 7:24). The Lord's brother summarized the Lord's edicts when he wrote: *For he shall have judgment without mercy, that hath shewed no mercy; and mercy rejoiceth against judgment* (Jas. 2:13).

Paul reminded the brethren in Rome, *we shall all* (meaning both Jew and Gentile) *stand before the judgment seat of Christ,* which served as a stern warning against passing judgments of condemnation toward one another. Saints are to judge according to works and fruits, they are forbidden to judge the motives of the heart.

---

[120] Robertson L. Whiteside.

# Commentary on Romans

**Verse 11.** *For it is written, As I live, saith the Lord, every knee shall bow to me, and every tongue shall confess to God.* The passage quoted is from Isaiah, who wrote: *I have sworn by myself, the word is gone out of my mouth in righteousness, and shall not return, That unto me every knee shall bow, every tongue shall swear* (Isa. 45:23). The Greek preposition translated "for" means "because" it is written—the Lord will call all men into account. Judgments must be well clad in mercy and righteousness, lest mercy and righteousness be withheld and withdrawn.

**Verse 12.** *So then every one of us shall give account of himself to God.* Here the word *so* equates to *wherefore* or *therefore*. Because all men must bow before the Lord, it behooves them to judge others as they wish for the Lord to judge them. It is well to observe all men will account for themselves. The goodness of one will not be imputed to another, as Ezekiel 18:20-24 shows.

> *The soul that sinneth, it shall die. The son shall not bear the iniquity of the father, neither shall the father bear the iniquity of the son: the righteousness of the righteous shall be upon him, and the wickedness of the wicked shall be upon him. But if the wicked will turn from all his sins that he hath committed, and keep all my statutes, and do that which is lawful and right, he shall surely live, he shall not die. All his transgressions that he hath committed, they shall not be mentioned unto him: in his righteousness that he hath done he shall live. Have I any pleasure at all that the wicked should die? saith the Lord God: and not that he should return from his ways, and live? But when the righteous turneth away from his righteousness, and committeth iniquity, and doeth according to all the abominations that the wicked man doeth, shall he live? All his righteousness that he hath done shall not be mentioned: in his trespass that he hath trespassed, and in his sin that he hath sinned, in them shall he die.*

No man can stand before God, depend upon the goodness of another, and be awarded eternal life. All men are judged by their own merits—not on those of others. *For we must all appear*

# Commentary on Romans

*before the judgment seat of Christ; that every one may receive the things done in his body, according to that he hath done, whether it be good or bad* (II Cor. 5:10).

**Verse 13.** *Let us not therefore judge one another any more: but judge this rather, that no man put a stumblingblock or an occasion to fall in his brother's way.* "If a man's eating meat as food led some brother to think he was eating it in honor of an idol, and was thereby led to eat meat in honor of an idol, his eating the meat became a stumblingblock over which his brother stumbled and fell. A man should never insist on exercising his rights or liberties, if harm comes of his doing so"[121] [sic].

Saints are not permitted to pass judgments that lack mercy. Paul's instruction for the saints at Rome to no longer *judge one another* was seated in the lack of mercy of the Jewish and Gentile converts.

*Judge this rather, that no man put a stumblingblock or an occasion to fall in his brother's way.* Far better to place stepping stones of assistance on the pathway of thy brother than to cast stones of stumbling before them. Those who place stones of stumbling shall give an account for each stone cast.

The context here remains with the eating of meats or the refusal thereof by the Christian Gentiles and Jews. "Let both the converted Jew and Gentile consider that they should labor to promote each other's spiritual interests, and not be a means of hindering each other in their Christian course; or of causing them to abandon the Gospel, on which, and not on questions of rites and ceremonies, the salvation of their soul depends"[122] [sic].

**Verses 14-15.** *I know, and am persuaded by the Lord Jesus, that there is nothing unclean of itself: but to him that esteemeth any thing to be unclean, to him it is unclean. But if thy brother be grieved with thy meat, now walkest thou not charitably. Destroy not him with thy meat, for whom Christ died.* The persuasion with which Paul was directed was inspired persuasion. The word *persuasion* means to be induced by and to have confidence in.

---

[121] Robertson L. Whiteside.
[122] Adam Clarke.

# Commentary on Romans

Paul was induced by inspiration and had confidence in what was revealed to him by inspiration.

Paul was instructing the saints of Rome by means of inspiration. Paul plainly stated he was *persuaded by the Lord Jesus.* When Paul was *persuaded* matters not, be it upon the occasion of his writing this epistle or an earlier time. The persuasion still came from *the Lord Jesus.* The importance of these things is first: as saints in the Lord's church, the converted Jew and Gentile should give great consideration to the fact Paul received his persuasion from the Lord. Second, in their efforts to be servants of the Lord they would be more provoked unto brotherly love.

That *there is nothing unclean of itself* does not categorize all things. The subject before the saints of Rome was the eating of meats; they understood the context in which Paul issued the statement. Paul lists the following as works of the flesh which are indeed unclean. *Now the works of the flesh are manifest, which are these; Adultery, fornication, uncleanness, lasciviousness, Idolatry, witchcraft, hatred, variance, emulations, wrath, strife, seditions, heresies, Envyings, murders, drunkenness, revellings, and such like: of the which I tell you before, as I have also told you in time past, that they which do such things shall not inherit the kingdom of God* (Gal. 5:19-21). None will assert the things listed by Paul are indeed profitable to the betterment of one's spiritual welfare. These things are indeed unclean.

Nothing God has provided for man's sustenance is to be refused. *For every creature of God is good, and nothing to be refused, if it be received with thanksgiving* (I Tim. 4:4). If, however, the conscience is violated, then he *that esteemeth any thing to be unclean, to him it is unclean.*

**Verse 15.** *But if thy brother be grieved with thy meat, now walkest thou not charitably. Destroy not him with thy meat, for whom Christ died.* The passage is not hard to understand. As Christians we must not cause our brethren grief. The context here refers to the eating of, or refraining from, things which grieved some brethren in the congregation at Rome.

Paul reminded the Jewish and Gentile converts they were breth-

# Commentary on Romans

ren, and it was for them as brethren that *Christ died.* Christ died for both—the Jew and the Gentile—and they should; therefore, regard their brothers in Christ as saints of great value and treat one another accordingly.

**Verse 16.** *Let not then your good be evil spoken of.* This verse too maintains its place within the confines of the eating or not eating of certain meats. It is better to refrain from the eating of anything than to engage in things which cast hindrances before one's brother. Those who know of a brother's opposition to a thing and continue to engage in such, ignoring his brother's conscience, casts obstacles before his brother. Doing so may cause a brother to lose his soul—not to mention his own as well. Better to do without and save both thyself and thy brother than to have a hand in the loss of both.

**Verse 17.** *For the kingdom of God is not meat and drink; but righteousness, and peace, and joy in the Holy Ghost.* The Kingdom of God is not a physical, but is spiritual in nature—ordained by the Father, headed and purchased by Christ, and revealed by the Holy Ghost. Jesus declared His Kingdom was not of this world—not physical—but spiritual (cf. Jno. 18:36). Paul stated the Kingdom of God is peace and joy in the Holy Ghost, meaning it was revealed by Him. Peace and joy are found in the Lord's church as revealed by inspired authors.

The phrase, *in the Holy Ghost*, has caused not a few troubles. Again, it serves students well to understand the context of the passage under consideration as well as seeking the definition of the word *in*, which is defined in part by implication, instrumentality, medially, or constructively. If, as some insist, peace and joy are found in the Holy Ghost, then it is the case there is no peace or joy to be had without the Holy Ghost. Such an argument fails miserably for there are many in the world of great wickedness who enjoy peace and joy. Many are at peace with their evil deeds. Many have great joy in wickedness. If there were no pleasure to be experienced in sin, Satan would refrain from the use of it. Moses chose *to suffer affliction with the people of God, than to enjoy the pleasures of sin for a season* (Heb. 11:25).

The peace and joy of which Paul speaks is spiritual peace and

## Commentary on Romans

joy, not the pleasures of peace and joy of the world. Further, keep in mind the mindset of the Jews and the Gentiles regarding their judgments of one another with respect to the eating or not eating of certain things. Both were forbidden to pride themselves in their eating or not eating. They were forbidden to rejoice and be at peace with themselves by passing judgments of condemnation on their fellow brethren. Rather, they were to seek the peace and joy of godliness revealed by the Holy Ghost.

Regardless of the difficulty some may have with this passage, it is vital to recall the setting of this passage is, first, within the age of inspiration. Second, the context addresses the casting forth of stumblingblocks before the brethren who comprised the church at Rome. Third, the peace and joy of which the apostle speaks refers to the peace and joy that should have existed between the Jewish and Gentile converts. It was through the Holy Ghost Paul revealed to the saints of Rome the eating of meats was not a spiritual matter, *for the kingdom of God is not meat and drink.*

The Lord gave no commandments regarding the eating of meats. However, the apostles addressed the matter and did so by inspiration. They forbade the eating of *meats offered to idols, and from blood, and from things strangled...* (Acts 15:29).

**Verse 18.** *For he that in these things serveth Christ is acceptable to God, and approved of men.* *These things* serving Christ refers to the peace and joy of the previous. Saints are to serve the Lord with both peace and joy. When men serve the Lord, they serve both their brethren and their fellow man.
For the Jewish and Gentile converts to serve their brethren and Christ proved them *acceptable to God.* To continue in condescending judgments against one another for the meats they ate or from which they refrained was not at all acceptable to the Father, nor was is serving Christ as they ought.

### Romans 14:19-23

*19 Let us therefore follow after the things which make for peace, and things wherewith one may edify another. 20 For meat destroy not the work of God. All things indeed are pure; but it is evil for that man who eateth*

# Commentary on Romans

*with offence. 21 It is good neither to eat flesh, nor to drink wine, nor any thing whereby thy brother stumbleth, or is offended, or is made weak. 22 Hast thou faith? have it to thyself before God. Happy is he that condemneth not himself in that thing which he alloweth. 23 And he that doubteth is damned if he eat, because he eateth not of faith: for whatsoever is not of faith is sin.*

The use of *us* means both Jew and Gentile which made up the body of Christ at Rome. Saints must be united in both mind and doctrine. The Lord prayed for unity and Paul besought it (Jno. 17:20-21; cf. I Cor. 1:10).

**Verse 19.** *Let us therefore follow after the things which make for peace, and things wherewith one may edify another.* Therefore shows the conclusion to all Paul addressed in this chapter. The two distinct objectives set forth here are peace and edification—peace first, because without it there can be no edification—then edification. Peace feeds edification and nurtures it to the betterment of unity among the brethren.

The phrase, *follow after*, means "to press on"; figuratively, of one who in a race runs swiftly to reach the goal. The aim of saints is to attain *the things which make for peace.*

Saints are forbidden to advocate strongly for the enforcement of opinions, doing so causes strife and division within the body of Christ. Christians must hotly pursue peace. Peace is a state of tranquility, exempt from rage, havoc, or war. Tranquility must have its place among the brethren for edification; without peace there is no tranquility or edification.

**Verse 20.** *For meat destroy not the work of God. All things indeed are pure; but it is evil for that man who eateth with offence.* Two imperatives are presented here. First, the destruction of the *work of God* is forbidden. Second, Paul forbids one to eat that which offends brethren.

*For meat* means for the sake of eating meat, which offends others. Scruples in Christian conduct are mandatory; they must not

# Commentary on Romans

be discarded. For the sake of having one's way in matters of opinion, one must be willing to step forward into the grace which makes for peace. For one to cause division and destruction within the body of Christ (because of preferences) works toward disunity, destruction, and is detrimental to the soul.

The word *destroy* means to demolish, as one would destroy a building. The church was built by the Lord, saints are *built upon the foundation of the apostles and prophets, Jesus Christ himself being the chief corner stone; In whom all the building fitly framed together groweth unto an holy temple in the Lord: In whom ye also are builded together for an habitation of God through the spirit* (Eph. 2:20-22). When one works toward the destruction of the Lord's church, he destroys His church. When brethren participate in destroying the Lord's building, the Lord no longer dwells therein.

A congregation without the Lord is one which journeys quickly toward eternal destruction. As members of the Lord's church, *we are laborers together with God: ye are God's husbandry, ye are God's building. According to the grace of God which is given unto me, as a wise masterbuilder, I have laid the foundation, and another buildeth thereon. But let every man take heed how he buildeth thereupon. For other foundation can no man lay than that is laid, which is Jesus Christ* (I Cor. 3:9-11).

The church is *the work of God*, and it behooves all Christians to contribute to the growth and progress of it. As saints, we either contribute to the spreading of borders of His Kingdom, or we are detrimental to it. *He that is not with me is against me: and he that gathereth not with me scattereth* (Lk. 11:23).

*All things indeed are pure.* The context of the "statement that 'all things are clean' applies to meats. The law declared certain animals unclean; that law was no longer binding. Legally no animal was now unclean, but it is evil to the man who eats with offense"[123] [sic]. Luke wrote:

> *On the morrow, as they went on their journey, and drew nigh unto the city, Peter went up upon the house-*

---
[123] Robertson L. Whiteside.

# Commentary on Romans

*top to pray about the sixth hour: And he became very hungry, and would have eaten: but while they made ready, he fell into a trance, And saw heaven opened, and a certain vessel descending unto him, as it had been a great sheet knit at the four corners, and let down to the earth: Wherein were all manner of fourfooted beasts of the earth, and wild beasts, and creeping things, and fowls of the air. And there came a voice to him, Rise, Peter; kill, and eat. But Peter said, Not so, Lord; for I have never eaten any thing that is common or unclean. And the voice spake unto him again the second time, What God hath cleansed, that call not thou common* (Acts 10:9-15).

The phrase, *but it is evil for that man who eateth with offence*, needs no voluminous commentary. "A Christian stumbles, or sins, when he violates his convictions; and it is evil for any one to lead a person to go against his convictions, no matter how innocent the act within itself may be"[124] [sic].

**Verse 21.** *It is good neither to eat flesh, nor to drink wine, nor any thing whereby thy brother stumbleth, or is offended, or is made weak.* Jamieson, Fausset, and Brown comment thus:

> **It is good not to eat flesh, nor to drink wine, nor any thing**—"nor to do any thing" **whereby**—"wherein" **thy brother stumbleth, or is offended, or is made weak**—rather, "is weak." These three words, it has been remarked, are each intentionally weaker than the other:—Which may cause a brother to stumble, or even be obstructed in his Christian course, nay—though neither of these may follow—wherein he continues weak; unable wholly to disregard the example, and yet unprepared to follow it." But this injunction to abstain from *flesh*, from *wine*, and from *whatsoever* may hurt the conscience of a brother, must be properly understood. Manifestly, the apostle is treating of the regulation of the Christian's conduct with reference simply to the prejudices of the weak in faith; and his directions are to be considered not as *prescriptions for*

---
[124] Robertson L. Whiteside.

> *one's entire lifetime*, even to promote the good of men on a large scale, but simply as cautions against the too free use of Christian liberty in matters where other Christians, through weakness, are not persuaded that such liberty is divinely allowed[125] (emph. theirs) [sic].

**Verse 22.** *Hast thou faith? have it to thyself before God. Happy is he that condemneth not himself in that thing which he alloweth.* Whiteside comments thus:

> The Christian who was well taught knew that the legal distinction between clean and unclean animals had been done away; he would therefore likely believe that he could eat any meat he chose to eat. Verse 22: "One man hath faith to eat all things." But the whole chapter shows that such faith must not be exercised under circumstances that might lead others to sin against their convictions. He might eat the meat in his own home in the presence of God. Bloomfield has this: "Keep this persuasion to yourself, and your God; use it when you have no other witness." A man condemns himself in what he approves, if in holding to it and practicing it he causes others to stumble[126] [sic].

The *faith* of which Paul speaks here is the faith possessed by the individual who ate his meat without violating his conscience. The *faith* which allowed one to eat meats by which others were troubled was not permitted to be forced upon others.

*Happy is he that condemneth not himself in that thing which he alloweth.* The word *happy* means "blessed." When one refrains from compelling others to adopt his opinions, he is blessed. Opinions forced on others become dogmas and are ills against the soul of the one dictating them, as well as those imposed upon. Matters of opinion are neither obligatory nor binding upon others. A Christian is condemned when he causes others to stumble even though his actions are not in themselves evil.

Paul summarized the matter when he wrote: *All things are lawful*

---

[125] Robert Jamieson, A.R. Fausset, and David Brown.

[126] Robertson L. Whiteside.

# Commentary on Romans

*unto me, but all things are not expedient: all things are lawful for me, but I will not be brought under the power of any* (I Cor. 6:12). *All things are lawful for me, but all things are not expedient: all things are lawful for me, but all things edify not* (I Cor. 10:23).

**Verse 23.** *And he that doubteth is damned if he eat, because he eateth not of faith: for whatsoever is not of faith is sin.* Whiteside correctly said: "The Jew who believed it wrong to eat certain meat, and yet ate the meat rather than to be called odd or foolish, sinned against himself and against God. If a man even has a doubt about the rightfulness of a certain thing, he should not engage in it. He is condemned if he does...."[127] [sic].

"This verse is a necessary part of the preceding, and should be read thus: But he that doubteth is condemned if he eat, because he eateth not of faith. The meaning is sufficiently plain. He that feeds on any kind of meats prohibited by the Mosaic law, with the persuasion in his mind that he may be wrong in so doing, is condemned by his conscience for doing that which he has reason to think God has forbidden"[128] [sic].

*For whatsoever is not of faith is sin.* If it is the case one cannot in good conscience engage in a thing, then it is sinful for him to do so even though the activity is not a sin. It may violate the conscience of someone to work in a place of business which makes alcohol available for purchase even though he serves not as a one who tends to the register or stocks shelves. Should such employment violate the conscience of an individual, then said individual would be in sin accepting employment with such an establishment.

## Romans 15:1-7

*1 We then that are strong ought to bear the infirmities of the weak, and not to please ourselves. 2 Let every one of us please his neighbour for his good to edification. 3 For even Christ pleased not himself; but, as it is written, The reproaches of them that reproached thee fell on me. 4 For whatsoever things were written afore-*

---
[127] Robertson L. Whiteside.
[128] Adam Clarke.

# Commentary on Romans

*time were written for our learning, that we through patience and comfort of the scriptures might have hope. 5 Now the God of patience and consolation grant you to be likeminded one toward another according to Christ Jesus: 6 That ye may with one mind and one mouth glorify God, even the Father of our Lord Jesus Christ. 7 Wherefore receive ye one another, as Christ also received us to the glory of God.*

The chapter break here is unfortunate, these verses are contextually assigned to the previous chapter. Paul began his conclusive arguments, saying, *let us therefore follow after the things which make for peace, and things wherewith one may edify another* (Rom. 14:19). The apostle spent no little time working to resolve the divisiveness which existed between the Jewish and Gentile converts.

**Verse 1.** *We then that are strong ought to bear the infirmities of the weak, and not to please ourselves.* The strong refers to those who had a faith which permitted them to eat the meats which were troublesome to others. The weakness of the Jews was their *infirmity.* The Jews were regulated by the Law of Moses—their first spiritual husband but, they were now married to Christ. *Wherefore, my brethren, ye also are become dead to the law by the body of Christ; that ye should be married to another, even to him who is raised from the dead, that we should bring forth fruit unto God* (Rom. 7:4). Strong attachment to the Old Law remained for many Jewish converts, for that reason the Gentile converts were instructed to ascend to higher degrees of compassion and sympathy for their Jewish brethren. The Gentiles were instructed to work toward unity in the church. They were not to please themselves through the eating of the meats which proved to be a stumblingblock for their Jewish brethren.

**Verse 2.** *Let every one of us please his neighbour for his good to edification.* Every one here refers to both the Jewish and Gentile converts. As Christians, we are to "do all in our power to please our brethren; and especially in those things in which their spiritual edification is concerned. Though we should not indulge men in mere whims and caprices, yet we should bear with their ignorance and their weakness, knowing that others had much to

# Commentary on Romans

bear with from us before we came to our present advanced state of religious knowledge"[129] [sic].

Pleasing our brethren is for their good and edification. Christians must seek to please their brethren in such a way to promote better things, not simply things which are good, rather things which are best. Many times saints seek to please others not for good, but for the advantage of themselves. Pleasing our brethren must be for their good and edification. Saints ought never contribute to the detriment of others.

*Edification* is an antonym of *destruction*. In 14:20, Paul spoke of destruction. The strong of the Lord's church have a great responsibility to edify the weak and build up the brethren. The burden of edification was employed more directly upon the Gentile converts. The Gentiles were charged heavily with the duty of promoting unity, edification, and harmony between the Jewish and Gentile converts, but the Jews were not exempt from the same.

**Verse 3.** *For even Christ pleased not himself; but, as it is written, The reproaches of them that reproached thee fell on me.* Christ did not seek to please Himself, rather He came to be about His Father's business (Lk. 2:49b). Jesus said: *My meat is to do the will of him that sent me, and to finish his work* (Jno. 4:34). *For I came down from heaven, not to do mine own will, but the will of him that sent me* (Jno. 6:38).

Paul refers the Roman saints to the Psalmist who wrote *as it is written, for the zeal of thine house hath eaten me up; and the reproaches of them that reproached thee are fallen upon me* (Psa. 69:9). With these words we are reminded of the fifty-third chapter of Isaiah. Indeed, Christ did not seek to please himself; rather, He gave way to the hope of others having the reproach of all men imputed to him.

**Verse 4.** *For whatsoever things were written aforetime were written for our learning, that we through patience and comfort of the scriptures might have hope.* Specifically the things *written aforetime* here refer to the words of the Psalm afore cited by

---
[129] Adam Clarke.

# Commentary on Romans

Paul. Yet, Paul intends for the Jews and Gentiles to understand all *things written aforetime were written for* their learning. There is an urgent and ever pressing need for saints to gain an in-depth knowledge of *the things written aforetime*—the Old Testament. The Old Testament is the New Testament concealed and the New Testament is the Old Testament revealed.

For the Jews who made up a large part of the congregation in Rome, a recollection of the things of the Law of Moses should have reminded them of the things from which they were delivered. For the Gentiles converts a good knowledge of the Old Testament would better help them in understanding the mindset of their Jewish brethren. The Scriptures always better equip the child of God in understanding, and better supplies him with compassion and a willingness to be a better servant to and for the brotherhood.

The need to conquer the intent of the apostle's words is essential. Paul said *that we through patience and comfort of the scriptures might have hope.* Observe first, Paul uses *we,* meaning Jew and Gentile.

Second, notice Paul spoke of *patience.* The *patience* of which the apostle spoke was the *patience* and *longsuffering* the brethren were to extend to one another regarding the eating of meats or the refusal to do so. The brethren were to be patient with one another regarding the matter of meats. Patience with the brethren is always commanded and must be extended with much generosity.

Further, Paul said, we through the *comfort of the scriptures might have hope.* Both Jews and Gentiles could find comfort through a better knowledge of the Scriptures. The *hope* of which Paul desired was the *hope* of unity among the brethren. Without knowledge of the Scriptures, there is no hope of peace. However, mere knowledge lacks success when it is not applied, coupled to a compassionate heart and seated in sincere love. Paul said to the saints in Corinth: *And though I have the gift of prophecy, and understand all mysteries, and all knowledge; and though I have all faith, so that I could remove mountains, and have not charity, I am nothing* (I Cor. 13:2).

# Commentary on Romans

**Verse 5.** *Now the God of patience and consolation grant you to be likeminded one toward another according to Christ Jesus.* The inspired wisdom of Paul shines brightly in this verse. As Paul made use of *patience and comfort* in verse 4, he does likewise here. In the previous passage, Paul urges *patience and comfort* to be extended. Here Paul informs the saints they have a *God of patience and consolation.* Just as the Lord is patient with His children, so they were to be with one another. When brethren extend kind patience to one another, they gain comfort from the same. The Lord does likewise when saints extend patience toward one another. God follows suit and rewards them with comfort, peace, and hope. When Christians are as *"likeminded,"* as God, they live *according to Christ Jesus.*

**Verse 6.** *That ye may with one mind and one mouth glorify God, even the Father of our Lord Jesus Christ.* This verse explains, when saints are long-suffering, patient, and comforting of one another as they ought, they are of the mindset they ought to be.

Saints must do the things that promote unity, peace, and comfort *that ye may with one mind and one mouth glorify God.* "Oneness is necessary if we would 'glorify the God and Father of our Lord Jesus Christ.' As Christ received us, so should we receive, or accept, one another, in spite of the fact that we do not all belong to the same race"[130] [sic].

**Verse 7.** *Wherefore receive ye one another, as Christ also received us to the glory of God.* This verse is the conclusion of the apostle's dissertation regarding the eating of meats. As saints, we are to *receive ye one another, as Christ also received us.*

The phrase, *to the glory of God*, refers to the purpose and degree by which and unto which the Lord received the saints of Rome. The Lord receives us today for and unto the same. We are to be a glory to the Lord and the Father.

"In the same manner, and with the same cordial affection, as Christ has received us into communion with himself, and has made us partakers of such inestimable blessings, condescending to be present in all our assemblies. And as Christ has re-

---
[130] Robertson L. Whiteside.

# Commentary on Romans

ceived us thus to the glory of God, so should we, Jews and Gentiles, cordially receive each other, that God's glory may be promoted by our harmony and brotherly love"[131] [sic].

## Romans 15:8-23

*8 Now I say that Jesus Christ was a minister of the circumcision for the truth of God, to confirm the promises made unto the fathers: 9 And that the Gentiles might glorify God for his mercy; as it is written, For this cause I will confess to thee among the Gentiles, and sing unto thy name. 10 And again he saith, Rejoice, ye Gentiles, with his people. 11 And again, Praise the Lord, all ye Gentiles; and laud him, all ye people. 12 And again, Esaias saith, There shall be a root of Jesse, and he that shall rise to reign over the Gentiles; in him shall the Gentiles trust. 13 Now the God of hope fill you with all joy and peace in believing, that ye may abound in hope, through the power of the Holy Ghost. 14 And I myself also am persuaded of you, my brethren, that ye also are full of goodness, filled with all knowledge, able also to admonish one another. 15 Nevertheless, brethren, I have written the more boldly unto you in some sort, as putting you in mind, because of the grace that is given to me of God, 16 That I should be the minister of Jesus Christ to the Gentiles, ministering the gospel of God, that the offering up of the Gentiles might be acceptable, being sanctified by the Holy Ghost. 17 I have therefore whereof I may glory through Jesus Christ in those things which pertain to God. 18 For I will not dare to speak of any of those things which Christ hath not wrought by me, to make the Gentiles obedient, by word and deed, 19 Through mighty signs and wonders, by the power of the Spirit of God; so that from Jerusalem, and round about unto Illyricum, I have fully preached the gospel of Christ. 20 Yea, so have I strived to preach the gospel, not where Christ was named, lest I should build upon another man's foundation: 21 But as it is written, To whom he was not spoken of, they shall see: and they that have not heard*

---
[131] Adam Clarke.

# Commentary on Romans

*shall understand. 22 For which cause also I have been much hindered from coming to you. 23 But now having no more place in these parts, and having a great desire these many years to come unto you.*

The apostle, in this chapter, continues the discourse of the former, concerning mutual forbearance in indifferent things; and so draws towards a conclusion of the epistle. Where such differences of apprehension, and consequently distances of affection, are among Christians, there is need of precept upon precept, line upon line, to allay the heat, and to beget a better temper. The apostle, being desirous to drive the nail home, as a nail in a sure place, follows his blow, unwilling to leave the subject till he has some hopes of prevailing, to which end he orders the cause before them and fills his mouth with the most pressing arguments. We may observe, in this chapter, I. His precepts to them. II. His prayers for them. III. His apology for writing to them. IV. His account of himself and his own affairs. V. His declaration of his purpose to come and see them. VI. His desire of a share in their prayers[132] [sic].

**Verse 8.** *Now I say that Jesus Christ was a minister of the circumcision for the truth of God, to confirm the promises made unto the fathers.* The meaning here is that Christ was a minister to the Jews to *confirm the promises made unto the fathers*, who were Abraham, Isaac and Jacob.

The universal scope of the Gospel was prophesied by Isaiah in various verses: *And the Gentiles shall see thy righteousness, and all kings thy glory: and thou shalt be called by a new name, which the mouth of the Lord shall name* (Isa. 62:2). *Nevertheless the dimness shall not be such as was in her vexation, when at the first he lightly afflicted the land of Zebulun and the land of Naphtali, and afterward did more grievously afflict her by the way of the sea, beyond Jordan, in Galilee of the nations. The people that walked in darkness have seen a great light: they that dwell in the land of the shadow of death, upon them hath the light shined* (Isa. 9:1-2, fulfilled in Matthew 4:14-16). *And in that day*

---
[132] Matthew Henry.

## Commentary on Romans

*there shall be a root of Jesse, which shall stand for an ensign of the people; to it shall the Gentiles seek: and his rest shall be glorious* (Isa. 11:10). The New Testament confirms what was prophesied—*That Christ should suffer, and that he should be the first that should rise from the dead, and should shew light unto the people, and to the Gentiles* (Acts 26:23).

The apostle concluded his discussion regarding meats with verse 7. Here he turns his attention to the Jewish mind again, reminding them the Lord *was a minister of the circumcision.* The intent here is the Lord preached to the circumcision—the Jews—in order *to confirm the promises made unto the fathers.*

> "The fathers were Abraham, Isaac, and Jacob; the promises are found in Gen. 12:1-3; 22:15-18; 26:3,4; 28:13,14. The part of these promises that referred particularly to Christ is this: *In thy seed shall all nations of the earth be blessed.* Paul makes this clear in Gal. 3: 16: *Now to Abraham were the promises spoken, and to his seed. He saith not, And to seeds, as of many; but as of one, And to thy seed, which is Christ*"[133] [sic].

**Verse 9.** *And that the Gentiles might glorify God for his mercy; as it is written, For this cause I will confess to thee among the Gentiles, and sing unto thy name.* This verse begins with the conjunction *and* which clearly shows the inseparable connection between this verse and the previous one. Together they show, not only was Jesus *a minister of the circumcision for the truth,* but He also opened the way for the Gentiles, providing them the avenue by which they could sing the song of their deliverance from the Patriarchal System.

Just as the Jews needed liberation from the Law of Moses, so the Gentiles needed deliverance from the Patriarchal Law. David prophesied of such when he wrote concerning the Gentiles being called unto the New Law of Christ. *O praise the Lord, all ye nations: praise him, all ye people. For his merciful kindness is great toward us: and the truth of the Lord endureth for ever. Praise ye the Lord* (Psa. 117:1-2).

---

[133] Robertson L. Whiteside.

# Commentary on Romans

Paul said, *for this cause*; for what *cause?* That God shall be confessed and songs of praises sung among the Gentiles for their deliverance from the Patriarchal System. Jesus confirmed this when He said to the Jews: *Your father Abraham rejoiced to see my day: and he saw it, and was glad* (Jno. 8:56). Abraham was a Patriarch not subject to the Law of Moses, for the Law of Moses was yet five hundred years distant. The coming of Christ was longed for by the Patriarchs just as His coming was longed for by the Jews.

*Now when Jesus was born in Bethlehem of Judaea in the days of Herod the king, behold, there came wise men from the east to Jerusalem, Saying, Where is he that is born King of the Jews? for we have seen his star in the east, and are come to worship him* (Matt. 2:1-2). The words rendered *wise men* is better translated *Magi,* "a term that designates an order of priests that originally referred to the Persians and Medes. There are numerous instances in the Old Testament wherein prophecies of Christ were revealed to Gentiles.

There were two priests of God of whom the Old Testament speaks who were Patriarchs. First, Melchizedek, king of Salem, was the priest of the most high God (Gen. 14:18). Second, Jethro was a priest of Midian (Exo. 18:1).

Further, the Old Testament informs us of Balaam who prophesied of Christ: *For from the top of the rocks I see him, and from the hills I behold him: lo, the people shall dwell alone, and shall not be reckoned among the nations. Who can count the dust of Jacob, and the number of the fourth part of Israel? Let me die the death of the righteous, and let my last end be like his* (Num. 23:9-10). Job said, *For I know that my redeemer liveth, and that he shall stand at the latter day upon the earth* (Job 19:25). Given the fact Paul said: *For this cause I will confess to thee among the Gentiles, and sing unto thy name* (v. 9), it is little wonder he informed the Jewish converts the Gentiles had good reason to praise God for their release from the Patriarchal System. The apostle quoted from the psalmist who prophesied: *Therefore will I give thanks unto thee, O Lord, among the heathen, and sing praises unto thy name* (Psa. 18:49).

# Commentary on Romans

Though Barnes was a denominationalist, many of his comments merit consideration.

> The meaning here is, that he would cause these blessings to be remembered by making a record of them in this song of praise; a song that would be used not only in his own age and in his own country, but also among other nations, and in other times. He would do all in his power to make the knowledge of these favors, and these proofs of the existence of the true God, known abroad and transmitted to other times. The apostle Paul uses this language Rom. 15:9 as expressing properly the fact that the knowledge of God was to be communicated to the Gentiles[134] [sic].
>
> Paul's use of the promise made to the fathers would not please the exclusive Jewish Christians; and so he quotes some Old Testament Scriptures to show that it had been God's plan through the ages to include the Gentiles in the blessings of the promised seed. This would show both Jew and Gentile that neither had any right to feel superior to the other, and such feelings would promote better fellowship between them. The passages in the order quoted are Ps. 18:49 (or 2 Sam. 22:50); Deut. 32:43; Ps. 117:1; Isa. 11:10. The Gentiles as well as the Jews, would praise Jehovah for his mercy, and would also enjoy the blessings of his rule. Paul quotes the passages to show that they were then being fulfilled; and that, as both Jew and Gentile were enjoying the same blessings and both were under the rule of the Messiah, there should be peace between Jewish Christians and Gentile Christians[135] [sic].

**Verses 10-12.** *And again he saith, Rejoice, ye Gentiles, with his people. And again, Praise the Lord, all ye Gentiles; and laud him, all ye people. And again, Esaias saith, There shall be a root of Jesse, and he that shall rise to reign over the Gentiles; in him shall the Gentiles trust.* These verses contain additional Old

---

[134] Albert Barnes.

[135] Robertson L. Whiteside.

# Commentary on Romans

Testament Scripture references which Paul used to solidify his argument.

**Verse 10** is a citation from the Law of Moses: *Rejoice, O ye nations, with his people: for he will avenge the blood of his servants, and will render vengeance to his adversaries, and will be merciful unto his land, and to his people* (Deut. 32:43). Paul tells us the word *nations* means the "Gentiles." When a New Testament author gives his inspired commentary on any Old Testament passage, there can be no disagreement as to what the passage means. The use of this passage should not be taken lightly. Paul quoted from the Law of Moses, which was an observation of which Jews would quickly take notice. Be it remembered the apostle was striving to solidify unity between the Jewish and Gentile converts. Paul's citation of the Old Law captured the Jewish mind and in so doing, Paul was showing the Jewish converts the Old Law prophesied of the Gentiles being a part of the New Law which was then yet to come. If the Jewish converts were as respectful to the Old Law as they claimed, they could not deny the prophecy Paul quoted from the Law. "The design of the quotation was to show that the Old Testament speaks of the Gentiles as called on to celebrate the praises of God; of course, the apostle infers that they are to be introduced to the same privileges as his people"[136] [sic.].

Another observation worthy of consideration here is the use of the term *New Testament*. The term occurs in six New Testament passages; the term *Old Testament* occurs but once. The use of these terms was devastating to the Jews. They were persuaded the Law of Moses was given to them for all time. To hear of a *New Testament,* which would replace the Law of Moses did not sit well with the Jews. It was even more problematic for the Jews to hear the term *Old Testament.* We can hardly grasp the impact the phrases, *Old and New Testaments*, had on the Jews. The terms were demoralizing to them. They could not comprehend how God would take the Law of Moses from them and issue a New Law. Yet it was the Old Law to which Paul referred to show the Jews God always intended to usher in His New Law and end the Old Law. Paul's inspired remarks in the Second Corinthian epistle shows that the Jews rejected the end

---
[136] Albert Barnes.

# Commentary on Romans

of the Old Law, even blinding themselves to it.

> But if the ministration of death, written and engraven in stones, was glorious, so that the children of Israel could not stedfastly behold the face of Moses for the glory of his countenance; which glory was to be done away. For even that which was made glorious had no glory in this respect, by reason of the glory that excelleth. For if that which is done away was glorious, much more that which remaineth is glorious (II Cor. 3:7, 10-11).

> Seeing then that we have such hope, we use great plainness of speech: And not as Moses, which put a vail over his face, that the children of Israel could not stedfastly look to the end of that which is abolished: But their minds were blinded: for until this day remaineth the same veil untaken away in the reading of the old testament; which veil is done away in Christ (II Cor. 3:12-14).

The Lord made first use of the term *New Testament*. *For this is my blood of the new testament, which is shed for many for the remission of sins* (Matt. 26:28; cf. Mk. 14:24; Lk. 22:20). Paul and the writer of Hebrews (if not Paul) also used the phrase: *After the same manner also he took the cup, when he had supped, saying, This cup is the new testament in my blood: this do ye, as oft as ye drink it, in remembrance of me* (I Cor. 11:25); *Who also hath made us able ministers of the new testament; not of the letter, but of the spirit: for the letter killeth, but the spirit giveth life* (II Cor. 3:6); *And for this cause he is the mediator of the new testament, that by means of death, for the redemption of the transgressions that were under the first testament, they which are called might receive the promise of eternal inheritance* (Heb. 9:15).

**Verse 11.** *And again, Praise the Lord, all ye Gentiles; and laud him, all ye people.* This verse is from David, who said, *O praise the Lord, all ye nations: praise him, all ye people. For his merciful kindness is great toward us: and the truth of the Lord endureth for ever. Praise ye the Lord* (Psa. 117). Again, Paul provided

# Commentary on Romans

inspired commentary on the passage quoted. The word *nations* in the Psalm means *Gentiles*, as declared in verse 11; with such we may not contend. See comments on verse 9.

**Verse 12.** *And again, Isaiah saith, There shall be a root of Jesse, and he that shall rise to reign over the Gentiles; in him shall the Gentiles trust.* This citation comes from two verses in Isaiah 11: *And in that day there shall be a root of Jesse, which shall stand for an ensign of the people; to it shall the Gentiles seek: and his rest shall be glorious* (Isa. 11:1, 10).

Because Jesus is called the *root and the offspring of David*, there could be no objection from the Jewish converts that Jesus was to *rise to reign over the Gentiles; in him shall the Gentiles trust. And one of the elders saith unto me, Weep not: behold, the Lion of the tribe of Judah, the Root of David, hath prevailed to open the book, and to loose the seven seals thereof.... I Jesus have sent mine angel to testify unto you these things in the churches. I am the root and the offspring of David, and the bright and morning star* (Rev. 5:5; 22:16).

Observe in verses 10-12 each verse begins with the word *again*. Verse 12 has the word *and* preceding the word *again*. *Again, again, and again* Paul refers to the Old Testament which goes to his statement made in verse 4.

**Verse 13.** *Now the God of hope fill you with all joy and peace in believing, that ye may abound in hope, through the power of the Holy Ghost.* The word *now* of verse 13 is a primary particle, meaning "but, and, also, and moreover." On verse 12 the ASV of 1901 reads: *And again, Isaiah saith, There shall be the root of Jesse, And he that ariseth to rule over the Gentiles; On him shall the Gentiles hope.*

> Concerning the Messiah Isaiah had said, "On him shall the Gentiles hope." In addition, so to the Gentiles as well as to the Jews God was the God of hope—he made hope possible even to those who formerly had been without God and without hope (Eph. 2:12). Without this hope there could be no joy and no peace —no peace of mind and no peace with one another.

# Commentary on Romans

But we are to be filled with joy and peace in believing, in continuous, active believing. And to be filled with joy and peace increases our hope[137] [sic].

We cite verse 12 from the ASV because the word *trust* is used in the KJV, the ASV uses the word *hope*. Whiteside has well presented the thought intended. Trust implies hope, and hope implies trust, the two work in harmony. In either translation the conclusion is the same: there is no doctrinal difference whether *trust* or *hope* is used.

The *hope* of which Paul spoke in this verse does not refer to an activity in which God was involved. This *hope* is the *hope* God provided for the Jews and the Gentiles in which they could be one; united in Christ and the avenue by which they could become a *new man in Christ*. God *abolished the law of commandments contained in ordinances* of the Old Law *to make in himself of twain one new man, so making peace* between the Jews and the Gentiles (Eph. 2:15).

So long as the Jews remained under the Old Law and the Gentiles remained under the Patriarchal Law, there could be no unity between them. Paul emphasized this matter to the church of Galatia: *There is neither Jew nor Greek, there is neither bond nor free, there is neither male nor female: for ye are all one in Christ Jesus* (Gal. 3:28). Whiteside comments that God

> made hope possible even to those who formerly had been without God and without hope (Eph. 2:12). Without this hope there could be no joy and no peace— no peace of mind and no peace with one another. But we are to be filled with joy and peace in believing, in continuous, active believing. And to be filled with joy and peace increases our hope. The power of the Holy Spirit made this hope and peace possible; for the Holy Spirit revealed all we know about God and Christ and the plan of salvation, and confirmed that revelation by signs and wonders. And the things the Holy Spirit revealed to us is the source of all our knowledge, joy,

---
[137] Robertson L. Whiteside.

# Commentary on Romans

peace, and hope[138] [sic].

**Verse 14.** *And I myself also am persuaded of you, my brethren, that ye also are full of goodness, filled with all knowledge, able also to admonish one another.* Paul was *persuaded*—convinced—by both Jewish and Gentile converts—they were *full of goodness, filled with all knowledge, able also to admonish one another.* Being filled with goodness and knowledge would produce admonitions of one another. Paul knew by inspiration the church at Rome was indeed endowed with goodness and knowledge.

Paul felt assured his instructions in the previous chapters provoking the Jewish and Gentile converts toward unity gave him the assurance they would admonish one another as they ought. Paul felt assured that they, even with their differences about observing days and eating meats, were good people. It is likely that only a small minority were disturbed about these things. In his words of praise Paul must have had the greater part of the church in mind. "Filled with knowledge" could not have been well applied to those who were so disturbed about the matters discussed in chapter 14. Spiritually gifted men in that church would be able to teach and admonish the weak. Paul's words of commendation would be encouraging to these brethren[139] [sic].

The previous chapter addressed matters that divided some of the saints in Rome; this chapter is Paul's effort to reunite them.

**Verses 15-16.** *Nevertheless, brethren, I have written the more boldly unto you in some sort, as putting you in mind, because of the grace that is given to me of God, That I should be the minister of Jesus Christ to the Gentiles, ministering the gospel of God, that the offering up of the Gentiles might be acceptable, being sanctified by the Holy Ghost.* Paul informed the saints he wrote with boldness because of the *grace* which he received from the Lord. The boldness with which Paul wrote was by inspiration, the Holy Ghost instructed Him to do so. In these verses, Paul addresses both the Jews and the Gentiles.

---

[138] Robertson L. Whiteside.
[139] Ibid.

# Commentary on Romans

The phrase, *in some sort*, has caused much commentary both written and spoken. Some have suggested it referred to a certain faction within the congregation. Others maintain the phrase refers to different parts of the Roman epistle; yet others suggest it refers to other subjects. Usually, it denotes separation or a departure from the current subject at hand. It is needful to remind the reader Paul had been addressing the Jewish and Gentile converts separately and at times collectively. In this chapter, Paul continues the pattern. In verses 8-12, he addressed the Jewish converts; this is made clear through the apostle's citation of Scriptures from the Old Testament. In verses 15 and 16, Paul speaks to both the Jews and the Gentiles.

Paul's stating he was a *minister of Jesus Christ to the Gentiles* served two purposes. First, it reminded the Jews that the Gentiles were called by the Gospel as well as the Jews. Second, the statement assured the Gentiles Paul was assigned as the apostle to the them, but his appointment was not to the Gentiles only (Acts 9:15). Because the apostle was specifically assigned, but not restricted to serve the Gentiles, they should have given greater heed unto the things Paul revealed. This helps one in understanding *putting you in mind* in verse 15.

The thought Paul expressed in the phrase, *because of the grace that is given to me of God*, is the same as he expressed in his address to the church at Ephesus, wherein he wrote: *Unto me, who am less than the least of all saints, is this grace given, that I should preach among the Gentiles the unsearchable riches of Christ* (Eph. 3:8).

What does *that the offering up of the Gentiles might be acceptable* mean? Some insist Paul means the Gentiles served as his offering up to God. Others assert it refers to the offerings the Gentiles offered up to God. The context forbids the former position. Many of Paul's efforts in this epistle have been to show the Jews and the Gentiles that God forever intended to extend the way of salvation unto the Gentiles. The Jews were beleaguered with having to give up the Old Law and obey the New Law of Christ. They were even more troubled having to accept the Gentiles were to be *grafted in* to the natural branches.

# Commentary on Romans

The *offering up of the Gentiles* refers to the fact that only through the Gospel could the Gentiles have their service to God offered up acceptably. Just as the Old Law had come to an end, so did the Patriarchal Law, which ended with the household of Cornelius, recorded in Acts 10. Some contend the Patriarchal Law ended before that event. However, such is not the case. Some insist Cornelius was a proselyte before his conversion. There are numerous reasons such cannot be true. First, Peter himself refuted the assertion at the counsel of the apostles and elders in Jerusalem.

> *And certain men which came down from Judaea taught the brethren, and said, Except ye be circumcised after the manner of Moses, ye cannot be saved. When therefore Paul and Barnabas had no small dissension and disputation with them, they determined that Paul and Barnabas, and certain other of them, should go up to Jerusalem unto the apostles and elders about this question. And being brought on their way by the church, they passed through Phenice and Samaria, declaring the conversion of the Gentiles: and they caused great joy unto all the brethren. And when they were come to Jerusalem, they were received of the church, and of the apostles and elders, and they declared all things that God had done with them. But there rose up certain of the sect of the Pharisees which believed, saying, That it was needful to circumcise them, and to command them to keep the law of Moses. And the apostles and elders came together for to consider of this matter* (Acts 15:1-6).

Notice carefully the next verse: *And when there had been much disputing, Peter rose up, and said unto them, Men and brethren, ye know how that a good while ago God made choice among us, that the Gentiles by my mouth should hear the word of the gospel, and believe* (Acts 15:7). Why did Peter use the word *Gentiles*? Peter identified those of the household of Cornelius as *Gentiles*, not proselytes, because Cornelius was not a convert to Judaism.

Another reason why Cornelius could not have been a proselyte

# Commentary on Romans

is that if he were, he was not the *first* Gentile convert. A third reason why Cornelius could not have been a proselyte is that proselytes were already part of the church. They are listed as those present on the day of Pentecost (Acts 2:10).

In that there were proselytes present on the day of Pentecost, and in that Nicolas of Antioch was a proselyte (Acts 6:5), and in that Peter identifies Cornelius as a Gentile, Cornelius could in no way have been a proselyte. Thus, the *offering up of the Gentiles* of which Paul spoke in verse 16 has reference to the conversion of the Gentiles which made it possible for their offerings to be *acceptable.*

In more than one lectureship it has been proclaimed from the pulpit, by *notable brethren,* Cornelius was a proselyte. Complete sermons have been presented in which numerous Old Testament passages were supplied to build the case that Cornelius was a proselyte. Yet the evidence shows he was not.

On the phrase, *sanctified by the Holy Ghost,* much has been asserted. Who or what was *sanctified by the Holy Ghost?* This question is imperative to understand and must not be considered lightly. There are only three plausible considerations. First, the sanctification of the Holy Ghost referred to the sanctification of the Gentiles. Second, the sanctification of the Holy Ghost refers to the sacrifices offered to God. Third, the sanctification refers to Paul. The first two considerations must be rejected because the Holy Spirit sanctified no one other than inspired men; therefore, the sanctification of the Holy Ghost cannot be applied to the Gentiles. More on this shall be addressed below. Second, the sanctification of the Holy Ghost cannot refer to the offerings of the Gentiles. Such a position would mean the offerings were sanctified, but not the Gentiles.

The sanctification of the Holy Ghost here refers to Paul who was *sanctified by the Holy Ghost* to preach the gospel by inspiration to the Gentiles that their offerings might be acceptable to God. Verse 16 is better understood by saying: *That I, being sanctified by the Holy Ghost, should be the minister of Jesus Christ to the Gentiles, ministering the gospel of God, that the offering up of the Gentiles might be acceptable.* Inspired men and women of

# Commentary on Romans

the first century church were sanctified—set apart by the Holy Spirit to reveal truth. Only inspired men were *sanctified by the Holy Ghost.* Men, who obey the Gospel, are only sanctified by the truth—the word of the Lord (Jno. 17:17).

**Verse 17.** *I have therefore whereof I may glory through Jesus Christ in those things, which pertain to God.* Therefore presents the conclusion of verses 15 and 16. Paul, having been *sanctified by the Holy Ghost* to preach the Gospel to the Gentiles, gloried in that task. Paul did not take his duty lightly. He realized if he did not preach the Gospel with all diligence and do so without remuneration, he had no justification for glorying in Christ. He wrote: *For though I preach the gospel, I have nothing to glory of: for necessity is laid upon me; yea, woe is unto me, if I preach not the gospel* (I Cor. 9:16)!

God had conferred upon Paul the most honorable title He can bestow upon a man—that of an apostle. He also had conferred upon him the noble distinction and duty to preach the Gospel. Today there are no greater duties placed upon man than of an elder, deacon, evangelist, or saint. Paul's glorying; however, was only through Jesus Christ. Paul truly considered himself blessed to be a part of *those things which pertain to God* as an inspired apostle.

**Verse 18.** *For I will not dare to speak of any of those things, which Christ hath not wrought by me, to make the Gentiles obedient, by word and deed.* It was through the preaching of the Gospel which worked toward the conversion of the Gentiles. Through Paul's preaching he was able *to make the Gentiles obedient* to God, should they obey it. It is vital to recall the first-century preaching was under the direction of inspiration. In order to confirm the message proclaimed by inspired men, there was the need of miraculous gifts. Paul's preaching was indeed confirmed by such as is set forth in verse 19.

**Verse 19.** *Through mighty signs and wonders, by the power of the Spirit of God; so that from Jerusalem, and round about unto Illyricum, I have fully preached the gospel of Christ.* Paul plainly stated he preached the Gospel; *through mighty signs and wonders, by the power of the Spirit of God.* From *Jerusalem, and*

# Commentary on Romans

*round about unto Illyricum* shows that preached the same Gospel wherever he went. He had said: *as I teach every where in every church* (I Cor. 4:17).

*I have fully preached the gospel of Christ.* Paul withheld nothing from his preaching. Paul reminded the elders of the church of Ephesus: *And how I kept back nothing that was profitable unto you, but have shewed you, and have taught you publicly, and from house to house.... For I have not shunned to declare unto you all the counsel of God* (Acts 20:20, 27).

Preachers of the Gospel must not withhold anything. It is not enough to preach the truth; *preachers must preach the needed truth*—the *whole the counsel of God* in its entirety. Endless lessons and sermons on love do a congregation no good if it is in need of lessons and sermons on evangelism, appropriate worship (authorized by God), or proper Christian conduct.

**Verse 20.** *Yea, so have I strived to preach the gospel, not where Christ was named, lest I should build upon another man's foundation.* This passage is not difficult. It implies the church at Rome was not established by another apostle—neither Peter nor anyone else. We refer the reader to the introduction for more regarding this matter.

Paul wanted no part of building on *another man's foundation.* There were some in the early church gravely jealous of Paul—so much so that many worked rejoiced in his sufferings, his persecutions, and even in his incarceration.

> *So that my bonds in Christ are manifest in all the palace, and in all other places; And many of the brethren in the Lord, waxing confident by my bonds, are much more bold to speak the word without fear. Some indeed preach Christ even of envy and strife; and some also of good will: The one preach Christ of contention, not sincerely, supposing to add affliction to my bonds: But the other of love, knowing that I am set for the defense of the gospel. What then? notwithstanding, every way, whether in pretense, or in truth, Christ is preached; and I therein do rejoice, yea, and will rejoice*

# Commentary on Romans

(Phil. 1:13-18).

**Verse 21.** *But as it is written, To whom he was not spoken of, they shall see: and they that have not heard shall understand.* As noted earlier, Paul often changes his audience from the Jews to the Gentiles; at times he speaks to both. With the words, *as it is written,* Paul here addresses the Jewish converts. Having conferred with both the Jews and Gentiles in the previous verses, he again refers to the Old Testament (with which the Jews were familiar) to solidify his inspired argument. It is interesting to note the number of times Paul refers to the Old Testament in this portion of his discourse.

Paul alludes to a passage from the prophet Isaiah: *So shall he sprinkle many nations; the kings shall shut their mouths at him: for that which had not been told them shall they see; and that which they had not heard shall they consider* (Isa. 52:15).

> Paul considered preaching to the Gentiles a high honor. He was honored to be the instrument through whom the Gentiles might come to a knowledge of the truth. It was needful for the Jewish converts to repeatedly hear what that of which the Old Testament prophesied regarding the Gentiles being awarded the way of salvation. Till the gospel was preached to them, no tidings had come to Gentiles. Paul was sent to open the eyes of the Gentiles, to turn them from darkness to the light, that they might see.[140]

Paul, in his defense before King Agrippa, declared:

> *At midday, O king, I saw in the way a light from heaven, above the brightness of the sun, shining round about me and them which journeyed with me. And when we were all fallen to the earth, I heard a voice speaking unto me, and saying in the Hebrew tongue, Saul, Saul, why persecutest thou me? it is hard for thee to kick against the pricks. And I said, Who art thou, Lord? And he said, I am Jesus whom thou persecutest. But rise, and stand upon thy feet: for I have*

---
[140] Robertson L. Whiteside.

# Commentary on Romans

> *appeared unto thee for this purpose, to make thee a minister and a witness both of these things which thou hast seen, and of those things in the which I will appear unto thee; Delivering thee from the people, and from the Gentiles, unto whom now I send thee, To open their eyes, and to turn them from darkness to light, and from the power of Satan unto God, that they may receive forgiveness of sins, and inheritance among them which are sanctified by faith that is in me* (Acts 26:13-18).

**Verse 22.** *For which cause also I have been much hindered from coming to you.* The *cause* he wrote of in chapter one: *Now I would not have you ignorant, brethren, that oftentimes I purposed to come unto you, (but was let hitherto,) that I might have some fruit among you also, even as among other Gentiles* (Rom. 1:13). The word *let* in this verse is defined as; prevented, forbidden, hindered, or kept from doing something.

Consider Luke's record from the following verses, which explains how Paul knew where to travel:

> *And a vision appeared to Paul in the night; There stood a man of Macedonia, and prayed him, saying, Come over into Macedonia, and help us. And after he had seen the vision, immediately we endeavored to go into Macedonia, assuredly gathering that the Lord had called us for to preach the gospel unto them.... And from thence to Philippi, which is the chief city of that part of Macedonia, and a colony: and we were in that city abiding certain days.... And when Silas and Timotheus were come from Macedonia, Paul was pressed in the spirit, and testified to the Jews that Jesus was Christ.... After these things were ended, Paul purposed in the spirit, when he had passed through Macedonia and Achaia, to go to Jerusalem, saying, After I have been there, I must also see Rome* (Acts 16:9-10, 12; 18:5; 19:21).

**Verse 23.** *But now having no more place in these parts, and having a great desire these many years to come unto you.* The

# Commentary on Romans

word *now* is the contrast to *hindered.* Paul in the past, was *hindered* by Divine design from going to Rome. Paul was permitted to go to Rome only when God determined it fitting.

> *Now when Festus was come into the province, after three days he ascended from Caesarea to Jerusalem Then the high priest and the chief of the Jews informed him against Paul, and besought him, Jerusalem, laying wait in the way to kill him. But Festus answered, that Paul should be kept at Caesarea, and that he himself would depart shortly thither. Let them therefore, said he, which among you are able, go down with me, and accuse this man, if there be any wickedness in him. And when he had tarried among them more than ten days, he went down unto Caesarea; and the next day sitting on the judgment seat commanded Paul to be brought. And when he was come, the Jews which came down from Jerusalem stood round about, and laid many and grievous complaints against Paul, which they could not prove. While he answered for himself, Neither against the law of the Jews, neither against the temple, nor yet against Caesar, have I offended any thing at all. But Festus, willing to do the Jews a pleasure, answered Paul, and said, Wilt thou go up to Jerusalem, and there be judged of these things before me? Then said Paul, I stand at Caesar's judgment seat, where I ought to be judged: to the Jews have I done no wrong, as thou very well knowest. For if I be an offender, or have committed any thing worthy of death, I refuse not to die: but if there be none of these things whereof these accuse me, no man may deliver me unto them. I appeal unto Caesar. Then Festus, when he had conferred with the council, answered, Hast thou appealed unto Caesar? unto Caesar shalt thou go* (Acts 25:1-12).

*Having no more place in these parts* means Paul knew his work in the area in which he was then working was completed. His remark was made by inspiration. The Lord determined to have to have Paul journey elsewhere.

# Commentary on Romans

## Romans 15:24-33

*24 Whensoever I take my journey into Spain, I will come to you: for I trust to see you in my journey, and to be brought on my way thitherward by you, if first I be somewhat filled with your company. 25 But now I go unto Jerusalem to minister unto the saints. 26 For it hath pleased them of Macedonia and Achaia to make a certain contribution for the poor saints which are at Jerusalem. 27 It hath pleased them verily; and their debtors they are. For if the Gentiles have been made partakers of their spiritual things, their duty is also to minister unto them in carnal things. 28 When therefore I have performed this, and have sealed to them this fruit, I will come by you into Spain. 29 And I am sure that, when I come unto you, I shall come in the fulness of the blessing of the gospel of Christ. 30 Now I beseech you, brethren, for the Lord Jesus Christ's sake, and for the love of the Spirit, that ye strive together with me in your prayers to God for me; 31 That I may be delivered from them that do not believe in Judaea; and that my service which I have for Jerusalem may be accepted of the saints; 32 That I may come unto you with joy by the will of God, and may with you be refreshed. 33 Now the God of peace be with you all. Amen.*

This portion of Paul's epistle has been the subject to much criticism from those who wish to cast doubts about Paul and his efforts to evangelize. There is no external historical record of the apostle ever having journeyed to Spain, nor is there any Biblical record. However, it remains true the apostle wrote these verses by inspiration.

Some insist there is evidence which lend to credence to Paul's journey to Spain, but these so-called proofs are without support. On the other hand, there are an equal number of arguments against Paul's ever having gone to Spain. It matters not whether he did. What is important is Spain did receive the Gospel within the lifetime of the apostles, as Paul declared in the epistle of Colossians: *If ye continue in the faith grounded and settled, and*

# Commentary on Romans

*be not moved away from the hope of the gospel, which ye have heard, and which was preached to every creature which is under heaven; whereof I Paul am made a minister* (Col. 1:23).

**Verse 24.** *Whensoever I take my journey into Spain, I will come to you: for I trust to see you in my journey, and to be brought on my way thitherward by you, if first I be somewhat filled with your company.* Paul intended to journey to Spain, and in so doing he planned to spend some time in Rome.

It is wildly asserted by many that the phrase, *I will come to you*, does not belong in the original text. Regardless, the comment is valid. If one were to read this verse without the phrase, there is no damage done to the point of the passage. Removing it would cause it to read: *Whensoever I take my journey into Spain I trust to see you in my journey, and to be brought on my way thitherward by you, if first I be somewhat filled with your company.* Elementary logic dictates the phrase is elliptical in nature and application. The passage contains the phrases, *I trust to see you in my journey,* and, *if first I be somewhat filled with your company.* How is it some deduce that *I will come to you* is damaging to the text when it is the case Paul expressed his hope of seeing the saints in Rome? Further, how is it some make strong efforts to explain away the apostle's hope to be *filled with the company* of the saints there? Was there some avenue by which Paul could have trusted to see the saints of Rome and be filled with their company without going to Rome? Not in the least. Being filled with the company of others and trusting to see said company requires presence. It is an absurdity to contend that *I will come to you* damages the text.

*For I trust to see you in my journey, and to be brought on my way thitherward by you.* Two matters to consider here: first, Paul had trust to see the saints of Rome during the proposed journey to Spain. Second, Paul expected to be monetarily assisted by the Roman saints as he traveled. Such was the custom of the early churches. We refer the reader to the following passages (Acts 15:3; 17:14-15; 20:38; 21:5; I Cor. 16:6 and 11, and III Jno. 8). On the phrase, *if first I be somewhat filled with your company,* it is well to note the word *first* here means "first and foremost." First and foremost, Paul expressed his wish to be *filled—*

# Commentary on Romans

satisfied. The word envelops the idea of taking one's fill. Literally, Paul intended the Roman saints to understand; he must first be filled with their company and receive a monetary gift from them by which he may continue his journey to Spain.

**Verses 25-26.** *But now I go unto Jerusalem to minister unto the saints. For it hath pleased them of Macedonia and Achaia to make a certain contribution for the poor saints which are at Jerusalem.* Paul is addressing both the Jewish and Gentile converts in these verses. He knew the congregation there maintained a treasury and had hoped to receive a benefit for his traveling purposes.

> Before visiting them on his intended journey into Spain, he had a mission to fulfill in Jerusalem. For sometime he had been stirring up the churches of the Gentiles to make contributions for the poor saints in Judea. Many facts concerning this collection for the saints may be learned from 1 Cor. 16:1-4; 2 Cor. 8:1-7; 9:1-15[141] [sic].

> Through the instrumentality of the Jews, yet in spite of some Jews, the Gentiles had received the gospel. These Gentile Christians felt an obligation therefore to do what they could to supply the material needs of the poor saints in Judea[142] [sic].

**Verse 25.** Adam Clarke offers the following comments:

> ...from this and the two following verses we learn that the object of his journey to Jerusalem was to carry a contribution made among the Gentile Christians of Macedonia and Achaia for the relief of the poor Jewish Christians at Jerusalem. About this affair he had taken great pains, as appears from 1 Co 16:1-4; 2 Co 8, and 2 Co 9:1-15. His design in this affair is very evident from 2 Co 9:12-13, where he says that the administration of this service not only supplieth the want of the saints, but is abundant also by many thanksgivings unto God; whiles, by the experiment of this ministration,

---
[141] Robertson L. Whiteside.
[142] Ibid.

# Commentary on Romans

they glorify God for your professed subjection unto the Gospel of Christ, and for your liberal distribution unto them and unto all men. The apostle was in hopes that this liberal contribution, sent by the Gentile Christians who had been converted by St. Paul's ministry, would engage the affections of the Jewish Christians, who had been much prejudiced against the reception of the Gentiles into the Church, without being previously obliged to submit to the yoke of the law. He wished to establish a coalition between the converted Jews and Gentiles, being sensible of its great importance to the spread of the Gospel; and his procuring this contribution was one laudable device to accomplish this good end. And this shows why he so earnestly requests the prayers of the Christians at Rome, that his service which he had for Jerusalem might be accepted of the saints[143] [sic].

**Verse 26.** *For it hath pleased them of Macedonia and Achaia to make a certain contribution for the poor saints which are at Jerusalem.* The saints of Macedonia were *pleased* to send monetary aid to the poor saints of Jerusalem. They did so cheerfully and with great desire; they were endowed with a strong compulsion to do so.

Paul wrote to the church at Corinth concerning the willingness of the Macedonian saints to send aid to the poor saints of Jerusalem, saying:

> *Moreover, brethren, we do you to wit of the grace of God bestowed on the churches of Macedonia; How that in a great trial of affliction the abundance of their joy and their deep poverty abounded unto the riches of their liberality. For to their power, I bear record, yea, and beyond their power they were willing of themselves; Praying us with much intreaty that we would receive the gift, and take upon us the fellowship of the ministering to the saints. And this they did, not as we hoped, but first gave their own selves to the Lord, and unto us by the will of God* (II Cor. 8:1-5).

---
[143] Adam Clarke.

# Commentary on Romans

**Verse 27.** *It hath pleased them verily; and their debtors they are. For if the Gentiles have been made partakers of their spiritual things, their duty is also to minister unto them in carnal things.* The Gentiles were debtors to the Lord for having been made partakers of their spiritual things; therefore, they had the spiritual duty to be of service to their Jewish brethren, and *minister unto them in carnal things.*

David wrote: *I have been young, and now am old; yet have I not seen the righteous forsaken, nor his seed begging bread* (Psa. 37:25). There are times when brethren are couched in bad times and sit in need. Saints are commanded to tend to the wants of those who need assistance. Good brethren are anxious to arise to such opportunities. A lesson this author learned long ago from a now-departed uncle is noted here in a few words regarding God's children who find themselves in straits of difficult times, be they monetary, physical, or spiritual. The uncle said: *When a child of God needs help, God sends a child of God.* Saints serve themselves best when they are first in line to assist those who need help. Helping others in times of want and need ought to be an opportunity for which the Christian seeks diligently.

**Verse 28.** *When therefore I have performed this, and have sealed to them this fruit, I will come by you into Spain.* Paul was not deterred from the duty of taking the funds needed by the saints in Jerusalem. There are times when one saint requires attention and action before another. The saints in Jerusalem were in deep need of physical things; the saints of Rome were in less need of such things. Brethren do well to understand which needs require attention first. It is not enough for one to do well; one must do well according to the degree of needs suffered.

Once Paul delivered the monetary aid he had gathered to the saints of Jerusalem, it would be considered *sealed*—faithfully delivered up, and a success of Paul's ministry. It would also serve as a proof of the conversion of the Gentile saints to God.

**Verse 29.** *And I am sure that, when I come unto you, I shall come in the fullness of the blessing of the gospel of Christ.* Paul had great confidence believing he would go to Rome; he did not realize, however, the circumstances under which he would go.

# Commentary on Romans

He went as a captive for the Lord and not as he had hoped.

> And Paul, earnestly beholding the council, said, Men and brethren, I have lived in all good conscience before God until this day. And the high priest Ananias commanded them that stood by him to smite him on the mouth. Then said Paul unto him, God shall smite thee, thou whited wall: for sittest thou to judge me after the law, and commandest me to be smitten contrary to the law? And they that stood by said, Revilest thou God's high priest? Then said Paul, I wist not, brethren, that he was the high priest: for it is written, Thou shalt not speak evil of the ruler of thy people. But when Paul perceived that the one part were Sadducees, and the other Pharisees, he cried out in the council, Men and brethren, I am a Pharisee, the son of a Pharisee: of the hope and resurrection of the dead I am called in question. And when he had so said, there arose a dissension between the Pharisees and the Sadducees: and the multitude was divided. For the Sadducees say that there is no resurrection, neither angel, nor spirit: but the Pharisees confess both. And there arose a great cry: and the scribes that were of the Pharisees' part arose, and strove, saying, We find no evil in this man: but if a spirit or an angel hath spoken to him, let us not fight against God. And when there arose a great dissension, the chief captain, fearing lest Paul should have been pulled in pieces of them, commanded the soldiers to go down, and to take him by force from among them, and to bring him into the castle. And the night following the Lord stood by him, and said, Be of good cheer, Paul: for as thou hast testified of me in Jerusalem, so must thou bear witness also at Rome (Acts 23:1-11).

The Lord gave Paul assurance he would indeed go to Rome, and he was instructed to *be of good cheer.*

> And when we came to Rome, the centurion delivered the prisoners to the captain of the guard: but Paul was suffered to dwell by himself with a soldier that kept

# Commentary on Romans

*him. And it came to pass, that after three days Paul called the chief of the Jews together: and when they were come together, he said unto them, Men and brethren, though I have committed nothing against the people, or customs of our fathers, yet was I delivered prisoner from Jerusalem into the hands of the Romans. Who, when they had examined me, would have let me go, because there was no cause of death in me. But when the Jews spake against it, I was constrained to appeal unto Caesar; not that I had ought to accuse my nation of. For this cause therefore have I called for you, to see you, and to speak with you: because that for the hope of Israel I am bound with this chain. And they said unto him, We neither received letters out of Judaea concerning thee, neither any of the brethren that came shewed or spake any harm of thee. But we desire to hear of thee what thou thinkest: for as concerning this sect, we know that every where it is spoken against. And when they had appointed him a day, there came many to him into his lodging; to whom he expounded and testified the kingdom of God, persuading them concerning Jesus, both out of the law of Moses, and out of the prophets, from morning till evening. And some believed the things which were spoken, and some believed not. And when they agreed not among themselves, they departed, after that Paul had spoken one word, Well spake the Holy Ghost by Esaias the prophet unto our fathers, Saying, Go unto this people, and say, Hearing ye shall hear, and shall not understand; and seeing ye shall see, and not perceive: For the heart of this people is waxed gross, and their ears are dull of hearing, and their eyes have they closed; lest they should see with their eyes, and hear with their ears, and understand with their heart, and should be converted, and I should heal them. Be it known therefore unto you, that the salvation of God is sent unto the Gentiles, and that they will hear it. And when he had said these words, the Jews departed, and had great reasoning among themselves. And Paul dwelt two whole years in his own hired house, and received all that came in unto him, Preaching the kingdom of God,*

# Commentary on Romans

*and teaching those things which concern the Lord Jesus Christ, with all confidence, no man forbidding him* (Acts 28:16-31).

**Verses 30-33.** *Now I beseech you, brethren, for the Lord Jesus Christ's sake, and for the love of the Spirit, that ye strive together with me in your prayers to God for me; That I may be delivered from them that do not believe in Judaea; and that my service which I have for Jerusalem may be accepted of the saints; That I may come unto you with joy by the will of God, and may with you be refreshed. Now the God of peace be with you all. Amen.*

Paul knew he had bitter enemies in Jerusalem, who would kill him if they got a chance. Even amongst the saints whose needs he was preparing to supply, there were bitter enemies of Paul. But he believed the prayers of others would be helpful, and so he begs the Roman brethren to strive together with him in praying that no harm befall him. People can sometimes be so antagonistic to others as to refuse all assistance from them. Paul feared the antagonism of the Jews to the Gentiles was so great his contributions from the Gentiles would not be accepted by the saints in Jerusalem. Therefore, he asked the saints at Rome to pray that his ministration would be accepted by the brethren at Jerusalem. This shows that the relations between Jewish churches and Gentile churches were much strained at the time. The theory has been advanced that one reason Paul was so anxious to collect much help for the poor saints in Judea was, to bring the Jewish churches to a better feeling toward Gentile churches. If the brethren of Judea would accept his gift, he could then go to Rome in joy through the will of God; that is, if it was God's will for him to go to Rome. And if the Judean saints did accept his collected contributions, one cause of great worry would be removed from his mind, and he could find rest at Rome[144] [sic].

The prophecy of Agabus was not only correct but fulfilled. Paul did in fact go to Rome, as both the Lord and Agabus declared.

---

[144] Robertson L. Whiteside.

# Commentary on Romans

Luke wrote regarding the prophecy of Agabus:

> *And as we tarried there many days, there came down from Judaea a certain prophet, named Agabus. And when he was come unto us, he took Paul's girdle, and bound his own hands and feet, and said, Thus saith the Holy Ghost, So shall the Jews at Jerusalem bind the man that owneth this girdle, and shall deliver him into the hands of the Gentiles. And when we heard these things, both we, and they of that place, besought him not to go up to Jerusalem. Then Paul answered, What mean ye to weep and to break mine heart? for I am ready not to be bound only, but also to die at Jerusalem for the name of the Lord Jesus. And when he would not be persuaded, we ceased, saying, The will of the Lord be done* (Acts 21:10-14).

There are times when our prayers are answered favorably, but oftentimes not as we hope or expect.

## Romans 16:1-27

> *1 I commend unto you Phebe our sister, which is a servant of the church which is at Cenchrea: 2 That ye receive her in the Lord, as becometh saints, and that ye assist her in whatsoever business she hath need of you: for she hath been a succourer of many, and of myself also. 3 Greet Priscilla and Aquila my helpers in Christ Jesus: 4 Who have for my life laid down their own necks: unto whom not only I give thanks, but also all the churches of the Gentiles. 5 Likewise greet the church that is in their house. Salute my well beloved Epaenetus, who is the firstfruits of Achaia unto Christ. 6 Greet Mary, who bestowed much labour on us. 7 Salute Andronicus and Junia, my kinsmen, and my fellowprisoners, who are of note among the apostles, who also were in Christ before me. 8 Greet Amplias my beloved in the Lord. 9 Salute Urbane, our helper in Christ, and Stachys my beloved. 10 Salute Apelles, approved in Christ. Salute them which are of Aristobulus' household. 11 Salute Herodion my kinsman. Greet*

# Commentary on Romans

*them that be of the household of Narcissus, which are in the Lord. 12 Salute Tryphena and Tryphosa, who labour in the Lord. Salute the beloved Persis, which laboured much in the Lord. 13 Salute Rufus chosen in the Lord, and his mother and mine. 14 Salute Asyncritus, Phlegon, Hermas, Patrobas, Hermes, and the brethren which are with them. 15 Salute Philologus, and Julia, Nereus, and his sister, and Olympas, and all the saints which are with them. 16 Salute one another with an holy kiss. The churches of Christ salute you. 17 Now I beseech you, brethren, mark them which cause divisions and offences contrary to the doctrine which ye have learned; and avoid them. 18 For they that are such serve not our Lord Jesus Christ, but their own belly; and by good words and fair speeches deceive the hearts of the simple. 19 For your obedience is come abroad unto all men. I am glad therefore on your behalf: but yet I would have you wise unto that which is good, and simple concerning evil. 20 And the God of peace shall bruise Satan under your feet shortly. The grace of our Lord Jesus Christ be with you. Amen. 21 Timotheus my workfellow, and Lucius, and Jason, and Sosipater, my kinsmen, salute you. 22 I Tertius, who wrote this epistle, salute you in the Lord. 23 Gaius mine host, and of the whole church, saluteth you. Erastus the chamberlain of the city saluteth you, and Quartus a brother. 24 The grace of our Lord Jesus Christ be with you all. Amen. 25 Now to him that is of power to stablish you according to my gospel, and the preaching of Jesus Christ, according to the revelation of the mystery, which was kept secret since the world began, 26 But now is made manifest, and by the scriptures of the prophets, according to the commandment of the everlasting God, made known to all nations for the obedience of faith: 27 To God only wise, be glory through Jesus Christ for ever. Amen.*

Matthew Henry wrote the following overview of this chapter:

> Paul is now concluding this long and excellent epistle, and he does it with a great deal of affection. As in the

# Commentary on Romans

main body of the epistle, he appears to have been a very knowing man, so in these appurtenances of it he appears to have been a very loving man. So much knowledge and so much love are a very rare—but (where they exist) a very excellent and amiable—composition; for what is heaven but knowledge and love made perfect? It is observable how often Paul speaks as if he were concluding, and yet takes fresh hold again. One would have thought that solemn benediction which closed the foregoing chapter should have ended the epistle; and yet here he begins again, and in this chapter he repeats the blessing (Rom. 16:20), "The grace of our Lord Jesus Christ be with you, Amen." And yet he has something more to say; nay, again he repeats the blessing (Rom. 16:24), and yet has not done; an expression of his tender love. Now, in this closing chapter, we may observe, I. His recommendation of one friend to the Roman Christians, and his particular salutation of several among them (v.1-16). II. A caution to take heed of those who caused divisions (Rom. 16:17-20). III. Salutations added from some who were with Paul (Rom. 16:21-24). IV. He concludes with a solemn celebration of the glory of God (Rom. 16:25-27)[145] [sic].

The Epistle concludes with various salutations. The "*names*'" which occur in this chapter are chiefly "Greek;" and the persons designated had been probably inhabitants of Greece, but had removed to Rome for purposes of commerce, etc. Possibly some of them had been converted under the ministry of the apostle himself during his preaching in Corinth and other parts of Greece. It is remarkable that the name of "Peter" does not occur in this catalog; which is conclusive evidence, contrary to the Papists, that Peter was not then known by Paul to be in Rome[146] [sic].

Before tending to our own remarks on this chapter the efforts of liberalism compels us to refute the damnable doctrine that as-

---
[145] Matthew Henry.
[146] Albert Barnes.

# Commentary on Romans

serts a woman may serve in the office of a deaconess based upon eisegetical efforts to discredit the truth regarding some of the roles women are to have in the Lord's church. Whiteside provided the following assessment.

> There has been much said for and against the possibility that Phoebe was an official deaconess of her home church. But the use of the word *diakonos*, here translated servant, does not prove that she occupied an official position. In these letters to the churches the word is used a number of times, but not in any official sense, unless in this one place. We let our minds run to officialism too much. On account of the social condition of women of that age, aged women of experience, piety and ability were needed to teach, encourage, and otherwise help young women. On this point, see 1 Tim. 5:3-16; Tit. 2:3-6. To select a person for a certain work does not necessarily make him an officer in the common acceptation of that term. To select a man to hold a series of meetings does not make him an officer, and no one thinks so. Selecting a song-leader does not make him an officer. Selecting certain women to attend to certain duties does not make them deaconesses in any official sense. *Diakonos* therefore had no official significance. It is thought by some that she was the bearer of Paul's letter to Rome, but that is not certain. She evidently went to Rome on certain business, for Paul urges the brethren to "assist her in whatever matter she may have need." To receive her in the Lord was to treat her as a worthy Christian should be treat-ed; "for she herself also hath been a helper of many, and of mine own self.'" Those who help others always commend themselves to the Lord[147] [sic].

Clarke wrote the following in his effort to promote the doctrine of women deacons.

> Phoebe is here termed a servant, διακονον, a deaconess of the Church at Cenchrea. There were deaconesses in the primitive Church, whose business it was to

---
[147] Robertson L. Whiteside

## Commentary on Romans

attend the female converts at baptism; to instruct the catechumens, or persons who were candidates for baptism; to visit the sick, and those who were in prison, and, in short, perform those religious offices for the female part of the Church which could not with propriety be performed by men. They were chosen in general out of the most experienced of the Church, and were ordinarily widows, who had borne children. Some ancient constitutions required them to be forty, others fifty, and others sixty years of age. It is evident that they were ordained to their office by the imposition of the hands of the bishop; and the form of prayer used on the occasion is extant in the apostolical constitutions. In the tenth or eleventh century the order be-came extinct in the Latin Church, but continued in the Greek Church till the end of the twelfth century[148] [sic].

Sadly, there are many liberally-minded members of the church who espouse the ungodly assertions set forth by Clarke. Not only have liberals echoed Clarke's doctrine, but they continue to mutilate and maul the Scriptures to justify this damnable doctrine. Those who engage in such are *unlearned and unstable* and *wrest, as they do also the other scriptures, unto their own destruction* (II Pet. 3:16).

Once a congregation succumbs to the doctrine of women deacons that congregation is but one step from women elders and women preachers. Not long after such things are embraced, steps toward woman prophets is sure to follow. Within the Lord's church, there are many who envelop themselves with all of these things. The Lord said, however, *wisdom is justified of all her children* (Lk. 7:35).

**Verses 1-26.** The word *salute* is found fifteen times in twelve verses of this chapter; it behooves us therefore, to consider the word in more depth. The word is defined as :to enfold in the arms, to welcome—embrace, greet, to draw to one's self toward, bid welcome, wish well for or to receive joyfully—welcome."

We divide this chapter into five sections: first, verses 1-15 which

---
[148] Adam Clarke

# Commentary on Romans

contain the *salutable*. Verse 16 describes the *saluting* itself. Verses 17 and 18 identify the *saluteless*. Verses 19-23 contain the *saluters*. Last, verses 25-27 shows us the salute. We ask that the *coining* of these few words be acceptable to better illustrate the matters following.

**In verses 1-15.** The *salutable* own the following traits and engage in the following conduct. They are those who provide a succor to the Lord's church. They are among those who are willing to lay down their lives for the cause of Christ. They are among the well beloved. They engage in much labor in the vineyard of Christ. They are worthy of note among the apostles. They are beloved in the Lord. They are approved in and by Christ. They are in the Lord and they are also chosen in the Lord.

**Verse 16.** The *saluting* involves kind affection. It demands the extension of the right hand of fellowship. It aspires the saints to greet one another in the manner of holiness.

**Verses 17-18.** The *saluteless* are those who must be marked. They are men who cause division in the Lord's church. They are offensive to the Lord, and walk contrary to the doctrine of Christ. They are also to be avoided.

**Verses 19-23.** These verses show us who the *salueters* were of whom Paul spoke. They were men who were obedient to the Lord, described as wise, and identified as work-fellows among the saints.
**Verses 21-23.** *Timotheus my workfellow, and Lucius, and Jason, and Sosipater, my kinsmen, salute you. I Tertius, who wrote this epistle, salute you in the Lord. Gaius mine host, and of the whole church, saluteth you. Erastus the chamberlain of the city saluteth you, and Quartus a brother.* Those mentioned here were likely with Paul at the time of this writing. On Erastus, the chamberlain of the city, Clarke provided the following information

> Treasurer of the city of Corinth, from which St. Paul wrote this epistle. This is supposed to be the same person as is mentioned Act 19:22. He was one of St. Paul's companions, and, as appears from 2 Ti 4:20,

## Commentary on Romans

was left about this time by the apostle at Corinth. He is called the chamberlain οικονομος, which signifies the same as treasurer; he to whom the receipt and expenditure of the public money were intrusted. He received the tolls, customs, etc., belonging to the city, and out of them paid the public expenses. Such persons were in very high credit; and if Erastus was at this time treasurer, it would appear that Christianity was then in considerable repute in Corinth. But if the Erastus of the Acts was the same with the Erastus mentioned here, it is not likely that he now held the office, for this could not at all comport with his travelling with St. Paul. Hence several, both ancients and moderns, who believe the identity of the persons, suppose that Erastus was not now treasurer, but that having formerly been so he still retained the title. Chrysostom thought that he still retained the employment[149] [sic].

**Verses 25-26.** Here we have the *salute* itself described. The salute is one of grace and power. It is to be based upon Biblical principles. Further, the salute helps to better establish the saints in the faith. It was revealed according to revelation. Lastly, the salute must be obeyed.

**Verse 27.** *To God only wise, be glory through Jesus Christ for ever. Amen.* Here we have Paul's closing doxology—the expression of praise to God the Father.

The phrase, *through Jesus Christ*, was a weighty matter, not for light consideration. To the Jews these words served as a reminder it was no longer through Moses that praises to God could be offered. For the Gentiles the phrase implied two things. First, for those converted from paganism, it served as the reminder that only through Christ could one offer praises to the Father. Second, it reminded them the Patriarchal Law was now defunct, and it was only through Christ their sacrifices and praises to the Father were made acceptable.

The epistle closes with the word *Amen*, an appropriate and most fitting conclusion. In early Christian assemblies, when a brother

---
[149] Adam Clarke.

# Commentary on Romans

had read a text, given a Divine discourse, or had offered up prayer to God, others responded by saying, *Amen*—thus making the substance of what was uttered their own. The word has been defined in numerous ways, we prefer: *As God has said it, so let it be done.*

Many matters were addressed by Paul in this epistle. Among them was Paul's effort to end the strife between the Jews and Gentiles, thus encouraging unity.

*To God only wise, be glory through Jesus Christ for ever. Amen* (Rom. 16:27).

> At its outset, this is an ascription of glory to the power that could do all this; at its close it ascribes glory to the wisdom that planned and that presides over the gathering of a redeemed people out of all nations. The apostle adds his devout "Amen," which the reader—if he has followed him with the astonishment and delight of him who pens these words—will fervently echo[150] [sic].

---

[150][sic]. Robert Jamieson, A.R. Fausset, and David Brown.

# Commentary on Romans

## Works Cited

**Barnes, Albert.** Notes On The New Testament Explanatory And Practical By Albert Barnes. Ed. By Robert Frew, D.D. Grand Rapids, MI: Baker Book House, 1949.

**Clarke, Adam.** Adam Clarke's Commentary on the Old and New Testaments A derivative of Adam Clarke's Commentary for the Online Bible produced by Sulu D. Kelley, Concord, NC.

**Coleridge, Samuel.** *Table Talk,* Oxford: Oxford University Pub., N.D.

**Coneybeare, W.J., and J.S. Howson.** *The Life and Epistles of St. Paul.* London: Longmans, Green, and Co., 1886.

**Godet F.** *Commentary on St. Paul's Epistle to the Romans.* Tr. and Ed. by Talbot W. Chambers, D.D. New York: Funk & Wagnals, 1883.

**Henry, Matthew.** *Matthew Henry's Commentary on the Whole Bible*, 6 Vols. Peabody, MA: Hendrickson Pub., 2014.

**Jamieson, Robert, A.R. Fausset, and David Brown.** *Commentary Critical and Explanatory on the Whole Bible.* Grand Rapids: Christian Classics Ethereal Library, 1871.

**Keil and Delitzsch.** 1996 ed.

**Little** XXXXXXXXXXXXXXXXXXXXX

**Mosher Keith.** Unpublished class notes on Romans. Memphis, TN: Memphis School of Preaching, 1989.

**Thayer Henry:** *Greek—English Lexicon of the New Testament.* Grand Rapids, MI: Baker Book House, 1977.

**Vine W. E.** *Vine's Complete Expository Dictionary of Old & New Testament Words.* Old Tappan, NJ: Fleming H. Revell, 1966.

**Wallace Foy E.** *The Book of Revelation.* Nashville, TN: The Foy E. Wallace, Jr. Publications, 1966.

**Whiteside Robertson L.** *Paul's Letter to the Saints at Rome* (4th ed.). Denton, TX: Miss Inys Whiteside,1955

# Commentary on Romans

## Scripture References

| Genesis | Page |
|---|---|
| 1:26-27 | 102 |
| 2:5-17 | 19 |
| 3:15 | 77 |
| 3:22-24 | 87-88 |
| 4:4 | 268 |
| 4:4-5 | 37 |
| 4:16 | 55 |
| 4:16-17 | 321 |
| 8:20 | 268 |
| 9:6 | 324 |
| 10:8-20 | 321-22 |
| 12:1-3 | 70-71, 185, 374 |
| 14:18 | 375 |
| 15:1-17 | 268-69 |
| 15:1-18 | 73-74 |
| 15:6 | 64-65 |
| 15:11 | 75 |
| 15:13 | 70 |
| 15:17 | 76 |
| 17:1-2, 4-5 | 72 |
| 17:1-14 | 72 |
| 17:10-11 | 48 |
| 17:16, 20 | 74 |
| 18:1-8 | 301 |
| 18:14 | 182 |
| 19:1 | 223 |
| 19:1-2 | 301 |
| 19:4-11 | 223-24 |
| 22:1-12 | 65 |
| 22:15-18 | 374 |
| 25:23 | 208 |
| 25:1-34 | 72 |
| 26:3-4 | 373 |
| 28:3 | 72 |
| 28:13-14 | 74, 374 |
| 31:19 | 21 |
| 31:54 | 269 |
| 32:28 | 201 |
| 35:1-4 | 21 |
| 38:12-30 | 88-89 |

| Exodus | |
|---|---|
| 2:24 | 183 |
| 4:22 | 201 |
| 6:5 | 183 |
| 10:3, 7 | 216 |

| Exodus | Page |
|---|---|
| 12:41 | 70 |
| 18:1 | 375 |
| 19:5 | 66 |
| 19:6 | 272 |
| 20:17 | 123 |
| 23:17 | 147 |
| 25:40 | 42 |
| 26:30 | 42 |
| 27:8 | 42 |
| 28:36 | 272 |
| 32:1-7 | 21-22 |
| 32:16 | 43 |
| 35:5 | 244 |
| 39:30 | 30, 272 |

| Leviticus | |
|---|---|
| 4:2, 13, 27 | 94 |
| 18:5 | 228 |
| 18:21 | 23 |
| 18:22 | 26 |
| 19:3 | 329 |
| 20:13 | 26 |
| 20:26 | 272 |
| 25:1-22 | 197 |
| 25:8-12 | 197-98 |

| Numbers | |
|---|---|
| 5:12-29 | xiv-xv |
| 8:4 | 42-43 |
| 15:24-25 | 27 |
| 16:28 | 159 |
| 19:13 | 140 |
| 22:5 | 25 |
| 23:9-10 | 375-76 |
| 23:19 | 264 |
| 24:1-13 | 160-61 |
| 25:1-2 | 24 |
| 35:11-15 | 146-47 |

**Deuteronomy**

# Commentary on Romans

| Reference | Page | Reference | Page |
|---|---|---|---|
| 4:13 | 202 | 9:7 | 48 |
| 7:7 | 263 | 19:10, 14 | 240 |
| 10:15 | 263 | 19:18 | 59 |
| 14:1 | 201 | 20:35-43 | 293-94 |
| **Deuteronomy** | **Page** | **II Kings** | **Page** |
| 18:10 | 23 | 16:3 | 23 |
| 18:15 | 125, 229 | | |
| 18:15-19 | 44, 112, 116-17, 148, 239, 241-42 | **I Chronicles** | |
| 23:2 | 88, 90 | 18:12-13 | 208 |
| 28:37 | 47 | 28:19 | 43 |
| 29:1 | 202 | | |
| 29:4 | 245 | **II Chronicles** | |
| 30:11-14 | 229 | | |
| 32:21 | 237 | 7:20 | 48 |
| 32:35 | 313 | 29:25 | xvii |
| 32:43 | 376-77 | | |
| 34:9 | 157 | **Ezra** | |
| **Joshua** | | 6:1-5 | 260-61 |
| 2:1-11 | 210-11 | **Job** | |
| 20:2 | 146 | | |
| 21:23, 27, 32 | 146 | 9:2 | vii |
| | | 19:25 | 61, 376 |
| **Judges** | | 22:2 | 217-18 |
| | | 40:2 | 218 |
| 16:23 | 24 | **Psalms** | |
| **Ruth** | | 18:49 | 388-89 |
| | | 19:1-4 | 21 |
| 4:18-22 | 89-90 | 34:14 | 312 |
| | | 35:5, 11 | 54 |
| **I Samuel** | | 37:21    3 | 32 |
| | | 37:25 | 352, 409 |
| 5:2 | 24 | 44:14 | 48 |
| 8:1-22 | 319-21 | 44:22 | 193 |
| 15:29 | 264 | 51:4 | 54 |
| 16;7 | 50 | 51:5 | 88 |
| 18:5, 7 | 52 | 55:13-14 | 54 |
| 23:12, 19-20 | 52 | 69:9 | 381 |
| | | 69:22-23 | 244-45 |
| **II Samuel** | | 89:34 | 19 |
| | | 89:35-36 | 264 |
| 15:6, 31 | 52 | 117 | 391 |
| 22:50 | 376 | 117:1 | 389 |
| 23:1-2 | 161. 194. 198 | 118:22 | 246 |
| 24:10, 18-25 | 269-70 | 119:89 | 19 |
| | | 133:1 | 306 |
| **I Kings** | | | |
| | | **Proverbs** | |

# Commentary on Romans

| | | | |
|---|---|---|---|
| 2:5 | 266 | 52:15 | 402 |
| 4:23 | 276 | 53:7 | 313 |
| 12:24 | 294 | 53:12 | 230 |
| 12:27 | 294 | 55:7 | 204 |
| 14:12 | 363 | 55:8-11 | 54 |
| 15:19 | 294 | 55:11 | 22, 200 |
| 16:4 | 212 | 59:1-2 | 192 |
| 16:18 | 308 | 59:20-21 | 260-61 |
| 16:25 | 22, 363 | 62:2 | 386 |
| 18:9 | 294 | 64:8 | 212 |
| 18:19 | 334 | 65:1-2 | 233 |
| 19:24 | 294 | 65:2 | 212 |
| 20:2 | 327 | | |
| 21:25 | 294 | **Jeremiah** | |
| 22:13 | 294 | 3:9 | 120 |
| 23:7 | 22 | 6:16 | 210 |
| 24:30 | 294 | 10:23 | 22-23, 363 |
| 25:21-22 | 316 | 12:5 | 299 |
| 26:13-15 | 316 | 18:36 | 212 |
| 28:13 | 204 | 20:8-9 | 296-97 |
| | | 20:9 | 14 |
| **Ecclesiastes** | | 25:11-12 | 324 |
| | | 29:10 | 324 |
| 8:2 | 329 | 31:9 | 120, 147, 197 |
| 10:4 | 314 | 31:31-34 | 126, 211 |
| 12:14 | 9, 37, 154, 350 | 34:12-22 | 62, 111, 117 |
| **Isaiah** | | **Lamentations** | |
| 1:1-19 | 240-41 | | |
| 1:11-16 | 273-74 | 2:15 | 48 |
| 2:2 | 5 | | |
| 2:2-3 | 201 | | |
| 5:21 | 308 | **Ezekiel** | |
| **Isaiah** | **Page** | | **Page** |
| 6:9-10 | 243 | 16:4 | 29 |
| 7:14 | 174 | 18:20-24 | 367, 268 |
| 9:1-2 | 386 | 18:26 | 47 |
| 9:6 | 175 | 22:26 | 47 |
| 10:20-23 | 216 | 23:37 | 120 |
| 11:1 | 54 | 24:14 | 264 |
| 11:1, 10 | 392 | | |
| 11:10 | 386, 389 | **Daniel** | |
| 28:16 | 226, 246 | 9:20-27 | 340 |
| 29:10 | 243 | 9:24-27 | 284 |
| 30:9 | 212 | 9:26-27 | 87 |
| 40:13-14 | 212 | | |
| 45:19 | 6, 263 | **Hosea** | |
| 45:23 | 367 | | |
| 52:5 | 48 | 4:1 | 266 |
| 52:7 | 230 | | |

# Commentary on Romans

| | | | |
|---|---|---|---|
| 2:23 | 215 | 8:14-15 | xii |
| 6:3 | 57 | 10:40 | 303 |
| 6:6 | 266 | 10:42 | 303 |
| 9:15 | 193 | 11:6 | 220 |
| 11:1 | 197 | 11:16 | 253 |
| 13:11 | 324 | 12:41-42 | 353 |
| | | 12:45 | 353 |
| **Joel** | | 13:13-15 | 243 |
| | | 15:15-18 | 35 |
| 2:28-32 | 227 | 16:18 | x |
| 2:30-32 | 353 | 16:18-19 | 3 |
| | | 17:2 | 276 |
| **Amos** | | 17:24-47 | 331 |
| | | 18:16 | 195 |
| 5:25-26 | 25 | 19:26 | 180 |
| 6:1-6 | xvii | 21:9 | 54 |
| | | 21:28-30 | 296 |
| **Habakkuk** | | 22:15-22 | 330 |
| | | 22:17-21 | 322 |
| 2:4 | 15-17 | 22:21 | 329 |
| | | 22:32 | 364 |
| **Zephaniah** | | 23:36 | 338, 353 |
| | | 23:38 | 108, 146-47 |
| 3:4 | 47 | 24:4-8 | 301 |
| 6:12 | 54 | 24;13 | 343 |
| | | 24:15 | 341, 349 |
| **Zechariah** | | 24:21 | 250, 34 |
| | | 24:27-30 | 340 |
| 13:1-7 | 284 | 24:30 | 346 |
| | | 24:33 | 343, 345-46 |
| **Malachi** | | 24:34 | 338, 353 |
| | | 24:24-30 | 293 |
| 3:8 | 313 | 25:41 | 305 |
| | | 25:43 | 303 |
| **Matthew** | **Page** | | |
| | | **Matthew** | **Page** |
| 2:1-2 | 388 | | |
| 2:23 | 54 | 26:28 | 391 |
| 3:1 | 182 | 27:12-14 | 313-14 |
| 3:9 | 44, 113, 202 | | |
| 4:14-16 | 386 | **Mark** | |
| 5:9 | 312 | | |
| 5:11-12 | 304 | 1:15 | 225 |
| 5:16 | 278 | 8:12 | 338, 354 |
| 5:39 | 314 | 8:38 | 338, 354 |
| 5:39-41 | 312 | 9:1 | 4 |
| 5:43-45 | 335 | 9:2 | 276 |
| 5:44 | 304 | 11:21 | 305 |
| 6:19-20 | 36 | 12:26 | 364 |
| 6:20 | 11 | 13:4 | 346 |
| 6:25-34 | 352 | 13:29 | 346 |
| 7:1-2 | 366 | 13:30 | 338, 354 |

410

# Commentary on Romans

| | | | |
|---|---|---|---|
| 14:24 | 391 | 12:44 | 135 |
| 16:15-16 | 347 | 13:4-6 | 230 |
| | | 13:34 | 6 |
| **Luke** | | 13:34,35 | 289-90 |
| 1:5-6 | 61, 150 | 13:35 | 333 |
| 1:13 | 82 | 14:6 | 22, 141 |
| 2:49 | 70, 295, 381 | 14:9 | 186 |
| 4:13 | 104 | 14:15 | 68, 274 |
| 6:27-28 | 304 | 15:4 | 68 |
| 7:35 | 428 | 15:2 | 255 |
| 7:31 | 338, 354 | 15:12 | 290 |
| 8:11 | 15 | 15:14 | 68 |
| 9:4-5 | 230 | 15:17 | 290, 333 |
| 9:57-62 | 296 | 16:8 | 87 |
| 10:16 | 279 | 16:13-14 | 87 |
| 11:1-4 | 181-82 | 17:4 | 4 |
| 11:23 | 374 | 17:17 | 399 |
| 11:29-32 | 253, 338, 354 | 17:20-21 | 306, 364, 373 |
| 11:50-51 | 338, 354 | 17:21 | 12 |
| 12:14 | 360 | 18:20 | 6, 263 |
| 14:26-29 | 194 | 18:31 | 148 |
| 16:8 | 338, 355 | 18:36 | 46, 201, 371 |
| 16:15 | 57 | 19:15 | 54 |
| 16:16 | 95 | | |
| 17:25 | 338, 355 | **Acts** | |
| 21:20 | 341 | | |
| 21:22 | 344 | 1:6 | 199 |
| 21:32 | 338, 355 | 1:8 | 233 |
| 22:20 | 391 | 2:1-10 | 397-98 |
| | | 2:10 | xii |
| **John** | | 2:1-11 | 231-32 |
| | | 2:8-11 | x |
| 1:11-17 | 95 | 2:9-11, 14-21 | 340 |
| 1:34-35 | 45, 238 | 2:19-21 | 353 |
| **John** | **Page** | **Acts** | **Page** |
| 3:1-2 | 5 | 2:23 | 58 |
| 3:16 | 7, 289 | 2:32-33 | 108 |
| 3:16-17 | 88 | 2:37 | 355 |
| 4:34 | 381 | 2:38 | 155-56, 347, 353 |
| 5:39 | 57, 63 | 2:39 | 201-203 |
| 6:28,29 | 70 | 2:40 | 339, 345, 355 |
| 6:38 | 381 | 2:41 | 231 |
| 7:24 | 35, 366 | 2:42 | 339 |
| 8:12 | 78 | 3:25 | 74 |
| 8:24 | 225 | 4:12 | 15 |
| 8:32 | 8, 173 | 5:1-4 | 288 |
| 8:44 | 144 | 5:36 | 281 |
| 8:56 | 63, 175, 387 | 5:1-10 | 38 |
| 9:5 | 78 | 6:1-5 | 397 |
| 10:28-29 | 192 | 7:37-38 | 171 |
| 10:30 | 186 | 7:42,43 | 24 |

411

# Commentary on Romans

| | | | |
|---|---|---|---|
| 8:1-3 | 303-304 | 22:3 | 125, 140 |
| 8:3 | 167 | 25:1-12 | 403, 404 |
| 8:14 | xii, 286-87 | 26:5 | 222 |
| 8:18 | 159, 183, 285 | 26:13-18 | 402 |
| 8:21-22 | x | 26:23 | 386 |
| 8:26-40 | 228-29 | 28:16-29 | 243-44 |
| 8:37 | 84 | 28:16-31 | 411-12 |
| 9:1-2 | 139, 167 | | |
| 9:10-16 | 279 | **Romans** | |
| 9;15 | 214, 395 | | |
| 9:11-16 | 2 | 1:5 | 5 |
| 10:3-4 | 398 | 1:11 | xii, 285 |
| 10:9-15 | 375 | 1:11-12,15 | xxiv |
| 11:23 | 292 | 1:13 | 403 |
| 11:27-30 | 301 | 1:15-16 | vii |
| 12:17 | x | 1:16 | 55, 62, 201, 232, 385 |
| 12:19 | x | | |
| 12:21-23 | 39 | 1:17 | vii |
| 13:6-12 | 39 | 1:18 | 213 |
| 13:42-47 | 247-48 | 1:25 | 19 |
| 13:46 | 245 | 2:1 | 49, 59, 62 |
| 15:1 | 56 | 2:4-6 | 213-14 |
| 15:2 | 287 | 3:3-4 | 99 |
| 15:3 | 406 | 3:8 | 251 |
| 15:1-5 | 106, 115 | 3:9 | 265 |
| 15:5 | 116, 131, 136, 160, 220 | 3:10 | 65 |
| | | 3:22-23 | 265 |
| 15:1-6 | 396-97 | 3:23 | ix |
| 15:6 | 65 | 5:7 | 196, 290-91 |
| 15:7 | 397 | 5:8 | 7 |
| 15:10 | 245 | 5:10 | 99 |
| 15:22-24 | 66 | 6:12 | 113 |
| 15:24-26 | 85 | 6:14-15 | 118-19 |
| 15:29 | 372 | 6:17 | 5, 84, 240-41 |
| **Acts** | **Page** | | |
| | | **Romans** | **Page** |
| 15:36-40 | 312 | | |
| 16:4-10 | 228 | 6:17-18 | 219 |
| 16:9-10,12 | 403 | 6:23 | 263, 272 |
| 17:10-11 | 231 | 7:4 | 105, 134, 141, 363, 380 |
| 17:14-15 | 406 | | |
| 17:30 | 42, 93 | 7:5-6 | 132 |
| 18:5 | 403 | 7:7 | 60, 150 |
| 19:21 | xi, 403 | 7:14-23 | 136 |
| 19:22 | 419 | 7:15-25 | 145 |
| 20:20, 27 | 401 | 7:19 | 138 |
| 20:28 | 286 | 8:2 | 92 |
| 20:38 | 406 | 8:4 | 61 |
| 21:5 | 406 | 8:9 | 156 |
| 21:10-14 | 413 | 8:15 | 164 |
| 23:1 | 195 | 8:16-17 | 39-40 |
| 23:1-11 | 410 | 8:24 | 279, 298 |

# Commentary on Romans

| Romans | Page | Romans | Page |
|---|---|---|---|
| 8:26 | 182 | 3:10 | 280 |
| 8:27 | 182-83, 190 | 4:17 | 400 |
| 8:27-29 | 184 | 6:2-3 | 50 |
| 8:33 | 2, 31, 64, 68-69, 93, 189 | 6:7 | 314 |
| | | 6:12 | 377 |
| 8:34 | 191 | 7:26 | 167, 244 |
| 8:35-39 | 299-300 | 9:16 | 13, 399 |
| 9:32 | 236 | 10:1-2 | 82 |
| 10:1-3 | 242 | 10:12 | 302 |
| 10:1-15 | 358-59 | 10:14-33 | 357 |
| 10:17 | 7, 230 | 10:23 | 377 |
| 11:1 | 125 | 11:25 | 391 |
| 11:12-15 | 257 | 12:4-12 | 283 |
| 11:21-25 | 396 | 12:25 | 300 |
| 12:4-5 | 300 | 12:27 | 171 |
| 12:5 | 293 | 12:31 | 10 |
| 12:6-8 | 177 | 13:2 | 382 |
| 12:9 | 333 | 13:5 | 335, 350 |
| 12:18 | 58 | 13:8-10 | 284 |
| 13:8 | 290, 332 | 14:15 | 179, 182 |
| 13:11-12 | 342-43 | 14:33 | 6 |
| 13:12 | 349 | 14:37 | 280 |
| 14:9 | 223 | 15:2 | vi |
| 14:12 | 9, 37, 154, 350 | 15:3-8 | 107 |
| 14:19 | 379 | 15:10 | 1 |
| 14:20 | 386 | 15:34 | 266 |
| 15:4 | 389 | 15:42-44 | 167 |
| 15:5 | 306 | 15:49-54 | 168 |
| 15:9 | 388 | 15:56,57 | 95 |
| 15:9-20 | xi | 16:1-3 | 302 |
| 15:15 | 280 | 16:1-4 | 407 |
| 15:18-23 | xxiv | 16:6, 11 | 406 |
| 15:24-27 | 301 | 16:13 | 297 |
| 16:1-3 | xi | | |
| 16:17-20 | 415 | | |

| Romans | Page | II Corinthians | Page |
|---|---|---|---|
| 16:20 | 343, 349, 415 | 1:3-7 | 299 |
| 16:21-27 | 415 | 1:3 | 272 |
| 16:26 | 5 | 1:22 | 176 |
| 16:27 | 421 | 3:6 | 391 |
| | | 3:6-7 | 142 |
| I Corinthians | | 3:7, | 10-11, 390-91 |
| | | 3:7-11 | 84, 170 |
| 1:10 | 12, 307, 373 | 3:12-14 | 391 |
| 1:10-11 | 300, 358 | 3:17 | 115 |
| 1:23 | 220 | 4:16 | 275 |
| 2:2 | 55 | 5:5 | 176 |
| 2:9-13 | 266 | 5:10 | 154, 350, 368 |
| 2:16 | 212 | 5:10-11 | 37 |
| 3:9-11 | 374 | 5:18 | 99 |

# Commentary on Romans

| | | | |
|---|---|---|---|
| 7:10 | 263 | 4:24-25 | 173 |
| 8:1-5 | 408-409 | 5:1 | 115, 173, 245 |
| 8:1-6 | 302 | 5:1-4 | 113 |
| 8:1-7 | 407 | 5:4 | 192 |
| 8:8 | 277, 278 | 5:13 | 290 |
| 8:21 | 309 | 5:14 | 113, 333 |
| 9:1-15 | 407 | 5:19-21 | 369-70 |
| 9:12-13 | 407 | 6:1 | 316 |
| 10:5 | 266 | 6:3 | 308 |
| 13:5 | 278 | 6:4 | 278 |
| 13:11 | 307 | 6:7-8 | 19-20 |
| | | 6:10 | 302 |

**Galatians**

**Ephesians**

| | | | |
|---|---|---|---|
| 1:4 | 275 | | |
| 1:6 | 116 | 1:3 | 33, 39, 229 |
| 1:6-7 | 106 | 1:5 | 187 |
| 1:6-9 | 14-15 | 1:7 | 214, 249 |
| 1:11-12 | 132-33 | 1:10-11 | 184-85 |
| 1:13 | 139, 195 | 1:13-14 | 176 |
| 1:13-14 | 98 | 1:18 | 214 |
| 2:1, 11 | 98 | 1:22 | xii |
| 2:4 | 115, 173, 245 | 1:22-23 | 171, 282 |
| 1:1, 11 | xi | 2:2 | 275 |
| 2:11-14 | 360 | 2:7 | 249 |
| 2:14 | xii | 2:8 | 263 |
| 2:16 | 40, 236-37 | 2:11-20 | 247 |
| 2:20 | 105 | 2:12 | 298, 393 |
| 3:19 | 57, 111 | 2:13-18 | 225 |
| 3:2 | 159 | 2:14 | 202 |
| 3:16 | 386 | 2:14-16 | 120 |
| 3:16-17 | 197 | 2:15 | 364, 393 |
| 3:19, 24 | 149 | 2:15-16 | 247 |
| 3:19:19-29 | 85, 99 | 2:14-19 | 216 |
| 3:23 | 163 | 2:20-22 | 374 |
| 3:23-26 | 236 | 3:8 | 5, 280, 396 |

| **Galatians** | **Page** | **Ephesians** | **Page** |
|---|---|---|---|
| 3:24 | 107, 134, 223 | 3:8-11 | 3 |
| 3:21-25 | 92 | 3:11 | 3, 325 |
| 3:21-26 | 64 | 3:15 | 293 |
| 3:24-25 | 56 | 3:13-15 | 159 |
| 3:26-27 | 83 | 3:16 | 214 |
| 3:26-28 | 251-52, 281 | 4:2 | 290 |
| 3:28-29 | 39 | 4:4 | 282 |
| 4:3 | 173 | 4:26-27 | 314 |
| 4:3, 9, 24-25 | 125 | 5:11 | 41 |
| 4:3, 9 | 163 | 5:14 | 347 |
| 4:4 | 172, 176 | 5:22-33 | 121 |
| 4:4-5 | 87, 170 | 6:17 | 355 |
| 4:9 | 173 | | |
| 4:10-11 | 362 | **Philippians** | |

# Commentary on Romans

| | | | |
|---|---|---|---|
| 1:13-18 | 401 | 1:13 | 1 |
| 1:15-16 | 12 | 1:15 | 223 |
| 1:15-18 | 251 | 2:5 | 104, 161, 182 |
| 2:1 | 272 | 2:5-6 | 191 |
| 2:2, 5 | 307 | 3:2 | 303 |
| 2:12 | 40, 69-70 | 4:1 | 26 |
| 3:4-6 | 125, 140 | 4:1-2 | 210 |
| 3:6 | 150 | 4:4 | 370 |
| 3:5-6 | 61 | 5:3-16 | 416 |
| 3:20-21 | 167-68 | 5:24 | 50 |
| 4:5 | 337 | 6:3-5 | 35 |
| 4:22 | xii | | |

**II Timothy**

| | | | |
|---|---|---|---|
| **Colossians** | | 2:15 | 8 |
| | | 2:21 | 214 |
| 1:5 | 298 | 3:12 | 304 |
| 1:9-10 | 266 | 4:20 | 419 |
| 1:13 | 4, 405 | | |
| 1;18 | 282 | **Titus** | |
| 1:23 | 232, 298 | | |
| 2:12 | 102 | 1:1 | 93 |
| 2:14 | 99, 107, 110, 120, | 1:2 | 264, 297 |
| | 125, 141, 171 | 1:8 | 303 |
| 2:16 | 362 | 1:9 | 288 |
| 3:4 | 167-68 | 2:3-6 | 416 |
| 3:5 | 27 | 2:11 | 95 |
| 3:12 | 272 | 2:14 | 297 |
| 3:17 | 9, 297 | 3:1 | 321 |
| 3:23 | 297 | 3:7 | 297 |

| | | | |
|---|---|---|---|
| **I Thessalonians** | | **Hebrews** | |
| 3:12 | 290, 333 | 1:1-2 | 184 |
| 4:4 | 214 | 2:15 | 173, 245 |
| 4:5 | 27 | 4:1 | 9 |
| **1 Thessalonians** | **Page** | **Hebrews** | **Page** |
| 4:9 | 290 | 4:15 | 104 |
| 4:15, 17 | 90 | 4:16 | 9 |
| 5:21 | 278 | 5:8-9 | vii, 32, 88 |
| 5:22 | 275, 291 | 5:9 | 17, 68-69, 187 |
| | | 6:4-6 | 97, 105 |
| **II Thessalonians** | | 6:6 | 344 |
| | | 6:10 | 317 |
| 2:10 | 28 | 6:18 | 264 |
| 2:14 | 6, 188, 227, 263 | 7:25 | 191 |
| 3:6, 14 | 35 | 8:5 | xv, 45 |
| 5:22 | | 8:6-13 | 111 |
| | | 8:8 | 149 |
| **I Timothy** | | 8:9 | 253 |
| | | 9:15 | 391 |

# Commentary on Romans

| | | | |
|---|---|---|---|
| 9:15-18 | 112 | 1:9 | 223, 273 |
| 9:24 | 191 | 1:14-15 | 276 |
| 9:27 | 89 | 1:16 | 273 |
| 10:1 | 45 | 1:22 | 290 |
| 10:1-8 | 151 | 2:6 | 226 |
| 10:18-26 | 109 | 2:7 | 83, 231 |
| 10:19 | 100 | 2:9 | 273 |
| 10:24 | 290, 333 | 2:13-15 | 321, 327 |
| 10:25 | 337, 342, 344 | 2:17 | 290, 333 |
| 10:26 | 97, 154 | 2:23 | 313 |
| 10:28 | 272 | 3:7 | 214 |
| 10:30 | 82, 344 | 3:8 | 290, 307, 333 |
| 10:37 | 344 | 3:15 | 1, 298 |
| 11:4 | 21, 40 | 3:21 | 347 |
| 11:7 | 50 | 4:7 | 337, 345 |
| 11:11-12 | 82 | 4:9 | 303 |
| 11:25 | 371 | 4:16-18 | 344 348-89 |
| 11:29 | 254 | 5:1-5 | xii |
| 11:30 | 82 | 5:3 | 287 |
| 12:14 | 312 | 5:8 | 108 |
| 12:26-29 | 344 | | |
| 12:29 | 18, 37, 254 | **II Peter** | |
| 13:1 | 333 | 1:1 | 10, 31 |
| 13:2 | 303 | 1:2-3, 8 | 266 |
| 13:4 | 26 | 1:3 | 32 |
| 13:6 | 9 | 2:6-7 | 246 |
| 13:12 | 343 | 2:6-8 | 217 |
| | | 2:9 | 19 |
| **James** | | 2:13-15 | 327 |
| | | 2:19 | 245 |
| 1:2-4 | 299 | 3:5 | 19, 29 |
| 1:11 | 11 | 3:9 | 210, 213, 385 |
| 1:13-15 | 130-31 | 3:14-16 | 231 |
| 1:14 | 103, 189, 210 | 3:16 | 126-27, 208, 347, 356, 417 |
| 1:17 | 264 | | |
| 1:21 | 15 | **II Peter** | **Page** |
| **James** | **Page** | | |
| | | 3:15-16 | 125 |
| 2:1-9 | 308 | 3:15-18 | ix |
| 2:10 | 223 | 3:18 | 266 |
| 2:13 | 366 | | |
| 2:17 | 83 | **I John** | |
| 2:19 | 15 | | |
| 2:20-24 | 67-68 | 2:1 | 191 |
| 2:24 | 40, 69 | 2:2 | 62 |
| 2:24, 26 | 70 | 2:15-17 | 11, 29 |
| 4:7 | 162, 180 | 3:2 | 167-68 |
| 5:8-9 | 337, 345 | 3:8 | 70 |
| | | 3:11 | 290, 333 |
| **I Peter** | | 3:14 | 333 |
| | | 3:16 | 291 |
| 1:2 | 187 | 3:23 | 290 |

416

# Commentary on Romans

| | | | |
|---|---|---|---|
| 4:7 | 290, 333 | Vs. 3 | 11-12, 69 |
| 4:8 | 254 | Vss. 16-19 | 311 |
| 4:10 | 62 | Vs. 21 | 193, 334 |
| 4:11, 20 | 333 | | |
| 4:11-12 | 290 | **Revelation** | |
| | | 1:3 | 343 |
| **II John** | | 1:9 | 4 |
| | | 2:14 | 26 |
| Vs. 5 | 290 | 2:23 | 182, 186 |
| Vss. 9-11 | 7, 35 | 3:16 | 192 |
| | | 5:5 | 392 |
| **III John** | | 19:17-18 | 78 |
| | | 20:2 | 19, 189 |
| Vss. 8-10 | 11-12, 406 | 22:12 | 337 |
| | | 22:16 | 392 |
| **Jude** | | 22:20 | 337 |
| Vs. 1 | 2, 31, 64, 68, 189 | | |

www.ingramcontent.com/pod-product-compliance
Lightning Source LLC
Chambersburg PA
CBHW062057280426
43673CB00085B/449/J